THE DEVELOPMENT OF AUTISM: PERSPECTIVES FROM THEORY AND RESEARCH

THE DEVELOPMENT OF AUTISM: PERSPECTIVES FROM THEORY AND RESEARCH

Edited by

Jacob A. Burack
McGill University, Montreal, Quebec, Canada

Tony Charman
Institute of Child Health, London, England

Nurit Yirmiya
Hebrew University of Jerusalem, Israel

Philip R. Zelazo
McGill University, Montreal, Quebec, Canada

LAWRENCE ERLBAUM ASSOCIATES, PUBLISHERS
2001 Mahwah, New Jersey London

Lawrence Erlbaum Associates, Inc., Publishers
10 Industrial Avenue
Mahwah, New Jersey 07430-2262

Cover design by Kathryn Houghtaling Lacey

Library of Congress Cataloging-in-Publication Data

The development of autism : perspectives from theory and research / Jacob A. Burack … [et al.].
p. cm.
"This volume is the product of a symposium on the development of autism that was presented at the Fifth European Congress of Psychology in Dublin in August 1997."
Includes bibliographical references and index.
ISBN 0-8058-3245-9 (cloth : alk. paper)
1. Autism--Congresses. 2. Autism--Etiology--Congresses. I. Burack, Jacob A. II. European Congress of Psychology : (5th : 1997 : Dublin, Ireland)

RCC553.A88 D48 2001
616.89'82--dc21 00-062298

Books published by Lawrence Erlbaum Associates are printed on acid-free paper, and their bindings are chosen for strength and durability

Printed in the United States of America
10 9 8 7 6 5 4 3 2 1

Dedication

The editors of this volume have graciously decided to dedicate it to the memory of Lisa Capps, a productive and imaginative researcher of childhood autism, who died in February 2000. The following paragraphs, summarizing Lisa's own view of her accomplishments in the field of autism and her plans for the future, were written at the end of November 1995 when she applied for an academic position at the University of California at Berkeley.

> My thinking has been shaped by dialogue between Clinical and Developmental Psychology from the start; I became involved in research as an undergraduate at Stanford University, where I worked with Dr. Anne Fernald on studies of mothers' use of intonation in communicating with infants. Concerned about how such communication might be altered in distressed relationships, I sought clinical experience with mothers and infants in a therapeutic nursery at Mt. Sinai Medical Center in New York City. At the same time I worked as a clinical research assistant at New York Psychiatric Institute, and on studies of narrative with Drs. Jerome Bruner and Carol Feldman at New York University.
>
> As a graduate student in Clinical Psychology at UCLA, my research with Dr. Marian Sigman on emotional relatedness and communication has challenged persistent notions about the nature of autistic impairment, for example, that autistic children are affectively flat and unable to form secure attachment relationships with caregivers. This work has significant clinical implications and offers insight into attachment theory. Additional research on high-functioning adolescents with autism suggested that they were

surprisingly able to identify a broad range of affective expressions and to recount times in which they had experienced various emotions. In contrast to non-autistic comparison subjects who described their emotional experiences with apparent ease, the task appeared laborious for those with autism, particularly in relation to complex emotions. Because task difficulty was negatively correlated with IQ, I became interested in the relationship between intellectual ability and the other aspects of social and emotional understanding. In another study with the same sample we found IQ was positively correlated with the ability to identify the emotions of videotaped protagonists and with parent reports of socially adaptive behaviors, but negatively correlated with adolescents' own perceptions of their social competence. These results suggest that autistic individuals with advanced intellectual abilities may have greater social and emotional understanding, engendering a heightened awareness of their limitations.

Dr. Sigman and I recently completed a book, *Autism, A Developmental Perspective* (1997). This book is unique in that it views autism through the lens of developmental psychopathology. Journeying from infancy through middle childhood and adolescence to adulthood, we demonstrate that understanding autism requires locating behavioral characteristics within a developmental frame, and that efforts to unravel the mysteries of autism enhance knowledge of normal development. We propose that autistic children suffer from deficits in social understanding that emerge in early infancy, and illuminate how these deficits organize the unfolding pattern of strengths and weaknesses displayed by individuals with autism over the course of their lives.

As evident from these paragraphs, Lisa was a magical writer whose work was embued with compassion and theoretical understanding of the highest order. She went on in her letter of application to outline her research goals in autism, "Adopting a developmental psychopathological perspective, I plan to develop a longitudinal research program that combines quantitative methods with naturalistic observation and discourse analysis to examine ... how linguistic practices, in particular, narrative style, relate to joint attention, social referencing, emotional understanding, and theory of mind among children with autism." She did go on to form a research group at UC Berkeley conducting studies of narrative in children with autism, elaborating on the kinds of discourse and conversation analysis she learned from Dr. Elinor Ochs as well as methodologies borrowed from Dr. Helen Tager-Flusberg and Dr. Judy Reilly. In two papers published recently, she reported that children with autism were less competent that children with developmental delays in informal, semi-structured conversations, although the two groups did not differ in narrative usage in stories told about a wordless picture book. Narrative abilities in both settings were related to performance on theory of mind tasks for the children with autism but not for the developmentally delayed group.

Her research group at Berkeley, composed of a number of excellent graduate students including Amy Busch, Molly Losh, and Lisa Rasco, has continued her work. Their papers will be appearing in the next few years and will keep an aspect of Lisa Capps with us for just a while longer.

The editors have asked me to write about Lisa's personal qualities but I find this impossible. Nothing that I can say about Lisa fully captures her brilliance, her compassion, her wit, her wisdom, her enthusiasm, her humility, or her beauty. Anyone reading these words who did not know Lisa will think that I exaggerate; those lucky enough to have known her will find that their own words fail them. Lisa enriched the life stories of all of us in ways that we are continuously discovering.

Marian Sigman, Ph.D.
Departments of Psychiatry and Psychology
UCLA

Contents

Preface

This volume is the product of a symposium on the development of autism that was presented at the Fifth European Congress of Psychology in Dublin, Ireland, in August 1997. All the participants in that symposium contributed to this volume, and other researchers were invited to submit chapters as well. The presentations in both the Dublin symposium and in this volume reflect a trend that began in the early 1990s toward the merging of three areas of psychological study—autism, general developmental processes, and developmental psychopathology. Accordingly, the contributions are largely influenced by the pioneers of psychological research on autism, such as Neil O'Connor, Beatte Hermelin, and Uta Frith, but are carried out within the larger contexts of traditional and contemporary developmental theories. This interplay is consistent with the premise of developmental psychopathology that the studies of typical and atypical development are mutually informative.

The contributors to this volume vary with regard to scholarly background: some are primarily involved in the study of autism, some in the broader context of developmental disorders, and others in mainstream developmental psychology. The collaborations among researchers with these varying backgrounds enhance our understanding of the behaviors and developmental characteristics of persons with autism. The adaptation of developmental theory, rigorous methodologies, and innovative experimental paradigms and procedures are all contributions from developmental psychology to the study of autism. The authors highlight the benefits of these contributions as they extend and broaden the range of domains of functioning considered in the developmental study of persons with autism, while uniting disparate areas of research within common developmental frameworks. They provide critiques and analyses of current areas of research and propose alternative frameworks for understanding characteristics of autism. This is all consistent with the Dublin symposium discussions, where participants stressed the need for collaboration among researchers in providing increasingly comprehensive profiles of the development of persons with autism.

The volume is divided into four sections. The first includes discussions of autism within the context of general developmental theories, behavioral genetics, and physiological evidence that are intended to provide background to the subsequent presentations regarding specific areas of functioning. The second section reflects extensions of the earlier focus on basic processes among persons with autism, and issues of attention and perception are considered. The third section includes critiques and analyses of theory of mind and the central coherence hypothesis—the two cognitive theories of autism that dominated much of the psychological research in autism during the 1990s. The fourth section represents the broadening of developmental foci of research and includes presentations on social adaptation and behavior.

The contributors cover a wide range of domains of functioning among persons with autism, but the quest to provide a comprehensive portrait of the development of persons with autism is far from complete. Researchers must continue to broaden the scope of research to include even more domains and to provide increasingly precise documentation of changes in behavior across the life span. This will best be accomplished by continued collaborations between experts on autism and experts on developmental psychology. We hope that this volume provides a base for subsequent work of this type.

We thank the contributors for providing innovative and provocative chapters that extend current thinking and knowledge about persons with autism. We thank our mentors, colleagues, and collaborators who taught us about the importance of a developmental perspective in the study of persons with autism and other neurodevelopmental disorders, notably Simon Baron-Cohen, Bob Hodapp, Marian Sigman, and Ed Zigler. We thank Judi Amsel, former executive editor at Lawrence Erlbaum Associates, who encouraged us to undertake this project and was a source of constant support throughout the process. Among the many at Erlbaum who participated in the preparation of this volume, we especially thank Sara Scudder, senior book production editor, and Bill Webber, developmental psychology editor. We also thank Beatriz Valdes, project manager at Argosy Publishing, for ensuring the timely publication of the volume. We thank Hanna Kovshoff, Natalie Russo, Tara Flanagan, and Yvette Delhommeau for their help in organizing and preparing the manuscript at various stages in the publication process.

Jake Burack thanks the Social Science and Humanities Research Council for financial support of his work on this volume, and the British Council for a travel grant that facilitated the initiation of this project. Tony Charman gratefully acknowledges the support of the University of London Central Research Fund, and thanks the Royal Society and British Academy for contributions to expenses at the conference where discussion with colleagues led to this volume. Nurit Yirmiya thanks the United States–Israel Binational Science Foundation and the Israel Science Foundation for their support of her work. Philip R. Zelazo thanks the Montreal Children's Hospital/McGill University Foundation for support of his work on autism.

Finally, we dedicate this volume to the memory of Lisa Capps who in her short life contributed significantly to both the professional and lay literatures about persons with autism. As a researcher, clinician, advocate, colleague, and friend, Lisa's contributions are valuable legacies to us all.

I

Introduction: Developmental, Neurobiological, Genetic, and Family Considerations

1

Development and Autism: Messages From Developmental Psychopathology

Jacob A. Burack
McGill University, Montreal, Quebec, Canada
Tony Charman
Institute of Child Health, London, England
Nurit Yirmiya
Hebrew University of Jerusalem, Israel
Philip R. Zelazo
McGill University, Montreal, Quebec, Canada

The theme of developmental perspectives in the study of autism is an example of the relatively new focus on the mutually informative relationship between the sciences of typical development and psychopathology (Cicchetti, 1984; Cicchetti & Cohen, 1995; Luthar, Burack, Cicchetti, & Weisz, 1997). This emergent area of study, generally referred to as *developmental psychopathology*, is at the crossroads between two distinct disciplines that involve disparate world views and empirical approaches (Burack, 1997). The traditional study of development involves both complex theorizing about and precise charting of continual changes of mechanisms and processes within elaborate, but universal, systems. In contrast, the study of psychopathology typically involves the precise examination of specific areas of functioning that uniquely differentiate one atypical group from other atypical groups as well as from the typical population. The differences in theoretical premises and constructs, empirical questions, and methodologies between these disparate frameworks contribute to the richness and innovativeness at the meeting point, but also necessitate that the two original disciplines must be transformed by their fledgling descendant.

The primary impetus for the emergence of developmental psychopathology is that each of the two primary contributing fields of study can enhance the other. Thus, Cicchetti's (1984) dictum, "that we can learn more about the normal functioning of an organism by studying its pathology, and likewise more about its pathology by studying its normal condition," is the essential "battle cry" of the discipline. Examples of atypical development, developmental histories, and environmental contexts provide developmentalists with cases of "experiments in nature" and "testing the limits" that are uniquely informative for understanding the essence and boundaries of typical development (e.g., Hodapp & Burack, 1990). They also afford opportunities to study the extent to which patterns of typical development are maintained, modified, or both, in circumstances with compelling theoretical and even philosophical implications that cannot be experimentally designed for ethical or other considerations (Burack, 1997; Sroufe & Rutter, 1984). Conversely, understanding the nature of psychopathology, or the behavioral effects of atypicality of any kind, can only be achieved by a consideration of the intricacies of the evolving typical organism (Enns & Burack, 1997; Hodapp, Burack, & Zigler, 1998; Zigler & Glick, 1986). In this manner, development serves as a guideline for understanding and assessing the occurrence and severity of delays or deviance among persons who are atypical in one or more ways (Wagner, Ganiban, & Cicchetti, 1990; Yirmiya, Erel, Shaked, & Solomonica-Levy, 1998).

Within this framework, persons with autism are studied together with typically developing persons as principles and methodologies from the study of general development are applied; the breadth of study includes all of these elements incorporated within the purview of mainstream developmental psychology. This intuitively appealing approach, however, is replete with challenges as studies must be designed to meet the theoretical and methodological standards of such disparate areas of study. The contributors to this volume represent a cohort of scholars dedicated to this undertaking in order to extend understanding of persons with autism and related developmental disorders. They contribute a body of literature that reflects their varied research interests, in the quest to provide a comprehensive understanding of the many aspects of development among persons with autism.

Autism and Developmental Theory

Autism was embraced by popular Western culture during the last decade or two of the past millennium. This fascination is evidenced by the popularity of trade books about persons with this disorder (e.g., Sacks, 1995), autobiographies by high-functioning persons with autism (e.g., Grandin & Sacks, 1996: Williams, 1992, 1994), and even "blockbuster" movies about or involving persons with autism or autistic features (e.g., *Rain Man* with Dustin Hoffman; *Mercury Rising* with Bruce Willis; and *What's Eating Gilbert Grape?* with Johnny Depp and

Leonardo DiCaprio). The common theme in these popular successes is that autism is a mystifying and debilitating disorder that is associated with some unusual cognitive strengths and behavioral idiosyncracies. However, consistent with the framework of developmental psychopathology, the focus of research is increasingly shifting from a primary consideration of the impairments identified among persons with autism toward an analysis of functioning within the context of typical development (Bowler, chap. 11, this volume; Frye, Zelazo, & Burack, 1999; Happé, chap. 12, this volume).

This revolution is most evident in the types of questions asked by researchers. Previously, the two most common questions were how are people with autism uniquely different from other persons? and what is the specific cause of this difference? Both questions were relevant to the atypicality inherent among persons with autism. These questions of "uniqueness" and "specificity" continue to be asked and are relevant to diagnostic issues (Charman, 2000) and to developing aspects of intervention with persons with autism (Zelazo, Burack, Boseovski, Jacques, & Frye, chap. 10, this volume). However, the task of understanding and facilitating the behavior of persons with autism and their relationships with others is now focused on issues of development. Such issues are central to understanding all people but can also be specifically geared toward attaining insights into this population. Within the ever broadening developmental framework, topics of study include evolving patterns of cognitive, neuropsychological, linguistic, and social development; genotype–phenotype associations; parent–child relationships; relationships with other family members; the child within the context of various aspects of the community; and others.

The study of autism is particularly associated with developmental issues because it is initially diagnosed early in childhood, continues to be evident throughout the life span, affects development in virtually all domains of functioning, and is typically (but not always) associated with delayed development. Questions are asked about specific developmental delays or deviancies in relation to general levels of functioning, the acquisition of abilities or skills throughout the developmental course, cross-domain relationships and the organization of development, the sequences of certain abilities or skills, and development within family and environmental contexts. In these endeavors, methodologies are adopted from studies of normal development, and notions such as developmental level are integrated into the experimental design.

Contributions of development to methodology in the study of autism are most often discussed with regard to strategies for matching persons with autism to those in the comparison groups, which can include typically developing persons, those with other disorders, or both. Matching persons with autism to others is complicated by the remarkable differences across areas of functioning among persons with autism, as evidenced by relative strengths in some domains, typical levels in others, and extreme deficits in still others. In order to account for this varied profile and for the common occurrence of global developmental delay, researchers typically use one or more measures of developmental level for matching (for discussions of the use of comparison groups, see Burack et al., in press; Mervis & Robinson, 1999; Sigman & Ruskin, 1999).

Developmental level is also essential to understanding the relevance of specific findings, as each developmental level is characterized by specific salient developmental issues and histories that are often quite different from those at other levels (Burack, 1997; Sroufe & Rutter, 1984; see Happé, chap. 12, this volume). Thus, group differences, similarities, or both, may be seen at one or more developmental levels but not at others. Concordantly, the current and long-term effects of specific problems are largely determined by developmental level associated with the impairment (i.e., whether the problematic ability is one relevant to infancy, childhood, adolescence, or adulthood). Problems at one point in development may be less relevant, or even inconsequential, at another.

Consistent with the framework of developmental psychopathology, the developmental study of persons with autism is informative for understanding basic developmental processes. For example, the dissociations among various areas of functioning—as highlighted by lowered levels of language abilities and theory of mind compared to other areas of cognitive functioning—are informative about the integrity of sequences of development, organization, and disorganization of the developing organism and the related notions of domain-general versus domain-specific modular development. Similarly, the severe social problems among persons with autism allow for the study of family dynamics in particularly stressful situations (Bauminger & Yirmiya, chap. 4, this volume). These examples may become windows of considerable insight into the understanding of typical developmental processes (Travis & Sigman, chap. 14, this volume), although the quest for illumination is likely to entail considerable interpretation in the extrapolation of characteristics from a population with so many severe developmentally related problems.

The Tenets of a Developmental Approach and the Study of Atypicality

Unlike the bygone years of the reign of Piaget, no single theoretical approach currently dominates developmental thought and research. As notions of development vary considerably among theorists and researchers, the whole discipline of developmental psychology is in considerable flux (Bronfenbrenner, Kessel, Kessen, & White, 1986; Chandler, 1997; Hodapp, Burack, & Zigler, 1990; Horowitz, 2000). Although the science of development is an evolving and burgeoning discipline (Frye, 1991), several theorists, including elders of the field, decry the end of development as a unified science within the current zeitgeist of postmodernist deconstruction and desolation (Bill Kessen and Sheldon White in Bronfenbrenner, Kessel, Kessen, & White, 1986; Kessen, 1984).

The theories of the early developmental workers, especially those of Jean Piaget and Heinz Werner, were constructivist at several levels. One, they were deemed universal to all persons and, at least for Werner (1948, 1957), applicable to all living things, societies, and concepts, not to just persons. Two, the focus was on understanding principles of organization and the evolving structural relationship among the whole and its parts. Three, development was portrayed as primarily teleological with coherent, invariant, and orderly growth to a universally adaptive endpoint. Four, development involved the organism within the entire context in which it evolved. This type of constructivist approach provided a complex but general framework for understanding the developing organism that is not optimal for the type of empirical work characterized by "postmodernist" psychology (Chandler, 1998). These early theories were criticized, deconstructed, reconstructed, or altered such that the discipline changed from one of relative unity to one of fragmentation.

Differences in interests and theoretical foundations among the early theorists are certainly sources of much of the current diversity among contemporary developmental frameworks. However, discrepancies in the subsequent interpretations and modifications of their work are even more directly responsible for the current landscape of vastly different theoretical frameworks and research emphases. This fragmentation of the field led eminent developmentalists, most notably Bill Kessen (1984), to declare that "the age of development" is ended. Other more optimistic theorists concur that there is little unity in the discipline, but argue that certain core themes of development continue to be relevant (Chandler, 1997; Frye, 1991) and that the failure to search for organization among these strands is "a cop-out" (Urie Bronfenbrenner in Bronfenbrenner et al., 1986).

Concern about the future of developmental psychology arose largely from disillusionment during the 1960s and 1970s with the monolithic frameworks of Piagetian and other developmental theories that dominated the landscape. Paradoxically, these early theories were viewed as too broad to incorporate individual differences or to be tested empirically, but too narrow with regard to the aspects of the developing organism that were included for study. The criticisms reflected a move away from constructivist grand theorizing in development. One, the adoption of Western societies' emerging interests in cultural and individual differences led to questions about the universalities inherent in the typically teleological theories of development. Two, the grandness of the developmental theories precluded an ability to account for the intricacies of both intra- and interindividual differences with and across the many domains of development. Thus, these theories were considered both too broad and too vague to generate testable hypotheses that, commensurate with the prevailing positivistic philosophy of science, are the basis of the fine-grained research endeavors of empirical psychology. The observational methods and conceptual musings of the elders were incompatible with the younger generations' scientifically conservative drift toward more sophisticated and precise paradigms in the empirical pursuit of ever smaller questions of study. This emphasis on empirical approaches also coincided with, and maybe even led to, a broadening of topics that could be considered under the rubric of development. Whereas the earlier, complex systems of development were generally limited to the relatively accessible, and apparently somewhat connected, domains of cognition, the newer and narrower approaches were capable of testing more disparate aspects of development, albeit within considerably more splintered frameworks.

The developmental revisionists were largely motivated by aspirations to formulate frameworks that facilitated scientific, conceptual, or both types of understanding of development and that incorporated the entire spectrum of behavioral functioning (e.g., cognitive, linguistic, emotional, social). This led to remarkably divergent approaches. Some revisionists emphasized the organism's transactions with a holistic environment, others considered individual differences and group differences, and still others systematized the empirical study of specific aspects of functioning. In some cases, the emphasis was on theoretical representations of reality, whereas others involved complex mathematical formulations. These revised frameworks reflect the paradoxical nature of concerns about the early developmental theories. For example, some are deemed improvements because they include more comprehensive frameworks of the entire person and environment, whereas others are intended to facilitate the more fine-grained study of specific aspects of functioning.

Perspectives From Developmental Psychopathology. Ironically, within this climate of uncertainty about the nature of development, researchers of developmental psychopathology are among the staunchest defenders of the faith (for a review, see Burack, 1997). Basic developmental standards were co-opted in the quest to provide a comprehensive and common framework for understanding evolving patterns of behavior for the many disparate groups of persons considered within the discipline (e.g., Cicchetti & Pogge-Hesse, 1982; Hodapp & Burack, 1990). Because the foci of the discipline are so varied as to account for individual and group differences in a wide range of disorders, biological problems, life experiences, or all of these, the identification of a few landmark components is necessary to maintain the integrity of the discipline. These include theoretical foundations that were initially articulated by early theorists and that remain hallmarks of contemporary work in this area as well as more contemporary issues that reflect new interests and the expansion of the discipline.

Among the traditional issues, teleological development entails an orderly progression toward increasingly adaptive levels of functioning and necessitates universal sequences of the acquisition of skills and abilities. Evidence of consistency in Piagetian sequences across different groups of persons with mental retardation (Weisz & Zigler, 1979) and autism (Burack & Volkmar, 1992; Morgan, 1986; Morgan, Cutrer, Coplin, & Rodrigue, 1989) is compelling evidence for the integrity of the orderliness of the emerging system. Similarly, the traditional notion of the developing organism as an integrated and organized system is relevant to issues of the inherent interconnectedness across domains of functioning. Although these issues arose from traditional developmental frameworks, the study of developmentally atypical populations necessitates an extended, or more "liberal" approach, to developmental principles (Cicchetti & Pogge-Hesse, 1982). For example, the severe problems displayed by persons with autism in certain areas of functioning are relevant both to issues of the acquisition of specific skills and abilities and to the organization of development across domains. In advocating a liberal approach, developmental psychopathologists retain the basic notions of traditional developmental frameworks, while adapting them to the unique characteristics of the specific groups to which they will be applied.

Within the ever expanding domain of developmental psychology, issues previously not considered central to developmental research are now integral to the discipline. For example, issues of social and emotional development, family relationships, and interactions with the environment—none of which were examined in great depth by the classic developmentalists—are now common foci of study (Dunn, 1996; Harris, 1994). These new areas provide a more comprehensive framework of development than did Piaget's primarily cognition-based focus. They reflect a growing interest in the unique aspects of individuals, in the growth of the self in areas beyond simple cognition, and in the role within and contributions to the world. This more fine-grained approach to development allows for a more comprehensive picture of the individual, but at the same time limits the generalizability of findings and theories across persons or groups of persons.

Thus, the notion of a developmental framework for the study of persons with autism, or any other group of persons, implies a wide range of research interests and involves the use of many disparate methodologies. However, the various emphases and foci can be integrated to provide a comprehensive, if somewhat mosaic, portrait of the many aspects of development of persons with autism and, in keeping with our motif, to inform about typical developmental processes across several domains of functioning. The diversity of this expanded developmental approach is evident in the variety of both the topics and methodologies delineated in the chapters in this volume.

The Study of Autism Within the Context of Developmental Psychopathology

As with other areas of the study of development, the developmental study of persons with autism is characterized by a multiplicity of foci, perspectives, and methodologies. In some cases, traditional developmental concepts, such as sequences, regressions, and cross-domain relations, are tested directly (Burack & Volkmar, 1992), but in most cases the developmental issues are embedded in research about specified domains of functioning. Influenced both by traditional paradigms of psychopathology and by the narrow emphases of positivistic approaches to science, the focus of autism research is typically on specific areas of functioning. The question inevitably (or at least, usually) is whether an area of behavioral deficit, or in some cases a strength, might be indicative of an impairment that is the core of, or at least an important source of, autistic behavior (Plaisted, chap. 8, this volume). In many cases, the behavioral characteristics are related to neurological or genetic markers (Bauminger & Yirmiya, chap. 4, this volume; Koenig, Tsatsanis, & Volkmar, chap. 5, this volume). Consistent with typical paradigms of psychopathology, these associations are considered strong evidence for the primacy of that specific dysfunction (for a discussion of the relation between behavioral and physiological research, see Yeung-Courchesne & Courchesne, 1997). The developmental influence on this type of research is as a guideline for identifying areas of deficit or assessing the extent of the impairment (Yirmiya et al., 1998). These methodological contributions entail the use of explicit developmental considerations such as rate and structure, but also implicit assumptions about precursors, sequences, and level of functioning (Charman, 2000).

The Study of Traditional Concepts of Development. The developmental notions of rate and structure are the common foundations of the framework used to identify basic characteristics of autism. The two issues are related to each other as well as to the concept of development and are relevant both to methodological considerations and theoretical queries. The rate question is pertinent to interindividual differences and asks whether level of functioning in a group within a specific domain is developmentally advanced, appropriate, or impaired in relation to expectations of performance within a similar developmental time frame (usually chronological age, CA or mental age, MA). The expectations are based on the typical rate of development for a specific ability among some comparison group, usually typically developing persons. In this manner, a common developmental framework can be used to chart the time frame for the attainment of a specific skill among persons with autism as compared to typically developing persons as well as other groups of atypical persons. The developmental point at which each skill is attained is significant for the ultimate efficiency of that skill, for the achievement of later skills for which the skill is a precursor, and for the relationship of the skill with others in the complex organismic system. Thus, the magnitude of the delay in attainment is likely indicative of the severity of the problem and the extent of the effect on subsequent development.

The question of structure is relevant to the intraindividual differences in levels of functioning among domains. Thus, it entails issues of rate in the various domains, but also includes the comparison of development across domains, in relation to global development, or both. As with virtually all diagnostic groups, persons with autism show identifiable patterns of development and disparities across domains; despite individual differences within the population, the discrepancies across domains are often large. These patterns of differences across domains within the individual are the essence of the behavioral diagnostic criteria of autism, and of all disorders.

The Disclaimer in the Study of Traditional Concepts—Are the Stages and Sequences Similar?

Both the issues of rate and structure are contingent on the not-necessarily-correct assumptions of similar stages and sequences through these stages—that the nature and order of abilities or milestones attained by persons with autism are qualitatively similar to those among typically developing persons. These assumptions are largely relics of the traditional developmental premise of universality, but maintain their usefulness in allowing for quantitative comparisons across groups. For example, if the attainment of an ability or milestone is always characterized by levels of efficiency or proficiency within some inherently common range, then cross-group comparisons of level of functioning are meaningful since the units of measurement are the same (or, at least similar). However, if the quality of functioning is not similar, then quantitative comparisons across groups with regard to level of attainment are no longer meaningful (Zelazo, chap. 3, this volume). Accordingly, problems in performance or behavior need to be viewed within the context of the diminished quality of particular skills or abilities rather than solely on quantitative notions of developmental delay or failure to attain a certain level. In this scenario, the picture of comparative development would be hopelessly muddled since the pathways of development emerging from the particular skill would be different across groups and would subsequently lead to increasingly divergent developmental patterns.

The common acceptance of cross-group similarities in the sequence of acquisition of stages thus allows researchers to equate the development of persons with autism to that of groups of other persons, including both those with histories of typical development and atypical development. Even in cases where the evidence suggests atypical development, such an interpretation is contingent on comparisons in which groups are matched on a developmental measure that is assumed to reflect a level of similarity between the groups. Accordingly, the veracity of these group comparison strategies is contingent on the level of intergroup similarity with regard to order of developmental stages or milestones (Happé, chap. 12, this volume), and on the specific relations between processes and attainment of skills (Bowler, chap. 11, this volume).

One alternative to cross-group comparisons is the delineation of within-group (or within-person) profiles (Mervis & Robinson, 1999). This strategy is beneficial because it eliminates the complexities inherent in choosing measures to match groups that differ considerably with regard to relative levels of functioning across domains. It capitalizes on these differences and delineates the cross-domain profiles within any given group. In this framework, each subject serves as a comparison for him or herself and each group for itself. This strategy is consistent with, and even implicit in, much of the research on relative strengths and weaknesses among persons with autism and on the relations in levels of functioning across domains (Happé, chap. 12, this volume; Hughes, chap. 13, this volume; Mottron & Burack, chap. 7, this volume).

Expanded Framework of Development and Autism. The history of developmental psychopathology is linked inextricably with the expansion of the traditional developmental framework. This includes increased attention to the impact of the environment on development and to a broadening of the foci of development to include noncognitive factors (e.g., Cicchetti, 1984; Luthar, 1997; Sameroff & Chandler, 1975; Sroufe & Rutter, 1984; Zigler, 1967). Piaget and Werner both acknowledged that environment was essential to development, but their focus was on the evolving organism, and little attention was paid to differences in environment or to their sequelae. Furthermore, their foci was typically on cognitive and, at least in Werner's (1957) case, more basic processes such as perception. The increase in attention to individual characteristics and group differences as opposed to common universals, however, highlighted the impact of a wide range of environmental factors on development and on the complexity of individuals that extended beyond the realm of the goings-on of the mind. This expansion of developmental focus was evident in several classic articles in the history of developmental psychopathology. For example, in initially defining a developmental approach to the study of persons with mental retardation, Zigler (1967) articulated the notion of studying the "whole child" including the consideration of personality and motivational factors that he linked to the unique life experiences and environmental backgrounds of these individuals. Similarly, in their landmark work on risk and protective factors among children, Sameroff and Chandler (1975) highlighted both the facilitative and detrimental effects of the environment and emphasized that, in many cases, the impact of these factors can override even physiological ones. These issues subsequently became central to the development of the emergent discipline of psychopathology.

The historical pattern of research on autism is similar to that of research on typical development. Although the disorder was initially viewed within the context of social relatedness, much of the early empirical work was focused on basic cognitive, or precognitive, processes (e.g., Frith, 1970, 1972; Hermelin & O'Connor, 1964) and was a precursor to current work on attention (Leekam & Moore, chap. 6, this volume) and perception (Mottron & Burack, chap. 7, this volume; Plaisted, chap. 8, this volume). The research on theory-of-mind and executive-function impairments that dominated the autism literature in the 1980s and 1990s pointed to the centrality of cognition (Tager-Flusberg, chap. 9, this volume), the complexities of the relation among cognitive process (Bowler, chap. 11, this volume; Zelazo, chap. 3, this volume; Zelazo et al., chap. 10, this volume), and the association between cognition and the social deficiencies that characterize autism (Happé, chap. 12, this volume; Hughes, chap. 13, this volume; Loveland, chap. 2, this volume). The broadening of developmental frameworks to extend beyond cognition is evidenced in recent work on social factors including social-communicative impairments (Charman & Swettenham, chap. 16, this volume; Travis & Sigman, chap. 14, this volume) and social relationships (Kasari, Chamberlain, & Bauminger, chap. 15, this volume), and on the implications of behavioral genetic (Bauminger & Yirmiya, chap. 4, this volume) and physiological (Koenig, Tsatsanis, & Volkmar, chap. 5, this volume) evidence.

In this volume we present varied perspectives about developmental issues in the study of persons with autism. Although it is not a comprehensive overview of the field, the volume reflects current research and theorizing about the development of individuals with autism. Our hope is that with this project, we present a meaningful mosaic of developmental issues that will be a guide to researchers, practitioners, family members, and others interested in understanding, treating, and living with persons with autism.

ACKNOWLEDGMENTS

Jake Burack's participation on this chapter was supported by a research award from the Social Sciences and Humanities Research Council of Canada.

Please address correspondence to Jake Burack, Department of Educational Psychology, McGill University, 3700 McTavish Street, Montreal, Quebec, H3A 1Y2, Canada.

REFERENCES

Bronfenbrenner, U., Kessel, F., Kessen, W., & White, S. (1986). Toward a critical social history of developmental psychology: A propaedeutic discussion. *American Psychologist, 41,* 1218–1230.

Burack, J. A., Pasto, L., Porporino, M., Iarocci, G., Mottron, L., & Bowler, D. (in press). Applying developmental principles to the study of autism. In E. Schopter, N. Yirmiya, C. Shulman, & L. Marcus (Eds.), *The research basis of autism: Implications for interverntion.* New York: Kluwer Academic Press/Plenum.

Burack, J. A. (1997). The study of atypical and typical populations in developmental psychopathology: The quest for a common science. In S. S. Luthar, J. A. Burack, D. Cicchetti, & J. R. Weisz (Eds.), *Developmental psychopathology: Perspectives on adjustment, risk and disorder* (pp. 139–165). New York: Cambridge University Press.

Burack, J. A., & Volkmar, F. R. (1992). Development of low- and high-functioning autistic children. *Journal of Child Psychology and Psychiatry, 33,* 607–616.

Chandler, M. (1997). Stumping for progress in a post-modern world. In E. Amsel & K. A. Renninger (Eds.), *Change and development: Issues of theory, method, and application* (pp. 1–26). Mahwah, NJ: Lawrence Erlbaum Associates, Inc.

Charman, T. (2000). Early diagnosis of autism. In S. Baron-Cohen, H. Tager-Flusberg & D. Cohen (Eds.), *Understanding other minds: Perspectives from autism and developmental neuroscience* (2nd ed.) (pp. 422–441). Oxford, UK: Oxford University Press.

Cicchetti, D. (1984). The emergence of developmental psychopathology. *Child Development, 55,* 1–7.

Cicchetti, D., & Cohen, D. J. (1995). (Eds.), *Developmental psychopathology, Vol. 2: Risk, disorder, and adaptation.* New York: Wiley.

Cicchetti, D., & Pogge-Hesse, P. (1982). Possible contributions of organically retarded persons to developmental theory. In E. Zigler & D. Balla (Eds.), *Mental retardation: The developmental—difference controversy* (pp. 277–313). Hillsdale, NJ: Lawrence Erlbaum Associates, Inc.

Dunn, J. (1996). The Emanuel Miller Memorial Lecture 1995. Children's relationships: Bridging the divide between cognitive and social development. *Journal of Child Psychology and Psychiatry, 37,* 507–518.

Enns, J. T., & Burack, J. A. (1997). Attention and developmental psychopathology: The merging of disciplines. In J. A. Burack & J. T. Enns (Eds.), *Attention, development, and psychopathology.* New York: Guilford.

Frith, U. (1970). Studies in pattern detection in normal and autistic children: II Reproduction and production of color sequences. *Journal of Experimental Child Psychology, 10,* 120–135.

Frith, U. (1972). Cognitive mechanisms in autism: Experiments with color and tone sequence production. *Journal of Autism and Childhood Schizophrenia, 2,* 160–173.

Frye, D. (1991). The end of development? In F. S. Kessel, M. H. Bornstein, & A. J. Sameroff (Eds.), *Contemporary constructions of the child: Essays in honor of William Kessen.* Hillsdale, NJ: Lawrence Erlbaum Associates, Inc.

Frye, D., Zelazo, P. D., & Burack, J. A. (1999). I. Cognitive complexity and control: Implications for theory of mind in typical and atypical populations. *Current Directions in Psychological Science, 7,* 116–121.

Grandin, T., & Sacks, O. W. (1996). *Thinking in pictures: And other reports from my life with autism.* New York: Vintage.

Harris, P. L. (1994). The child's understanding of emotion: Developmental change and the family environment. *Journal of Child Psychology and Psychiatry, 35,* 3–28.

Hermelin, B., & O'Connor, N. (1964). Effects of sensory input and sensory dominance on severely disturbed autistic children and subnormal controls. *British Journal of Psychiatry, 55,* 201–206.

Hodapp, R. M., & Burack, J. A. (1990). What mental retardation teaches us about typical development: The examples of sequences, rates, and cross-domain relations. *Development and Psychopathology, 2,* 213–225.

Hodapp, R. M., Burack, J. A., & Zigler, E. (1990). The developmental perspective in the field of mental retardation. In R. M. Hodapp, J. A. Burack, & E. Zigler (Eds.), *Issues in the developmental approach to mental retardation* (pp. 3–26). New York: Cambridge University Press.

Hodapp, R. M., Burack, J. A., & Zigler, E. (1998). Developmental approaches to mental retardation: A short introduction. In J. A. Burack, R. M. Hodapp, & E. Zigler (Eds.), *Handbook of mental retardation and development.* New York: Cambridge University Press.

Horowitz, F. D. (2000). Child development and the PITS: Simple questions, complex answers and developmental theory. *Child Development, 71,* 1–10.

Kessen, W. (1984). Introduction: The end of the age of development. In R. Sternberg (Ed.), *Mechanisms of cognitive development.* San Francisco: Freeman.

Luthar, S. S., Burack, J. A., Cicchetti, D., & Weisz, J. R. (Eds.). (1997). *Developmental psychopathology: Perspectives on adjustment, risk, and disorder.* New York: Cambridge University Press.

Luthar, S. S. (1997). Sociodemographic disadvantage and psychosocial adjustment: Perspectives from developmental psychopathology. In S. S. Luthar, J. A. Burack, D. Cicchetti, & J. R. Weisz (Eds.), *Developmental psychopathology: Perspectives on adjustment, risk, and disorder* (pp. 459–485). New York: Cambridge University Press.

Mervis, C. B., & Robinson, B. F. (1999). Methodological issues in cross-syndrome comparisons: Matching procedures, sensitivity, and specificity. *Monographs of the Society for Research in Child Development, 64,* 115–130.

Morgan, S. B. (1986). Autism and Piaget's theory: Are the two compatible? *Journal of Autism and Developmental Disorders, 16,* 441–457.

Morgan, S. B., Cutrer, P. S., Coplin, J. W., & Rodrigue, J. R. (1989). Do autistic children differ from retarded and normal children in Piagetian sensorimotor functioning? *Journal of Child Psychology and Psychiatry, 30,* 857–864.

Sacks, O. W. (1995). *An anthropologist on Mars.* London, UK: Picador.

Sameroff, A. J., & Chandler, M. (1975). Reproductive risk and the continuum of caretaker casualty. In F. D. Horowitz, M. Hetherington, S. Scarr-Salapatek, & G. Siegel (Eds.), *Review of child development research* (Vol. 4, p. 187–244). Chicago, University of Chicago Press.

Sigman, M., & Ruskin, E. (1999). Continuity and change in the social competence of children with autism, Down syndrome, and developmental delays. *Monographs of the Society for Research in Child Development, 6,* v–114.

Sroufe, L. A., & Rutter, M. (1984). The domain of developmental psychopathology. *Child Development, 55,* 17–29.

Wagner, S., Ganiban, J. M., & Cicchetti, D. (1990). Attention, memory and perception in infants with Down syndrome: A review and commentary. In D. Cicchetti & M. Beeghly (Eds.), *Children with Down syndrome: A developmental perspective* (pp. 147–179). New York: Cambridge University Press.

Weisz, J. R., & Zigler, E. (1979). Cognitive development in retarded and nonretarded persons: Piagetian tests of the similar sequence hypothesis. *Psychological Bulletin, 86,* 831–851.

Werner, H. (1948). *Comparative psychology of mental development* (Rev. ed.). New York: Follett.

Werner, H. (1957). The concept of development from a comparative and organismic point of view. In D. Harris (Ed.), *The Concept of development.* Minneapolis: University of Minnesota Press.

Williams, D. (1992). *Nobody nowhere: The extraordinary autobiography of an autistic.* New York: Doubleday.

Williams, D. (1995). *Somebody somewhere: Breaking free from the world of autism.* New York: Doubleday.

Yeung-Courchesne, R., & Courchesne, E. (1997). From impasse to insight in autism research: From behavioral symptoms to biological explanations. *Development and Psychopathology, 9,* 389–419.

Yirmiya, N., Erel, O., Shaked, M., & Solomonica-Levy, D. (1998). Meta-analyses comparing theory of mind abilities of individuals with autism, individuals with mental retardation, and normally developing individuals. *Psychological Bulletin, 124,* 283–307.

Zigler, E. (1967). Familial retardation: A continuing dilemma. *Science, 155,* 292–298.

Zigler, E., & Glick, M. (1986). *A developmental approach to adult psychopathology.* New York: Wiley.

2

Toward an Ecological Theory of Autism

Katherine A. Loveland
Center for Human Development Research
Department of Psychiatry and Behavioral Sciences
University of Texas-Houston, Medical School

In this chapter I propose a different way of viewing autism, a developmental disorder that affects social behavior, communication, and cognition. My aim is to sketch a theory of autism that is consistent with the principles of an ecological psychology as proposed by James J. Gibson (1979). Such a theory offers not only a different epistemological stance than other current approaches to autism, but also the potential to draw together the diverse and sometimes scattered pieces of this puzzling developmental disorder on multiple levels of explanation. I first discuss some of the assumptions present in current theories of autism and go on to suggest an alternative view.

Current Approaches to Explaining Autism

Although there are a number of competing views of autism, most of these views share certain assumptions about how a disorder such as autism should be explained. Most theories of autism deal with the disorder primarily on one of two levels of explanation.

Top-down explanations have to do with cognition or other mental activity, particularly hypothetical cognitive modules, structures, and representations, e.g., impairment of a Theory of Mind (ToM) module. Psychological explanations of the essential social deficits in autism remain somewhat controversial, with most investigators favoring the view that a cognitive deficit is responsible (e.g., Baron-Cohen,

1995) and others the view that early affective attunement or social awareness deficits are involved (Hobson, 1993; Meltzoff & Gopnik, 1993; Waterhouse & Fein, 1989). Most, though not all, investigators explain the social deficits of people with autism as resulting from failures of the ability to understand what others think, know, believe, or feel. Thus, a failure to understand (or represent) the internal states (or mental representations) of other people results in autistic behavior. Such explanations take developmental or psychiatric disorders in general to be the manifestations of impaired mental activity. Mental activity is assumed to consist of manipulation or processing of mental contents (representations or structures); thus, explanations of autism on this level will include descriptions of the impaired mental contents and their relationships to observed characteristics of the syndrome. If the brain is invoked, it is assumed to be the locus of mental contents and the cognitive modules that process them; in this way, one can reify the mental modules and contents through establishing a locus or loci of brain impairment. Therefore, in this type of theory, if we can identify a mental structure or module whose impairment is necessary and sufficient to account for the behavioral deficits observed in autism, we will then have explained autism.

Bottom-up explanations have to do with impaired brain structures and their effects on behavioral functioning. Among these are explanations that link social-affective deficits to impairments of the medial temporal lobe (Bachevalier & Merjanian, 1994; Dawson, Meltzoff, Osterling, & Rinaldi, 1998; Loveland, Bachevalier, & Nemanic, 1998); deficits in visuospatial attention to impairment of the cerebellum and parietal lobe (Townsend, Courchesne, & Egaas, 1996); deficits in executive functioning to impairment in the frontal lobe (Ozonoff, Pennington, & Rogers, 1991); and abnormalities of the hippocampus, amygdala, and sensory cortex with social-affective, cognitive, and attentional deficits (Dawson & Lewy, 1989; Waterhouse, Fein, & Modahl, 1996). Such explanations assume that developmental or psychiatric disorders are the manifestations of underlying brain disorders. Thus, explanations of autism on the neurobiological or neuropsychological level will consist mainly of descriptions of impaired brain structures and their relationships to behavioral deficits. If mental-behavioral functioning is invoked, it is to help locate the relevant brain structures through careful study of functional impairments. Thus, in this view, if we can locate a brain structure or circuit that is definitely impaired in autism and show that it is necessary and sufficient to bring about the syndrome, we will then have explained autism.

Both these approaches to solving the problem of autism have merit, and both have contributed a great deal to our understanding of autism through large bodies of useful empirical work. Both have the potential to provide a developmental account of autism. However, each, by itself, suffers from a tendency to focus on some aspects of the phenomenon of autism while neglecting others. Both also tend to assume that the important relationship disrupted in autism is unidirectional, i.e., either the brain or the mind (or both) causes behavior. In pure form they lead to the conclusion that either the brain or the mind is what is "really important" about autism, but not both—i.e., reductionism or mentalism. Significantly, both share the assumption that autism can be described as something that is located within the person with autism. When viewed this way, autism tends to be reified as a thing (a static syndrome or deficit) that afflicts a person and remains throughout life; thus, the person is said to "have autism," rather than to have autistic characteristics or behaviors.

There have been efforts more recently to link these two general approaches to autism by connecting laboratory tasks that measure cognitive or affective functioning with neuropsychological or neurobiological measures of brain integrity. The study of brain-behavior relationships (neuropsychology) has been recognized as fundamental to understanding autism (Dawson, 1996), and most significantly, there have been attempts to connect current cognitive theory about autism with possible neural substrates for the disorder. For example, a number of studies have linked ToM deficits with impaired executive functioning and thence to impaired frontal-lobe functioning via specific neuropsychological testing (e.g., Hughes, Russell, & Robbins, 1994; McEvoy, Rogers, & Pennington, 1993; Ozonoff, 1995; Ozonoff & McEvoy, 1994; Rogers & Pennington, 1991). Others have linked ToM task performance to frontal-lobe functioning through functional magnetic resonance imaging (MRI) (Baron-Cohen et al., 1999; Frith & Frith, 1999; Gallagher et al., 2000; Stone, Baron-Cohen, & Knight, 1998;), or empathy to medial-temporal-lobe functioning through neuropsychological testing (Dawson, 1996). These and similar efforts are a first step toward defining an approach to autism that avoids the polarizing effects of the two approaches just described.

Despite the salutary effects of these recent studies on the field, it is nonetheless plain that the shared assumptions undergirding cognitive and neurobiological approaches have not changed: i.e., if autism is a disorder that happens in the head, then thanks to recent research we will soon be able to tell exactly where it is taking place!

Is autism located within the person? In a certain sense this must be so, in that there are behavioral characteristics that people with autism typically have that people without autism typically do not, and we assume that these are related to developmental differences within the person. I would argue that this view is incomplete, because it fails to account for the neurobehavioral embeddedness of the person with autism within his or her environment over development. In the following sections I propose an alternative to mentalistic and reductionistic ways of explaining autism: one that locates autism not within the head of the autistic person, but in the disordered relationship of person and environment over development.

An Ecological Alternative: Basics of an Ecological Approach

I base this proposal on the theoretical work of James J. Gibson (1979), who developed what he called an ecological approach to visual perception and to psychological explanation more generally. Several principles characterize the ecological approach (see Mace, 1977; Michaels & Carello, 1981; Reed, 1988; and Reed & Jones, 1982; for excellent reviews of ecological principles and their history in greater depth than is possible here). It asserts, first, that perception of the world is direct rather than mediated by mental representations. This assertion rests on the idea that there is information available in the structured stimulation we receive that is specific to what is perceived. An ecological approach assumes a direct realist epistemology rather than the indirect and constructivist view more common in developmental psychology (although cf. E. Gibson 1997; Dent-Read & Zukow-Goldring, 1997; and Loveland, 1986; for examples of the application of ecological principles to developmental psychology), in that it does not suppose that raw, meaningless sensory stimulation must be rearranged, processed, enriched, or otherwise massaged before it can be understood.

An ecological realist psychology also does not assume that cognition causes behavior, and in fact denies the necessity of postulating mental constructs to account for behavior (cf. Watkins, 1990, for a related argument dealing with memory). It is thus functionalistic rather than mentalistic in orientation. However, such an approach also rejects reductionism and behaviorism, in that behaviors or neural substrates alone are not the focus of study, nor is it assumed that the person is a passive receiver of stimuli (stimulus-response). The human person (or any other organism) is instead seen as part of an *organism-environment system*. Thus, for the ecologically minded behavioral scientist, the appropriate unit of study is neither the individual, nor the contents of the individual's head (mind or brain), nor a set of environmental stimuli, but the interaction of person and environment.

This point is best understood with respect to the *perception-action cycle*, which is the continuous reciprocal process by which the organism both perceives and acts on the environment: Perception guides action, and action both directs perception and affects what is there to be perceived. For example, as a baby reaches for a dangling string, vision guides reaching; the act of reaching also guides what is perceived, as the baby orients to the string and ultimately touches it. The baby, like any other organism, exists as an embedded part of its environment, and its development can be viewed as a continual process of adjustment between the two. For this reason, numerous theorists writing from an ecological view have argued that the appropriate unit of analysis for studies of human behavior is not the individual person, but the person-environment system (e.g., Baron & Misovich, 1993; cf. also the "radical contextualist" approach of Fogel et al., 1992). This emphasis on embeddedness of the organism within the environment is, of course, the reason that such an approach is called "ecological."

The perception/action cycle in turn gives rise to the concept of *affordances* (Gibson, 1979; see also Gibson's writings on this topic as published in chap. 4.9 of Reed & Jones, 1982). Gibson used the term *affordances* to describe the opportunities for action and perception that the environment offers to an individual: i.e., the functional meaning of objects, events, persons, and so forth for an individual, depending on his or her current needs and effectivities. He argued that affordances are directly perceived and that they are derived from the interaction of the organism and environment rather than being properties located within either one. Thus, for example, whether an object affords lifting for me depends on the interaction of my characteristics (e.g., how strong I am, whether I have hands to grasp it, etc.) with those of the object (e.g., how much it weighs, its shape and size, etc.). Discovering and acting on available affordances is an essential process in development for individuals of any animal species. (See J. Gibson, 1979; Heft, 1989; Mace, 1977; and Loveland, 1991; for further discussion of the concept of affordances.)

Over the past twenty years numerous investigators have adopted Gibson's view wholly or in part and have elaborated on it in diverse ways (e.g., Neisser, 1992; Shaw & Bransford, 1977). In particular, there have been some attempts to apply Gibson's theory of affordances to understanding the ways in which humans navigate the social as well as the physical (inanimate) environment (Baron & Misovich, 1993; Heft, 1989; Loveland, 1991; McArthur & Baron, 1983; Reed, 1988; Van Acker & Valenti, 1989). Gibson himself acknowledged the need for this type of analysis but never delved deeply into its implications or limitations:

> A populated environment is not just a terrestrial environment with a special set of animated social objects in it. People *are* animated objects, to be sure, with complex affordances for behavior; but they are more than that. People are not only *parts* of the environment but also *perceivers* of the environment. Hence a given perceiver perceives other perceivers. And he also perceives *what* others perceive. In this way each observer is aware of a shared environment, one that is common to all observers, not just *his* environment. (J. Gibson, unpublished manuscript, 1974, later published in Reed & Jones, 1982) (p. 411)

Efforts to apply ecological principles to social psychology have been controversial, but they have contributed to lively debate and a growing body of empirical work dealing with the ability of humans to perceive what other humans afford them (Ginsburg, 1990). Much of the controversy has revolved around whether social behavior and intentions can truly be perceived directly or whether some form of mediating mental constructs must be postulated to account for our understanding of them. Clearly, there is evidence that a great deal of what we know about one another can be learned through direct observation, even without the benefit of mediating verbal information. In fact, there is an extensive literature on nonverbal behavior and its perception and expression by children and adults that is too large to review here. (See DePaulo, 1991; and Feldman, Philippot, & Custrini, 1991; for interesting discussions of some of this literature.) A few examples of findings from research done from an ecological viewpoint must suffice.

For example, beginning with Runeson and Frykholm's (1983) work on "kinematic specification of dynamics," there is considerable evidence that humans can perceive complex social intentions, such as one child's degree of willingness to play with another or to share, simply by observing nonverbal behavior (Loveland, Tunali-Kotoski, Ortegon, Pearson, & Gibbs, 1997a; Van Acker & Valenti, 1989). Other research has shown the ability of observers to perceive the gender of a walking figure specified only by a series of lights placed on key areas of the body (point-light walkers) (Koslowski & Cutting, 1977) and their ability to pick up information in craniofacial structure that specifies growth, aging, and facial attractiveness (e.g., Alley, 1988; Berry, 1990; Carello, Grosofsky, Shaw, Pittenger, & Mark, 1989). Still other research has shown that adults can identify others' intentions through observing body motion and facial expressions (Valenti, 1989; Valenti & Wagner, 1991) and others' emotions through observing gait (Montepare, Goldstein, & Clausen, 1987). Children as young as 11 years can detect, without verbal information, which two of three independently videotaped people were interacting with each other (Dornbush, Melendez, & Pick, 1995). Even infants less than a year old, as a large literature shows, can readily detect characteristics such as the gender and age of persons across visual and auditory modalities (Bahrick, Netto, & Hernandez-Reif, 1998; Walker-Andrews, Bahrick, Raglioni, & Diaz, 1991).

These examples do not, in themselves, prove that perception of others' personal characteristics, behavioral intentions, or mental states is direct and unmediated by mental representations. In fact most investigators in the nonverbal behavior field seem to rely on either an information-processing model or a vague assumption of mediating mental representations to explain how social and affective behavior is perceived and understood (cf. Feldman et al., 1991). However, these examples do illustrate the success of an ecological psychology framework in generating research on social behavior and social perception, and, more important for the present discussion, they demonstrate that many rather complex aspects of human social life are specified in perceptually available information. It is this approach that I wish to apply to understanding the abnormal development of social perception and social behavior in individuals with autism.

An Ecological View of Autism?

In an earlier paper (Loveland, 1991) I argued that the theory of affordances offers a way to understand the failure of persons with autism to interact with their environments, particularly their social and cultural environments, in ways we would ordinarily expect. Within this framework, people with autism can be described as failing to perceive and act upon the same affordances (or functional meanings) as other people, particularly with respect to "social affordances," i.e., the possibilities for action offered by other persons. I wish now to elaborate on this position and to clarify its contribution to the understanding of autism.

Seen within the ecological framework, autism is not a static condition existing within a person, but a developmental process that can only be understood as taking place through the interaction of person and environment. Thus, autism is located not "within the head" of the person with autism, but in a disordered relationship between person and environment. Can such an approach really account for what we know about social behavior and social understanding in autism?

There is a great deal of research on the social cognition and affective awareness of people with autism, but relatively less on their social behavior and still less on their understanding of complex social situations. In the great tradition of experimental psychology, we have tended to search where the light is brightest; thus, much of what we know about the social-affective skills of people with autism comes from laboratory studies using simplified stimuli and situations. These studies are often intriguing and illuminating, but they usually focus on fairly narrow samples of behavior exhibited under special conditions (my own laboratory is no exception!). In short, they tend to lack "ecological validity." Not surprisingly, it has been difficult for such studies to capture much of what are recognized as the clinical manifestations of the social deficit in autism. What do we know about the social understanding of people with autism, and can what we know be viewed within the ecological framework?

As demonstrated by numerous Theory of Mind studies, persons with autism are often wrong about what other people think, know, or believe, although they seem to be able to identify desires (Baron-Cohen, 1995). These results are usually interpreted as showing that the cognitive module responsible for the metacognitive process of mindreading is defective in persons with autism, such that performance on these tasks is developmentally delayed. Viewed within an ecological psychology framework, experimental tasks such as these might be interpreted somewhat differently. Although poorer performance on ToM tasks in persons with autism is well documented, one need not accept the assumption that all such tasks are solved through metacognitive means (i.e., cognition about cognition). The term "theory of mind" itself implies a conceptual level of understanding and explicit reasoning about what others know or believe. From an ecological perspective one might instead say that false belief and deception tasks, such as those typically used to measure the presence of ToM, actually measure the subject's ability to perceive directly what a particular situation affords another person.

Even though persons with autism as a group usually do more poorly on ToM tasks than do other people, studies have clearly shown that performance on these tasks varies with developmental level, such that more developed persons with autism can often successfully reason about what others know or believe. This fact has necessitated the adoption of more complex ToM tasks and other, less typical social cognition tasks thought to be more challenging for very bright people with autistic spectrum disorders, such as the labeling of eyes-only pictures thought to correspond to cognitive, not emotional, states (Baron-Cohen, Joliffe, Mortimore, & Robertson, 1997) and the stretching of the ToM construct to cover these tasks. These studies tend to show that even bright persons with autism have trouble identifying the mental states of others ("mind reading") when conditions are made sufficiently complex. The studies using eye-only pictures are of particular interest to the ecological psychologist because they suggest that people with autism have a deficit in detecting the affordances (functional significance) of certain kinds of facial gestures.

We know from other research that people with autism frequently appear to misinterpret facial expressions and other human affective signals, though not under all conditions (e.g., Hobson, 1986a, 1986b; Klin et al., 1999; Loveland et al., 1995; Snow, Hertzig, & Shapiro, 1987; Weeks & Hobson, 1987). When compared with children without autism of similar age and IQ, they are sometimes found to do more poorly on emotion recognition and emotion-matching tasks. Often when they are compared with others of similar verbal level, however, no differences are found. For example, they can often identify facial expressions corresponding to simple emotions such as happy or sad about as well as nonautistic persons of similar language level (Loveland et al., 1997b; Ozonoff, Pennington, & Rogers, 1990; Prior, Dahlstrom, & Squires, 1990). Thus, merely being able to identify or label this kind of display is not necessarily enough to allow one to interact smoothly with others. Most likely, the deficits of persons with autism on both emotion recognition and ToM tasks are relative rather than absolute.

Some studies have looked at more complex social perception than that examined in typical affect-recognition research on autism. Moore, Hobson, & Lee (1997), for example, used a point-light walker technique to explore the ability of persons with autism to perceive animateness, actions, and attitudes (e.g., mental states, affects, tendencies to behave). Although persons with autism were able to perceive the figure as human and could identify its actions about as well as typically developing persons and nonautistic persons with mental retardation, they were poorer at recognizing the attitudes portrayed in the figures' actions. Loveland et al. (1997a) examined the ability of verbal persons with autism and nonautistic comparison subjects to determine videotaped children's intention to share or not share some candy in an arranged, but real, situation. Judgments were compared with those of a nondisabled adult group, whose ratings established 19 silent-video segments with significant agreement on whether the child depicted did or did not want to share. Nonautistic comparison subjects were significantly more accurate than those with autism in determining which children did not want to share. Both these studies suggest that persons with autism have difficulty detecting the affordances of other people's behavior, i.e., what the opportunities for action are in response to the behavior.

Phillips, Baron-Cohen, and Rutter (1998), working from a different theoretical stance, found that young people with autism were delayed in their understanding of the intention to carry out a specific act. These results concerning identifying attitudes and intentions are of particular interest because they contrast with findings on children without autism. For example, Van Acker and Valenti (1989) found that children with mild handicapping conditions such as learning disabilities were as able as typically developing children to detect a child's social intention (to play or not play) toward another child by viewing video clips.

Meltzoff (1995) found that children as young as 18 months could correctly infer what an adult intended to do when the adult was shown trying but failing to complete a specific action. Studies such as these show that children without autism are quite adept at detecting what other people's behaviors afford them.

Other investigators have examined the ability of persons with autism to make judgments about the appropriateness of behavior in social situations. For example, Surian, Baron-Cohen, and Van der Lely (1996) found that verbal children with autism were less able than controls to identify utterances in a conversational exchange that violated pragmatic expectations for appropriateness (Gricean conversational maxims). Children with autism also performed near chance overall. Loveland et al. (1996) found that verbal children and adolescents with autism could distinguish inappropriate from appropriate social behavior in videotaped clips at greater than chance levels, but that they did so significantly less often than controls without autism. Moreover, even when subjects with autism correctly identified inappropriate behaviors, they often could not tell why the behavior was inappropriate. These results suggest that children with autism may in part lack understanding of the implications of behavior (their own and others') for other people.

Despite clear difficulties with social understanding and social behavior, persons with autism do, to varying extents, have social interest and awareness, and studies suggest they can detect at least some of what is going on in social interactions (e.g., Loveland et al., 1997b). In fact, many people with autism display considerable interest in getting along with others and considerable distress at their failure to do so. For example, studies of attachment indicate that most children with autism do attach to caregivers, contrary to what was once thought (Sigman & Mundy, 1989; Sigman & Ungerer, 1984). If people with autism possess some of the building blocks of social interaction, then why is it so consistently reported that they are emotionally odd or socially inappropriate (e.g., Tantam, Holmes, & Cordess, 1993; Yirmiya, Kasari, Sigman, & Mundy, 1989)?

The standard view is that autistic persons' perception of other persons is not impaired; only their conceptual understanding of other persons' internal states is defective. (This view rests on the assumption that socially meaningful things cannot be directly perceived, and so they must all be explained on the conceptual level.) Thus failure to think of other persons as perceivers, knowers, or experiencers leads to failure to understand much of what goes on in the human social world. If people with autism are poorer at identifying mental contents than are other people, then they are wrong more often about what others know, believe, feel, or intend, and what limited ability they do have to identify the mental contents of others breaks down in more complex, cognitively challenging situations (such as advanced ToM tests, or dinner parties).

I agree with the numerous investigators who assert that there is something missing in the innate ability of the person with autism to experience other persons and to share feelings and thoughts with them in meaningful ways, and that this lack contributes to deficits in accurately predicting what others believe, know, intend, or feel in particular situations. Unfortunately, this account does not answer the question of exactly how these deficits result in inappropriate behavior, and so it is incomplete. To this account I would add several things.

The social deficit of autism involves not only failure to understand others but also a failure to regulate one's own behavior appropriately in response to a complex and rapidly changing social world (cf. Cicchetti & Tucker, 1994, for discussion of self-regulation as a principle in human development). That is, even when people with autism can identify emotions and other important aspects of social situations and are motivated to interact with others, they nevertheless fail to monitor and to continuously adapt their own social behavior appropriately. If people with autism have trouble not only in identifying the internal states of others but in using this and other information to self-regulate social behavior, then we may say that they have failed to accurately detect the opportunities for action that others afford them. In this way an important instance of the perception-action cycle in human behavior has gone awry. A failure not only to detect reliably and accurately what is present in the social world but to correctly identify its implications for action could account for the ability of many higher functioning individuals with autism to pass certain emotion recognition and ToM tasks, while still behaving very oddly in real situations. Thus, for example, a person who observes a large man approaching with a wooden bat in hand might conclude that an attack is imminent and run away unless he also observes the man smiling and carrying a baseball. To know what the large man affords (danger or play) depends on the ability to pick up enough of the right information from that which is available. It also depends on having already discovered what baseball bats *can* afford and recognizing that while they are chiefly good for hitting, the presence of a baseball makes it likely that it is the ball, and not oneself, that is about to be hit (cf. Loveland, 1991, for discussion of the use of cultural learning to select among available affordances). To give a simpler example, whether an animal chooses to fight or flee from another animal depends in part on size ratio, as Baron & Misovich (1993) have pointed out in their discussion of individual traits as possibilities for action.

Do people with autism have difficulty with self-regulating social behavior in response to changing conditions they perceive? Some research suggests that people with autism have trouble interpreting the functional meaning of what others say and do (i.e., its implications for their own behavior) and that this can lead to inappropriate behavior. For example, research on empathy in children with autism indicates that they are less responsive than are comparison groups to other people's distress even when they notice the distress (Bacon, Fein, Morris, Waterhouse, & Allen, 1998; Loveland & Tunali, 1991; Sigman, Kasari, Kwon, & Yirmiya, 1992; Yirmiya, Sigman, Kasari, & Mundy, 1992). Corona, Dissanayake, Arbelle, Wellington, & Sigman (1998) found that the failure of children with autism to respond to an examiner's distress did not seem to be related to avoiding something aversive, but rather to a failure to understand the significance of what they were seeing.

Such studies provide a clue to the way that poor "mentalizing" ability contributes to disruption of the perception/action cycle for individuals with autism. If others' feelings, thoughts, and motives are opaque or confusing, then an important source of information is unavailable or corrupted. The result can be a failure to accurately detect what other people afford in particular situations. Of course, some affordances of the person or situation may be detected (bats afford hitting), but maybe not the same ones that would be detected by nonautistic persons in the same situation. As a result, the perceived possibilities for action are limited or skewed, and unusual behavior takes place. Unusual behavior, in turn, affects one's social environment. It is well known, for example, that caregivers of children with autism modify their speech and social behavior toward greater directiveness, in response to difficulty in communicating with the child (Landry & Loveland, 1989). Moreover, the unusual affective, social, and communicative behavior of children with autism, such as incongruous facial expressions, may negatively affect the behavior of caregivers, resulting in differences such as less smiling toward the child (Dawson, Hill, Spencer, Galpert, & Watson, 1990; Loveland et al., 1994; McGee, Feldman, & Chernin, 1991; Snow et al., 1987; Yirmiya et al., 1989). Children with autism, therefore, experience a distinctly different social world than that experienced by other children from a very early age, as their unusual behavior affords different sorts of interactions from those that other children usually experience. Not only do they experience or understand the world differently from other children, their world really is different from that of other children, simply because they are in it.

The failure or disruption of the perception-action cycle as it pertains to interpersonal relations is part of a larger developmental picture for autism. The failure of the perception-action cycle is not a single event but a continuous process that affects development not only on the behavioral but on the neurobiological level. I would argue that the disruption of the person with autism's relationship with the human social world is both a product of early neurobiological impairment and an important factor in shaping subsequent neurobehavioral development.

Can an Ecological Approach to Autism Encompass the Neurobiological Level of Explanation?

The approach to autism I propose is not strictly Gibsonian, because it acknowledges the importance of the neurobiological level of explanation. Gibson, along with many subsequent theorists within an ecological view, eschewed theorizing about the brain. He did this in part to avoid reductionism and in part to avoid the "little man in the head"—infinite regression paradox in perception. Gibson's realist epistemology is inconsistent with the ancient but still widely accepted assumption that the nervous system, peripheral and central, serves as a kind of conduit to reality, by means of which the mind (or the little man in the head) receives raw sensory material to be constructed into percepts and concepts. The information so delivered is usually assumed to be more or less veridical, but the world is always known "at second hand." This view has roots in ancient philosophy but is closely identified in modern times with Johannes Müller's theory of specific nerve energies, which asserted that our knowledge of the world is shaped and limited by the qualitative capacities of our specialized sensory nerves. Many versions of this view, which can be described as indirect realism, can be found today in the fields of developmental psychology, cognitive psychology, neuropsychology, and neuroscience (cf. Katz & Wilcox, 1990). Gibson, by contrast, ascribed no special status to the brain at all, viewing it instead as one component in a larger perceptual system that included not only sense organs and the nervous system but the organism's entire body. For example, the head and torso turn when we orient to a sound. Thus, the muscular systems of the body are essential to the active perceptual exploration of our environment through the perception-action cycle. This point is more important than it may appear, for the ability of the organism to adjust continuously to the changing conditions of the environment in which it lives is essential to survival.

Although Gibson had some valid reasons for avoiding the brain in building his theory, I believe that explanations on multiple levels are needed, not so that we can reduce our models to the lowest level of explanation, but so that we can understand human functioning in its entirety. Moreover, it is not necessary to posit indirect realism to discuss the relationship of brain and behavior (cf. Neisser, 1992).

Much current work on autism examines relationships between brain and behavior and aims to link the cognitive with the neurobiological level of explanation. Some regions of the brain that are impaired in a significant number of persons with autism have been identified, and based on the functions these regions are thought to subserve, they can be linked to at least some of the clinical manifestations of autism (Dawson, 1996). A particularly interesting candidate is the orbital region of the prefrontal cortex, which along with the amygdala and other limbic structures forms a circuit that subserves emotional and social functioning (Anderson, Bechara, Damasio, Tranel, & Damasio, 1999, 2000). This brain circuit is by no means the only possible substrate for autism, nor does it necessarily account for all the behavioral manifestations of the syndrome. However, there is mounting evidence that this circuit is probably involved in the development of autism. I use it here as an example of the way in which an ecological approach to autism can be compatible with the neurobiological level of explanation. There is evidence from both human and animal studies that impairment of this brain circuit can result in deficient social-emotional understanding and behavior (e.g., Steklis & Kling, 1985; Stone et al., 1998). A number of investigators working from clinical, neuropathological, and animal experimental evidence have hypothesized that this circuit or its component structures are centrally involved in autism

(Bachevalier & Merjanian, 1994; Bauman & Kemper, 1994; Bishop, 1993; Damasio & Maurer, 1978; Fein, Pennington, & Waterhouse, 1987; Loveland et al., 1998; Waterhouse et al., 1996). Jocelyne Bachevalier and colleagues (Bachevalier & Merjanian, 1994) found that rhesus monkeys with neonatal lesions of the medial temporal lobe showed numerous social-emotional abnormalities similar to those of autism as they matured, including passivity and withdrawal, stereotypies, and impaired communication.

In general, the amygdala and related medial-temporal-lobe structures are thought to be involved in emotional response to environmental events, as well as to perception of emotional states in others, while the orbitofrontal region of the brain is thought to be involved in the ongoing adjustment of behavior in response to environmental stimuli and to the possible consequences of behavior. If the orbitofrontal-amygdala circuit is deeply involved in the ability not only to detect (perceive) the nature of social-emotional conditions, but to rapidly and appropriately adjust one's behavior in response to changes, then we have aptly described the neurobiological substrate for a perception/action cycle that may be disordered in autism. In particular, this circuit may be described as one that subserves the detection of social affordances. It will be recalled that affordances are opportunities for action. The ventral brain circuit in question mediates detection of the social-affective meaning or valence (for the perceiver) of objects, events, and so on, including other humans and their behavior. It further serves to continuously regulate behavior in response to the changing opportunities for action, which change in part because of the actions of the perceiver. This description, while incomplete, is nonetheless consistent with an ecological description of the larger process of perception and action. How may it be applied to autism?

I argued earlier that the person with autism has difficulty not only with understanding the thoughts, feelings, motives, and so on of other persons, but also with continuously regulating behavior in response to them. It is this failure of the perception/action cycle—a failure in not accurately detecting the opportunities for action that other people afford—that results in the odd social and affective behavior of persons with autism, including their tendency to fail ToM tasks. Developmental impairment of the orbitofrontal-limbic circuit of the brain may therefore offer a description of this same process on the neurobiological level of explanation by suggesting how and why the relationship of person and environment is disrupted in this way.

How is this disordered relationship affected by the development of the person with autism? The brain develops by cycles of synaptic surplus followed by synaptic pruning (Black, 1998; Greenough, Black, & Wallace, 1987), guided in part by the interaction of the child and the environment. The frontal lobes are hypothesized to play an important role by affecting the pruning of more posterior synapses. For example, Thatcher (1997) argued that as nerve growth factor "sweeps across the brain" causing growth of new synapses to be pruned, behavioral discontinuities develop, because functionally different anatomical regions of the brain mature at different rates and ages. This process could give rise to observed developmental "stages," with periods of obvious growth and periods of plateau in certain functions: "Each stage or period represents rapid synaptic growth within functionally differentiated neural systems, and, as a consequence, neural plasticity involves the genetically driven overproduction of synapses and the environmentally driven maintenance and pruning of synaptic connections." (p. 110)

What might such a process mean for autism? We can speculate that the impaired perception/action cycle of autism feeds into the process of "sculpting" the neurons of the brain in the following way: If it is assumed that autism originates in brain impairments present very early in life, then these impaired structures as they mature will in turn adversely affect later-developing structures to which they project. This would be the case for early impairment in the medial temporal region, which projects to the later-developing prefrontal cortex. However, because the orbitoprefrontal-amygdala circuit is involved in regulating social-emotional behavior in response to a changing social environment, it is therefore continuously engaged in detecting the opportunities for action (social affordances) offered by that environment. When this process is disrupted, abnormal, maladapted (autistic) behavior results. Autistic behavior, in turn, leads to abnormal feedback from the environment. If the processes of synaptic maintenance and pruning are indeed "environmentally driven," then abnormal input from the environment will contribute to further impairment of the orbitoprefrontal cortex, which could in turn affect the pruning of synapses in more posterior regions. If pruning is disrupted, affected structures may be expected to develop improperly, to contribute to dysregulation of other structures, and to lead to more abnormal perception and action. Such a process would tend to "snowball" over time if not interrupted, with the person becoming more different from typically developing peers as development proceeds.

Although the prospect of tying developmental impairment of a particular brain circuit to deficits in perceiving and acting on social affordances in autism is tantalizing and exciting, much further research remains to be done before this prospect can be realized. Very little is really known about brain development in autism, although there is now intense interest and activity in this field of study. Investigators of diverse backgrounds and viewpoints have brought a variety of techniques to bear and have, perhaps unsurprisingly, found evidence of various brain differences in autism (e.g., Mottron et al., 1997; Townsend et al. 1996). Which of these findings will be reliable and which helpful in explaining the behavioral manifestations of autism over development will be apparent only in the future. Moreover, the picture of brain development in autism is likely to be highly complex and difficult to sort out because of the heterogeneity and variability of the autistic spectrum over development (Loveland & Tunali-Kotoski, 1997).

Conclusions

If we accept that the ecological view of autism is, at the least, an alternative approach offering a coherent account of the known phenomena of autism, what advantages does such a view confer? An example will serve to illustrate this point. As discussed earlier in this chapter, a great deal of recent research on autism has employed various ingenious laboratory tests of social cognition (usually false belief) to measure the presence of ToM. In a typical first-order ToM task, the subject sees something being hidden in the presence of an observer, who then leaves. When the observer has gone, the object is moved to a new location. The subject is then asked where the observer will look for the object when she or he returns. Those subjects who fail at this task are said not to have developed an adequate ToM, since they have failed to correctly predict what the observer's mental state (knowledge or belief) will be. From an ecological perspective, however, such tasks do not directly measure ToM at all. This point resembles one I made in an earlier paper on perceiving the affordances of reflecting surfaces (Loveland, 1986). In that paper I argued that the commonly used rouge-marking tests for mirror self-recognition, claimed to measure the acquisition of a self-concept in humans and other primates, actually measure the ability to use the mirror as a tool for viewing things not ordinarily visible from the observer's perspective (such as one's own face). The hypothetical construct of self-concept or self-schema is an inference added by the investigator to explain the subject's observed behavior of seeing and touching the rouge-mark. Similarly, the ToM is a theoretical construct added by the investigator to explain, for example, why children do or do not accurately perceive what others can perceive and thus infer what they are likely to do. This argument applies equally to strong and weak forms of the ToM—that is, those that do or do not take it to be a true "theory."

Why is such a construct so commonly invoked? Many investigators in developmental psychology and related fields accept that perception is indirect and that it depends on the active construction of meaningless sensory data into percepts (a kind of mental structure) and of percepts into concepts (which unlike percepts are thought to be truly meaningful). Many also accept that cognition causes behavior. Hence, they must not only postulate a mental structure to account for an observed behavior, they must also postulate it at the conceptual level. To some extent this tendency in developmental theory-making may also result from the fact that it is simply rather easy to invoke a corresponding concept, representation, mental schema, or cognitive module whenever a behavioral function or deficit is under study. As a result, the theoretical landscape of developmental psychology has become littered with hypothetical constructs particular to various theories and fields of study. The functionalism of the ecological approach, by contrast, offers some relief from the proliferation of hypotheticals. In so doing it also offers a cleaner approach to the study of phylogenetic continuities and differences in behavior.

The differences between an ecological view of autism and those built on a more conventional cognitive or neuropsychological framework lie at a very deep level—that of epistemology. Like differences of religion or politics, these fundamental philosophical differences may not in principle be resolved by empirical test. As Bill Mace has observed (1977), "The overall approach to perception in terms of ecology that Gibson takes is probably best thought of as a metatheory rather than a theory in the sense of offering specific, falsifiable hypotheses. The overall approach and its subcomponents such as ecological optics should be evaluated in terms of their fruitfulness. No one will ever be able to claim truth or falsity for it. However, the work conducted within a subspeciality such as ecological optics is full of testable and tested hypotheses." (p. 54) So it is with an ecological theory of autism.

The fruitfulness of an ecological approach to autism will be reflected in the extent to which research and theory growing from such an approach are able to advance our understanding of this fascinating disorder, as well as the extent to which they contribute to an understanding of autism on multiple levels of scientific analysis. Moreover, autism may provide a unique opportunity to examine Gibson's theory of affordances, through the study of the perception of social affordances and its possible neural substrates.

ACKNOWLEDGMENTS

The author thanks Jake Burack, Stuart Shanker, Emese Nagy, and Jocelyne Bachevalier for their comments on earlier drafts of this chapter. Any errors or omissions are entirely my own. Preparation of this chapter was supported in part by grant number P01 HD35471 from the National Institute on Child Health and Human Development.

Author information: Katherine A. Loveland, Ph.D. Center for Human Development Research, Department of Psychiatry and Behavioral Sciences, University of Texas, Houston - Medical School, 1300 Moursund Street, Houston, Texas 77030; katherine.a.loveland@uth.tmc.edu. Phone: 713-500-2587.

REFERENCES

Alley, T. (1988). Social and applied aspects of face perception: An introduction. In T. R. Alley (Ed.), *Social and applied aspects of perceiving faces* (pp. 1–9). Hillsdale, NJ: Lawrence Erlbaum Associates, Inc.

Anderson, S. W., Bechara, A., Damasio, H., Tranel, D., & Damasio, A. R. (1999). Impairment of social and moral behavior related to early damage in human prefrontal cortex. *Nature Neuroscience, 2,* 1032–1037.

Anderson, S. W., Bechara A., Damasio, H., Tranel, D., & Damasio, A. R. (2000). I. Acquisition of social knowledge is related to the prefrontal cortex. *Journal of Neurology, 247,* 72.

Bachevalier, J., & Merjanian, P. (1994). The contribution of medial temporal lobe structures in infantile autism: A neurobehavioral study in primates. In M. L. Bauman & T. L. Kemper (Eds.), *The neurobiology of autism* (pp. 146–169). Baltimore: Johns Hopkins.

Bacon, A., Fein, D., Morris, R., Waterhouse, L., & Allen, D. (1998). The responses of autistic children to the distress of others. *Journal of Autism & Developmental Disorders, 28,* 129–142.

Bahrick, L. E, Netto, D., & Hernandez-Reif, M. (1998). Intermodal perception of adult and child faces and voices by infants. *Child Development, 69,* 1263–1275.

Baron, R. M., & Misovich, S. J. (1993). Dispositional knowing from an ecological perspective. *Personality and Social Psychology Bulletin, 19,* 541–552.

Baron-Cohen, S. (1995). *Mindblindness: An essay on autism and theory of mind.* Cambridge, MA: MIT Press/Bradford Books.

Baron-Cohen S., Joliffe T., Mortimore C., & Robertson M. (1997). Another advanced test of theory of mind: Evidence from very high functioning adults with autism or Asperger syndrome. *Journal of Child Psychology & Psychiatry, 38,* 813–822.

Baron-Cohen, S., Ring, H. A., Wheelwright, S., Bullmore, E. T., Brammer, M. J., Simmons, A., & Williams, S. C. (1999). Social intelligence in the normal and autistic brain: An fMRI study. *European Journal of Neuroscience, 11,* 1891–1898.

Bauman, M. L., & Kemper, T. L. (1994). Neuroanatomic observations of the brain in autism. In M. L. Bauman & T. L. Kemper (Eds.), *The neurology of autism* (pp. 119–145). Baltimore: Johns Hopkins.

Berry, D. (1990). What can a moving face tell us? *Journal of Personality and Social Psychology, 58,* 1004–1014.

Bishop, D. V. M. (1993). Annotation: Autism, executive functions, and Theory of Mind: A neuropsychological perspective. *Journal of Child Psychology and Psychiatry, 54,* 279–293.

Black, J. E. (1998). How a child builds its brain: Some lessons from animal studies of neural plasticity. *Preventive Medicine, 27,* 168–171.

Carello, C., Grosofsky, A., Shaw, R., Pittenger, J., & Mark, L. (1989). Attractiveness of facial profiles is a function of distance from archetype. *Ecological Psychology, 1,* 227–251.

Cicchetti, D., & Tucker, D. (1994). Development and self-regulatory structures of the mind. *Development and Psychopathology, 6,* 533–549.

Corona, R., Dissanayake, C., Arbelle, S., Wellington, P., & Sigman, M. (1998). Is affect aversive to young children with autism? Behavioral and cardiac responses to experimenter distress. *Child Development, 69,* 1494–1502.

Damasio, A., & Maurer, R. (1978). A neurological model for childhood autism. *Archives of Neurology, 35,* 777–786.

Dawson, G. (1996). The neuropsychology of autism. *Journal of Autism and Developmental Disorders, 26,* 179–184.

Dawson, G., Hill, D., Spencer, A., Galpert, L., & Watson, L. (1990). Affective exchanges between young autistic children and their mothers. *Journal of Abnormal Child Psychology, 18,* 335–345.

Dawson, G., & Lewy, A. (1989). Arousal, attention, and the socio-emotional impairments of individuals with autism. In G. Dawson (Ed.), *Autism: Nature, diagnosis and treatment* (pp. 49–74). New York: Guilford.

Dawson, G., Meltzoff, A. N., Osterling, J., & Rinaldi, J. (1998). Neuropsychological correlates of early symptoms of autism. *Child Development, 69,* 1276–1285.

DePaulo, B. (1991). Nonverbal behavior and self-presentation. In R. S. Feldman & B. Rimé (Eds.), *Fundamentals of nonverbal behavior* (pp. 351–397). New York: Cambridge University Press.

Dent-Read, C., & Zukow-Goldring, P. (Eds.). (1997). *Evolving explanations of development.* Washington, DC: American Psychological Association.

Dornbush, M. L., Melendez, P., & Pick, A. D. (1995, March/April). *An ecological approach to perceiving social interactions.* Paper presented at the biennial meeting of the Society for Research in Child Development, Indianapolis, IN.

Fein, D., Pennington, B., & Waterhouse, L. (1987). Implications of social deficits in autism for neurological dysfunction. In E. Schopler & G. B. Mesibov (Eds.), *Neurobiological issues in autism* (pp. 127–144). New York: Plenum.

Feldman, R. S., Philippot, P., & Custrini, R. (1991). Social competence and nonverbal behavior. In R.S. Feldman & B. Rimé (Eds.), *Fundamentals of nonverbal behavior.* New York: Cambridge University Press.

Fogel, A., Nwokah, E., Dedo, J. Y, Messinger, D. S., Dickson, L., Matusov, E., & Holt, S. (1992). Social process theory of emotion: A dynamic systems approach. *Social Development, 1,* 122–142.

Frith, C. D., Frith, U. (1999). Interacting minds—a biological basis. *Science, 286,* 1692–1695.

Gallagher, H. L., Happe, F., Brunswick, N., Fletcher, P. C., Frith, U., & Frith, C. D. (2000). Reading the mind in cartoons and stories: An fMRI study of "theory of mind" in verbal and nonverbal tasks. *Neuropsychologia, 38,* 11–21.

Gibson, E. (1997). An ecological psychologist's prolegomena for perceptual development: A functional approach. In C. Dent-Read & P. Zukow-Goldring (Eds.), *Evolving explanations of development* (pp. 23–54). Washington, DC: American Psychological Association.

Gibson, J. J. (1979). *The ecological approach to visual perception.* Boston: Houghton-Mifflin.

Ginsburg, G. P. (1990). The ecological perception debate: An affordance of the *Journal for the Theory of Social Behaviour. Journal for the Theory of Social Behaviour, 20,* Special issue, 347–364.

Greenough, W. T., Black, J. E., Wallace, C. S. (1987). Experience and brain development. *Child Development, 58,* 539–559.

Heft, H. (1989). Affordances and the body: An intentional analysis of Gibson's ecological approach to visual perception. *Journal for the Theory of Social Behavior, 19,* 1–30.

Hobson, R. P. (1986a). The autistic child's appraisal of expressions of emotion. *Journal of Child Psychology and Psychiatry, 27,* 321–342.

Hobson, R. P. (1986b). The autistic child's appraisal of expressions of emotion: A further study. *Journal of Child Psychology and Psychiatry, 27,* 671–680.

Hobson, R. P. (1993). *Autism and the development of mind.* Hove, UK: Lawrence Erlbaum Associates, Ltd.

Hughes, C., Russell, J., & Robbins, T. (1994). Evidence for executive dysfunction in autism. *Neuropsychologia, 32,* 477–492.

Katz, S., & Wilcox, S. (1990). Do many private worlds imply no real world? An analysis of the comparative argument in psychology. *Journal of the Theory of Social Behavior, 9,* 289–301.

Klin A., Sparrow S. S., de Bildt A., Cicchetti D. V., Cohen D. J., & Volkmar F. R. (1999). A normed study of face recognition in autism and related disorders. *Journal of Autism and Developmental Disorders, 29,* 499–508.

Koslowski, L., & Cutting, J. (1977). Recognizing the sex of a walker from a dynamic light-point display. *Perception and Psychophysics, 21,* 575–580.

Landry, S., & Loveland, K. (1989). The effect of social context on the functional communication skills of autistic children. *Journal of Autism and Developmental Disorders, 19,* 283–299.

Loveland, K. (1986). Discovering the affordances of a reflecting surface. *Developmental Review, 6,* 1–24.

Loveland, K. (1991). Social affordances and interaction: Autism and the affordances of the human environment. *Ecological Psychology, 3,* 99–119.

Loveland, K., Bachevalier, J., & Nemanic, S. (1998). *Amygdala dysfunction in autism: A preliminary study.* Paper presented to the International Society for the Study of Behavioral Development meeting, Berne, Switzerland, July, 1998.

Loveland, K., & Tunali, B. (1991). Social scripts for conversational interactions in autism and Down syndrome. *Journal of Autism and Developmental Disorders, 21,* 177–186.

Loveland, K., & Tunali-Kotoski, B. (1997). The school-aged child with autism. In D. Cohen and F. Volkmar (Eds.), *The Handbook of Autism and Pervasive Developmental Disorders,* (2nd ed., pp. 283–308). New York: Wiley.

Loveland, K., Tunali-Kotoski, B., Chen, R., Brelsford, K., Ortegon, J., & Pearson, D. (1995). Intermodal perception of affect in persons with autism or Down syndrome. *Development and Psychopathology, 7,* 409–418.

Loveland, K., Tunali-Kotoski, B., Chen, R., Ortegon, J., Pearson, D. A., Brelsford, K., & Gibbs, M. C. (1997b). Affect recognition in autism: Verbal and non-verbal information. *Development and Psychopathology, 9,* 579–593.

Loveland, K., Tunali-Kotoski, B., Ortegon, J., Pearson, D. A., & Gibbs, M. C. (1997a, April). *Social perception in persons with high-functioning autism: Perceiving the intention to share.* Presented at the Society for Research in Child Development meeting, Washington, DC.

Loveland, K., Tunali-Kotoski, B., Pearson, D., Brelsford, K., Ortegon, J., & Chen, R. (1994). Imitation and expression of facial affect in autism. *Development and Psychopathology, 6,* 433–444.

Loveland, K. A., Tunali-Kotoski, B., Pearson, D. A., Chen, R., Ortegon, J., & Gibbs, M. G. (1996, August). *Judgments of social appropriateness by high-functioning persons with autism.* Paper presented to the XIVth Biennial Conference of the International Society for the Study of Behavioural Development, Quebec City, Quebec, Canada.

Mace, W. M. (1977). James J. Gibson's strategy for perceiving: Ask not what's inside your head, but what your head's inside of. In R. Shaw, & J. Bransford, (Eds.), *Perceiving, acting and knowing.* (pp. 43–65). Hillsdale, NJ: Lawrence Erlbaum Associates.

McArthur, L., & Baron, R. (1983). Toward and ecological theory of social perception. *Psychological Review, 90,* 215–238.

McEvoy, R. E., Rogers, S. J., & Pennington, B. F. (1993). Executive function and social communication deficits in young autistic children. *Journal of Child Psychology and Psychiatry, 34,* 563–578.

McGee, G., Feldman, R., & Chernin, L. (1991). A comparison of emotional facial display by children with autism and typical preschoolers. *Journal of Early Intervention, 15,* 237–245.

Meltzoff, A. (1995). Understanding the intentions of others: Re-enactments of intended acts by 18-month-old children. *Developmental Psychology, 31,* 838–850.

Meltzoff, A., & Gopnik, A. (1993). The role of imitation in understanding persons and developing a theory of mind. In S. Baron-Cohen, H. Tager-Flusberg, & D. J. Cohen (Eds.), *Understanding other minds: Perspectives from autism* (pp. 335–366). Oxford, UK: Oxford University Press.

Michaels, C., & Carello, C. (1981). *Direct perception.* New York: Prentice Hall.

Montepare, J. M., Goldstein, S. B., & Clausen, A. (1987). The identification of emotions from gait information. *Journal of Nonverbal Behavior, 11,* 33–42.

Moore, D. G., Hobson, R. P., & Lee, A. (1997). Components of person perception: An investigation with autistic, non-autistic retarded and typically developing children and adolescents. *British Journal of Developmental Psychology, 15,* 401–423.

Mottron, L., Mineau, S., Decarie, J., Jambaque, I., Labreque, R., Pepin, J., & Aroichane, M. (1997). Visual agnosia with bilateral temporo-occipital brain lesions in a child with autistic disorder: A case study. *Developmental Medicine and Child Neurology, 39,* 699–705.

Neisser, U. (1992). Two themes in the study of cognition. In H. L. Pick, Jr., P. Van Den Broek, & D. C. Knill (Eds.), *Cognition: Conceptual and methodological issues* (pp. 333–340). Washington, DC: American Psychological Association.

Ozonoff, S. (1995). Executive functions in autism. In E. Schopler & G. B. Mesibov (Eds.), *Learning and Cognition in Autism* (pp. 199–215). New York: Plenum.

Ozonoff, S., & McEvoy, R. A. (1994). Longitudinal study of executive function and theory of mind development in autism. *Development and Psychopathology, 6,* 415–43.

Ozonoff, S., Pennington, B., & Rogers, S. (1990). Are there specific emotion perception deficits in young autistic children? *Journal of Child Psychology and Psychiatry, 31,* 343–361.

Ozonoff, S., Pennington, B., & Rogers, S. (1991). Executive function deficits in high-functioning autistic children: Relationship to theory of mind. *Journal of Child Psychology and Psychiatry, 32,* 1081–1105.

Phillips, W., Baron-Cohen, S., & Rutter, M. (1998). Understanding intention in normal development and in autism. *British Journal of Developmental Psychology, 16,* 337–348.

Prior, M., Dahlstrom, B., & Squires, T. (1990). Autistic children's knowledge of thinking and feeling states in other people. *Journal of Child Psychology and Psychiatry and Allied Disciplines, 31,* 587–601.

Reed, E. S. (1988). The affordances of the animate environment: Social science from the ecological point of view. In T. Ingold (Ed.), *What is an animal?* (pp. 110–126). London, UK: Allen & Unwin.

Reed, E. S., & Jones, R. (Eds.). (1982). *Reasons for realism: Selected essays of James J. Gibson.* Hillsdale, NJ: Lawrence Erlbaum Associates.

Rogers, S. J., & Pennington, B. F. (1991). A theoretical approach to the deficits in infantile autism. *Development and Psychopathology, 3,* 137–162.

Runeson, S., & Frykholm, G. (1983). Kinematic specification of dynamics as an informational base for person and action perception: Expectation, gender, and deceptive intention. *Journal of Experimental Psychology: General, 112,* 580–610.

Shaw, R., & Bransford, J. (1977). *Perceiving, acting and knowing.* Hillsdale, NJ: Lawrence Erlbaum Associates.

Sigman, M. D., Kasari, C., Kwon, J. H., & Yirmiya, N. (1992). Responses to the negative emotions of others by autistic, mentally retarded, and normal children. *Child Development, 63,* 796–807.

Sigman, M., & Mundy, P. (1989). Social attachments in autistic children. *Journal of the American Academy of Child and Adolescent Psychiatry, 28,* 74–81.

Sigman, M., & Ungerer, J. A. (1984). Attachment behaviors in autistic children. *Journal of Autism and Developmental Disorders, 14,* 231–244.

Snow, M., Hertzig, M., & Shapiro, T. (1987). Expression of emotion in young autistic children. *Journal of the American Academy of Child and Adolescent Psychiatry, 26,* 836–838.

Steklis, H. D., & Kling, A. (1985). Neurobiology of affiliative behavior in non-human primates. In M. Reite & T. Field (Eds.), *The psychobiology of attachment and separation* (pp. 93–129). New York: Academic Press.

Stone, W., Baron-Cohen, S., & Knight, R. (1998). Frontal lobe contributions to Theory of Mind. *Journal of Cognitive Neuroscience, 10,* 640–656.

Surian, L., Baron-Cohen, S., & Van der Lely, H. (1996). Are children with autism deaf to Gricean maxims? *Cognitive Neuropsychiatry, 1,* 55–71.

Tantam, D., Holmes, D., & Cordess, C. (1993). Nonverbal expression in autism of Asperger type. *Journal of Autism and Developmental Disorders, 23,* 111–133.

Thatcher, R. W. (1997). Human frontal lobe development: A theory of cyclical cortical reorganization. In N. A. Krasnegor, G. A. Lyon, & P. S. Goldman-Rakic (Eds.), *Development of the prefrontal cortex. Evolution, neurobiology, and behavior* (pp. 85–113). Baltimore: Paul H. Brookes.

Townsend, J., Courchesne, E., & Egaas, B. (1996). Slowed orienting of covert visual-spatial attention in autism: Specific deficits associated with cerebellar and parietal abnormality. *Development & Psychopathology, 8,* 563–584.

Valenti, S. S. (1989). Ecological social psychology: Illustrative experiments on the perception of intention and intercoordination in human social walking. *Perceiving and Acting Workshop Review, 4,* 28–32.

Valenti, S. S., & Wagner, K. (1991). Three experiments on children's and adults' perception of intention from facial expression and body motion. *Posters presented at the VIth International Conference on Event Perception and Action.* Amsterdam, The Netherlands, August 25-30.

Van Acker, R., & Valenti, S. S. (1989). Perception of social affordances by children with mild handicapping conditions: Implications of social skills research and training. *Ecological Psychology, 1,* 383–405.

Walker-Andrews, A. S., Bahrick, L. E., Raglioni, S. S., & Diaz, I. (1991). Infants' bimodal perception of gender. *Ecological Psychology, 3,* 55–75.

Waterhouse, L., & Fein, D. (1989). Social or cognitive or both? Crucial dysfunctions in autism. In C. Gillberg (Ed.), *Diagnosis and treatment of autism* (pp. 53–61). New York: Plenum.

Waterhouse, L., Fein D., & Modahl, C. (1996). Neurofunctional mechanisms in autism. *Psychological Review, 103,* 457–89.

Watkins, M. J. (1990). Mediationism and the obfuscation of memory. *American Psychologist, 45,* 328–335.

Weeks, S., & Hobson, R. P. (1987). The salience of facial expression for autistic children. *Journal of Child Psychology and Psychiatry, 28,* 137–151.

Yirmiya, N., Kasari, C., Sigman, M., & Mundy, P. (1989). Facial expressions of affect in autistic, mentally retarded, and normal children. *Journal of Child Psychology and Psychiatry, 30,* 725–736.

Yirmiya, N., Sigman, M., Kasari, C., & Mundy, P. (1992). Empathy and cognition in high-functioning children with autism. *Child Development, 63,* 150–160.

3

A Developmental Perspective on Early Autism: Affective, Behavioral, and Cognitive Factors

Philip R. Zelazo
Department of Psychology
McGill University Montreal, Quebec, Canada and the Montreal Children's Hospital, Quebec, Canada

Early valid diagnosis and intensive intervention carry a greater likelihood for ameliorating the effects of autism (e.g., Rogers, 1998) and can lead to a clearer perspective on etiology as well (Zelazo, 1997a, 1997b). Some researchers (e.g., Baird et al., 2000; Baron-Cohen, Allen, & Gillberg, 1992; Baron-Cohen et al., 1996) recognized the significance of early identification of autism and their attempts to produce a valid screening tool represented an important first step. Others have studied early social behaviors among children with autism to better understand the development of the disorder (Leekam & Moore, chap. 6, this volume; Mundy, Sigman, & Kasari, 1994). Early identification and treatment are important because as time advances constraints on plasticity increase. Just as the distances between the spokes of a wheel increase as they recede from the hub, so too the later we diagnose and treat autism, the more distant the children drift from normal development and their nonhandicapped peers.

In this chapter, I review key factors of normal psychological development through the first and second years of life and suggest ways that development may go awry in the case of autism. I suggest that there are cascading effects from seemingly innocent early behavioral aberrations in development that produce adverse affective, linguistic, cognitive, and social behaviors that define autism in the DSM–IV (APA, 1994), and ICD–10 (WHO, 1993) classifications. The role of cognitive factors, including delays in mental development that result in mental retardation in the majority of cases, is neither well researched nor well understood. I suggest that the distinction between intelligence and the development of expressive abilities requires greater clarification because it is frequently confused theoretically. Conventional tests used to measure mental ability are confounded with the disabilities seen in young children with autism. Virtually all of these tests require functional object use, expressive language, and compliance with an examiner's requests to infer mental ability. Autism, in large part, is defined by delays and difficulties in these very areas: delayed object use (functional and symbolic play), delayed expressive language, and behavioral and social difficulties that diminish the likelihood of compliance with an examiner's requests. This profile can only depress the child's scores on conventional tests and does not provide an unbiased measure of mental processing. This confounded situation has implication for both the etiology of autism and intervention strategies. An alternative approach to the assessment of mental ability is presented along with evidence supporting this developmental psychopathology model. The fact that a psychological model of the etiology of early autism has not been considered widely is addressed.

Developmental Psychopathology and Early Autism

Despite the classification of autism as a pervasive developmental disorder, the role of psychological development in its etiology is rarely acknowledged, particularly outside the field of psychology (D'Alessandro & Zelazo, 2000). Two factors are critical to this omission. First, the dominance of medicine, particularly psychiatry and neurology, in the early diagnosis of autism has led to a bias toward biological explanations. Second, developmental psychologists have not had ready access to children with autism early in the course of the disorder—particularly during the critical first three years of life. As stated in the DSM–IV (APA, 1994), "the disturbance must be manifest by delays or abnormal functioning in at least one of the following areas prior to age 3 years: Social interaction, language as used in social communication, or symbolic or imaginative play ... " (p. 67). The link between age and diagnosis of autism is stated even more explicitly: "By definition, if there is a period of normal development, it cannot extend past age 3 years" (p. 67). The significance of early assessment and treatment is strongly reinforced by evaluation research showing that early psychological interventions including, but not limited to, applied behavioral analysis (ABA) have a greater likelihood of success if begun before 5 years of age (Rogers, 1998; Rogers & Lewis 1989; Zelazo, 1997a, 1997b). Clearly, if psychological developmental factors are involved in the etiology of autism, they must occur within the first 3 years and psychologists must study their development earlier than has been the case generally.

Developmental psychopathology includes the notion that disorders involving mental retardation may involve delayed, but not necessarily deviant, development—a view that has been acknowledged for over 30 years (Zigler, 1967). Cicchetti (1984) and his colleagues (Cicchetti & Pogge-Hesse, 1982) and Hodapp and Zigler (1990) argued for and demonstrated the utility of the developmental psychopathology perspective to biologically based forms of mental retardation, such as Down syndrome. One of the fundamental tenets of this expanded perspective is that typical and atypical development are intimately intertwined (Burack, 1990; Cicchetti, 1984). The study of atypical development in light of typical development informs researchers about factors central to both domains. Thus, the study of typical cognitive and neuromotor development, from birth through the second year, may shed light on the etiology of autism. At the very least, knowledge of typical development can indicate more precisely where development goes awry in autism and can identify hypotheses for future research. Moreover, it is expected that knowledge of typical cognitive development will clarify the association between early autism and later mental retardation.

Normal Development During the First Two Years

Neonatal and Infant Development

Information Processing. The mental world of the neonate and the infant throughout most of the first year can be characterized as a state of minimal consciousness (Zelazo, P. D., 1996; Zelazo P. R., & Zelazo, P. D., 1998)—a state like that of implicit learning in the adult. This view holds that although the infant records its experiences throughout the first year by creating mental representations, its awareness is seriously limited. It is not until the end of the first year, when a major cognitive metamorphosis occurs, that the infant becomes a toddler and acquires many of the characteristics that define us as a species. P. R. Zelazo and P. D. Zelazo (1998) argue that these changes in behavior are driven by a profound cognitive change that permits qualitatively different information processing.

Zelazo, P. R., Weiss, and Tarquinio (1991) summarized a series of experiments on neonatal information processing indicating that neonates create mental representations for their experiences. This process occurs by at least the second day of life and, most likely, begins during the last trimester of the fetal period (DeCasper & Spence, 1991). The capacity to create mental representations—neural correlates—of its visual, auditory, and apparently neuromotor experiences continues throughout the first year (Cohen, 1991, 1998; Zelazo, P. R., 1998). However, processing of mental representations by neonates and infants is qualitatively different from processing by the adult or even the year-old infant (Zelazo, P. R., 1982; Zelazo P. R., & Leonard, 1983). The neonate's mental representations direct his or her neuromotor patterns—turning toward or away from sound sources, for example—and thus can motivate approach and avoidance behaviors (Weiss, Zelazo, P. R., &

Swain, 1988). However, neonates and infants throughout most of the first year remain unreflective and cannot recall, but can only recognize, stimuli that they experience. As such, neonates and infants are stimulus-bound and present-oriented. Moreover, infants make no reference to an explicit sense of self (Zelazo, P. R., & Zelazo, P. D., 1998). The infant's mental world is restricted, in large part, by its inability to recall associations to guide its actions (Diamond, 1985).

Cohen (1991, 1998) summarized data from an extensive series of studies on visual information processing with infants to show that the unit of information that is processed increases over the course of the first year. For example, as an infant gains visual experience, a triangle is processed as a whole unit rather than as three unconnected angles. The net effect is that speed of information processing improves with age over the first year as it does during the second and third years (Zelazo, P. R., Kearsley, & Stack, 1995) and throughout the first 26 years of life (Kail, 1991). The infant's information-processing ability remains qualitatively similar throughout most of the first year, although processing gets increasingly more efficient and rapid because myelination increases and higher order units of information are formed (Cohen, 1991, 1998). Nonetheless, the infant remains nonreflective and, thus, qualitatively different from the toddler. It is this limited level of awareness that is captured by the phrase, "minimal consciousness" (Zelazo, P. D., 1996).

Neuromotor Development. There appears to be a parallel pattern of development for neuromotor behavior. Neonates and infants appear to gain cortical control of initially hardwired neuromotor patterns with use and they appear to become integrated into higher order units, but remain limited qualitatively. P. R. Zelazo (1976, 1998) argued that with use neonates and infants gain instrumental control of complex neuromotor patterns such as the stepping pattern and thus effectively contribute to their own "neurological wiring." Zelazo, P. R., Zelazo, N. A., and Kolb (1972) demonstrated that daily elicitation of the neuromotor stepping pattern resulted in a sharp increase in stepping. N. A. Zelazo, P. R. Zelazo, Cohen, and P. D. Zelazo (1993) replicated this finding and extended the result to the neonatal sitting pattern identified by Katona (1989). N. A. Zelazo, P. R. Zelazo, Cohen, and P. D. Zelazo (1994) demonstrated that smiling increases during the last 4 of 7 weeks of training for infants who received active stimulation of the stepping pattern relative to infants receiving practice with sitting or no practice at all. The results for smiling while stepping implied that the development of higher order control was at the cortical level. Independent research on smiling (Kagan, 1967; Sroufe & Waters, 1976; Zelazo, P. R. & Komer, 1971) strongly supports the notion that smiling occurs when there is a match between an external event and a mental representation of that event following some effort.

Based on these results, P. R. Zelazo, Robaey, and Bonin (1999) examined the development of the lateralized readiness potential (LRP) for the stepping foot—a precisely located, anticipatory movement-related brain potential that occurs about 500 milliseconds prior to the lifting of the foot. The results revealed clear increases in the LRP over the third, fifth, and seventh weeks of training relative to untrained controls. These results demonstrate that the level of control that develops with practice is cortical, consistent with the original suggestion that with practice the neonate gains instrumental control of the initially hardwired neuromotor patterns (Zelazo, P. R., 1976, 1983). This view is contrary to Thelen's (1983, 1995; Thelen & Fisher, 1982) argument that neonatal stepping is a strictly peripherally based phenomenon that can be explained by biomechanical principles alone.

Throughout the first year reflexive neuromotor behaviors improve and become integrated with use much as Piaget (1952) described the process for circular reactions. Existing reflexive behaviors such as reaching (Rochat & Goubet, 1995), grasping (Touwen, 1984), and rooting appear to expand and become integrated so that the infant comes to mouth, wave, and bang objects as its dominant form of object use by $9^1/_2$ months (Belsky & Most, 1981). Approximately 88% of all toy manipulations in a free-play context at $9^1/_2$ months involve stereotypical use of objects independent of their functions (Fig. 3.1; Zelazo, P. R., & Kearsley, 1980).

To summarize, it appears that neuromotor behaviors expand from smaller to larger integrated units of behavior (Zelazo, P. R., 1998) just as visual processing expands from smaller to higher order units of information (Cohen, 1991, 1998). Moreover, just as the neonate processes visual and auditory information at the cortical level, so it appears that the neonate processes and gains control of some of its neuromotor patterns at the cortical level as well—and long before generally believed possible (Thelen, 1995; Zelazo, P. R. et al., 1999). In addition, the development of neuromotor behaviors throughout the first year, like the processing of visual and auditory information, remains qualitatively limited for the infant relative to the toddler.

The Toddler: The Dawn of Active Thought and the Development of Expressive Abilities

At the end of the first year of life, from about 9 to 12 months, there is a major change in cognitive development—a change so profound that I have referred to it as the "dawn of active thought" (Zelazo, P. R., & Leonard, 1983). A host of new behaviors emerge in ontogeny that define us as a species: naming, protodeclarative pointing, functional object use, social referencing, bipedal locomotion, and deferred imitation, to name a few (Zelazo, P. R., 1982). P. R. Zelazo and P. D. Zelazo (1998) suggest that there is an underlying concomitant change in consciousness from the stimulus-bound minimal consciousness of the infant (Zelazo, P. D., 1996) to the recursive consciousness of the toddler.

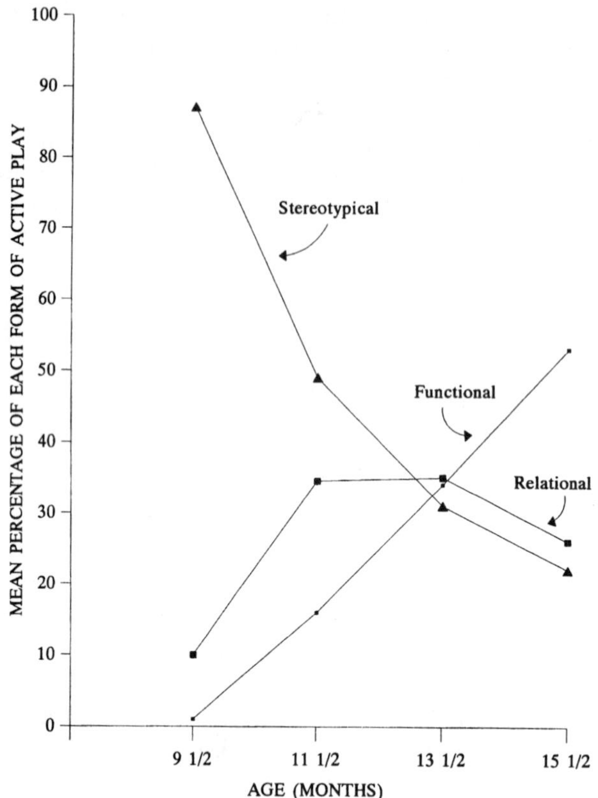

FIG. 3.1. Stereotypical, relational, functional, and the average sum of play for $9\frac{1}{2}$, $11\frac{1}{2}$, $13\frac{1}{2}$, and $15\frac{1}{2}$-month-old children. (From P. R. Zelazo & R. B. Kearsley (1980). The emergence of functional play in infants: Evidence for a major cognitive transition. *Journal of Applied Developmental Psychology, 1*, 95–117.

The tight interval synchrony with which these profound changes occur—literally from $9^1/_2$ to $11^1/_2$ months for many behaviors that we have studied—strongly implicates both a central determinant and a maturational influence. It appears that only a central cognitive influence could so radically affect such disparate areas of development as expressive language, gross and fine-motor development, and social behavior. Similarly, it seems likely that only a maturational change could produce such qualitatively different changes over such a short period of time (Zelazo, P. R., 1982; Zelazo P. R., & Leonard, 1983). P. R. Zelazo and P. D. Zelazo (1998) argued that maturational and cognitive experiences interact to produce functional increases in speed of processing. Increased processing speed within a fixed psychological window—the infant's consciousness—yields the capacity to be aware of two mental representations simultaneously and permits two-step behaviors, such as turning toward and reaching for the swimming pool wall (Weiss & Zelazo, P. R., 1981, 1982). This emergent capacity for two-step functions appears to underlie the many new expressive abilities that occur at the end of the first year of life and possibly the development of intentional actions generally (Zelazo, P. D., Astington, & Olson, 1999). The emergence of this transition has independent research support (Carpenter, Nagel, & Tomasello, 1998; Kagan, 1972; Moore & Corkum, 1994; Tomasello, 1999, 2000).

P. R. Zelazo and P. D. Zelazo (1998) suggest that the capacity to hold mental representations in consciousness simultaneously can be modeled as a recursive loop, much as Edelman (1989) suggested. If at least one of these mental representations involves an acquired action, recursive consciousness can allow for stored memories to override prepotent reflexive-like neuromotor patterns. This phenomenon is illustrated most clearly in the transition from stereotypical to functional object use (Zelazo P. R., & Kearsley, 1980). Only five $9^1/_2$-month-old children in a sample of 16 normally developing children displayed only one functional act in a 15-minute free-play setting, whereas all $13^1/_2$-month-old children in a comparable sample displayed multiple functional acts. Just as the capacity for holding two mental representations in consciousness directs the telephone to the ear rather than the mouth (i.e., functional object or tool use), so this capacity permits naming (that is "ball," for example), protodeclarative pointing (Butterworth & Morissette, 1996), social referencing (Moore & Corkum, 1994), deferred imitation (Meltzoff, 1988), and a host of other expressive abilities. Thus, the cognitive metamorphosis occurring toward the end of the first year produces a qualitatively different child—one who is able to express him or herself with culturally appropriate actions, words, and social conventions.

One principal implication of this analysis bears directly on the interplay between nature and nurture. Some researchers have emphasized the innate aspects of the developments associated with this cognitive transition; others have emphasized culture (Tomasello, 2000). The view presented here acknowledges both biological and experiential influences (Zelazo, P. R., 1982, 1998; Zelazo P. R., & Zelazo, P. D., 1998). The basis for the numerous psychological changes seen between 9 and 12 months appears to be maturational rather than experiential and central rather than modular in origin (Fodor, 1983). However, the realization of the abilities inherent in recursive consciousness—the development of expressive abilities—is heavily dependent on experience and culture. Toddlers must have opportunities to observe the functional uses of objects, if not actually play with them, if they are to acquire functional play. They must hear specific words and be inclined to repeat them if they are to speak the language of their culture. Perhaps most pointedly, they must imitate—be it words or actions—if they are to either speak or use objects appropriately. Normally all systems develop in synchrony. What then happens with the autistic child?

Development of Autistic Behaviors During the Second Year

Development in the autistic child turns abruptly abnormal during the second year. A number of problems occur but usually there is a failure to name objects (or, if naming occurs initially, words may be lost at around 18 months) and the emergence of serious behavior problems, frequently in the form of noncompliance to requests, with the most extreme case in the form of temper tantrums. Researchers cannot say for certain whether behavior problems are the cause or the consequence of arrested language development; we only know that they co-occur with close interval synchrony. An empirical answer is difficult to attain for at least two reasons. First, it is nearly impossible to accurately reconstruct development retrospectively. Second, because the incidence of autism is relatively low, it is difficult to know which children will be autistic, and it is impractical to carefully monitor the large numbers necessary to identify a few. Nonetheless, prospective efforts at large-scale screening for autism hold the potential to address this question (e.g., Baron-Cohen et al., 1996).

Fortunately, there are both logical and clinical reasons to believe, contrary to the widely accepted view, that behavior problems may be the cause and not the result of arrested expressive language development. Logically, if there is a causal relation, it is as reasonable to expect that disruptive and noncompliant behavior may arrest expressive language development as it is to expect that disruptive behavior is the result of frustration caused by the inability to talk. The strongest case for behavior as the cause of arrested language development is the fact that treatment to facilitate compliance yields improved expressive language development (Zelazo, P. R., 1997b; Zelazo, P. R., & Kearsley, 1984). In the design of the study by P. R. Zelazo & Kearsley (1984), treatment is an independent variable that is guided by a theoretical perspective and yields predicted improvements. Clinically, it makes greater sense to correct noncompliant behavior as a first step toward facilitating expressive language than it does to stimulate expressive language in a noncompliant child who, by definition, is uncooperative with most attempts to stimulate language. Unlike motor actions that can progress with the physical assistance of an adult, expressive language requires cooperation from the child. Indeed, that is the principal challenge with a nontalking two-year-old child with autism who is generally avoidant to task demands: How does one stimulate expressive language? Not without the compliance of the child. Because compliance is essential for verbal imitation to occur, it is prudent to proceed as though noncompliant resistant behavior plays an initial, if not causal, role in delayed expressive language development in children with autism.

How may noncompliant behavior arrest expressive language development? I suggest that attempts at naming may stop during the early part of the second year—a time when toddlers typically display vocal excitement to moderately discrepant information (Zelazo, P. R., Kagan, & Hartmann, 1975). If, for a variety of reasons, the environment either does not reinforce word approximations or reinforces an incompatible behavior such as crying, this propensity for speech may decline or even be replaced with an alternative form of communication. When a child cries because of the pain associated with recurrent otitis media or another illness, for example, and is rewarded by the parents' attention, there is an increased risk that crying will replace attempts at naming, even when the pain is resolved. Moreover, in the case of recurrent otitis media, hearing is diminished temporarily during the course of the illness. However, crying does not arrest expressive language development in the majority of cases, so other factors, either in the child or in the environment, must contribute to delayed talking among children with autism.

Once crying or avoidance is established as the prepotent response, three serious consequences occur. First, crying or other forms of avoidance preempt efforts at verbal communication; crying and avoidance are virtually incompatible with talking and do not easily co-occur, particularly for inexperienced talkers. Second, affective development—specifically self-regulation (Kopp, 1989)—is arrested just as expressive development is stifled. Immediate crying is an expressive avoidant reaction that precludes the development of stress or frustration tolerance because it permits escape from the stressors. Avoidance eliminates the task demand, reduces the stress to the child, and therefore reinforces a pattern of escape. Of necessity, stressors must be confronted if self-regulation is to develop. Third, because self-regulation does not develop, even the slightest request from an adult produces avoidance and noncompliance (Rogers, 1997; Rogers, Zelazo, Mendelson, & Rotsztein, 1998), presumably because task demands themselves are stressors (Carr & Newsom, 1985).

This pattern of avoidance—a noncompliant reaction to adult requests—precludes imitation, which is an implicit request for compliance. Because imitation—either immediate or deferred—is an essential though not final step in the development of expressive language (Speidel & Nelson, 1989), naming itself is arrested. This cascading pattern of behavior arrests the development of the toddler's expressive and communicative capabilities—be they talking, object use, or social interaction (Zelazo, P. R., 1989). Thus, from this developmental perspective, it is the inability to tolerate even the slightest frustration (stresses to task demands) that elicits escape behaviors and, thus, prevents normal expressive language development; it is not that arrested expressive language development leads initially to frustration and subsequently to behavior problems, although that may happen in some instances.

This characterization of development in children with autism is consistent not only with clinical experience but with the primary traits reported in the DSM–IV (APA, 1994). Autism is characterized by "severe and extensive impairments in reciprocal social interaction and communication, hyperactivity, short attention span, impulsivity, aggressiveness, self-injurious behaviors, and particularly in young children, temper tantrums" (p. 67). A developmental perspective on early autism emphasizes the role of avoidant responses including temper tantrums as defining behaviors. Observation of children with Pervasive Developmental Disorders (PDD) and autistic toddlers in a structured teaching session where demands are placed on them by their parents reveals that noncompliant and resistant behaviors occur with greater frequency than for typically developing children (Rogers, 1997; Rogers et al., 1998). In this study, demands (easy, moderate, and difficult) were determined individually for children with autism and for two samples of same-aged typically developing children who served as comparison groups.

Temper tantrums and milder forms of noncompliant and oppositional behaviors, including simply ignoring adult requests, terminate task demands and allow the child to escape the stresses associated with them (Carr & Durand, 1985; Carr & Newsom, 1985; Rogers, 1997; Rogers et al., 1998). This behavioral pattern can truncate normal parent–child interactions and reduce learning opportunities that promote development of expressive language and appropriate object use. This scenario in no way suggests fault, because both parents and children become victims of circumstances that they are neither aware of nor understand. It simply illustrates that behavioral patterns can become entrenched and can carry profound developmental consequences. Indeed, Francis, Diorio, Liu, and Meaney (1999) have even demonstrated nongenomic transmission of maternal behavior and stress responses across generations in the rat. Their study demonstrates clearly that acquired behaviors can be as persistent as genetic effects.

The Role of Mental Assessment

The DSM–IV (APA, 1994) indicates that approximately 75% of children with Autistic Disorder function in the range of mental retardation, a fact that deserves greater prominence in the discussion of this disorder. The cascading of developmental difficulties associated with autism extends to the assessment of mental ability in young children. I have argued that the measures used on conventional tests to infer mental ability are confounded with the primary disabilities presented for intellectual assessment during the first three years of life (Zelazo, P. R., 1979, 1989). This argument is especially true for early autistic disorder. Conventional tests, such as the Bayley Scales of Infant Development (Bayley, 1993), measure gross and fine-motor facility explicitly during the first year of life and indirectly for receptive language and nonverbal imitative items during the second and third years. Expressive language is required for naming items during the second and third years. Moreover, implicit in virtually all forms of conventional testing is a necessity for compliance with adult requests—compliance to task demands. Even nonverbal tests measure similar domains of development—expressive language, age-appropriate object use, and social-emotional behaviors. The primary difference is that they are assessed using parental report. Unfortunately, children with autism have behavioral difficulties, are noncompliant to adult requests, and have delays with expressive language and play—the primary measures used to infer mental ability. Difficulties in any one of these areas will depress estimates of mental ability. Moreover, as the child gets older, expressive language plays a dominant role in tests of intelligence and contributes significantly to further cognitive development. Thus, conventional tests alone are inappropriate for children with PDD and autistic disorder. The tragedy is that, in many instances—75% of the cases in a study by P. R. Zelazo and Kearsley (1984)—the use of conventional tests may result in identifying children as mentally retarded when they are not. Because there is no known cure for mental retardation, such an assessment can severely depress the prognosis for a child with autism; hope is deflated and expectations are lowered.

Ironically, the need for alternative procedures for assessing mental development among young children with known mental retardation has been recognized. Cicchetti and Beeghly (1990) explicitly called for alternative assessment procedures to address the limitations of conventional testing for children with Down syndrome. Fortunately, an alternative is possible and there is substantial literature examining the information-processing ability of infants and young children. Data from a host of studies show that recovery of attention to a novel stimulus during infancy using either paired-comparison or habituation-recovery paradigms has greater predictability to intelligence tests at 2, 4, and 7 years of age (r's ranging from .46 to .64) than conventional tests themselves (Bornstein & Sigman, 1986; Fagan & McGrath, 1981; Lewis & Brooks-Gunn, 1981; Zelazo, P. R., 1997a).

P. R. Zelazo (1979, 1989) and P. R. Zelazo, Kearsley, and Stack (1995) adapted a procedure to assess information-processing ability that was used initially by Kagan, Kearsley, and P. R. Zelazo (1978) to examine infant and toddler attention to visual and auditory events. The adapted information-processing procedure assesses the child's capacity to create mental representations for complex visual and auditory sequences at age-appropriate rates. A Standard Transformation Return (STR) paradigm was developed in which an initial event is repeated so that an expectancy can be formed (a mental representation), followed by a discrepant variation that effectively poses a simple perceptual-cognitive problem that is also repeated. The original event is reintroduced and repeated. This STR procedure measures speed of information processing—a dimension that can distinguish children over the first three years of life (Lewis, Goldberg, & Campbell, 1969) and that P. R. Zelazo et al. (1995) have shown can discriminate children between 22, 27, and 32 months of age.

The STR paradigm does not require expressive language, object manipulation, or compliance with an examiner's requests, and therefore, circumvents the confounded measures inherent in conventional tests of mental development. Thus, when used in combination with conventional tests, which will almost invariably reveal delayed development among children with autism, a differential diagnosis can be made. Delayed development with delayed information processing implies true mental retardation. Delayed development with age-appropriate information processing implies normal intelligence and points to delays with the expression of that intelligence—expressive language and object use—and a noncompliant resistant response to adult requests.

This analysis received support from a study by P. R. Zelazo and Kearsley (1984; Zelazo, 1997a) in which a sample of 44 children with PDD and autism were sorted into intact and impaired processors using the information-processing procedures. Both groups were given intensive parent-implemented developmental behavioral therapy designed to foster compliance with actions, object use, and expressive language over a 10-month period (P. R. Zelazo et al., 1984). In this design, treatment is effectively an experimental manipulation applied equally to both groups with a differential outcome predicted for intact and impaired information processors.

Two findings were particularly striking. First, 61% of the children with normal information-processing ability achieved mental ages that equaled or exceeded their chronological ages on conventional tests (conducted blindly) 18 months following the 10-month therapy program. Nine of 10 "impaired processors" increased rather than reduced their delays despite intensive therapy. These results provide experimental validity for the information-processing assessment. Second, 75% of the sample of children with delays on conventional tests had intact (age-appropriate) information-processing ability. These results cast serious doubt on the finding that 75% of children with autism are mentally retarded—at least within the first three years. To some degree, their retardation may be acquired—in part, due to the confounded tests of early mental development, the resulting lowered expectations, and the persistence of the maladaptive pattern of development set in motion.

The finding that many children with PDD and autism may not be mentally retarded gained indirect support with a sample of 21 children with intact information-processing ability who received a shorter period of treatment—6 months (Lalinec, Zelazo, P. R., Rogers, & Reid, 1995; Lalinec-Michaud, 1995). This study used a before–after design and cross-lagged comparisons of younger children following treatment with same-aged older children beginning treatment that were recruited using identical criteria. Clear reductions in delays were found on conventional tests (a conservative measure) following treatment relative to their initial scores and relative to same-aged older children beginning treatment. Improvements with expressive language and play were obtained as well using the same comparisons. These results should be replicated using random assignment to an immediate treatment or a delayed treatment group that is assessed before and after their wait to commence treatment. Such a design would minimize ethical difficulties because delays due to shortages of services are unavoidable. Similar results showing that delayed children with PDD and autism with age-appropriate information processing can significantly increase their intelligence test scores would radically improve the prognosis for autism. Not only would the comorbidity of childhood psychosis and mental retardation be severed in some cases, but one path toward an effective therapy would be implicated.

A Theoretically Guided Developmental-Behavioral Program for Autism

Learning to speak: A manual for parents (Zelazo, P. R., et al., 1984) was developed as a therapeutic program to overcome delays with expressive development. This treatment program is consistent with the overall theoretical view presented in this chapter. The same four factors are central to both the diagnosis of autism and this theoretical formulation. Moreover, in conventional tests of mental development, these four factors are confounded with the disabilities inherent in autism. The assessment of information-processing ability is designed to overcome these confounds. To complete the consistency, the same four factors are the core behaviors addressed in the therapeutic intervention. This consistency is presented across five process categories in Table 3.1.

The outward appearance, guiding principles, and language used to describe the treatment program are of applied behavioral analysis (ABA). The Skinnerian technique for shaping behavior is of central importance for changing noncompliant and resistant behaviors to compliant ones and for stimulating expressive language development. A less obvious but equally important emphasis in this program is on early child development research—particularly the development of information-processing ability—and on neuromotor development including object use and play, early expressive language acquisition, and social-emotional development.

The developmental underpinnings serve a central but largely invisible role in this treatment program. They determine the critical set of behaviors to be targeted during the daily parent-implemented therapy sessions that are adjusted by the therapists on a biweekly basis. The target behaviors, which represent the new behaviors to be encouraged over the immediate two weeks of treatment, literally drive progress. Developmental factors provide the standard that the child must achieve within each domain of development and impart a dynamic quality to the program because the developmental target must change constantly.

The Role of Stress Tolerance. At the heart of this program is the concept of noncompliant resistant behavior and its relation to the development of stress tolerance and self-regulation (Kopp, 1989). There is clear evidence from our own research (Zelazo, P. R., 1997b; Zelazo P. R., & Kearsley, 1984) and from ABA approaches, in particular (e.g., Carr & Durand, 1985; Lovaas, 1987; McEachin, Smith, & Lovaas, 1993), that gaining compliance to instruction leads to significant improvement with social-communicative development. However, two primary theoretical questions are not addressed convincingly by ABA

TABLE 3.1

Theoretical consistency of a developmental psychopathological view of early autism

		Mental Assessment		
Diagnostic Criteria	*Psychological Theory of Etiology*	*Confounding Factors in Conventional Tests*	*Processing of Visual and Auditory Information*	*Therapeutic Plan*
1. Non-compliant behavior (non-imitative, disruptive behavior, atypical social interactions).	1. Non-compliant behavior → avoidance of all demands and arrested development of stress tolerance: non-imitative, protest to demands and atypical social interactions.	1. Demands for compliance with examiner testing a non-compliant and non-imitative child.	1. Minimal demands for compliance with examiner and testing context. Imitation not required.	1. Shape compliance to ever-increasing task demands to increase stress tolerance.
2. Delayed development of object use (functional and symbolic play/proto-declarative pointing).	2. Delayed development of object use in severe cases: non-imitative and avoidant of demands.	2. Measurement of object use and language comprehension, imitation, and pointing.	2. Object use not required.	2. Shape object use in a developmental sequence from stereotypical to functional to symbolic use.
3. Delayed expressive language development.	3. Delayed development of expressive language: non-imitative and avoidance of demands.	3. Measurement of spoken vocabulary.	3. Measurement of spoken vocabulary not required.	3. Shape expressive language in a developmental sequence.
4. Delayed mental development.	4. Arrested development of expressive ability.	4. Delayed mental development confounded with delayed expressive development.	4. Allows differential diagnosis to determine whether delays are with processing or expressive development.	4. Stimulate age-appropriate expressive development to allow catch-up on conventional test for <<intact>> information processors.

approaches. They do not explain why noncompliant behaviors develop or how they can arrest further development. P. R. Zelazo et al. (1984) suggest that noncompliant children have low frustration tolerance. Rogers (1997) compiled existing data to show that compliance is a "keystone behavior" that can lead to changes in a variety of domains (e.g., Russo, Cataldo, & Cushing, 1981; Soutor, Houlihan, & Young, 1994). This argument, coupled with the earlier suggestion that noncompliant resistant behavior permits the child to escape from task demands and the literature indicating that task demands increase noncompliant behavior (Carr & Durand, 1985), lead to a precise theoretical position. Resistant and noncompliant behaviors permit the child to escape from task demands and, as such, preclude the development of stress (frustration) tolerance and self-regulation (Kopp, 1989).

Rogers (1997; Rogers et al., 1998) tested delayed and nondelayed typically developing children on both verbal and visual-perceptual (nonverbal) tasks at three levels of task difficulty—low, moderate, and high. Level of task difficulty was determined individually for each child in preliminary testing. The delayed children, all of whom were diagnosed with PDD other or autism and were untestable previously, had received 8 months of parent-implemented developmental-behavioral therapy (Zelazo, P. R., et al., 1984) and had demonstrated sufficient improvement with compliance and development (Lalinec-Michaud, 1995; Lalinec, Zelazo, P. R., Rogers, & Reid, 1995) to permit participation in the Rogers et al. (1998) study. Two groups of same-age typically developing children—one group that attended day care and another that did not—served as comparison children.

There were two major findings. First, both delayed and typically developing children displayed less compliance to verbal than to nonverbal (visual-perceptual) tasks—a factor assumed in ABA and developmental programs, but not demonstrated previously. Second, delayed children were increasingly less compliant to moderately and highly difficult tasks. There was no difference between delayed and nondelayed children on easy visual-perceptual tasks. These results indicate that delayed children, even after considerable therapy and improvement, show low stress tolerance to task demands, implying that stress tolerance and an insufficient capacity for self-regulation are critical factors in PDD and autism (Rogers et al., 1998).

Information-Processing Assessment and the Question of "Catch-Up"

It is one of Nature's cruelest tricks that delayed children must develop faster than normal if they are ever to "catch up"—ever to reduce the magnitude of their developmental delays. Thus, there must be a premium on efficiency if the seemingly impossible is to be achieved. Fortunately, "catch-up" is a reasonable expectation if, as determined by the assessment of information-processing ability (Zelazo, P. R., 1979; 1997a), some delayed children have normal intelligence with delayed expressive development (Zelazo, P. R., 1989; 1997b). That is the significance of the finding that 61% of the 33 children with "intact" information-processing ability achieved mental ages equal to or greater than their chronological ages following treatment (Zelazo, P. R., 1997b; Zelazo P. R., & Kearsley, 1984). The goal of catch-up on conventional tests in this study was to demonstrate the validity of the information-processing assessment that permitted a differential diagnosis. If intact information processing was a valid indicator of normal intelligence, catch-up was possible because delays were with expressive development not intelligence. In these cases, care providers did not make the children smarter, they only helped them to express what they knew. Of course, catch-up is not the only measure of benefit; it is, however, possible in some cases and it is explicable theoretically.

Conclusions and Implications

A broadly based developmental psychopathological view of the etiology of early autism has been conspicuously absent (D'Alessandro & Zelazo, 2000). Where developmental psychopathological views of autism exist, they have not been sufficiently encompassing in their account to be persuasive, nor have they addressed problems sufficiently early to account for etiology (Rutter, 1996). I have proposed a developmental-behavioral view of early autism that rests on an empirical account of mental (information-processing) and neuromotor abilities in normally developing children from birth through the second year of life. Central to this view is the notion that the development of mental ability and the capacity to express that ability may become decoupled in the development of autism during the second year of life.

A critical factor in the emergence of autism is the development of noncompliance to task demands that results in arrested expressive development including delayed object use and expressive language, but especially stress tolerance and emotion regulation. Because these domains of development are prerequisites for the assessment of intelligence in young children and because delays in these same areas are among the defining characteristics of autism, as many as 75% of young children with autism appear to be mentally retarded as well. The information-processing procedures used to assess mental ability are designed to correct for these limitations and have produced evidence for normal processing and intelligence despite delays with expressive development. The treatment program *Learning to Speak* is designed to stimulate these same three domains of expressive development—compliance to adult requests, functional and symbolic play, and expressive language. These treatment procedures produced reductions in delays on conventional tests of mental development and improved compliance, play, and expressive language with young delayed children who have normal information-processing ability. The consistency across the defining characteristics of autism, the difficulties with conventional tests of intelligence, the assessment and treatment procedures to correct for these limitations, the theoretical formulation, and the quasi-experimental nature of the research design lends theoretical consistency and converging evidence to support this formulation.

Moreover, this developmental psychopathological view can account for why ABA approaches produce positive results in some instances. The heavy emphasis on encouraging compliance is perhaps the most important factor. However, the developmental-behavioral view presented here accounts for why compliance is an important behavior to be modified and why it can alter other behaviors. Changing noncompliant behavior to compliant behavior fosters stress tolerance and eventually changes the child's state from stressful and avoidant to pleasant and compliant. This view offers clearly testable predictions and suggests methods to reduce noncompliance and foster development in ways that are not obvious from other theoretical views. A key factor in this program is the information-processing procedure to assess intelligence. It is more precise than the therapeutic trial often used by ABA therapists to identify noncompliant children with "normal intelligence" and has greater empirical validity as a measure of intellectual ability.

A variety of early interventions including ABA approaches and our developmental-behavioral therapy program produce positive outcomes (Rogers, 1998). The question for future research is not whether the behavior and development of young children with autism can be improved, but rather, which approaches yield the most thorough improvement. Even if further research establishes a clear genetic basis for autism (Rutter, 1996), developmental-behavioral approaches can yield marked benefit. The developmental psychopathological approach presented here involves the manipulation of theoretically guided variables and holds the potential to inform us about typical development as Cicchetti (1984) and Burack (1990) have argued.

This theoretical view can account for subsequent behaviors displayed by children with autism, including the association with mental retardation and the reason some children have been able to escape this fate. Other features of autism, such as self-stimulating behaviors, can be accounted for as well. If low stress tolerance is a core factor among children with autism, then self-stimulatory behaviors would be expected to develop as primitive attempts at emotional self-regulation. From this perspective, it would be predicted that arousal from either positive or negative circumstances would elicit self-stimulation. Behaviors such as hand flapping would occur as uncontained discharges of excitement resulting from arousal. Other defining characteristics of autism, such as the absence of imitative behaviors or symbolic play, also become explicable. Functionally, imitation and compliance to task demands are synonymous, and noncompliance occurs as escape from the stress of task demands. Symbolic play is dependent on imitation (compliance) and on acquiring functional play in a developmental sequence. Other behaviors, particularly appropriate social interactions, are dependent on compliance to task demands as well. These and other explanations from this model lend themselves to precise empirically testable statements. Future research will determine the ultimate validity of the model.

ACKOWLEDGMENTS

P. R. Zelazo's time and the materials required for the preparation of this manuscript were supported, in part, by a grant from the Unique Lives Program of the Montreal Children's Hospital Foundation/McGill University to P. R. Zelazo and a grant from the Natural Sciences and Engineering Research Council of Canada (Grant No. 06PO173069) to Philip R. Zelazo and Philippe Robaey. I thank Philip David Zelazo, Peta Leclerc, and my fellow editors, Jake Burack, Tony Charman, and Nurit Yirmiya, for helpful detailed comments and suggestions on earlier drafts of this manuscript.

Please address correspondence to the Montreal Children's Hospital/McGill University, Department of Psychology, 2300 Tupper St., Montreal, Quebec.H3H 1P3, Canada, or e-mail Peta.Leclerc@muhc.McGill.ca.

REFERENCES

American Psychiatric Association. (1994). *Diagnostic and statistical manual of mental disorders* (4th ed.). Washington, DC: Author.

Baird, G., Charman, T., Baron-Cohen, S., Cox, A., Swettenham, J., Wheelwright, S., Drew, A., & Kemal, L. (2000). A screening instrument for autism at 18 months of age: A six year follow-up study. *Journal of the American Academy of Child and Adolescent Psychiatry, 39,* 694–702.

Baron-Cohen, S., Allen, J., & Gillberg, C. (1992). Can autism be detected at 18 months? The needle, the haystack, and the CHAT. *British Journal of Psychiatry, 161,* 839–843.

Baron-Cohen, S., Cox, A., Baird, G., Swettenham, J., Nightingale, N., Morgan, K., Drew, A., & Charman, T. (1996). Psychological markers in the detection of autism in infancy in a large population. *British Journal of Psychiatry, 168,* 158–163.

Bayley, N. (1993). *Bayley scales of infant development* (2nd ed.). San Antonio, TX: Psychological Corporation.

Belsky, J., & Most, R. K. (1981). From exploration to play: A cross-sectional study of infant free-play behavior. *Developmental Psychology, 17,* 630–639.

Bornstein, M. H., & Sigman, M. D. (1986). Continuity in mental development from infancy. *Child Development, 57,* 251–274.

Burack, J. A. (1990). Differentiating mental retardation: The two-group approach and beyond. In R. M. Hodapp, J. A. Burack, & E. Zigler (Eds.), *Issues in the developmental approach to mental retardation* (pp. 27–48). New York: Cambridge University Press.

Butterworth, G., & Morissette, P. (1996). Onset of pointing and the acquisition of language in infancy. *Journal of Reproductive and Infant Psychology, 14,* 219–231.

Carpenter, M., Nagel, K., & Tomasello, M. (1998). Social cognition, joint attention and communicative competence from 9 to 15 months of age. *Monographs of the Society for Research in Child Development, 63,* (No. 4, Serial No. 255). Malden, MA: Blackwell Publishers, Inc.

Carr, E. G., & Durand, V. M. (1985). The social-communicative basis of severe behavior problems in children. In S. Reiss and R. Bootzin (Eds.), *Theoretical issues in behavior therapy* (pp. 219–254). Orlando, FL: Academic Press.

Carr, E. G., & Newsom, C. D. (1985). Demand-related tantrums: Conceptualization and treatment. *Behavior Modification, 9,* 403–426.

Cicchetti, D. (1984). The emergence of developmental psychopathology. *Child Development, 55,* 1–7.

Cicchetti, D., & Beeghly, M. (1990). An organizational approach to the study of Down syndrome: Contributions to an integrative theory of development. In D. Cicchetti & M. Beeghly (Eds.), *Children with Down syndrome: A developmental perspective* (pp. 29–62). New York: Cambridge University Press.

Cicchetti, D., & Pogge-Hesse, P. (1982). Possible contributions of the study of organically retarded persons to developmental theory. In E. Zigler & D. Balla (Eds.), *Mental retardation: The developmental-difference controversy* (pp. 277–318). Hillsdale, NJ: Lawrence Erlbaum Associates.

Cohen, L. (1991). Infant attention: An information processing approach. In M. J. Weiss & P. R. Zelazo (Eds.), *Newborn attention: Biological constraints and the influence of experience* (pp. 1–21). Norwood, NJ: Ablex.

Cohen, L. (1998). An information-processing approach to infant perception and cognition. In F. Simion & G. Butterworth (Eds.), *The development of sensory, motor and cognitive capacities in early infancy: From perception to cognition* (pp. 277–300). Sussex, UK: Lawrence Erlbaum Associates.

D'Alessandro, D., & Zelazo, P. R. (2000). *Autism as a pervasive developmental disorder: Where has the development gone?* Manuscript submitted for publication.

DeCasper, A. J., & Spence, M. J. (1991). Auditory mediated behavior during the perinatal period: A cognitive view. In M. J. Weiss & P. R. Zelazo (Eds.), *Newborn Attention* (pp. 142–176). Norwood, NJ: Ablex.

Diamond, A. (1985). Development of the ability to use recall to guide action, as indicated by infants' performance on AB. *Child Development, 56,* 868–883.

Edelman, G. (1989). *The remembered present: A biological theory of consciousness.* New York: Basic Books.

Fagan, J., & McGrath, S. K. (1981). Infant recognition memory and later intelligence. *Intelligence, 5,* 121–130.

Fodor, J. (1983). *Modularity of mind.* Cambridge, MA: MIT Press.

Francis, D., Diorio, J., Liu, D., & Meaney, M. (1999). Non-genomic transmission across generations of maternal behavior and stress responses in the rat. *Science, 286,* 1155–1158.

Hodapp, R. M., & Zigler, E. (1990). Applying the developmental perspective to individuals with Down syndrome. In D. Cicchetti & M. Beeghly (Eds.), *Children with Down syndrome: A developmental perspective* (pp. 1–28). New York: Cambridge University Press.

Kagan, J. (1967). On the need for relativism. *American Psychologist, 22,* 131–142.

Kagan, J. (1972). Do infants think? *Scientific American, 226,* 74–82.

Kagan, J., Kearsley, R.B., & Zelazo, P. R. (1978). *Infancy: Its place in human development.* Cambridge, MA: Harvard University Press.

Kail, R. (1991). Developmental changes in speed of processing during childhood and adolescence. *Psychological Bulletin, 109,* 490–501.

Katona, F. (1989). Clinical neuro-developmental diagnosis and treatment. In P. R. Zelazo & R. G. Barr (Eds.), *Challenges to developmental paradigms* (pp. 167–187). Hillsdale, NJ: Lawrence Erlbaum Associates.

Kopp, C. B. (1989). Regulation of distress and negative emotions: A developmental view. *Developmental Psychology, 25(3),* 343–354.

Lalinec, C., Zelazo, P. R., Rogers, C.- L., & Reid, C. (1995). *Developmental delay: Impact of six-month parent-implemented behavioral treatment.* Poster presented at the Annual Meeting of the American Psychological Association, New York, August 11–15.

Lalinec-Michaud, C. (1995). Impact of a 6-month parent-implemented behavioral intervention for children with developmental language delays of unknown etiology. Unpublished doctoral dissertation, McGill University, Montreal, Quebec, Canada.

Lewis, M., & Brooks-Gunn, J. (1981). Visual attention at three months as a predictor of cognitive functioning at two years of age. *Intelligence, 5,* 131–140.

Lewis, M., Goldberg, S., & Campbell, H. (1969). A developmental study of information processing within the first three years of life: Response decrement to a redundant signal. *Monographs of the Society for Research in Child Development, 34,* (9, Serial No. 133).

Lovaas, O. I. (1987). Behavioral treatment and normal educational and intellectual functioning in young autistic children. *Journal of Consulting and Clinical Psychology, 55,* 3–9.

McEachlin, J. J., Smith, T., & Lovaas, O. I. (1993). Long-term outcome for children with autism who received early intensive behavioral treatment. *American Journal of Mental Retardation, 97,* 359–372.

Meltzoff, A. N. (1988). Infant imitation after a 1-week delay: Long-term memory for novel acts and multiple stimuli. *Developmental Psychology, 31(5),* 1–16.

Moore, C., & Corkum, V. (1994). Social understanding at the end of the first year of life. *Developmental Review, 14,* 349–372.

Mundy, P., Sigman, M., & Kasari, C. (1994). Joint attention, developmental level, and symptom presentation in autism. *Development and Psychopathology, 6,* 389–401.

Piaget, J. (1952). *The origins of intelligence in children.* New York: International Universities Press. (French Edition, 1936).

Rochat, P., & Goubet, N. (1995). Development of sitting and reaching in 5- to 9-month-old infants. *Infant Behavior and Development, 18(1),* 53–68.

Rogers, C.- L. (1997). *Behavioral, affective, and attentional responses of developmentally delayed and nondelayed preschoolers to task difficulty.* Unpublished doctoral dissertation, McGill University, Montreal, Quebec, Canada.

Rogers, C.- L., Zelazo, P. R., Mendelson, M., & Rotsztein, B. (1998). Behavioral, affective and attentional responses of developmentally delayed and nondelayed pre-schoolers to task difficulty. *Infant Behavior and Development, 21.* [Abstract].

Rogers, S. J. (1998). Empirically supported comprehensive treatments for young children with autism. *Journal of Clinical Child Psychology, 27,* 168–179.

Rogers, S. J., & Lewis, H. (1989). An effective day treatment model for young children with pervasive developmental disorders. *Journal of the American Academy of Child and Adolescent Psychiatry, 28,* 207–214.

Russo, D. C., Cataldo, M. F., & Cushing, P. J. (1981). Compliance training and behavioral covariation in the treatment of multiple behavior problems. *Journal of Applied Behavior Analysis, 14,* 209–222.

Rutter, M. (1996). Autism research: Prospects and priorities. *Journal of Autism and Developmental Disorders, 26(2),* 257–275.

Rutter, M., MacDonald, H., Le Couteur, A., Harrington, R., Bolton, P., & Bailey, A. (1990). Genetic factors in child psychiatric disorders: II. Empirical findings. *Journal of Child Psychology and Psychiatry and Allied Disciplines, 31,* 39–83.

Slater, A., & Morison, V. (1991). Visual attention and memory at birth. In M. J. Weiss & P. R. Zelazo (Eds.), *Newborn attention* (pp. 256–277). Norwood, NJ: Ablex.

Soutor, T. A., Houlihan, D., & Young, A. (1994). An examination of response covariation on the behavioral treatment of identical twin boys with multiple behavioral disorders. *Behavioral Interventions, 9(3),* 141–155.

Speidel, G. E., & Nelson, K. E. (Eds.). (1989). *The many faces of imitation in language learning.* New York: Springer-Verlag.

Sroufe, A., & Waters, E. (1976). The ontogenesis of smiling and laughter: A perspective on the organization of development in infancy. *Psychological Review, 83,* 173–189.

Thelen, E. (1983). Learning to walk is still an "old" problem: A reply to Zelazo. *Journal of Motor Behavior, 15,* 139–161.

Thelen, E. (1995). Motor development: A new synthesis. *American Psychologist, 50,* 79–95.

Thelen, E., & Fisher, D. (1982). Newborn stepping: An explanation for a "disappearing reflex." *Developmental Psychology, 18,* 760–775.

Tomasello, M. (1999). Having intentions, understanding intentions, and understanding communicative intentions. In P. D. Zelazo, J. W. Astington, & D. R. Olson (Eds.), *Developing theories of intention: Social understanding and self-control* (pp. 63–75). Mahwah, NJ: Lawrence Erlbaum Associates.

Tomasello, M. (2000). Culture and cognitive development. *Current Directions in Psychological Science, 9,* 37–40.

Touwen, B. C. (1984). Primitive reflexes: Conceptual or semantic problem. In H. Prechtl (Ed.), *Continuity of neurofunctions to postnatal life* (pp. 115–125). Oxford, UK: Blackwell Scientific.

Weiss, M. J., & Zelazo, P. R. (1981, April). *Development of mobility in water during infancy.* Paper presented at the Annual Meeting of the Eastern Psychological Association, New York.

Weiss, M. J., & Zelazo, P. R. (1982, January). *Facilitation of swimming during infancy: Evidence for "plasticity" of motor development.* Paper presented at the Annual Meeting of the American Association of Science, Washington, DC.

Weiss, M. J., Zelazo, P. R., & Swain, I. U. (1988). Newborn response to auditory stimulus discrepancy. *Child Development, 59,* 1530–1541.

World Health Organization. (1993). *The ICD–10 classification of mental and behavioral disorders. Diagnostic criteria for research.* Geneva, Switzerland: Author.

Zelazo, N. A., Zelazo, P. R., Cohen, K., & Zelazo, P. D. (1993). Specificity of practice effects on elementary neuromotor patterns. *Developmental Psychology, 29,* 686–691.

Zelazo, N. A., Zelazo, P. R., Cohen., K., & Zelazo, P. D. (1994). Infant smiling during stimulation of stepping and sitting. *Sixth European Regional Conference of Rehabilitation International,* Budapest, Hungary, September 5.

Zelazo, P. D. (1996). Towards a characterization of minimal consciousness. *New Ideas in Psychology, 14,* 63–80.

Zelazo, P. D., Astington, J. W., & Olson, D. R. (1999). (Eds.), *Developing theories of intention.* Mahwah, NJ: Lawrence Erlbaum Associates.

Zelazo, P. R. (1976). From reflexive to instrumental behavior. In L. Lipsitt (Ed.), *Developmental psychobiology: The significance of infancy* (pp. 87–104). Hillsdale, NJ: Lawrence Erlbaum Associates.

Zelazo, P. R. (1979). Reactivity to perceptual-cognitive events: Application to infant assessment. In R. B. Kearsley & I. Sigel (Eds.), *Infants at risk: Assessment of cognitive functioning* (pp. 49–83). Hillsdale, NJ: Lawrence Erlbaum Associates.

Zelazo, P. R. (1982). The year-old infant: A period of major cognitive change. In T. Bever (Ed.), *Regressions in development: Basic phenomena and theoretical alternatives* (pp. 47–79). Hillsdale, NJ: Lawrence Erlbaum Associates.

Zelazo, P. R. (1983). The development of walking: New findings and old assumptions. *Journal of Motor Behavior, 15,* 99–137.

Zelazo, P. R. (1989). Infant-toddler information processing and the development of expressive ability. In P. R. Zelazo & R. G. Barr (Eds.), *Challenges to developmental paradigms: Implications for theory, assessment and treatment* (pp. 93–112). Hillsdale, NJ: Lawrence Erlbaum Associates.

Zelazo, P. R. (1997a). Infant-toddler information processing treatment of children with pervasive developmental disorder and autism: Part I. *Infants and Young Children, 10(1),* 1–14.

Zelazo, P. R. (1997b). Infant-toddler information processing assessment for children with pervasive developmental disorder and autism: Part II. *Infants and Young Children, 10(2),* 1–13.

Zelazo, P. R. (1998). McGraw and the development of unaided walking. *Developmental Review, 18,* 449–471.

Zelazo, P. R., Kagan, J., & Hartmann, R. (1975). Excitement and boredom as determinants of vocalization in infants. *Journal of Genetic Psychology, 126*, 107–117.

Zelazo, P. R., & Kearsley, R. B. (1980). The emergence of functional play in infants: Evidence for a major cognitive transition. *Journal of Applied Developmental Psychology, 1,* 95–117.

Zelazo, P. R., & Kearsley, R. B. (1984). The identification of intact and delayed information processing: An experimental approach. *Infant Behavior and Development, 7,* 393.

Zelazo, P. R., Kearsley, R. B., & Stack, D. M. (1995). Mental representations for visual sequences: Increased speed of central processing from 22 to 32 months. *Intelligence, 20,* 41–63.

Zelazo, P. R., Kearsley, R. B., & Ungerer, J. A. (1984). *Learning to speak: A manual for parents.* Hillsdale, NJ: Lawrence Erlbaum Associates.

Zelazo, P. R., & Komer, M. J. (1971). Infant smiling to non-social stimuli and the recognition hypothesis. *Child Development, 41,* 1327–1339.

Zelazo, P. R., & Leonard, E. (1983). The dawn of active thought. In K. Fischer (Ed.), *Levels and transitions in children's development* (pp. 37–50). San Francisco: Jossey-Bass.

Zelazo, P. R., Robaey, P., & Bonin, M. (1999). *The development of movement-related lateralized brain potentials with exercise of the neuromotor stepping pattern in 7- to 14-week-old infants.* Poster presented at the SRCD Biennial Meetings, Albuquerque, NM, April 15–20.

Zelazo, P. R., Weiss, M. J., & Tarquinio, N. (1991). Habituation and recovery of neonatal orienting to auditory stimuli. In M. J. Weiss & P. R. Zelazo (Eds.), *Newborn attention: Biological constraints and the influence of experience* (pp. 120–141). Norwood, NJ: Ablex.

Zelazo, P. R., Zelazo, N. A., & Kolb, S. (1972). Walking in the newborn. *Science, 176,* 314–315.

Zelazo, P. R., & Zelazo, P. D. (1998). The emergence of consciousness. In H. H. Jasper, L. Descarries, V. F. Castellucci, & S. Rossignol (Eds.), *Advances in neurology: Vol. 77. Consciousness: At the frontiers of neuroscience* (pp. 149–165). Philadelphia: Lippincott-Raven.

Zigler, E. (1967). Familial retardation: A continuing dilemma. *Science, 155,* 292–298.

4

The Functioning and Well-Being of Siblings of Children With Autism: Behavioral-Genetic and Familial Contributions

Nirit Bauminger
School of Education
Bar-Ilan University, Ramat Gan, Israel
Nurit Yirmiya
Department of Psychology and School of Education
Hebrew University of Jerusalem, Israel

The disorder of autism is associated with a strong genetic component (Bailey, Palferman, Heavey, & Le Couteur, 1998; Szatmari, Jones, Zwaigenbaum, & MacLean, 1998) and with a unique environmental-familial experience (Rutter et al., 1997) requiring adjustment on all levels. On the average, children in the same family share 50% of their genes. Environmentally, the shared component is defined as that part of the environment that makes siblings similar to each other (e.g., social-economic status, parental characteristics), whereas the nonshared component refers to the independent aspects of the sibling environment (e.g., living with a sibling with a disability) (Anderson, Hetherington, Reiss, & Howe, 1994). Thus, due to the combined effects of these factors, siblings of children with autism have a higher risk for the development of impairments on a genetic and environmental basis.

The first aim of this chapter is to review findings regarding the cognitive, academic, and social-emotional abilities and impairments of children with a sibling with autism. Next, the behavioral-genetic and the family-system perspectives are discussed. Within the behavioral-genetic perspective, autism is considered the most severe manifestation of a disorder on a continuum of impairments. Thus, difficulties in the cognitive, academic, and social-emotional functioning of siblings are considered as a lesser variant or a broader phenotype of autism that is genetically determined. Within the family-system perspective, the family environment is considered an important contributor to the development of cognitive and emotional functioning of siblings. Therefore, at least some of the difficulties experienced by siblings of individuals with autism may be associated with living with an atypically developing sibling. Following the presentation of these two perspectives, the diathesis-stress model to psychopathology is introduced. Based on this model, the behavioral-genetic and the family-system perspectives are integrated in an attempt to achieve a more in-depth and dynamic understanding of the transaction between genetics and environment and how it may affect the development of children who have a sibling with autism.

SIBLINGS' COGNITIVE AND ACADEMIC PROFILE

Many researchers have focused on the cognitive and academic abilities and impairments of siblings of children with autism using various comparison groups. Cognitive abilities are typically examined with evaluations of verbal and nonverbal intelligence, and academic skills are evaluated with an emphasis on reading and writing. The data pertaining to these two domains are then reviewed in consideration of the various comparison groups employed.

The nature of the comparison group with which the siblings of children with autism are compared is important because different comparison groups "control" for different genetic and environmental aspects, or for both. For example, Down syndrome is a specific chromosomal disorder. Because relatives of children with Down syndrome are not expected to be at a greater genetic risk (Piven, Palmer, Jacobi, Childress, & Arndt, 1997), a comparison group of siblings of children with Down syndrome does not control for the genetic basis. However, it does control for some of the environmental-familial effects of growing up with a sibling with a severe handicap. Mental retardation of unknown etiology controls for the environmental effects and also may control for the heterogeneity of organic etiology, which, similar to autism, may include genetic components. Learning disabilities have a genetic basis (DeFries, Fulker, & LaBuda, 1987; Faraone, Biederman, Krifcher, & Lehman, 1993; Wadsworth, DeFries, Fulker, & Plomin, 1995), and therefore comparing siblings of children with autism to siblings of children with learning disabilities may enable the specification of a particular phenotype for the genetic basis of autism that differs from the phenotype for learning disabilities. However, children with learning disabilities most typically do not manifest mental retardation and in many ways are easier to care for than a child with mental retardation or with autism. Thus, a comparison group of siblings of children with learning disabilities enables some control of genetic risk, but the control for environmental effects is less than optimal. Finally, a comparison group of typically developing children allows comparison with normative development.

Verbal and Nonverbal Intelligence

Comparisons With Siblings of Children With Down Syndrome. Szatmari et al. (1993) compared the cognitive functioning of siblings of children with autism to that of groups of siblings of both children with Down syndrome and children born at low birth weight using the Revised Stanford–Binet Intelligence test, the Benton Test of Facial Recognition, and the Wisconsin Card Sorting Test (WCST). They concluded that siblings of children with autism do not reveal cognitive impairments and even show superiority on verbal reasoning, abstract-visual reasoning, and full-scale IQ. Similarly, Fombonne, Bolton, Prior, Jordan, and Rutter (1997) reported higher verbal and full-scale IQ scores achieved by siblings of children with autism than by siblings of children with Down syndrome on the Wechsler Intelligence Scale for Children–Revised (WISC–R) test. Within the group of siblings of children with autism, Fombonne et al. found significantly lower verbal IQ scores in the siblings affected with the broader phenotype versus unaffected siblings.

Leboyer, Plumet, Goldblum, Perez-Diaz, and Marchaland (1995) and Plumet, Goldblum, and Leboyer (1995) reported that siblings—especially brothers—of children with autism scored lower than siblings of children with Down syndrome on a standardized assessment of verbal abilities but not on visuospatial abilities. Folstein et al. (1999) employing the Wechsler Adult Intelligence Scale–Revised (WAIS–R) or the WISC–R also found no significant differences between groups. In sum, the aforementioned studies are inconclusive. Some researchers revealed significant differences indicating poorer skills in siblings of children with autism than in siblings of probands with Down syndrome. However, other researchers suggested no significant differences, or even higher scores for the siblings of children with autism.

Comparisons With Siblings of Children With Developmental Delay of Unknown Etiology. Hughes, Plumet, and Leboyer (1999) reported a significant difference on executive-function tests between siblings of children with autism and siblings of children with developmental delay. More siblings of children with autism experienced difficulties on two of the four administered tasks compared to siblings in the comparison group. In contrast to the poorer performance on the executive tasks,

Hughes et al. reported higher spatial-span and rote-recall abilities in siblings of children with autism than in the comparison group.

Comparisons With Siblings of Probands With Learning Disabilities. Ozonoff, Rogers, Farnham, and Pennington (1993) reported no differences between siblings of children with autism and siblings of children with learning disabilities on six subtests of the WISC–R or the WAIS–R (information, similarities, vocabulary, comprehension, block design, and object assembly). On tests of executive function, they reported lower scores for the siblings of children with autism on the Tower of Hanoi test but not on the WCST.

Comparisons With Siblings of Children With Typical Development. Smalley and Asarnow (1990) reported no significant group differences between siblings of children with autism and typically developing children on the WISC–R and WAIS–R. However, the siblings of children with autism scored higher on the block design subtest of the WISC–R/WAIS–R and significantly higher on the Benton Test of Line Orientation. Hughes et al. (1999) also compared the performance of siblings of children with autism to that of siblings of children with typical development. Results were similar to those of the comparison between siblings of children with autism and siblings of children with developmental delay of unknown etiology: Siblings of children with autism showed poor executive-function ability and superior rote-recall and spatial-span ability.

Freeman et al. (1989), working with a large sample ($N = \lambda 53$) of siblings of children with autism, did not find any cognitive impairments or lower than average scores on the WPPSI, WISC–R, or the WAIS. Furthermore, the typically reported superiority in performance as compared to verbal abilities among persons with autism was not found for the siblings. This is inconsistent with the findings of Minton, Campbell, Green, Jennings, and Samit (1982), who reported that verbal scores were significantly lower than performance scores, although 40 of the 50 siblings achieved Standford-Binet and Wechsler scores within the normal range (similar to the findings of Leboyer et al., 1995, and Plumet et al., 1995).

In sum, studies employing different comparison groups and normative data do not present a clear picture. With only two exceptions (Hughes et al., 1999; Ozonoff et al., 1993), all the previously mentioned studies present nonsignificant and sometimes even higher nonverbal abilities (Smalley & Asarnow, 1990) in siblings of children with autism as measured by IQ, visuospatial, or executive-function tests. Findings are even more inconclusive when verbal difficulties are examined. Lower verbal abilities of siblings of children with autism were reported in some studies (Hughes et al., 1999; Leboyer et al., 1995; Plumet et al., 1995), whereas no differences were reported in others (Folstein, et al., 1999; Ozonoff et al.; Smalley & Asarnow) and some reported even higher abilities among siblings of children with autism (Fombonne et al., 1997; Szatmari et al., 1993).

Thus, examination of the data while considering the various comparison groups does not by itself assist in achieving a coherent picture. It may be that the divergent and at times contradictory findings are associated with additional methodological inconsistencies such as the inclusion of siblings of different ages, the use of different outcome measures within the domain of intellectual abilities (various IQ tests, specialized tests for dyslexia, or both), the employing of different diagnostic criteria with the probands, or the use of different designs (aggregation of familial data as in the Szatmari et al., 1993, study vs. no aggregation). We were not able to review the potential effects of variables such as the age of siblings or the types of measures used to assess specific outcomes due to the limited number of studies within each category of the comparison group employed. In the future, as more studies are published, these issues should be addressed in an attempt to achieve a more in-depth understanding of the cognitive abilities and impairments of siblings of children with autism compared with siblings of children with diagnoses other than autism.

Academic Abilities

Academic abilities are commonly assessed by parental interviews regarding the developmental and educational history of children and by the need for special education services, as well as by direct testing of performance on various ability and achievements tests. August, Stewart, and Tsai (1981) interviewed parents about their child's academic progress and about the need for special educational services and administered the Wide Range Achievement Test (WRAT) to evaluate academic achievements in reading, spelling, and arithmetic. Four of the 71 siblings (5.6%) of the children with autism presented gross disturbance in language acquisition and 9 of the 71 children (12.7%) displayed IQ scores below 80. Of these 9 children, 7 children (9.8%) needed special educational services for children with mental retardation and the remaining 2 children (2.8%) exhibited learning disabilities in reading. In contrast, only one child among the siblings of children with Down syndrome had an IQ lower than 70 and was in a special class for children with mild mental retardation. Similarly, based on maternal report, Piven et al. (1990) found an even higher percentage of language, reading, and spelling difficulties in siblings of probands with autism—8 of 67 siblings were affected, representing 11.9% of the sample. However, in a recent study, Folstein et al. (1999) found no significant differences between siblings of children with autism and siblings of children with Down syndrome on tests of reading and spelling (the Schonell test, the Kaufman, the Gray Oral Reading Test, and on one of the subtests of the Woodcock-Johnson Psychoeducational Battery), as well as no significant differences in reported reading and language history.

Using similar methodologies, Boutin et al. (1997) and Gillberg, Gillberg, and Steffenburg (1992) did not find higher rates of language, reading, and spelling problems among siblings of probands with autism. Boutin et al. compared siblings of probands with autism with siblings of children with mental retardation, whereas Gillberg et al. included a comparison group of typically developing children and another group of siblings of children with attention, motor control, and perception difficulties. Narayan, Moyes, and Wolff (1990) also found that none of the 28 siblings of high-functioning children with autism had global or specific reading, spelling, or language delay. Similarly, Mates (1990) reported nonsignificant findings with both the WRAT and with measures assessing school adjustment. In sum, as in the cognitive realm, no specific academic profile emerged among siblings of children with autism. It may be that the heterogeneity of the findings pertaining to cognitive and academic abilities is due to the transaction between genetic factors on the one hand and environmental-familial factors (e.g., fewer resources) on the other hand, which operate differently in different families.

SOCIAL ADJUSTMENT AND EMOTIONAL FUNCTIONING

Researchers investigating the social adjustment and emotional well-being of siblings of children with autism focused on the self-concept of these children, their overall social adjustment, and on the degree of depression they exhibited. Using the Piers–Harris Self Concept Scale (PHSCS), Berger (1980) reported that the siblings of children with autism scored significantly higher than the normal population, regardless of age and gender. However, other researchers suggest no differences. For example, Mates (1990) examined whether gender or family size (e.g., two-child families as compared with multichild families) are significant factors in the adjustment among oldest, nondisabled siblings of children with autism. No significant differences emerged between brothers and sisters on measures of self-concept, home, and school adjustment. Furthermore, there were no significant differences among male siblings from a two-child family, female siblings from a two-child family, male siblings from a multichild family, and female siblings from a multichild family and between normative data on any of the measures. Kolvin, Ounsted, Richardson, and Garside (1971) found that none of the 68 siblings of children with infantile psychosis (the term used at that time for autism) had infantile psychosis, late-onset psychosis, or schizophrenia. In contrast, Creak and Ini (1960), in one of the earliest reports on siblings of children with autism, found siblings of children with autism at high risk for social-emotional dysfunction. Nineteen of the 79 families (24%) had another child who was maladjusted. In a more recent study, Piven et al. (1990) presented a high rate (17.9%) of social-emotional dysfunction in adult siblings of children with autism.

Of the 67 adult siblings, 2 displayed severe social dysfunction, 9 needed treatment for affective disorder (depression or mania), and 1 was diagnosed with both.

In contrast to the aforementioned studies, which did not include comparison groups, several researchers did include comparison groups. Piven et al. (1997) reported a higher rate of social deficits in siblings of children with autism compared with the rate of social deficits in siblings of children with Down syndrome (33% vs. 0%, respectively). Gold (1993) found that 22 siblings of boys with autism scored significantly higher than did a comparison group of 34 siblings of typically developing boys on scores of depression but not on problems of social adjustment.

Three other findings in Gold's (1993) study are of interest and may shed light on the transactions between genetic liability and environmental-familial contributions. First, although no gender differences were found, depression was associated with different variables for male and female siblings of boys with autism. Among sisters, higher depression scores were significantly associated with specific characteristics of the boy with autism, including his age, the length of time since his diagnosis, and if the sister was younger than the boy with autism. For brothers, higher depression scores were significantly associated with reports that there was nothing good about having a brother with autism. A main effect was found for age of the sibling. Adolescent siblings were more depressed than those under 12 years of age. With regard to social support, siblings who reported that they did not have anyone to talk to about their affected sibling scored significantly higher on the depression inventory than those who reported having someone close to whom they could speak about their sibling. DeMyer (1979) and Sullivan (1979) described siblings of children with autism as responsible, mature, and socially well adjusted, but burdened. Also, Szatmari et al. (1993) did not find social deficits in siblings of probands with pervasive developmental disorder (PDD) when compared to siblings of children with Down syndrome or with low birth weight.

Employing various comparison groups is important in the social-emotional realm because, for example, the higher rate of depression reported in siblings of individuals with autism may be explained differently using the behavior-genetic and environmental-familial perspectives. From a behavior-genetic perspective, it may be suggested that higher rates of depression have a genetic basis associated with autism; whereas from the environmental-familial perspective, it may be suggested that some siblings will possibly develop depression as a reaction to living with an autistic sibling. Until specific genes that link depression and autism are identified, employing various comparison groups may be helpful in specifying the genetic and the environmental-familial contributions.

Mediating Factors

In addition to the type of comparison group employed in studying the abilities and impairments of siblings of children with autism, other variables—such as developmental level and gender of the probands with autism, gender of the siblings, family size, and socioeconomic status (SES)—may be important for our understanding of the findings. Examining these variables is important because it may assist in identifying a group of siblings (e.g., siblings of low-functioning individuals with autism compared with siblings of high-functioning individuals with autism, or female siblings of male probands versus another group of siblings) that is at a higher risk for cognitive-academic, social-emotional, or both types of impairments. Furthermore, it may assist in clarifying whether the genetic transmission of autism and associated difficulties is similar or different among groups of siblings.

Probands' IQ. The association between probands' IQ and cognitive and academic functioning of the siblings was examined across a range of functioning in some studies (August et al., 1981; Baird & August, 1985; Boutin et al., 1997; Piven et al., 1990; Szatmari et al., 1993) and within more restricted ranges in others (high-functioning probands: Bartak et al., 1975; Narayan et al., 1990; Smalley & Asarnow, 1990; low-functioning probands: Plumet et al., 1995). Piven et al. (1990) and Szatmari et al. (1993) did not find any association between probands' IQ and the cognitive and academic functioning of the siblings of low-functioning, high-functioning, or both types of probands with autism. In contrast, August et al., (1981), Baird and August (1985), and Boutin et al. (1997) reported a higher rate of cognitive disabilities in siblings of low-functioning probands with autism than in siblings of high-functioning probands with autism.

Narayan et al. (1990) and Smalley and Asarnow (1990) found no differences between a sample of siblings of high-functioning probands with autism and a sample of siblings of children with different types of mental retardation and with typically developing children. Similarly, Bartak et al. (1975) reported comparable rates of reading and language problems in siblings of high-functioning probands with autism and in siblings of children with language disorders—a higher rate of these problems than in the normative population. Thus, although the high-functioning probands with autism were carefully diagnosed in the three studies, findings are inconsistent. In the one study investigating mainly low-functioning probands with autism, a significant association was found between the siblings' cognitive functioning and the probands' IQ (Plumet et al., 1995).

Social and emotional functioning of siblings as a function of the IQ of probands with autism was investigated only by Piven et al. (1990), who reported a nonsignificant relationship between the IQ of probands with autism and the social deficits of the siblings. Due to the paucity of studies examining IQ of the probands as a moderator variable in explaining sibling's abilities and impairments, especially in the social-emotional realm, future studies should continue to examine this variable.

Gender of the Proband With Autism. Boutin et al. (1997) and Tsai and Beisler (1983) found higher rates of cognitive deficits in first-degree relatives (including siblings) of female probands with autism than in first-degree relatives of male probands with autism. Leboyer et al. (1995) and Plumet et al. (1995) reported higher rates of verbal difficulties in siblings of females with autism than in siblings of females with Down syndrome. Smalley and Asarnow (1990) found no noticeable cognitive disability among male siblings of probands with autism compared with male siblings of typically developing probands. These findings imply that siblings of female probands with autism are at a higher risk of developing cognitive impairments compared with siblings of male probands with autism. However, this conclusion needs to be viewed with caution, partly because it is based on studies with probands of only one gender. Thus, a comparison of male versus female probands with autism was not possible. August et al. (1981) included both male and female probands with autism but did not find an association between gender of the proband and siblings' cognitive profile.

The association between the probands' gender and social-emotional deficits in siblings is still unclear due to paucity of empirical evidence. Gold (1993) included a sample of only boys with autism, and found higher depression scores in brothers and sisters compared with brothers and sisters of typically developing children, but no comparison to a sample of siblings of female probands was performed.

Siblings' Gender. Leboyer et al. (1995) and Plumet et al. (1995) found that low verbal abilities of brothers of probands with autism, as compared with brothers of children with Down syndrome accounted for the differences in cognitive abilities between the two groups. Thus, based on these findings, higher rates of cognitive disabilities are manifested in brothers than in sisters of probands with autism when compared with siblings of children with Down syndrome. Berger (1980), Mates (1990), and Gold (1993) did not find significant differences between brothers and sisters of probands with autism. However, Gold (1993) reported that different variables were correlated with depression for female versus male siblings of probands with autism.

Family Size and SES. The association between family size and siblings' cognitive, academic, or social-emotional functioning is less clear in the studies of families of children with autism (Boutin et al., 1997; Mates, 1990; Narayan et al., 1990). This is most likely due to the stoppage effect (i.e., choosing not to have any more children after a child is diagnosed with autism) in some families. However, low SES (assessed using the Hollingshead's two-factor index of social position) was found to be associated with cognitive disabilities in siblings of children with autism in one study (Boutin et al.). Yet, this was not unique to the group with autism because family members from low-SES backgrounds of both probands with autism and probands with mental retardation showed higher rates of cognitive disabilities compared with high-SES families (Boutin et al.). In general, the literature regarding siblings of children with disabilities suggests that the adjustment of siblings in larger families is better than that of siblings in smaller families (Gath, 1974; McHale, Simeonsson, & Sloan, 1984). This issue, therefore, should be investigated in future studies.

POSSIBLE EXPLANATIONS FOR THE FINDINGS

The Behavioral-Genetic Perspective

The previously described findings of significant or nonsignificant differences between siblings of probands with autism and other siblings were mostly discussed in the original reports as evidence or lack of evidence for a genetic liability associated with autism. Autism is considered a syndrome with a strong genetic component (Rutter et al., 1997). The genetic basis of any disorder may be inferred from genetic studies linking specific genes to the disorder or by behavioral-genetic studies in which certain phenotypes are identified for a given disorder. These phenotypes are thought to represent specific genes associated with the disorder that are not yet identified.

Using the behavioral-genetic approach, several sources of information are required to establish the genetic basis for any disorder. Among these sources, family, twin, and adoption studies are used in most cases. Family studies are important because they provide an estimate of the risk for the disorder in the relatives compared with the risk in other comparison groups, including the normal population. The drawback of family studies is that the estimate of risk may include genetic and environmental contributions. In twin studies, the rate of the disorder (or its variants) between monozygotic and dizygotic pairs is compared to allow some methodological control since genes are 100% shared for the monozygotic pair, but only 50% shared for the dizygotic pair. Adoption studies are crucial for untangling the genetic and environmental contributions. In adoption studies, the rate of any disorder (e.g., autism or its lesser variant) among siblings of children with autism who grow up with adoptive parents (who most likely are free of the genetic liability for autism) and without having to cope with the sibling with a disorder is compared to the rate of the same condition among siblings of children with the disorder who remain with their biological family. If genetic components are operative in the disorder, the rate of the examined condition in the siblings should be the same for both groups. However, if environmental factors are operative, the rate of the condition among the adoptive children should be lower than the rate of the condition in the siblings who remain with their biological parents and affected sibling. Thus, adoption studies may provide the strongest support for a genetic component in any disorder.

Only twin and family studies using the behavioral-genetic perspective have been carried out in the field of autism. In twin studies, the concordance rate for autism ranges from 36% to 91% in monozygotic twins, and between 0% to 24% in dizygotic twins (Bailey et. al., 1995; Folstein & Rutter, 1977; Ritvo, Freeman, Mason-Brothers, Mo, & Ritvo, 1985; Steffenburg, Gillberg, Hellgren, & Anderson, 1989). The reoccurrence rate of autism in siblings is 2.9% to 7.0%, representing a greater risk rate than the risk for autism in the general population, which is 0.03% to 0.05% (Gillberg, Steffenburg, & Jakobsson, 1987; Jorde, et al., 1990; Smalley, 1997; Smalley, Asarnow, & Spence, 1988; Piven et al., 1990). The risk for any form of PDD in siblings of probands with autism is even higher than the risk for autism (Szatmari et al., 1998). The strongest support for genetic liability in autism stems from behavioral-genetic studies of twins and siblings in which the concordance rate for autism in twins and the rate of autism in siblings of children with autism were investigated. Unfortunately, the rare occurrence of autism precludes adoption studies, which theoretically could provide the strongest support for genetic liability because they enable an independent assessment of genetic and environmental contributions.

Behavior geneticists assume that autism represents the most severe phenotype of a genetically determined disorder that may have less severe phenotypes. These less severe phenotypes involve impairments in one or more of the three core areas of dysfunction manifested in autism: communication and language, social and emotional functioning, and circumscribed interests. Thus, assuming that autism has a genetic basis, siblings of probands with autism who share 50% of their genes, are expected to be at a greater risk not only for autism but also for the less severe phenotype, which is called the lesser variant or the broad phenotype of autism. Therefore, findings such as those reviewed here—indicating developmental disorders, learning disorders, psychopathology, and lower cognitive and social-emotional functioning—are interpreted as being genetically determined and as supporting the genetic hypothesis of autism.

However, in contrast to the clear picture regarding the higher concordance rate for autism in monozygotic versus dizygotic twins and the higher rate of autism in families who already have one child with autism, the review of the literature regarding the broad phenotype is less consistent. As presented in this review, the data are mixed with regard to the similarities among siblings with a stronger database, suggesting that being a male sibling of a child with autism, and more specifically of a female with autism, carries a high risk for development difficulties.

One explanation for the aforementioned findings is genetic. However, our review reveals that cognitive disabilities in siblings of probands with autism are associated with low-SES families (Boutin et al., 1997) and that depression levels in siblings are significantly correlated with the ability to share feelings about having a sibling with autism (Gold, 1993). Also, in Mates' (1990) study, parent participation in the

TEACCH (Treatment and education of autistic and communication-handicapped children) program is mentioned as a possible protective factor for sibling adjustment. In fact, Henderson and Vandenberg (1992) found that family adjustment was linked with a supportive social network. They also reported that parental characteristics (such as internal locus of control) and the severity of the disability of the child with autism are associated with family adjustment. Higher degrees of family adjustment were linked with less severe disability and with a more internal locus of control among parents. On the whole, Henderson and Vandenberg present a complicated picture of the factors that contribute to family adjustment. These factors include the parents' characteristics, the child with autism's degree of disability, and the level of external social support. Henderson and Vandenberg did not identify the unique personal factors contributing to siblings' adjustment in contrast to the family as a whole. However, based on their findings and those of others (such as Mates; Gold; and Boutin et al.), it is clear that family-process variables should be taken into consideration to obtain a more in-depth understanding of siblings' functioning and well-being.

Family-Systems Theory and Siblings' Functioning

According to the family-systems theory, a family is a "developing social system of physically separate people" (Kaye, 1985, p. 39). The unique characteristics and course of development of each family member are nested and interrelated with the development of the family as a whole (Kaye, 1985; Minuchin, 1985). Thus, siblings' functioning should be studied in the context of the relations within the family (e.g., parent–child interaction with the disabled and nondisabled child, marital interaction, and siblings' relationships) and in the context of social networks and cultural groups (Bell, 1971; Bronfenbrenner, 1979; Hinde, 1987, 1992). Rather than focusing solely on the child, the unit of analysis should be the child within the specific family and society. Although this perspective is appealing, empirical testing of its multiple levels as a whole is difficult. As yet, few studies have begun to examine parts of this model in families of children with autism in relation to the functioning of the children with autism themselves and of other family members as well.

Parent Interaction. Studies focusing on typically developing children reveal that children are highly responsive to emotional interactions between significant others, such as parents, and to the quality of the relationships within the family, such as the marital relationship (for reviews, see Dunn, 1993, and Erel & Burman, 1995). Therefore, parents with good marital relationships (e.g., marriages characterized by reciprocity and the sharing of responsibilities and feelings) are more likely to cope successfully with an atypically developing child than are parents whose marital relationships are less optimal. Supporting this notion, Rodrigue, Geffken, and Morgan (1993) found that higher marital satisfaction among parents of children with autism is associated with higher levels of self-esteem in the nonaffected children. However, Fisman et al. (1996) reported that marital satisfaction and family cohesiveness operate as protective factors for siblings of children with Down syndrome and for typically developing children but not for siblings of children with PDD. Thus, marital satisfaction and family cohesiveness may be important factors, but they cannot be regarded as protective or risk factors in relation to autism. Indeed, Fisman et al. (1996) suggest a transactional model in which the interrelations among different factors that influence siblings' adjustment (e.g., the unique characteristics, such as temperament, of the child with autism and of the nondisabled siblings; the parents' personalities, resources, and marital satisfaction) are examined to evaluate their comprehensive influences on siblings' adjustment.

Parents' Perception. According to Dunn (1993), children observe the interactional patterns of parents with their other children, observations which may have immediate and lasting effects on the patterns of interaction that they develop with their siblings. The degree to which parents resolve their feelings of acceptance of their child with autism affects whether and how siblings accept the child with autism (Simeonsson & McHale, 1981; McHale, Simeonsson, & Sloan, 1984; McHale, Sloan, & Simeonsson, 1986).

Based on clinical experience with families of children with autism, Harris (1982) identified four types of parental attitudes that lead to four different coping strategies that may influence the relationships within these families. The first type is the "poor sick child" pattern in which children with autism are perceived as sick and therefore not responsible for their behavior. A pattern of "mother is with the child with autism" is then established and other members of the family (father and siblings) are abandoned. A second type is the "it's just the three of us" pattern, in which the mother and the father take care of the child with autism and neglect their other children. The third type is "this child has come between us" pattern, in which parents are in conflict because one is overly involved with the child with autism. The fourth and last type is the "mother's little helper" pattern that is evident when the mother pulls in one of the siblings to help her take care of the child with autism while other family members are left out. DeMyer (1979) reports that one third of the parents of children with autism feel they neglect their nonhandicapped children because of the attention given to the child with autism. However, the adjustment of siblings whose parents reported that they neglected them was not compared to the adjustment of siblings whose parents reported that they did not neglect them.

Siblings' Responsibilities. An important mediator in siblings' adjustment is the degree of responsibility that they have to their sibling with the disability. Problems in adjustment are more likely to occur in families in which the nondisabled children take over parental duties for the child with a disability, with older girls in the family at greater risk to experience "role tension" (McHale et al., 1984). This issue has not yet been investigated with siblings of children with autism, but has been studied with siblings of children with mental retardation (Cleveland & Miller, 1977; Gath, 1974). Fromberg provides anecdotal evidence about his life with a brother with autism. He writes, "Being Steve's brother meant I was a part-time parent—but without the maturity or experience of our real parent" (Fromberg, 1984, p. 344). Fromberg describes the need to share responsibilities for his brother with his parents as a confusing and very painful experience.

Coping Style of Siblings. Siegel (1996) describes three (not mutually exclusive) prototypical coping strategies of siblings, based on clinical experience with families of children with autism. The first coping style is that of the parentified child, in which the sibling acts more like a parent than like a sibling toward the sibling with autism. Acting like a parent can deprive the sibling of his or her own childhood and can be worrisome when the child gives up his or her own needs too easily. However, assuming a parental role may also help the child to develop a more caring, empathic, and altruistic personality. The second coping style is that of the withdrawn child, in which the sibling puts a wall between his or herself and the child with autism. In most cases, these siblings are younger than the child with autism and have never experienced a period of development in which they were the primary focus of their parent's attention. They are at risk to develop depression as they grow older. The third coping style is that of the superachiever or family mascot. Siblings who are more extroverted tend to adapt by compensating the parents for their loss in having a child with autism. Adopting this coping style is not worrisome as long as the child is not pushed to achieve beyond his or her talents. The mascot child is the one who resorts to using humor or acting funny in order to get parental attention.

According to Siegel (1996), siblings choose one of these coping styles—predisposed by their personality (e.g., introverted vs. extroverted)—to gain parental attention. Thus, Siegel's description portrays an interaction between family factors (parents' attention to the nonaffected sibling) and the child's unique personality.

The family-systems theory raises important questions about possible influences on siblings' adjustment (e.g., parents' perception, parental attention, marital relationships; see Morgan, 1988). However, systematic studies of these influences are still in preliminary stages. Also, rather than looking for a single protective or risk factor, researchers should investigate transactional influences on the child with autism (e.g., gender, degree of severity of symptoms, age, level of IQ), parental characteristics such as personality and marital relationship, and siblings' characteristics such as age and gender.

Rutter et al. (1997), in referring to genetics and environmental effects, note that "genetics effects have to be manifest with respect to organisms developing in a particular environmental milieu, and environmental effects have to operate on organisms that differ with respect to genetically influenced individual characteristics" (p. 336). Therefore, the diathesis-stress model, which incorporates genetic factors as the diathesis component and environmental factors as the stress component, may be helpful in achieving a more in-depth understanding of how genetic and environmental factors transact in the functioning and well-being of siblings of children with autism.

The Diathesis-Stress Model

The diathesis-stress model (Brown & Harros, 1989; Burke & Elliott, 1999; Gottesman, 1991; Rende & Plomin, 1992; Rosenthal, 1970; Walker & Diforio, 1997; Walker, Downey, & Bergman, 1989; Walker, Neumann, Baum, & Davis, 1996; Zubin & Spring, 1977) integrates the biological-genetic and environmental-family approaches. Based on this model, a diathesis expressed as a genetic predisposition may be essential but not necessarily sufficient for its expression as a phenotype. The liability may be modified by many environmental factors, or as suggested by Gottesman, "Nature proposes and Nurture disposes."

The higher rates of the lesser variant or broader phenotype reported for siblings of children with autism may be a result of genetic involvement for some of the siblings. However, these characteristics might also be associated with environmental effects such as parental availability for the nonautistic children. This does not imply that environmental-familial variables necessarily cause the impairments, but rather that within "a window of opportunity" these variables may operate as additional risk or protective factors. The transaction between the genetic liability and environmental factors may be such that for some siblings, the genetic predisposition may be strong enough that under all environments, even the most optimal ones, these children will manifest impairments. For other siblings, the genetic predisposition may be so weak that unless strong environmental factors are operative, these children will not be diagnosed with the lesser variant. For yet other siblings, the genetic predisposition and environmental factors are both operative and can result in multiple impairments. Even if autism is genetically determined in some families, environmental factors may also significantly affect siblings' difficulties or strengths. It is important to note that these environmental factors do not necessarily have to be specific to the one parent who may have transmitted the genetic liability.

Until specific genes are identified for at least some of the families of a child with autism, research efforts should focus on manifested phenotypes in the context in which they appear. The transactional components inherent in this model challenge our research methodologies. However, research could benefit from conceptualizing programs based on the behavioral-genetic and family-systems theories, which include measures of intra- and interfamilial variables. Such studies would examine how these variables are associated with the siblings' developmental trajectories and well-being.

METHODOLOGICAL LIMITATIONS AND FUTURE DIRECTIONS

As noted throughout this chapter, several issues still need to be examined to obtain a more thorough understanding of siblings' cognitive, academic, and social-emotional development and functioning. The first issue relates to what is termed cognitive disability, lesser variant, or the broader phenotype of autism. These labels include different constructs and variables (e.g., language delay, IQ, reading and spelling difficulties, problem-solving abilities, and social-emotional and visuospatial abilities). Future studies may benefit from "unpacking" these terms and working on an agreed-upon definition.

In line with the diathesis-stress model, we also suggest that researchers implement a more comprehensive transactional model of inquiry that takes into account the environmental as well as genetic influences on siblings' functioning. Researchers have started to investigate how parents' perception of their child with autism may influence siblings' functioning and how marital relationships influence the nondisabled sibling's adjustment. However, the influence of the nonhandicapped sibling on the parents has not been studied at all. Perhaps when mothers assume more responsibilities for the child with autism, fathers are more available for the nondisabled children. Furthermore, the family-systems theory may provide a good frame of reference for developing prevention and intervention programs for siblings. Such programs may, for example, be aimed at enhancing open communication among family members about how it is to have a sibling with autism and at offering support during vulnerable phases. Finally, some of our knowledge concerning the influences of family variables on siblings' adjustment is based on clinical experience (Harris, 1982; Siegel, 1996), anecdotal data (e.g., Fromberg, 1984), or studies that lack a comparison group (Berger, 1980; Mates, 1990). Thus, a more extensive empirical investigation with well-controlled studies is needed to broaden our understanding of the environmental influences on siblings' adjustment.

A third neglected issue in the understanding of siblings' development and well-being is the paucity of longitudinal research and lack of long-term evaluations. Whether siblings' functioning changes over the years and if siblings are at greater risk during specific developmental periods (e.g., early childhood, adolescence) remains to be explored. Furthermore, the interactions between siblings' characteristics and those of the child with autism (e.g., severity of autistic symptoms, presence of self-injurious behavior, level of intelligence) need to be further explored. It may be that as children with autism mature, siblings experience some relief. Alternatively, it may be that after years of living with a sibling with autism, siblings may become tired and frustrated and therefore may function less well. On the whole, longitudinal studies and multiple evaluations of the family members may provide important information about the development and well-being of the siblings and the process of long-term coping with a sibling with autism.

ACKNOWLEDGMENTS

Nurit Yirmiya's work on this chapter was supported in part by the United States–Israel Binational Science Foundation and by the Israel Science Foundation founded by the Israel Academy of Sciences and Humanities.

REFERENCES

Anderson, E. R., Hetherington, E. M., Reiss, D., & Howe, G. (1994). Parents' non-shared treatment of siblings and the development of social competence during adolescence. *Journal of Family Psychology, 8,* 303–320.

August, G. J., Stewart, M. A., & Tsai, L. (1981). The incidence of cognitive disabilities in the siblings of autistic children. *British Journal of Psychiatry, 138,* 461–422.

Bailey, A., Le Couteur, A., Gottesman, I., Bolton, P., Simonoff, E., Yuzda, E., & Rutter, M. (1995). Autism as a strongly genetic disorder: Evidence from a British twin study. *Psychological Medicine, 25,* 63–77.

Bailey, A., Palferman, S., Heavey, L., & Le Couteur, A. (1998). Autism: The phenotype in relatives. *Journal of Autism and Developmental Disorders, 28,* 369–392.

Baird, T. D., & August, G. J. (1985). Familial heterogeneity in infantile autism. *Journal of Autism and Developmental Disorders, 15,* 315–321.

Bartak, L., Rutter, M., & Cox, A. (1975). A comparative study of infantile autism and specific developmental receptive language disorder: I. The children. *British Journal of Psychiatry, 126,* 127–145.

Bell, R. Q. (1971). Stimulus control of parent or caretaker behavior by offspring. *Developmental Psychology, 4,* 63–72.

Berger, E. W. (1980). *A study of self-concept of siblings of autistic children.* Unpublished Doctoral dissertation, University of Cincinnati.

Boutin, P., Maziade, M., Merette, C., Mondor, M., Bedard, C., & Thivierge, J. (1997). Family history of cognitive disabilities in first-degree relatives of autistic and mentally retarded children. *Journal of Autism and Developmental Disorder, 27,* 165–176.

Bronfenbrenner, U. (1979). *The ecology of human development.* Cambridge, MA: Harvard University Press.

Brown, G. W., & Harros, T. O. (1989). *Life events and illness.* New York: Guilford.

Burke, P., & Elliott, M. (1999). Depression in pediatric chronic illness: A diathesis-stress model. *Psychosomatics, 40,* 5–17.

Cleveland, D. W., & Miller, N. (1977). Attitudes and comments of older siblings of mentally retarded adults: An exploratory study. *Mental Retardation, 15,* 38–41.

Creak, M., & Ini, S. (1960). Families of psychotic children. *Journal of Child Psychology and Psychiatry, 1,* 156–175.

DeFries J. C., Fulker, D. W., & LaBuda, M. C. (1987). Evidence for a genetic etiology in reading disability of twins. *Nature, 329,* 537–539.

DeMyer, M. K. (1979). *Parents and children with autism.* New York: Wiley.

Dunn, J. (1993). *Young children's close relationships: Beyond attachment.* Newbury Park, CA: Sage.

Erel, O., & Burman, B. (1995). Inter-relatedness of marital and parent-child relations: A meta-analytic review. *Psychological Bulletin, 118,* 108–132.

Faraone, S. V., Biederman, J., Krifcher, B., & Lehman, B. (1993). Evidence for the independent familial transmission of attention deficit hyperactivity disorder and learning disabilities: Results from a family genetic study. *American Journal of Psychiatry, 150,* 891–895.

Fisman, S., Wolf, L., Ellison, D., Gillis, B., Freeman, T., & Szatmari, P. (1996). Risk and protective factors affecting the adjustment of siblings of children with chronic disabilities. *Journal of the American Academy of Child and Adolescent Psychiatry, 35,* 1532–1541.

Folstein, S. E., Gilman, S. E., Landa, R., Hein, J., Santangelo, S. L., Piven, J., Lainhart, J., & Worzek, M. (1999). Predictors of cognitive test patterns in autism families. *Journal of Child Psychology and Psychiatry, 40,* 1117–1128.

Folstein, S. E., & Rutter, M. L. (1977). Infantile autism: A genetic study of 21 twin pairs. *Journal of Child Psychology and Psychiatry, 18,* 297–321.

Fombonne, E., Bolton, P., Prior, J., Jordan, H., & Rutter, M. (1997). A family study of autism: Cognitive patterns and levels in parents and siblings. *Journal of Child Psychology and Psychiatry, 38,* 667–683.

Freeman, B. J., Ritvo, E. R., Mason-Brothers, A., Pingree, C., Yokota, A., Jenson, W., McMahon, W., Peterson, B., Mo, A., & Schroth, P. (1989). Psychometric assessment of first-degree relatives of 62 autistic probands in Utah. *American Journal of Psychiatry, 146,* 361–364.

Fromberg, R. (1984). The sibling's changing role. In E. Schopler & G. B. Mesibov (Eds.), *The effect of autism on the family* (pp. 327–342). New York: Plenum.

Gath, A. (1974). Sibling reactions to mental handicap: A comparison of brothers and sisters of mongol children. *Journal of Child Psychology and Psychiatry, 15,* 187–198.

Gillberg, C., Gillberg, I. C., & Steffenburg, S. (1992). Siblings and parents of children with autism: A controlled population-based study. *Developmental Medicine and Child Neurology, 34,* 389–398.

Gillberg, C., Steffenburg, S., & Jakobsson, G. (1987). Neurobiological findings in 20 relatively gifted children with Kanner-type autism or Asperger syndrome. *Developmental Medicine and Child Neurology, 29,* 641–649.

Gold, N. (1993). Depression and social adjustment in siblings of boys with autism. *Journal of Autism and Developmental Disorders, 23,* 147–163.

Gottesman, I. (1991). *Schizophrenia genesis: The origins of madness.* New York: Freeman.

Harris, S. (1982). A family system approach to behavioral training with parents of autistic children. *Child and Family Behavior Therapy, 4,* 21–35.

Henderson, D., & Vandenberg, B. (1992). Factors influencing adjustment in the families of autistic children. *Psychological Report, 71,* 167–171.

Hinde, R. A. (1987). *Individuals, relationships and culture.* Cambridge, UK: Cambridge University Press.

Hinde, R. A. (1992). Developmental psychology in the context of other behavioral sciences. *Developmental Psychology, 28,* 1018–1029.

Hughes, C., Plumet, M., & Leboyer, M. (1999). Towards a cognitive phenotype for autism: Increased prevalence of executive dysfunction and superior spatial span amongst siblings of children with autism. *Journal of Child Psychology and Psychiatry, 40,* 705–718.

Jorde, L. B., Mason-Brothers, A., Waldmann, R., Ritvo, E. R., Freeman, B. J., Pingree, C., MacMahon, W. M., Peterson, B., Jenson, W. R., & Mo, A. (1990). The UCLA-University of Utah epidemiologic survey of autism: Genealogical analysis of familial aggregation. *American Journal of Medical Genetics, 36,* 85–88.

Kaye, K. (1985). Toward a developmental psychology of the family. In L. L'bate (Ed.), *The handbook of family psychology and therapy* (Vol. 1). Homewood, IL: Dorsey Press.

Kolvin, I., Ounsted, C., Richardson, L. M., & Garside, R. F. (1971). The family and social background in childhood psychoses (III). *British Journal of Psychiatry, 118,* 396–402.

Leboyer, M., Plumet, M. H., Goldblum, M. C., Perez-Diaz, F., & Marchaland, C. (1995). Verbal versus visuospatial abilities in relatives of autistic females. *Developmental Neuropsychology, 11,* 139–155.

Mates, T. E. (1990). Siblings of autistic children: Their adjustment and performance at home and in school. *Journal of Autism and Developmental Disorders, 20,* 545–553.

McHale, S. M., Simeonsson, R. J., & Sloan, J. L. (1984). Children with handicapped brothers and sisters. In E. Schopler & G. B. Mesibov (Eds.), *The effect of autism on the family* (pp. 327–342). New York: Plenum.

McHale, S. M., Sloan, J. L., & Simeonsson, R. J. (1986). Sibling relationships of children with autistic, mentally retarded, and nonhandicapped brothers and sisters. *Journal of Autism and Developmental Disorders, 16,* 399–413.

Minton, J., Campbell, M., Green, W. H., Jennings, S., & Samit, C. (1982). Cognitive assessment of siblings of autistic children. *Journal of the American Academy of Child Psychiatry, 21,* 256–261.

Minuchin, S. (1985). Families and individual development: Provocation from the field of family therapy. *Child Development, 56,* 289–302.

Morgan, S. B. (1988). The autistic child and family functioning: A developmental-family systems perspective. *Journal of Autism and Developmental Disorders, 18,* 263–280.

Narayan, S., Moyes, B., & Wolff, S. (1990). Family characteristics of autistic children: A further report. *Journal of Autism and Developmental Disorders, 20,* 523–535.

Ozonoff, S., Rogers, S. J., Farnham, J. M., & Pennington, B. F. (1993). Can standard measures identify subclinical markers of autism? *Journal of Autism and Developmental Disorders, 23,* 429–441.

Piven, J., Gayle, J., Chase, J., Fink, B., Landa, R., Wrozek, M., & Folstein, S. E. (1990). A family history study of neuropsychiatric disorders in the adult siblings of autistic individuals. *Journal of the American Academy of Child and Adolescent Psychiatry, 29,* 177–183.

Piven, J., Palmer, P., Jacobi, D., Childress, D., & Arndt, S. (1997). Broader autism phenotype: Evidence from a family history study of multiple-incidence autism families. *American Journal of Psychiatry, 154, 185*–190.

Plumet, M. H., Goldblum, M. C., & Leboyer, M. (1995). Verbal skills in relatives of autistic females. *Cortex, 31,* 723–733.

Rende, R., & Plomin, R. (1992). Diathesis-stress models of psychopathology: A quantitative genetic perspective. *Applied and Preventive Psychology, 1,* 177–182.

Ritvo, E. R., Freeman, B. J., Mason-Brothers, A., Mo, A., & Ritvo, A. M. (1985). Concordance for the syndrome of autism in 40 pairs of afflicted twins. *American Journal of Psychiatry, 142,* 74–77.

Rodrigue, J. R., Geffken, G. R., & Morgan, S. B. (1993). Perceived competence and behavioral adjustment of siblings of children with autism. *Journal of Autism and Developmental Disorders, 23,* 665–674.

Rosenthal, D. (1970). *Genetic theory and abnormal behavior.* New York: McGraw Hill.

Rutter, M., Dunn, J., Plomin, R., Simonoff, E., Pickles, A., Maughan, B., Ormel, J., Meyer, J., & Eaves, L. (1997). Integrating nature and nurture: Implications of person-environment correlations and interactions for developmental psychopathology. *Development and Psychopathology, 9,* 335–364.

Siegel, B. (1996). *The world of the autistic child: Understanding and treating* autistic spectrum disorders. New York: Oxford University Press.

Simeonsson, R. J., & McHale, S. M. (1981). Review: Research on handicapped children: Siblings' relationships. *Child Care and Health Development, 7,* 153–171.

Smalley, S. L. (1997). Genetic influences in childhood-onset psychiatric disorders: Autism and attention-deficit/hyperactivity disorder. *American Journal of Human Genetics, 60,* 1276–1282.

Smalley, S. L., & Asarnow, R. F. (1990). Brief report: Cognitive subclinical markers in autism. *Journal of Autism and Developmental Disorders, 20,* 271–278.

Smalley, S. L., Asarnow, R. F., & Spence, M. (1988). Autism and genetics: A decade of research. *Archives of General Psychiatry, 45,* 953–961.

Steffenburg, S., Gillberg, C., Hellgren, L., & Anderson, L. (1989). A twin study of autism in Denmark, Finland, Iceland, Norway and Sweden. *Journal of Child Psychology and Psychiatry and Allied Disciplines, 30,* 405–416.

Szatmari, P., Jones, M. B., Tuff, L., Bartolucci, G., Fisman, S., & Mahoney, W. (1993). Lack of cognitive impairment in first-degree relatives of children with pervasive developmental disorders. *Journal of the American Academy of Child and Adolescent Psychiatry, 32,* 1264–1273.

Szatmari, P., Jones, M. B., Zwaigenbaum, L., & MacLean, J. E. (1998). Genetics of autism: Overview and new directions. *Journal of Autism and Developmental Disorders, 28,* 351–368.

Sullivan, R. C. (1979). Siblings of autistic children. *Journal of Autism and Developmental Disorders, 16,* 399–413.

Tsai, L. Y., & Beisler, J. M., (1983). The development of sex differences in infantile autism. *British Journal of Psychiatry, 142,* 373–378.

Wadsworth, S. J., DeFries, J. C., Fulker, D. W., & Plomin, R. (1995). Cognitive ability and academic achievement in the Colorado Adoption Project: A multivariate genetic analysis of parent–offspring and sibling data. *Behavior Genetics, 25,* 1–15.

Walker, E., Downey, G., & Bergman, A. (1989). The effects of parental psychopathology and maltreatment on child behavior: A test of the diathesis-stress model. *Child Development, 60,* 15–24.

Walker, E. F., & Diforio, D. (1997). Schizophrenia: A neural diathesis-stress model. *Psychological Review, 104,* 667–685.

Walker, E. F., Newman, C. C., Baum, K., & Davis, D. M. (1996). The developmental pathways to schizophrenia: Potential moderating effects of stress. *Development and Psychopathology, 8,* 647–665.

Zubin, J., & Spring, B. (1977). Vulnerability: A new view of schizophrenia. *Journal of Abnormal Psychology, 86,* 103–126.

5

Neurobiology and Genetics of Autism: A Developmental Perspective

Kathleen Koenig
Katherine D. Tsatsanis
Fred R. Volkmar
Yale Child Study Center
New Haven, CT

Autism is a neurodevelopmental disorder characterized by impaired social functioning, impaired communication, and restricted and repetitive behaviors. Although in the first two decades following its initial description by Kanner there was relatively little awareness regarding the neurobiological aspects of the disorder, it is now clear that autism is associated with a number of features that suggest abnormal nervous system functioning and that implicate genetic factors. Over the past two decades interest in these aspects of the condition has increased markedly, and there is a consensus on the importance of these factors in syndrome pathogenesis (Rutter, 2000).

Genes involved in central nervous system development regulate cell growth and synaptogenesis; there is evidence for the contribution of neurotransmitters, neuromodulators, and hormones to this process as well. Normative developmental data on brain formation—including neuron growth, axon and dendrite formation, synaptogenesis, pruning and programmed cell death, are available based on work with primates, and experimental evidence provides information on the timing of these events during gestation. Consequently, information regarding the neuropathological and neurochemical abnormalities seen in autism can provide specific clues about the timing of developmental events that have gone awry and the possible mechanisms involved in aberrant processing of information.

Similarly, neurophysiological and neuroimaging studies may help to localize areas of brain abnormality; such localization will be more precise when the relevant genes are identified.

Perhaps the most difficult task in the investigation of the genetic and neurobiological underpinnings of autism is linking this information to behavioral data. Although autism is defined by impairment in three specific domains of functioning, considerable variation can exist in clinical presentation. Adding to the complexity of varied presentation is the fact that developmental stage impacts the presentation of symptoms. Each aspect of behavior or physiology in autism must be considered with regard to ongoing developmental processes. Pathology cannot be viewed in isolation, but must be integrated into our understanding of typical development, including the changes in neurochemistry, brain structure, and brain function that occur over time.

In this chapter we review the most recent discoveries regarding the neurobiology of autism. We begin with a discussion of genetic factors and then move from the level of cell and brain pathology to studies of the neuroimaging, neurophysiology, and neurochemistry of autism. Throughout the chapter the need to integrate experimental findings within a developmental context is emphasized, and links from empirical data to behavioral manifestations are presented whenever possible.

Genetic Factors

Interest in possible genetic mechanisms in autism followed Folstein and Rutter's (1977) paper describing much higher rates of the disorder in monozygotic (identical) twins as compared with dizygotic (fraternal) twins. Also, although the recurrence risk in siblings (roughly 2% in many studies) was relatively low, it was at least 50-fold in excess of what would be expected based on chance alone. Other work suggested a potentially broader pattern of difficulties in siblings, such that genetic vulnerability might not be limited only to autism (Rutter, 2000). An increase in social and communicative impairments in family members was noted, as were increased rates of particular comorbid psychiatric conditions (Bailey et al., 1995; Smalley, McCracken, & Tanguay, 1995). There is now widespread agreement on the genetic basis of at least some cases of autism (Rutter, 2000).

A potential difficulty in identifying genetic loci in a disorder with heterogeneous presentation is that brain development occurs in probabalistic fashion, such that a specific phenotype cannot be predicted (Cook Jr., 1998). The most productive method of untangling the complexities of phenotypic heterogeneity may be to identify groups of individuals with autism with specific behavioral features for genetic investigation, rather than to use diagnoses alone. Latent class analysis methods have been used to estimate that probably 2 to 5 genes act in concert to produce an autistic phenotype. However, as many as 10 to 12 genes may be implicated, and it is not predicted that the same genes would consistently be involved (State, Lombroso, Pauls, & Leckman, 2000).

Linkage studies investigate families in which there is co-occurrence of a gene locus and the condition under investigation. The affected sibling pair method is a particularly potent methodology for identifying linkage; three groups have reported significant results. In a genome wide screen of 83 sibling pairs, the International Molecular Genetics of Autism Consortium (1998) reported suggestive linkage between the autism phenotype and a region on the long arm of chromosome 7. Two other groups have subsequently identified areas of interest on chromosome 7 as well as regions on chromosome 6 and 1 (Philippe et al, 1999; Risch et al, 1999). Linkage has been reported for the GABRB3 gene (Cook. et al., 1997), which is of special interest given the role of GABA receptors in relation to anxiety and seizures.

The association of autism with particular medical conditions has long been a topic for exploration and debate. The literature on this issue is plagued by a number of methodological problems, such as bias in ascertainment, small sample sizes and overreliance on case reports, issues in the diagnosis of autism, and ambiguities regarding causal medical conditions. The relevant issue is not whether autism is ever associated with some particular medical condition, but whether the frequency is greater than what would be expected based on chance alone (Bolton et al., 1991).

The strongest data to date suggest important, but limited, associations with two conditions, both of which have a strong genetic component: fragile-X syndrome and tuberous sclerosis (Dykens & Volkmar, 1997). Physical features of fragile-X syndrome include characteristic facial appearance, enlarged testicles, associated mental retardation, and some autistic features including poor eye contact, attentional problems, impulsivity, anxiety, and hypersensitivity to noise. About 1% of individuals with autism are affected with fragile-X. Tuberous sclerosis is an autosomal dominant disorder characterized by abnormal tissue growth in various organs associated with mental retardation and seizure disorder; rates of autism reported in these cases are from 0.4% to 2.8% of cases (Dykens & Volkmar, 1997). As with fragile-X, these rates, although accounting for only a small number of cases of autism, are significantly elevated relative to the rate of autism in the general population.

Case reports of specific deletions or translocations also highlight potential areas of interest. For example, Ishikawa-Brush et al. (1997) identified an individual with comorbid autism and multiple exostosis with a translocation of X;8. A break in a gene with high levels of expression in the limbic system was identified on chromosome X. A second case report of interest was a translocation of 7;20, in which a novel gene was found to cross the chromosome 7q11.2 breakpoint (State et al., 2000). This gene, subsequently named Autism Related Gene–1 (ARG–1), is highly expressed in fetal and adult brains. Other reports have noted proximal 15q deletions or duplications in persons with autism (Cook et al., 1998) and a mutated gene responsible for at least part of the phenotype in Rett's syndrome (Amir et al., 1999). Identification of the Rett's gene provides ground for further characterization of the biochemical effects of the mutation in structural and functional terms. Case reports identify critical regions for the selection of candidate genes.

A number of candidate genes have been examined for contribution to the autistic phenotype. These include genes regulating the expression of dopamine, genes involved in serotonergic abnormalities, genes involved in specific epilepsy syndromes, genes of the HLA region (related to the immunological system), and the GABA gene on chromosome 15, previously identified via a linkage study as associated with autism (Cook, 1998).

Consideration of the broader phenotype of the disorder, with an emphasis on examining the dimensional aspects of each symptom domain, may help to identify whether a "dosing effect" impacts the relative contribution of cognitive, language, or regulatory impairment to overall presentation in an individual with a lesser variant of autism (Rutter, 2000). Again, the need for precise characterization of subtypes within the spectrum is highlighted, in that patterns of cognitive strategies, language, onset, presence, and degree of stereotypic or repetitive behavior need to be described in ways that lend themselves to an understanding of the underlying neurobiological mechanisms.

Neuropathology

Neuropathologic study permits an examination of the brain at the level of the cell; in its detail, it can provide the foundation for interpreting the findings arising from neuroimaging, electrophysiologic, and genetic studies. Only a small number of postmortem studies have been reported in the autism literature to date. The findings overall are consistent for observations of increased brain weight as well as neuroanatomic abnormalities confined to the brain stem and cerebellum (Bailey et al., 1998; Bauman & Kemper, 1994, 1996; Ritvo et al., 1986). Bauman and Kemper (1985) reported reduced neuronal cell size and increased cell-packing density in several regions of the brain. Such abnormalities serve as potential markers for when the normal processes of neural development are affected and offer a preliminary framework for neurological models of autism. Findings were obtained in the hippocampus, subiculum, entorhinal cortex, amygdala, mammilary body, anterior cingulate, and septum. These regions of the limbic system are known to have a principal role in memory and emotional functioning. Bilateral damage to the amygdala, hippocampus, and adjacent cortical areas (e.g., entorhinal cortex) in infant monkeys produces patterns of behavior that are similar to autistic behavior (e.g., reduced eye contact, social withdrawal, expressionless faces) (Bachevalier & Merjanian, 1994). Early deficits in the capacity to assign emotional significance to stimuli may have a later impact on the meaning and organization of experiences for persons with autism. The designation of affective valence creates a strong link between people or events and contexts. The ongoing integration of these experiences builds up a cumulative structure of meaning that informs future decisions and actions.

Through this internal feedback system, selective attunement toward persons versus other elements in the environment may confer the greatest advantage.

The cerebellum and related inferior olivary nucleus are also sites of cellular abnormality. A significant decrease in the number of Purkinje cells and a more variable decrease in granule cells was found throughout the cerebellar hemispheres, most notably in the posterolateral cortex and adjacent archicerebellar cortex (Arin, Bauman, & Kemper, 1991; Bauman & Kemper, 1994). The cerebellum has been identified as an important structure in the coordination of attention and arousal systems (e.g., Courchesne, Yeung-Courchesne, Press, Hesselink, & Jernigan, 1988). From this perspective, well-functioning attentional systems are an integral component of social development. Shared or joint attention and an ability to make selective and rapid shifts in attention in response to social signal are paramount. Although there is no doubt that this aspect of functioning is relevant to understanding autism, the role of the cerebellum is less certain.

Taken together, these reports provide evidence of developmental neuropathology, but do not provide consistent evidence of localized abnormalities or the timing of neurodevelopmental events. Bauman and Kemper (1994) suggested that the more general pattern of small, densely packed neurons is comparable to the pattern seen during earlier stages of brain maturation and may represent a curtailment of normal development. Similarly, the cortical abnormalities reported by Bailey et al. (1998) are expected to be associated with a disruption of normal cortical developmental processes. These findings suggest that multiple events early in brain development converge to produce the abnormalities in brain organization and function that are present in autism.

Neuroimaging

Neuroimaging research is used to represent the structural landscape of the brain and to identify the association between structure and function (e.g., brain-behavior pathways). This is a rapidly growing area of study with increasing methodological sophistication. A limitation of this technology is that the developmental effects of early lesions can only be inferred. The main findings are, in different ways, suggestive of altered patterns of neuronal organization and axonal connections in this disorder.

Two neuroimaging investigations provide evidence for brain enlargement in autism compared to an age-, sex-, and nonverbal-IQ-matched comparison group (Filipek et al., 1992; Piven et al., 1995). Further analysis revealed selective enlargement of occipital, parietal, and temporal lobes, but not of the frontal cortex in the autism group (Piven, Arndt, Bailey, & Andreasen, 1996). Other investigations reported increased total brain volume on MRI (Filipek et al. ,1992), consistent with postmortem findings of increased brain weight (Bailey et al., 1998; Bauman & Kemper, 1994) as well as observations of increased head circumference in autism (Lainhart et al., 1997).

The presence of brain enlargement in autism suggests an aberration in the normal mechanisms associated with brain development. These processes include neuronal proliferation, neuronal migration and differentiation, and synaptogenesis, as well as programmed cell death, axonal elimination, and synaptic pruning. Disruption of any of these major processes may lead to increases in brain size that, in turn, also have implications for the organization and refinement of connections in the brain. Increasing brain size has an effect upon the degree of interconnection between neurons such that there are physical constraints on how large the brain can grow while still maintaining adequate levels of connectedness (Ringo, 1991). This may be reflected in greater specialization with increasing brain size. An implication of the finding of enlarged brain size in autism may be greater modularity of function.

Several findings suggest that enlargement of cortical regions does not extend to other regions of the brain, and that a corresponding functional dissociation may in fact exist. In this view, "higher order" centers and "lower," regions are "disconnected," such that social-affective and cognitive processes are not well integrated. Considered along developmental lines, the diminished regulatory influence of regions such as the caudate, amygdala, and thalamus can be seen to affect the functioning of the system as a whole. Structural imaging studies reveal increased volume of cortical regions in autism, but other areas of the brain appear to show no difference or are significantly decreased in size in individuals with autism relative to a comparision group. Imaging studies have not revealed differences in cross-sectional area or volume of the hippocampus (Piven, Bailey, Ranson, & Arndt, 1998; Saitoh, Courchesne, Egaas, Lincoln, & Schreibman, 1995) or size differences in the cross-sectional area of the caudate nuclei (Creasey et al., 1986; Gaffney, Kuperman, Tsai, & Minchin, 1988) or volume of the thalamus (Creasey et al., 1986). A recent MRI study reported significant enlargement of the caudate in autism, proportional to brain volume (Sears et al., 1999). Our recent investigation of the thalamus suggests that it is significantly decreased in volume in larger brained persons with high-functioning autism (Tsatsanis, Rourke, Klin, Volkmar, & Schultz, submitted). There are no published reports examining the volume of the amygdala using MRI, although there is evidence for its involvement in autism (e.g., Bachevalier & Merjanian, 1994; Bauman and Kemper, 1994).

Two independent reports of reduced cross-sectional area of the corpus callosum in autism, specifically in posterior subregions (Egaas, Courchesne, & Saitoh, 1995; Piven, Bailey, Ranson, & Arndt, 1997), are important because the corpus callosum represents a central pathway for interhemispheric communication of information. The anterior cingulate, which is implicated in emotional and executive functioning, was also found to be significantly smaller in relative volume and metabolically less active in high-functioning persons with autism. A recent study of twin boys discordant for the strictly defined phenotype for autism revealed smaller caudate, amygdala, hippocampus, and cerebellar lobules VI and VII in the affected twin, accounting for brain size (Kates et al., 1998). This finding underscores the importance of subcortical pathways in the expression of autism.

The cerebellum has received considerable attention following consistent reports of abnormalities in vermal lobules VI and VII using MRI (Courchesne et al., 1994; Courchesne et al., 1988; Murakami, Courchesne, Press, Yeung-Courchesne, & Hesselink, 1989). This finding has been replicated by one other group (Hashimoto, Tayama, Miyazaki, Murakawa, & Kuroda, 1992; Hashimoto et al., 1995), but not by others (Filipek et al., 1992; Holttum, Minshew, Sanders, & Phillips, 1992; Kleiman, Neff, & Rosman, 1992). Several studies (e.g., Courchesne et al., 1994; Filipek, 1995; Filipek et al., 1992; Piven & Arndt, 1995) suggest an association between IQ and hypoplasia of cerebellar vermal lobules. In a recent investigation, cerebellar lobules VIII-X were reported to be significantly smaller in cross-sectional area in a group of high-functioning children with autism relative to a typically developing comparison group (Levitt et al., 1999). A confounding effect of IQ was also observed for these results. In addition to these discrepancies, the neuropathologic evidence indicated a reduced number of Purkinje cells in the cerebellum, which was not specific to the vermal lobules, but was most characteristic of the cerebellar hemispheres (Bauman & Kemper, 1996).

The findings from the structural imaging studies are suggestive of a lack of correspondence between total brain volume and the volume of subcortical and limbic regions. There is also evidence of a functional disconnection between "higher" and "lower" centers of the brain from metabolic imaging studies. Two early positron emission tomography (PET) studies indicated a global increase in resting glucose metabolism in adult males with autism (Horwitz, Rumsey, Grady, & Rapoport, 1988; Rumsey et al., 1985), which may provide indirect support for structural findings of increased total brain volume, although negative findings have also been reported (Devolder, Bol, Michel, Congneau, & Goffinet, 1987; Herold, Frackowiak, LeCouteur, Rutter, & Howlin, 1988; Siegel et al., 1992). Horwitz et al. (1988) analyzed regional intercorrelations for cerebral metabolic rates and found differences in functional associations between frontal and parietal regions and marked differences between the two cortical regions and subcortical areas, particularly the basal ganglia and thalamus. The authors speculated that this altered pattern of metabolism is representative of an altered pattern of connections in the brain.

Chugani et al. (1997) demonstrated atypical patterns of serotonin synthesis in the brain in seven boys with autism. Decreased serotonin synthesis was observed in the left frontal cortex and thalamus, whereas elevated levels were found in the contralateral dentate nucleus of the cerebellum. In a more recent study, Single Photon Emission Tomography (SPET) images also showed marked hypoperfusion in the cerebellar hemisphere and thalamus of children with autism (Ryu et al., 1999). These findings are consistent with other results indicating abnormalities in these structures; the finding by Chugani and colleagues is also noteworthy given that serotonin has long been implicated in autism and that there is a report of linkage in a serotonin transporter gene (Cook et al., 1997).

Taken together, these findings may represent a disconnection between cortical and subcortical regions in autism, manifest in a pattern of reduced size of some subcortical structures in the context of enlarged cortical volume. Functionally, this abnormality appears to be represented in an altered pattern of connections and regulation of activity through diminished subcortical influences on refinement and organization of the cortex.

Functional imaging techniques have been used increasingly to examine potential differences in neural pathways activated while subjects are engaged in a cognitive activity. Notably, there is some overlap between regions identified in the structural and functional imaging studies, further supporting their role as part of abnormal neural pathways relevant to understanding autism. For example, in a relatively early PET study, Buchsbaum et al. (1992) investigated attentional processes using a visual vigilance task. Whereas there was no significant difference in performance on this task, a comparison group showed greater metabolic rates in the right versus the left cortex, whereas autistic subjects showed virtually equal metabolic rates in the right and left cortices. Significantly decreased activity in the right putamen and right thalamus was observed. An examination of brain activation during auditory perception and language tasks using PET (Müller et al., 1998; Müller et al., 1999) revealed less activation in the dorsolateral prefrontal area, thalamus, and cerebellum in the autism group compared with the normal comparison group during receptive and expressive language tasks.

In addition to revealing differences in particular regions of the brain, functional imaging studies have pointed to differences in the manner in which information is processed. A functional MRI (fMRI) study of performance on the Embedded Figures Task (EFT) showed differential activation despite relatively similar levels of performance (Ring et al., 1999). There was generally greater activity during task performance in the right dorsolateral prefrontal and bilateral dorsal parietal regions in the controls than in the group with autism. In the autism group, increased activity was observed in the right ventral occipitotemporal regions as well as cuneus, lingual gyrus, and fusiform gyrus. This differential pattern of activation was interpreted to suggest a different strategy for completing the task. Specifically, the autism group may have performed the EFT by using mental imagery, placing fewer demands on working memory, thus showing greater activity in some of the regions involved in object perception. In the normal group, the approach appeared to be more global and to involve the use of working memory.

Baron-Cohen and colleagues (1999) examined the attribution of mental states using fMRI and found that typically developing individuals showed greater task accuracy relative to individuals with autism with respect to both gender recognition and theory of mind. In the autism group, frontal components were activated less extensively compared with controls and the amygdala was not activated at all. In the control group, activation was greatest in the left amygdala, right insula, and left inferior frontal gyrus. The autism group showed greater power of response in bilateral superior temporal gyrus, which was suggestive of a greater processing load on verbally labeling visual stimuli. Similarly, functional abnormalities were indicated in persons with autism on a face and object-recognition task using fMRI, (Schultz et al., 2000). The autistic group showed less fusiform gyrus and more inferior temporal gyrus activity when performing person-identity tasks. The inferior temporal gyrus showed the greatest activity when a comparison group performed the object discrimination task, suggesting that subjects with autism were using object regions for processing faces.

At present, there is no consistent evidence of a specific neuroanatomical abnormality in autism to account for its expression. This finding serves to underscore the centrality of neural pathways in explaining the disorder. In this context, the developmental processes involved in the formation and refinement of connections in the brain are pivotal. A disruption in the self-organizational processes that characterize brain development is likely to produce an altered pattern of connectivity and consequent functional disturbances. The aforementioned findings support the notion that the brains of persons with autism are organized differently, which affects how information is processed.

Neurophysiology

Electroencephalographic studies provide a map of brain electrical activity with characteristic waveforms indicating slow or rapid activity in particular brain regions. These patterns change with development, corresponding to spurts and lags in brain growth, and some attempts have been made to link EEG waveforms to changes in information-processing strategies in healthy children (Ornitz, 1996). The use of this method to compare patterns of information processing in children with autism to normative developmental patterns could provide critical information regarding atypical information-processing strategies. For example, a critical period of cortical maturation is between 15 and 24 months, which is often the time when autistic symptomatology is first noted. EEG waveforms that are inconsistent with those typically occurring during this period can provide clues regarding specific regions of interest.

Some investigators have contended that the atypical EEG patterns found in individuals with autism reflect maturational delays, but this remains controversial (Cantor, Thatcher, Hrybyk, & Kaye, 1986; Dawson, Klinger, Panagiotides, Lewy, & Castelloe, 1995). Moreover, the view of maturational delay as a source of the abnormalities seen in autism rests on the assumption that similar patterns reflect a similar developmental course, a view that can be contested. In fact, atypical neural pathways are likely to develop in the immature brain, given its malleability, in ways that compensate for unalterable deficits (Dunn, 1994).

Two thirds of all persons with autism show abnormal EEGs, although no consistent pattern of focal deficits has emerged. Diffuse or focal spikes and slowing and paroxysmal spike wave activity are observed; such increased abnormalities are associated with lower intelligence (Dunn, 1994). A lack of the asymmetry found in the typical brain, with usual greater left hemisphere activity than right, is observed in the majority of studies that show symmetry in the left and right hemisphere, or greater right hemisphere activity (Dunn, 1994). This is not surprising given the role of the left hemisphere in language production, an area of central deficit in autism. Children with autism exhibit normal patterns of hemispheric activation during spatial tasks, for which the right hemisphere plays a more central role (Dawson, Warrenburg, & Fuller, 1983). In terms of consistent abnormalities in the topography of the brain, all regions of the cerebral cortex have been implicated.

Dawson et al. (1995) studied patterns of electrical activity in relation to subtypes of individuals with autism (described by Wing), including the aloof, passive, and active-but-odd groups, compared to an age-matched group and a language-matched group. The autistic group showed reduced power in all regions, and reduced activity in frontal regions—particularly the left frontal region—was noted for the passive group as compared with the active-but-odd group. Studies of nonautistic children and adults show a correlation between left and right frontal lobe activity and social approach and withdrawal (Dawson, 1994). This finding suggests a mechanism for understanding the aberrant social behavior found in autism; the data are consistent with recent models of autism that postulate impairment in temporal-limbic, and limbic-frontal systems (Bachevalier & Merjanian, 1994).

Recent work using evoked response potential (ERP) postulates links between patterns of electrical activity in response to exogenous stimuli to specific behavioral responses seen in autism. These patterns of electrical activity reflect abnormalities of neuronal development that are suggestive of a developmental syndrome rather than a discrete lesion in a particular system (Minshew, Sweeney, & Bauman, 1997). Evoked response potential (ERP) studies have not addressed the core social and language deficits in autism directly because information regarding the generators of this data in typically developing individuals is unknown (Minshew et al.). Rather, investigations have targeted responses to auditory and visual stimulation and to systems involved in processing information—for example, orienting to novelty, selective, and sustained attention, and modulation of attention.

Unusual sensitivity to auditory stimuli in autism, suggesting brain-stem dysfunction, has led to several studies exploring the integrity of the auditory brainstem pathway using brain-stem auditory-evoked responses (BAER)—an evoked potential generated within the subcortical auditory pathways from ear to brain stem. Results have been inconsistent, but when studies control for IQ and the presence of neurological disease, most show no abnormalities (Dunn, 1994). Studies of middle latency responses, reflecting the integrity of the thalamocortical system for both visual and auditory modalities, have revealed few abnormalities apart from some differences in habituation to stimuli (Buchwald et al.,

1992; Grillon, Courchesne, & Akshoomoff, 1989); this may be reflected in the unusual sensory responses some persons with autism show, even toward stimulation to which they should presumably have become accustomed.

Significant developmental differences are noted in long latency responses in typically developing children and adults. Experimental paradigms comparing behavioral response and ERPs using frequent, familiar, infrequent, or novel stimuli have been used in an attempt to understand unusual behavioral responses. Although no differences are apparent in response to frequent stimuli, studies suggest that individuals with autism have decreased responses in terms of amplitude to novel stimuli in the auditory and visual mode (Ciesielski, Courchesne, & Elmasian, 1990; Courchesne, Kilman, Galambos, & Lincoln, 1984; Dawson, Finley, Phillips, Galpert, & Lewy, 1988; Courchesne, Lincoln, Kilman, & Galambos, 1985). The implication is that smaller amplitudes reflect reduced processing and perhaps reduced discrimination of salient and relevant information. In a series of studies, Lincoln and colleagues demonstrated that the responses of children with autism to frequent auditory stimuli were aberrant in that the waveforms typically indicative of anticipation of auditory stimuli and maintenance of attention toward the task were reduced (Lincoln, Courchesne, Harms, & Allen, 1993; Lincoln, Courchesne, Harms, & Allen, 1995). Taken together, these data suggest that persons with autism have difficulty processing novel stimuli, even though it is accurately perceived, and have trouble anticipating or predicting when stimuli will occur based on probabilities.

Evidence for impairment of attentional systems is observed when subjects with autism are asked to alternatively attend and not attend to visual and auditory stimuli. No differences in waveform were seen between these two conditions in the group with autism, whereas in the control group significant differences in waveform reflected different task requirements (Ciesielski et al., 1990). Despite these differences, some subjects with autism performed exactly as controls on behavioral measures. This striking finding highlights the likely differences in neurophysiological processing that exist between the two groups.

In summary, evoked response potential studies show clear differences in the processing of information between autistic and nonautistic individuals, notably in attention to and categorization of stimuli, and possibly in decreased depth of processing of stimuli. Responses to novel and rare stimuli are most unusual, suggesting that persons with autism may not anticipate and react to novel events as typically developing persons do. Difficulties with selective attention and attention to the most salient (linguistic) stimuli are two examples of this lack of ability to respond to and categorize important stimuli.

Neurochemistry

Neurotransmitters, neuromodulators, and hormones are involved in guiding the growth of the central nervous system as well as providing communication in mature neural systems (Rakic, 1996; Whitaker-Azmitia, Lauder, Shemmer, & Azmitia, 1987). Given the diverse symptomatology manifest in autism it is likely that the neurochemical alterations involved are neither unique nor specific to autism and may be common to developmental disabilities or other neuropsychiatric disorders. This possibility has led to the view that specific behavioral profiles and symptoms should be the focus of neurochemical investigation, rather than a more global focus on the larger diagnostic category of autism.

Investigations in neurochemical processes have been particularly fraught with methodological problems and difficulties in making comparisons across studies. Methods for investigation include measurement of neurotransmitter and hormonal levels in plasma and cerebral spinal fluid (CSF), measurement of neurotransmitter and hormone metabolites in urine, neuroendocrine challenges, and psychopharmacological responses. The major problem for interpretation is that inferences regarding central nervous system functioning must be made based on measurements of plasma and urine or behavioral data from psychopharmacological intervention, which may have little relation to central nervous system levels. A second methodological issue is that existing studies have not considered the profound role of development and individual differences in the interpretation of the data. Changes in neurotransmitter and hormonal systems occur throughout development, and age, gender, race, and cognitive ability influence the characteristics of these systems (McBride et al., 1998). A further confound for cross comparisons is changes in diagnostic practices over the past decades.

Serotonin and the catecholamines, peptides, and hormones within the hypothalamo-pituitary-adrenal axis have been the focus of investigation in autism. Serotonin is widely distributed in brain systems and plays a role as a regulator of neuronal growth and a modulator of affiliative behavior, arousal, mood states, and hormone release (Anderson & Hoshino, 1997; Petty, Davis, Kabel, & Kramer, 1996; Whitaker-Azmitia et al., 1987). Approximately 25% of individuals with autism show elevated levels of plasma serotonin (Anderson, Horne, Chatterjee, & Cohen, 1990; Schain & Freedman, 1961). Increased serotonin levels are found in family members of hyperseretonemic individuals, suggesting common genetic underpinnings (Cook, Leventhal, & Freedman, 1988; LeBoyer et al., 1999). The meaning of this well replicated finding is unclear, however, since peripheral (specifically, platelet) serotonin levels may or may not reflect central levels. Nevertheless, it is likely that altered levels of serotonin play a role in the alteration of affilitative behavior and the dysregulation of arousal manifest in autism.

Interest in the underlying genetic mechanisms of the serotonin system in autism has focused on the role of the polymorphic serotonin transporter gene (Cook et al., 1997). No conclusive information regarding the mechanisms underlying increased platelet serotonin—including increased production in the gut, uptake, and storage in the platelet—or decreased metabolism has been reported (Cook et al., 1988; McBride et al., 1989; Minderaa, Anderson, Volkmar,

Akkerhuis, & Cohen, 1987; Yuwiler et al., 1992). Identification of the mechanism responsible for alteration of the platelet will lead to identification of biological markers for the disorder, as well as identification of relevant proteins, gene probes, and chromosomal locations.

Serotonin synthesis may be altered in autism, as suggested by research using positron emission tomography (PET). Individuals with autism show a smaller decrement in serotonin synthesis capacity in the frontal lobe during childhood and adolescence, as compared with that of typically developing individuals (Chugani et al., 1999). This finding is consistent with models of autism that postulate frontal lobe impairment (Damasio, 1978). Data regarding the development of serotonin systems as regulatory mechanisms in the developing embryo and the disarray of serotonin synthesis are the strongest leads available for making sense of the hyperseretonemic pattern in some individuals with autism.

Dopamine has been implicated in the pathogenesis of autism because of the prominence of motor stereotypies in the clinical picture and because of the reduction of these symptoms with the use of neuroleptics, which act to block the action of dopamine at receptor sites. Studies of dopamine have included measurement of the dopamine metabolite homovanillic acid (HVA) in CSF, plasma, and urine. Only 25% of HVA found in plasma and urine represents central metabolic activity, as even CSF contains HVA released from the adrenal and sympathetic systems (Anderson, 1994). Most studies show no increase in HVA in individuals with autism versus controls (Anderson & Hoshino, 1997; Minderaa, Anderson, Volkmar, Akkerhuis, & Cohen, 1989), and dopamine metabolism does not appear to be altered (Martineau et al., 1994). Alternatively, the alterations in dopamine metabolism may be so subtle as to be undetectable at this level of measurement.

An early report of reduced levels of MHPG, the metabolite of central norepinephrine (NE), in the urine of a small sample of boys with autism raised interest in the role of this neurotransmitter in autism (Young, Cohen, Caparulo, Brown, & Maas, 1979). Because norepinephrine has a likely impact on arousal and stress responses, a central role for brain-stem involvement was postulated in light of the altered levels of arousal and unusual sensory responses that have long been noted in autism (Ornitz, Atwell, Kaplan, & Westlake, 1985). However, more recent investigations have not targeted the brain stem to the exclusion of other subcortical and cortical systems, and subsequent investigations of MHPG levels in CSF have not replicated this finding (Minderaa et al., 1994).

Aberrant responses to stress and decreased sensitivity to pain as well as the high frequency of self-injurious behavior in the autistic population have stimulated investigation of brain opiod systems and of the integrity of the hypothalamic-pituitary-adrenal axis. Some, but not all, studies have supported the finding that beta-endorphin levels are increased in children with autism (Sandman, Barron, Chicz-DeMet, & DeMet, 1990; Tordjman et al., 1997). Comparison across studies is compounded by the fact that β-endorphin in cerebral spinal fluid is derived from central sources, whereas plasma β-endorphin is derived from the pituitary and does not cross the blood-brain barrier. Thus, central β-endorphin may be considered relevant for understanding brain opiod systems whereas peripherally derived β-endorphin is an indicator of the stress response generated by the pituitary-adrenal complex (Tordjman et al., 1997).

Sandman et al. (1990) concluded that beta-endorphin levels are generally lower in developmentally delayed individuals than in control subjects and that increased levels are associated with the presence of self-injurious behavior. In contrast, Tjordman et al. (1997) found elevated β-endorphin levels in individuals with autism, unrelated to intellectual level or to the presence of self-injurious behavior. Plasma adrenocorticotropic hormone (ACTH) and beta-endorphin levels were highly correlated in subjects with autism as compared with mentally retarded or typically developing controls, suggesting that levels of these substances are reflective of acute hyperarousal in response to stress (Tordjman et al., 1997). In addition, B-endorphin levels were correlated with autism severity as measured by the Autism Diagnostic Observation Schedule (ADOS). This finding suggests that dysregulation of the stress response, with exquisite sensitivity and exaggerated physiological responses to stress, contributes to the severity of some behavioral manifestations in autism, such as difficulty with novelty and resistance to change.

Increased plasma cortisol levels would be expected in persons with chronically heightened responses to stress, but this finding has not been borne out in most investigations of plasma cortisol (Nir et al., 1995; Tordjman et al., 1997). Cortisol levels reflect overall stress response over time, and increases in response to specific events have a fairly long latency period (Tordjman et al., 1997). Thus, findings of normal cortisol levels in individuals with autism suggest typical baseline adrenal functioning. This is consistent with other measures of basal sympathetic nervous system functioning, including levels of epinephrine and norepinephrine in plasma and CSF.

Conclusions

Although the genetic and neurobiological mechanisms involved in the pathology of autism remain unclear, certain inferences can be made from the existing evidence. Statistical modeling of genetic factors suggests that 4 to 12 genes are involved. The impact of these genetic abnormalities is not immediately apparent, but becomes evident over time as brain development progresses in the infant and very young child. Abnormalities in the development of the cortex including increased cortical thickness, high neuronal density, and neuronal disorganization have been described. Immature and abnormal neurons in some regions (notably the hippocampus, amygdala, subiculum, entorhinal cortex, anterior cingulate, and cerebellum) create a context for a lack of appropriate connectivity. Abnormal pathways develop in response to these aberrant processes, or normative pathways do not develop as strongly as would be needed for normal functioning.

One example of abnormal circuitry is the frontal-temporal circuit, which has been implicated in social and emotional functioning. This is supported by pathology studies showing abnormalities in temporal regions, as well as by an animal model demonstrating that lesions to these frontal-temporal circuits can model some of the behavioral manifestations seen in autism. Further, this is illustrated by functional MRI studies showing differences in brain activation in regions noted for face recognition and by evoked potential studies demonstrating atypical responses to novel stimuli.

Integration of information regarding normal developmental processes is crucial in understanding both the genesis and the unfolding of the deficits that occur in autism. Normative data regarding brain development, cognitive development, affective development, and other functional systems (motor and regulatory) and the timing of the development of these systems can be used to understand the aberrant behavioral manifestations seen in autism. Experiential factors and the individual's place as an active agent in his or her development must not be neglected. The pathways from gene to brain to behavior can be seen not only to converge, but to exert reciprocal influence.

Although a hetereogeneous etiology is presumed in autism, the final common pathways for abnormalities are demonstrated by the domains of impairment in socialization, communication, and restricted and repetitive behaviors. Yet diversity in presentation reflects the reality of this disorder, and better characterization of these domains in dimensional terms is the best way to track the pathological mechanisms. At present, one can only speculate about the links between known brain pathology and behavioral manifestations because the normative functions of existing brain systems are crudely delineated, and the sensitivity of these systems to minute change may produce functional changes that are not easily detected by current investigational techniques. Advances in molecular genetics with application to animal models, functional imaging, and imaging studies using techniques for measurement of neurochemicals are the new frontiers for investigation of the neurobiological events leading to typical and atypical development.

ACKNOWLEDGMENTS

From the Child Study Center and the Children's Clinical Research Center, Yale University School of Medicine, New Haven, CT. The support of NICHD grants 1-P01 HD3582-01 and 2-P01 HD3008-33 is gratefully acknowledged.

REFERENCES

Amir, R. E., Van den Veyver, I. B., Wan, M., Tran, C. Q., Franke, U., & Zoghi, H. (1999). Rett syndrome is caused by mutations in X-linked MECP2, encoding methyl-CpG-binding protein 2. *Nature Genetics, 23,* 185–188.

Anderson, G. (1994). Studies on the neurochemistry of autism. In M. L. Bauman & T. L. Kemper (Eds.), *The Neurobiology of Autism* (pp. 227–239). Baltimore: Johns Hopkins.

Anderson, G. M., Horne, W. C., Chatterjee, D., & Cohen, D. J. (1990). The hyperserotonemia of autism. *Annals of the New York Academy of Science, 600,* 331–40.

Anderson, G. M., & Hoshino, Y. (1997). Neurochemical studies of autism. In D. J. Cohen & F. R. Volkmar (Eds.), *Handbook of Autism and Pervasive Developmental Disorders* (pp. 325–343). New York: Wiley.

Arin, D. M., Bauman, M. L, & Kemper, T. L. (1991). The distribution of Purkinje cell loss in the cerebellum in autism. *Neurology, 41,* 307 (Abstract No. 676P).

Bachevalier, J., & Merjanian, P. M. (1994). The contribution of medial temporal lobe structures in infantile autism: A neurobehavioral study in primates. In M. L. Bauman & T. L. Kemper (Eds.), *The Neurobiology of Autism* (pp. 146–169). Baltimore: Johns Hopkins.

Bailey, A., Le Couteur, A., Gottesman, I., Bolton, P., Simonoff, E., Yuzda, E., & Rutter, M. (1995). Autism as a strongly genetic disorder: Evidence from a British twin study. *Psychological Medicine, 25,* 63–77.

Bailey, A., Luthert, P., Dean, A., Harding, B., Janota, I., Montgomery, M., Rutter, M., & Lantos, P. (1998). A clinicopathological study of autism. *Brain, 121,* 889–905.

Baron-Cohen, S., Ring, H. A., Wheelwright, S., Bullmore, E. T., Brammer, M. J., Simmons, A., & Williams, S. C. (1999). Social intelligence in the normal and autistic brain: An fMRI study. *European Journal of Neuroscience, 11,* 1891–1898.

Bauman, M. L., & Kemper, T. L. (1985). Neuroanatomic observations of the brain in early infantile autism. *Neurology, 35,* 866–874.

Bauman, M. L., & Kemper, T. L. (1994). Neuroanatomic observations of the brain in autism. In M. L. Bauman & T. L. Kemper (Eds.), *The neurobiology of autism* (pp. 119–145). Baltimore: Johns Hopkins.

Bauman, M. L., & Kemper, T. L. (1996). Observations on the Purkinje cells in the cerebellar vermis in autism. *Journal of Neuropathology and Experimental Neurology, 55,* 613 (Abstract No. 34).

Bolton, P., MacDonald, H., Murphy, M., Scott, S., Yuzda, E., Whitlock, B., Pickles, A., & Rutter, M. (1991). Genetic findings and heterogeneity in autism. *Psychiatric Genetics, 2* (S7a/2).

Buchsbaum, M. S., Siegel, B. V., Jr., Wu, J. C., Hazlett, E., Sicotte, N., Haier, R., Tanguay, P., Asarnow, R., Cadorette, T., Donoghue, D., Lagunas-Solar, M., Lott, I., Paek, J., & Sabalesky, D. (1992). Brief report: Attention performance in autism and regional brain metabolic rate assessed by positron emission tomography. *Journal of Autism and Developmental Disorders, 22,* 115–125.

Buchwald, J. S., Erwin, R., Van Lancker, D., Guthrie, D., Scwafel, J., & Tanguay, P. (1992). Midlatency auditory evoked responses: P1 abnormalities in adult autistic subjects. *Electroencephalography and Clinical Neurophysiology, 84,* 164–171.

Cantor, D. S., Thatcher, R. W., Hrybyk, M., & Kaye, H. (1986). Computerized EEG analyses of autistic children. *Journal of Autism and Developmental Disorders, 16,* 169–187.

Chugani, D. C., Muzik, O., Behen, M., Rothermel, R., Janisse, J. J., Lee, J., & Chugani, H. T. (1999). Developmental changes in brain serotonin synthesis capacity in autistic and nonautistic children. *Annals of Neurology, 45,* 287–295.

Chugani, D. C., Muzik, O., Rothermel, R., Behen, M., Chakraborty, P., Mangner, T., da Silva, E. A., & Chugani, H. T. (1997). Altered serotonin synthesis in the dentatothalamocortical pathway in autistic boys. *Annals of Neurology, 42,* 666–669.

Ciesielski, K. T., Courchesne, E., & Elmasian, R. (1990). Effects of focused selective attention tasks on event-related potentials in autistic and normal individuals. *Electroencephalography and Clinical Neurophysiology, 75,* 207–220.

Cook, E. H. J., Courchesne, R., Lord, C., Cox, N. J., Yan, S., & Lincoln, A. (1997). Evidence of a linkage between the serotonin transporter and autistic disorder. *Molecular Psychiatry, 2,* 247–250.

Cook, E. H. J., Leventhal, B. L., & Freedman, D. X. (1988). Free serotonin in plasma: Autistic children and their first-degree relatives. *Biological Psychiatry, 24,* 488–491.

Cook Jr., E. H., Lindgren, V., Leventhal, B. L., Courchesne, R., Lincoln, A., Shulman, C., Lord, C., & Corchesne, E. (1997). Autism or atypical autism in maternally but not paternally derived proximal 15q duplication. *American Journal of Human Genetics, 60,* 928–934.

Cook, E. H., Courchesne, R. Y., Cox, N. J., Lord, C., Gonen, D. Guter, S. J., Lincoln, A., Nix, K., Haas, R., Leventhal, B., & Courchesne, E. (1998). Linkage-disequilibrium mapping of autistic disorder, with 15q11–13 markers. *American Journal of Human Genetics, 62,* 1077–1083.

Cook Jr., E. H. (1998). Genetics of autism. *Mental Retardation and Developmental Disabilities Research Reviews, 4,* 113–120.

Courchesne, E., Kilman, B. A., Galambos, R., & Lincoln, A. J. (1984). Autism: Processing of novel auditory information assessed by event-related brain potentials. *Electroencephalography and Clinical Neurophysiology, 59,* 238–248.

Courchesne, E., Lincoln, A. J., Kilman, B. A., & Galambos, R. (1985). Event-related brain potential correlates of the processing of novel visual and auditory information in autism. *Journal of Autism and Developmental Disorders, 15,* 55–75.

Courchesne, E., Saitoh, O., Yeung-Courchesne, R., Press, G. A., Lincoln, A. J., Haas, R. H., & Schreibman, L. (1994). Abnormality of cerebellar vermian lobules VI and VII in patients with infantile autism: Identification of hypoplastic and hyperplastic subgroups with MR imaging. *American Journal of Roentgenology, 162,* 123–130.

Courchesne, E., Yeung-Courchesne, R., Press, G. A., Hesselink, J. R., & Jernigan, T. L. (1988). Hypoplasia of cerebellar vermal lobules VI and VII in autism. *New England Journal of Medicine, 318,* 1349–1354.

Creasey, H., Rumsey, J. M., Schwartz, M., Duara, R., Rapoport, J. L., & Rapoport, S.I. (1986). Brain morphometry in autistic men as measured by volumetric computed tomography. *Archives of Neurology, 43,* 669–672.

Damasio, A. R., & Maurer, R. G. (1978). A neurological model for childhood autism. *Archives of Neurology, 35,* 777–786.

Dawson, G. (1994). Development of emotional expression and emotion regulation in infancy: Contributions of the frontal lobe. In G. Dawson & K. W. Fischer (Eds.), *Human Behavior and the Developing Brain* (pp. 346–379). New York: Guilford.

Dawson, G., Finley, C., Phillips, S., Galpert, L., & Lewy, A. (1988). Reduced P3 amplitude of the event-related brain potential: Its relationship to language ability in autism. *Journal of Autism and Developmental Disorders, 18,* 493–504.

Dawson, G., Klinger, L. G., Panagiotides, H., Lewy, A., & Castelloe, P. (1995). Subgroups of autistic children based on social behavior display distinct patterns of brain activity. *Journal of Abnormal Child Psychology, 23,* 569–583.

Dawson, G., Warrenburg, S., & Fuller, P. (1983). Hemispheric functioning and motor imitation in autistic persons. *Brain and Cognition, 2,* 346–354.

Devolder, A., Bol, A., Michel, C., Congneau, M., & Goffinet, A. M. (1987). Brain glucose metabolism in children with the autistic syndrome: Positron tomography analysis. *Brain Development, 9,* 581–587.

Dunn, M. (1994). Neurophysiological observations in autism and their implications for neurological dysfunction. In M. L. Bauman & T. L. Kemper (Eds.), *The Neurobiology of Autism* (pp. 45–65). Baltimore: Johns Hopkins.

Dykens, E., & Volkmar, F. (1997). Medical conditions associated with autism. In D. Cohen & F. Volkmar (Eds.), *Handbook of Autism and Pervasive Developmental Disorders,* (2nd ed., pp. 388–410). New York: Wiley.

Egaas, B., Courchesne, E., & Saitoh, O. (1995). Reduced size of corpus callosum in autism. *Archives of Neurology, 52,* 794–801.

Filipek, P. A. (1995). Quantitative magnetic resonance imaging in autism: The cerebellar vermis. *Current Opinion in Neurology, 8,* 134–138.

Filipek, P. A., Richelme, C., Kennedy, D. N., Rademacher, J., Pitcher, D. A., Zidel, S., & Caviness, V. S. (1992). Morphometric analysis of the brain in developmental language disorders and autism. *Annals of Neurology, 32,* 475 (Abstract No. 166).

Folstein, S., & Rutter, M. (1977). Infantile autism: A genetic study of 21 twin pairs. *Journal of Child Psychology and Psychiatry, 18,* 297–321.

Gaffney, G. R., Kuperman, S., Tsai, L. Y., & Minchin, S. (1988). Morphological evidence for brainstem involvement in infantile autism. *Biological Psychiatry, 24,* 578–586.

Grillon, C., Courchesne, E., & Akshoomoff, N. (1989). Brainstem and middle latency auditory evoked potentials in autism and developmental language disorders. *Journal of Autism and Developmental Disorders, 19,* 255–269.

Hashimoto, T., Tayama, M., Miyazaki, M., Murakawa, M., & Kuroda, Y. (1992). Brainstem and cerebellar vermis involvement in autistic children. *Journal of Child Neurology, 7,* 149–152.

Hashimoto, T., Tayama, M., Murakawa, M., Yoshimoto, T., Miyazaki, M., Harada, M., & Kuroda, Y. (1995). Development of the brainstem and cerebellum in autistic patients. *Journal of Autism and Developmental Disorders, 25,* 1–18.

Herold, S., Frackowiak, R. S., LeCouteur, A., Rutter, M., & Howlin, P. (1988). Cerebral blood flow and metabolism of oxygen and glucose in young autistic adults. *Psychological Medicine, 18,* 823–831.

Holttum, J. R., Minshew, N. J., Sanders, R. S., & Phillips, N. E. (1992). Magnetic resonance imaging of the posterior fossa in autism. *Biological Psychiatry, 32,* 1091–1101.

Horwitz, B., Rumsey, J. M., Grady, C. L., & Rapoport, S. I. (1988). The cerebral metabolic landscape in autism: Intercorrelations of regional glucose utilization. *Archives of Neurology, 45,* 745–755.

International Molecular Genetics of Autism Consortium. (1998). A full genome screen for autism with evidence for linkage to a region on chromosome 7. *Human Molecular Genetics, 7,* 571–578.

Ishikawa-Brush, Y., Powell, J. F., Bolton, P., Miller, A. P., Francis, F., Willard, H. F., Lehrach, H., & Monaco, A. (1997). Autism and multiple exotoses associated with and X;8 translocation occurring within the GPPR gene and 3' to the SDC2 gene. *Human Molecular Genetics, 6,* 1241–1250.

Kates, W. R., Mostofsky, S. H., Zimmerman, A. W., Mazzocco, M. M., Landa, R., Warsofsky, I. S., Kaufmann, W. E., & Reiss, A. L. (1998). Neuroanatomical and neurocognitive differences in a pair of monozygous twins discordant for strictly defined autism. *Annals of Neurology, 43,* 782–791.

Kleiman, M. D., Neff, S., & Rosman, N. P. (1992). The brain in infantile autism: Are posterior fossa structures abnormal? *Neurology, 42,* 753–760.

Lainhart, J. E., Piven, J., Wzorek, M., Landa, R., Santangelo, S. L., Coon, H., & Folstein, S. E. (1997). Macrocephaly in children and adults with autism. *Journal of the American Academy of Child and Adolescent Psychiatry, 36,* 282–290.

LeBoyer, M., Phillippe, A., Bouvard, M., Guilloud-Bataille, M., Bondoux, D., Tabuteau, F., Feingold, J., Mouren-Simeoni, M. C., & Launay, J. -M. (1999). Whole blood serotonin and plasma beta-endorphin in autistic probands and their first-degree relatives. *Biological Psychiatry, 45,* 158–163.

Levitt, J. G., Blanton, R., Capetillo-Cunliffe, L., Guthrie, D., Toga, A., & McCracken, J. T. (1999). Cerebellar vermis lobules VIII–X in autism. *Progress in Neuro-Psychopharmacology and Biological Psychiatry, 23,* 625–633.

Lincoln, A. J., Courchesne, E., Harms, L., & Allen, M. (1993). Contextual probability evaluation in autistic, receptive developmental language disorder, and control children: Event-related potential evidence. *Journal of Autism and Developmental Disorders, 23,* 37–58.

Lincoln, A. J., Courchesne, E., Harms, L., & Allen, M. (1995). Sensory modulation of auditory stimuli in children with autism and receptive developmental language disorder: Event-related potential evidence. *Journal of Autism and Developmental Disorders, 25,* 521–539.

Martineau, J., Herault, J., Petit, E., Guerin, P., Hameury, L., Perrot, A., Mallet, J., Sauvage, D., Lelord, G., & Muh, J. (1994). Catecholaminergic metabolism and autism. *Developmental Medicine and Child Neurology, 36,* 688–697.

McBride, P. A., Anderson, G., Hertzig, M. E., Snow, M. E., Thompson, S. M., Khait, V. D., Shapiro, T., & Cohen, D. J. (1998). Effects of diagnosis, race, and puberty on platelet serotonin levels in autism and mental retardation. *Journal of the American Academy of Child and Adolescent Psychiatry, 37,* 767–776.

McBride, P. A., Anderson, G. M., Hertzig, M. E., Sweeney, J. A., Kream, J., Cohen, D., & Mann, J. (1989). Seretonergic responsivity in male young adults with autistic disorder. *Archives of General Psychiatry, 46,* 213–221.

Minderaa, R. B., Anderson, G. M., Volkmar, F. R., Akkerhuis, G. W., & Cohen, D. (1987). Urinary 5-hydroxyindoleacetic acid and whole blood serotonin and tryptophan in autistic and normal subjects. *Biological Psychiatry, 22,* 933–940.

Minderaa, R. B., Anderson, G. M., Volkmar, F. R., Akkerhuis, G. W., & Cohen, D. J. (1989). Neurochemical study of dopamine functioning in autistic and normal subjects. *Journal of the American Academy of Child and Adolescent Psychiatry, 28,* 190–194.

Minderaa, R. B., Anderson, G. M., Volkmar, F. R., Akkerhuis, G. W., & Cohen, D. (1994). Noradrenergic and adrenergic functioning in autism. *Biological Psychiatry, 36,* 237–241.

Minshew, N., Sweeney, J., & Bauman, M. (1997). Neurological aspects of autism. In D. Cohen & F. Volkmar (Eds.), *Handbook of Autism and Pervasive Developmental Disorders* (2nd ed., pp. 344–369). New York: Wiley.

Müller, R. A., Behen, M. E., Rothermel, R. D., Chugani, D. C., Muzik, O., Mangner, T. J., & Chugani, H. T. (1999). Brain mapping of language and auditory perception in high-functioning autistic adults: A PET study. *Journal of Autism and Developmental Disorders, 29,* 19–31.

Müller, R. A., Chugani, D. C., Behen, M. E., Rothermel, R. D., Muzik, O., Chakraborty, P. K., & Chugani, H. T. (1998). Impairment of dentate-thalamo-cortical pathway in autistic men: Language activation data from positron emission tomography. *Neuroscience Letters, 245,* 1–4.

Murakami, J. W., Courchesne, E., Press, G. A., Yeung-Courchesne, R., & Hesselink, J. R. (1989). Reduced cerebellar hemisphere size and its relationship to vermal hypoplasia in autism. *Archives of Neurology, 46,* 689–694.

Nir, I., Meir, D., Zilber, N., Knobler, H., Hadjez, J., & Lerner, Y. (1995). Brief report: Circadian melatonin, thyroid-stimulating hormone, prolactin, and cortisol levels in serum of young adults with autism. *Journal of Autism and Developmental Disorders, 25,* 641–653.

Ornitz, E. M. (1996). Developmental aspects of neurophysiology. In Melvin Lewis (Ed.), *Child and Adolescent Psychiatry: A Comprehensive Textbook,* (2nd ed., pp. 39–50). Baltimore: Williams & Wilkins.

Ornitz, E. M., Atwell, C. W., Kaplan, A. R., & Westlake, J. R. (1985). Brain-stem dysfunction in autism. *Archives of General Psychiatry, 42,* 1018–1025.

Petty, F., Davis, L. L., Kabel, D., & Kramer, G. L. (1996). Serotonin dysfunction disorders: A behavioral neurochemistry perspective. *Journal of Clinical Psychiatry, 57* (suppl. 8), 11–16.

Philippe, A., Martinez, M., Guilloud-Bataille, M., Gillberg, C., Rastam, M., Sponheim, E., Coleman, M., Zappella, M., Aschauer, H., van Malldergerme, L., Penet, C., Feingold, J., Brice, A., Leboyer, M., & study group, P. A. R. I. S. P. (1999). Genone-wide scan for autism susceptibility genes. *Human Molecular Genetics, 8,* 805–812.

Piven, J., & Arndt, S. (1995). The cerebellum in autism [Letter to the editor]. *Neurology, 45,* 398–399.

Piven, J., Arndt, S., Bailey, J., & Andreasen, N. (1996). Regional brain enlargement in autism: A magnetic resonance imaging study. *Journal of the American Academy of Child and Adolescent Psychiatry, 35,* 530–536.

Piven, J., Arndt, S., Bailey, J., Havercamp, S., Andreasen, N. C, & Palmer, P. (1995). An MRI study of brain size in autism. *American Journal of Psychiatry, 152,* 1145–1149.

Piven, J., Bailey, J., Ranson, B. J., & Arndt, S. (1997). An MRI study of the corpus callosum in autism. *American Journal of Psychiatry, 154,* 1051–1056.

Piven, J., Bailey, J., Ranson, B. J., & Arndt, S. (1998). No difference in hippocampus volume detected on magnetic resonance imaging in autistic individuals. *Journal of Autism and Developmental Disorders, 28,* 105–110.

Rakic, P. (1996). Development of the cerebral cortex in human and nonhuman primates. In M. Lewis (Ed.), *Child and Adolescent Psychiatry: A Comprehensive Textbook,* (2nd ed., pp. 9–29). Baltimore: Williams & Wilkins.

Ring, H. A., Baron-Cohen, S., Wheelwright, S., Williams, S. C., Brammer, M., Andrew, C., & Bullmore, E. T. (1999). Cerebral correlates of preserved cognitive skills in autism: A functional MRI study of Embedded Figures Task performance. *Brain, 122,* 1305–1315.

Ringo, J. L. (1991). Neuronal interconnection as a function of brain size. *Brain, Behavior, and Evolution, 38,* 1–6.

Risch, H., Spiker, D., Lotspeich, L., Nouri, N., Hinds, D., Hallmayer, J., Kalaydjieve, L., McCague, P., Dimiceli, S., Pitts, T., Nguyen, L., Yang, J., Harper, C., Thorpe, D., Vermeer, S., Young, H., Hebert, J., Lin, A., Fergeson, J., Chiotti, C., Wiese-Slater, S., Rogers, T., Salmon, B., Nicholas, P., Petersen, P. B., Pingree, C., McMahon, W., Wong, D. L., Cavalli-Sforza, L. L., Kraemer, H. C., & Myers, R. M. (1999). A genomic screen of autism: Evidence for a multilocus etiology. *American Journal of Human Genetics, 65,* 493–507.

Ritvo, E., Freeman, B. J., Scheibel, A., Duong, T., Robinson, H., Guthrie, D., & Ritvo, A. (1986). Lower Purkinje cell counts in the cerebella of four autistic subjects: Initial findings of the UCLA-NSAC autopsy research report. *American Journal of Psychiatry, 143,* 862–866.

Rumsey, J. M., Duara, R., Grady, C., Rapoport, J. L., Margolin, R. A., Rapoport, S. I., & Cutler, N. R. (1985). Brain metabolism in autism: Resting cerebral glucose utilization rates as measured with positron emission tomography. *Archives of General Psychiatry, 42,* 448–455.

Rutter, M. (2000). Genetic studies of autism: From the 1970s into the millenium. *Journal of Abnormal Child Psychology, 28,* 3–14.

Ryu, Y. H., Lee, J. D., Yoon, P. H., Kim, D. I., Lee, H. B., & Shin, Y. J. (1999). Perfusion impairments in infantile autism on technetium-99m ethyl cysteinate dimmer brain single-photon emission tomography: Comparison with findings on magnetic resonance imaging. *European Journal of Nuclear Medicine, 26,* 253–259.

Saitoh, O., Courchesne, E., Egaas, B., Lincoln, A. J., & Schreibman, L. (1995). Cross-sectional area of the posterior hippocampus in autistic patients with cerebellar and corpus callosum abnormalities. *Neurology, 45,* 317–324.

Sandman, C. A., Barron, J. L., Chicz-DeMet, A., & DeMet, E. M. (1990). Plasma B-endorphin levels in patients with self-injurious behavior and stereotypy. *American Journal on Mental Retardation, 95,* 84–92.

Schain, R. J., & Freedman, D. X. (1961). Studies on 5-hydroxyindole metabolism in autistic and other mentally retarded children. *Pediatrics, 58,* 315–320.

Schultz, R. T., Gauthier, I., Klin, A., Fulbright, R. Anderson, A. W., Volkmar, F., Skudlarski, P., Lacadie, C., Cohen, D. J., & Gore, J. C. (2000). Abnormal ventral temporal cortical activity among individuals with autism and Asperger syndrome during face discrimination. *Archives of General Psychiatry, 37,* 331–340.

Sears, L. L., Vest, C., Mohamed, S., Bailey, J., Ranson, B. J., & Piven, J. (1999). An MRI study of the basal ganglia in autism. *Progress in Neuro-Psychopharmacology and Biological Psychiatry, 23,* 613–624.

Siegel Jr., B. V., Asarnow, R., Tanguay, P., Call, J. D., Abel, L., Ho, A., Lott, I., & Buchsbaum, M. S. (1992). Regional cerebral glucose metabolism and attention in adults with a history of childhood autism. *Journal of Neuropsychiatry and Clinical Neurosciences, 4,* 406–414.

Smalley, S., McCracken, J., & Tanguay, P. E. (1995). Autism, affective disorders, and social phobia. *American Journal of Medical Genetics, 60,* 19–26.

State, M. W., Lombroso, P. J., Pauls, D. L., & Leckman, J. F. (2000). The genetics of childhood psychiatric disorders: a decade of progress. *Journal of the American Academy of Child and Adolescent Psychiatry, 39,* 946–962.

Tordjman, S., Anderson, G., McBride, A., Hertzig, M. E., Snow, M. E., Hall, L. M., Thompson, S., & Ferrari, P. (1997). Plasma B-endorphin, adrenocorticotropic hormone, and cortisol in autism. *Journal of Child Psychology and Psychiatry, 38,* 705–715.

Tsatsanis, K. D., Rourke, B. P., Klin, A., Volkmar, F., & Schultz, R. T. (2000). A volumetric evaluation of the thalamus in high-functioning individuals with autism using MRI. Manuscript submitted for publication.

Whitaker-Azmitia, P. M., Lauder, J. M., Shemmer, A., & Azmitia, E. C. (1987). Postnatal changes in serotonin1 receptors following prenatal alterations in serotonin levels: Further evidence for functional fetal serotonin1 receptors. *Developmental Brain Research, 33,* 285–289.

Wing, L., & Gould, J. (1979). Severe impairments of social interaction and associated abnormalities in children: Epidemiology and classification. *Jounal of Autism and Developmental Disorders, 9,* 11–29.

Young, J. G., Cohen, D. J., Kavanagh, M. E., Landis, H. D., Shaywitz, B. A., & Maas, J. W. (1981). Cerebral spinal fluid, plasma and urinary MHPG in children. *Life Sciences, 28,* 2837–2845.

Yuwiler, A., Shih, J. C., Chen, C. -H., Ritvo, E. R., Hanna, G., Ellison, G. W., & King, B. H. (1992). Hyperseretonemia and antiserotonin antibodies in autism and other disorders. *Journal of Autism and Developmental Disorders, 22*(1), 33–45.

II

Attention and Perception

6

The Development of Attention and Joint Attention in Children With Autism

Sue Leekam
University of Durham, England
Chris Moore
Dalhousie University, Halifax, Nova Scotia, Canada

Children are rarely diagnosed with autism in the first two years of life, as the full range of symptoms required for a diagnosis is usually not evident before this time. Yet early signs of autism are apparent in infants of one year old and less (Baranek, 1999; Osterling & Dawson, 1994; Wing, 1971). These early signs include a range of abnormalities in initiation and response to other people, imitation, eye contact, smiling, social and nonsocial play, use of gesture and speech, interactions with objects, motor stereotypies, and unusual sensory preoccupations. The earliest and most marked of these impairments, however, are those that relate to early social interaction and communication. Of these, one of the most discriminating is the impairment in *joint attention*—the ability to coordinate attention between people and objects (Baron-Cohen et al., 1996; Cox et al., 1998; Curcio, 1978; Lord, 1995; Loveland & Landry, 1986; Mundy, Sigman, Ungerer, & Sherman, 1986).

The aim of our research has been to try to trace the developmental origins and consequences of this joint-attention impairment. Working with a model of typical infant development, we have studied the interdependence between the development of joint attention and the development of attentional control in the first year of life. Understanding both the origins and the consequences of the joint-attention impairment requires a clear developmental perspective. The evidence suggests that the impairment is not absolute and is subject to developmental change depending on the ability and experience of the child. Any explanation of joint-attention impairment, therefore, needs to address the question of how and why such developmental changes occur.

What is Joint Attention?

Joint attention is a term that refers to a complex of interactional behaviors including gaze following, in which the child turns to look where another person is looking and other prelinguistic communicative acts such as pointing and showing objects to others. The characteristic components of these interactional episodes are a sharing of experience (i.e., *joint*ness) and *attention* to some third object or event apart from the two participants in the interaction.

In order to understand the impairment of joint attention in autism, it is helpful to look at how joint-attention behaviors appear in the course of typical development. These behaviors emerge within a context of social interaction that has been in place from early in the first year of life. Initially, during the first three months, typically developing infants spend much of their time in dyadic face-to-face interaction with other people, engaging in mutual gaze, vocal interchange, and turn-taking games. After the first few months, they progressively start to attend to objects outside of the dyadic interaction and by the age of 6 months, their attention to the mother has declined in favor of attention to objects (Trevarthen & Hubley, 1978; Bakeman & Adamson, 1984).

Triadic joint-attention behaviors involving both people and objects become established between 6 months and 12 months. One such behavior is gaze-following—looking where another person is looking by following another's head turn or eye direction. These gaze-following behaviors may be found earlier than 6 months when there are objects in the visual field. Even infants as young as 3 to 6 months will follow another's head turn when there is an object already visible. However, it is not until later, from 9 months, that infants use the other's head turn alone as a cue to search for an object in a particular location (Butterworth & Cochran, 1980; Corkum & Moore, 1998). Other triadic behaviors include pointing and showing objects to others. From 9 months, infants point to objects and hold up objects to show to others, alternating eye contact between person and object (Butterworth, 1995). By 18 months, infants can also follow head turns to the space behind them and can use eye movements alone as cues to follow gaze direction (Butterworth & Jarrett, 1991).

The contrast between the behaviors of typically developing infants and children with autism is made clear in the following descriptions by the parent of a typically developing 18-month-old and the parent of the much older 7-year-old child with autism of their child's ability to follow another person's pointing gesture and to show objects to other people. These descriptions are taken from an interview study with parents (Leekam, Hunnisett, & Moore, 1998) using an adaptation of an interview designed by Reddy (1991).

Typically developing child aged 18 months. "If I see something of interest and turn my head and point to it, he'll go 'Ah!' and point as well. He'll look at what I'm pointing at and look back at my eyes or face. Around his first birthday he started to hold out objects to show, looking at the object and then look up for my reaction."

Child with autism aged 7 years (verbal mental age 4 years 11months). "A few weeks ago he started for the first time to follow where I was pointing. A lot of the time he would ignore us unless we made a really sharp 'Look at that!' He'd look at the object or my hand. Not at my face. He doesn't often show things to me. If he does, he thrusts the object under my nose. He looks at the object or at his own hand when he's showing. He started showing objects to me for the first time less than a year ago."

These descriptions illustrate that behaviors that are common in infants are absent in children with autism of the same age. If they do appear, these behaviors emerge very late in development and do not have the same quality of shared, affective interaction shown by other children (Kasari, Sigman, Mundy, & Yirmiya 1990). The lack of joint attention in children with autism has been well documented not only in parent interviews but also in a number of research studies using observational and experimental techniques (for example, Baron-Cohen, 1989; Leekam, Baron-Cohen, Perrett, Milders, & Brown, 1997; Loveland & Landry, 1986; McEvoy, Rogers, & Pennington 1993; Mundy et al., 1986; Mundy, Sigman, & Kasari, 1994).

The lack of joint attention in the early years therefore seems to be central part of the disorder. What is the cause of this impairment? Broadly speaking, two main views have emerged. One view is that the origin of this impairment is affective. Taking the components of joint attention described earlier, it is the "jointness" component that is first affected. Autism is seen as the result of a deficit in intersubjective relatedness (Hobson, 1993) or a deficit in regulating social-emotional approach (Mundy, 1995). The prediction from this approach is that dyadic (child–other) as well as triadic (child–other–object) interactions are impaired. Such dyadic impairment would therefore show itself in problems with face-to-face gaze, initiating acts of joint attention, and the patterning of behavior within interactions.

The other view is that the origin of this impairment is cognitive. According to this view, what is impaired is the child's understanding of both his or her own and another person's attention to a third object. Joint-attention impairment arises because children cannot represent the psychological relation of seeing or attending that links the adult with the object; and this is part of a larger "theory of mind" impairment (Baron-Cohen, 1995; Baron-Cohen, Leslie, & Frith, 1985). This approach focuses on the problems in triadic joint-attention behaviors such as pointing to show and gaze-following. These behaviors indicate the child's awareness of the other person's attention to an object. When combined with gaze alternation, these behaviors also seem to show understanding of the "joint" nature of joint attention in the sense that the child seems aware that both his or her self and the other person are attending to an object.

The affective and cognitive approaches suggest that children with autism fail to engage in joint-attention behaviors either because they fail to share experiences with another person or because they fail to understand that another person is attending to an object. According to these explanations, the underlying capacity for either affective sharing or awareness of another's mental state of attention is evidenced by behaviors such as pointing and gaze following. However, the relationship between surface behavior and underlying function is not as straightforward as it appears. Studies of the development of pointing in infants, for example, demonstrate that the same surface behavior can have two different functions. One is to share interest or affect with another (declarative pointing) (Bates, Camaioni, & Volterra, 1975). It is this function that is also associated with the representation of another's mental state. The other function is to request an object or event (imperative pointing), a function that does not necessarily involve sharing affect or representation of another's mental state. There is evidence that it is the declarative rather than the imperative function that is specifically impaired for children with autism (Baron-Cohen, 1989; Charman, 1998; Curcio, 1978; Mundy et al., 1986). Pointing behaviors, therefore, may be occurring without the child necessarily sharing affect or representing another's mental state.

A similar separation between form and function can also be seen in the case of gaze following. Gaze following—turning to look where another person is looking—serves the function of sharing another person's focus of attention and experience. It may therefore indicate an underlying capacity to represent another's mental state or to engage in affective sharing. Yet gaze following also serves a useful function in enabling the individual to obtain something he or she wants. A gaze-following strategy can be acquired by noting the usefulness of other people's bodily movements as cues to the location of interesting objects or events. Perhaps the most compelling support for this proposal is that chimpanzees show quite sophisticated gaze-following strategies (e.g., Povinelli & Eddy, 1997). However, they show no attempts to initiate joint attention by pointing or showing (Tomasello, Kruger, & Ratner, 1993). This suggests that gaze following could occur without evidence of representing the other's state of attention or sharing their affective experience.

Given that gaze following is a useful strategy for obtaining desired objects and is the earliest joint-attention behavior to emerge in typical infancy, we were surprised to note the degree of impairment in gaze following reported in children with autism. When we started our enquiry in the mid-1990s, the literature on joint-attention skills in autism tended to emphasize impairment rather than ability (Baron-Cohen, 1989; Loveland & Landry, 1986; Mundy et al., 1986). What seemed odd to us in the case of gaze following was that children with autism were not using some kind of instrumental gaze-following strategy. Why would they not show surface gaze-following behavior even if this behavior took place without any underlying capacity of affective sharing or awareness of others?

Our initial hypothesis was that children with autism might fail to engage in gaze-following behavior for some other reason, maybe because of some perceptual or attentional problem that would affect their ability to make a response to another's head and eye movements. The focus for our enquiry was on the possibility of a low-level attentional dysfunction.

An explanation in terms of attentional dysfunction seemed to support a third major theoretical view for the underlying impairment of autism, which contrasts with the affective and cognitive views just described. This explanation is the executive function theory of autism. Executive functions are thought to encompass a range of subskills related to goal-directed action. The range of competencies incorporated within the term "executive functions" include planning, sequencing, ability to sustain attention, resistance to interference, utilization of feedback ability to coordinate simultaneous activity, cognitive flexibility, and response to novelty (Crawford, 1998). The specific executive components that appear to be impaired in autism are those related to flexibility (Ozonoff, Strayer, McMahon, & Filloux, 1994).

Executive-dysfunction explanations of autism would suggest that there are problems in one type of attentional orienting; the disengaging and shifting of visual attention (Pennington & Ozonoff, 1996; Russell 1996). Courchesne and colleagues (Courchesne et al., 1994) also claim that people with autism have specific problems with disengaging and shifting attention. However the evidence for executive impairments in very young children with autism is not conclusive. Despite earlier evidence for an association between executive-functioning impairments and joint-attention impairment in children with autism (McEvoy, Rogers, & Pennington, 1993), more recent research has failed to find autism-specific deficits in executive-functioning tasks involving shifting attention and working memory (Griffith, Pennington, Wehner, & Rogers, 1999). The relationship between joint attention and problems of disengaging and shifting of attention, therefore, remains to be clearly established. By studying the attentional components of joint attention, our enquiry promised to throw further light on this relationship.

In our attempt to explain the role of the attentional impairment in the development of joint attention, it was not sufficient for us to simply explain a general absence of gaze following in children with autism. In recent years, researchers have demonstrated that the lack of joint-attention behavior in autism is not absolute. Some children with autism do show joint-attention behaviors. Studies by DiLavore and Lord (1995); Mundy, Sigman, and Kasari (1994); and Sigman and Ruskin (1999) demonstrate how developmental factors such as age and developmental level might influence the acquisition of a range of joint-attention behaviors. In our research, therefore, we used a model of typical development to attempt to trace changes in the emergence of joint-attention behaviors in children with autism. We also looked at developmental factors of age and developmental level for gaze following.

Gaze Following and Attention in Typical Development

The question that intrigued us was why children with autism should have difficulty with gaze following when chimpanzees do not. This question set us thinking about another group of individuals who fail to engage in gaze following—young infants in the early months of life. Gaze-following ability emerges only gradually across the first year of life; very young infants, therefore, do not show this skill. The literature suggested that this period of development coincides with a critical period of development in attentional control (Johnson, 1990). If impairments in autism reflect extreme developmental delay, it is possible that children with autism might have a low-level attentional dysfunction that affects their ability to orient toward objects or people, or both. This proposed dysfunction might affect orienting in a general way or might be confined either to a particular type of orienting response (e.g., disengaging from a central head-turn cue) or to a particular type of stimulus (e.g., social versus nonsocial).

To examine the link between attention and joint attention in autism, we first looked at the developmental literature on attentional-orienting behaviors in the first year of life and compared this with the literature on gaze following during the same period (for review, see Moore, 1999). Although it might be expected that research on topics of infant attentional orienting and gaze following might belong to the same literature, these two areas of research have, for historical reasons, taken rather different directions and used different methodologies. Research on the development of attentional control in infancy has tended to focus on nonsocial stimuli in contrast to the social stimuli studied in the gaze-following literature. We report the findings of these research studies in the following section and later consider the possible importance of distinguishing between social and nonsocial attentional orienting.

The literature on attentional orienting to nonsocial stimuli shows that orienting behaviors start early. Even in the first few months, infants make a reflexive, involuntary orienting response by turning their heads or eyes toward a stimulus such as a flash of light or a sound. However, in the first months of life, infants also show difficulties in shifting to look at a target if they are simultaneously attending to a central stimulus (Aslin & Salapatek, 1975; Atkinson, Hood, Wattam-Bell, & Braddick, 1992; Harris & MacFarlane, 1974), a phenomenon known as "obligatory attention." Comparing this with evidence on the development of joint attention, it is clear that gaze following does not start at birth. Infants in the first few months spend most of their time in face-to-face interactions and tend not to shift away to look at objects in the periphery.

The attention-orienting literature shows that a change occurs at around 3 months, when infants are more able to disengage from a central stimulus and shift attention to a peripheral target. This was tested in visual-orienting studies by Atkinson et al. (1992), who measured infants' shifts of gaze to computer-generated patterns. When infants needed to disengage attention from a competing central stimulus, 3-month-olds performed significantly better than did 1-month-olds. The joint-attention literature shows something similar. Infants of 3 months, rather than exclusively attending to another person, progressively come to attend to objects outside of the dyadic interaction (Bakeman & Adamson, 1994).

Evidence from attentional orienting studies suggests that a new development occurs around the age of 3 to 6 months as infants start to use information from cues, which facilitates shifts of attention to objects within the visual field. Studies of cued attention typically use computer displays. For example, a briefly presented cue (e.g., a triangle) appears on a screen, followed, after a short delay, by the presentation of a target (e.g., a square). Hood (1995) found that 6-month-olds react faster to targets appearing in cued peripheral locations than to targets appearing in uncued peripheral locations. Three-month-olds did not. Johnson, Posner, and Rothbart (1994) also showed that 4-month-old infants were significantly faster to orient to a target when it appeared 100 ms later in the same peripheral location as the cue. After 3 months of age, then, infants appear to use cues to search for targets presented in the immediate visual field. Comparisons with joint-attention studies of gaze following also reveal that infants are beginning to use another person's head turn as a cue to locate objects. Studies by Butterworth and Cochran (1980) and D'Entremont, Hains, and Muir (1997) show that 3- to 6-month-old infants will follow gaze when there are target objects in the immediate visual field. There is some evidence that this ability may start even younger than 3 months when face-like stimuli are used (Hood, Willen, & Driver, 1998).

Attention in the early months of life is thought to be under exogenous control—that is, characteristics of the stimuli "capture" the infant's attention. Lauwereyns (1998) describes the distinction between exogenous and endogenous control in terms of the distinction between automatic and goal-oriented information processing. Exogenous orienting seems to reflect a reflexive system driven by physical characteristics of information in the visual field. Endogenous orienting in contrast seems to reflect a goal directed system involving cognitive interpretation—the formation and maintenance of expectations. In adult studies of attentional orienting, endogenous orienting is often tested using a central "symbolic" cue that contains meaning or information about the location—for example, an arrow that indicates spatial direction (Spence & Driver 1996). This cue predicts the location of a target that subsequently appears elsewhere in the visual field. Adults characteristically detect a target faster if it appears in the valid location predicted by the arrow cue and are slower if it appears in a different location (Posner, 1980).

The tasks administered to adults to test endogenous orienting involve verbal instruction and a computer-key-press decision task. Although these tests cannot be administered to infants, other evidence has been used to argue that increased endogenous control is developing in the second half of the first year. This evidence is based on measures of overt looking behavior. For example, Gilmore and

Johnson (1995) used an oculomotor-delayed response paradigm to show that infants at 6 months are able to learn and retain information from a briefly presented cue. After a delay of up to 5 seconds before targets were presented, infants successfully looked to the location where the cue had appeared earlier, suggesting that they had formed and retained an expectation from the cue.

The head-turn cue in a gaze-following situation can be likened to a symbolic cue used in a test of endogenous orienting. The infant has to predict the potential for a target from the indicating properties of the head turn alone. Several studies show that infants from the age of 9 months will reliably follow gaze even though there are no targets in the immediate visual field (Butterworth & Cochran, 1980; Butterworth & Jarrett 1991; Corkum & Moore, 1998; Moore, Angelopoulos, & Bennett, 1997). Moore (1999) suggests that infants who follow gaze in the absence of targets may be using endogenous control of attention. Their responses suggest that they have some understanding of the meaning of the other's head-turning behavior as a potential for indicating a target. There is no direct parallel for this finding in the traditional attention literature as cued-attention tasks rely on the presentation of targets.

Developments in Gaze Following and Attention

To summarize, when comparing attention and gaze following in typically developing infants, at least three phases are apparent. These are shown in Table 6.1. In the first phase, before about 2 months of age, the infant is able to orient but may have difficulty disengaging attention from what he or she is already looking at in order to shift attention elsewhere. At the second stage, from about 3 months, the infant seems able to disengage and shift attention from a competing central stimulus toward a stimulus located in the peripheral visual field and can use a cue to locate an exogenous target. Finally, from about 9 months, the infant can make use of the facilitating effects of another's head turn in a more "endogenous" way by searching away from the head-turn cue even if there is no target in the visual field.

The distinction between social and nonsocial orienting is orthogonal to this developmental scheme. As mentioned earlier, much of the research testing exogenous and endogenous orienting uses nonsocial stimuli, and studies have not tended to directly compare social and nonsocial stimuli in traditional attentional-orienting tasks. An important issue, therefore, is the extent to which there are differences in responding to social and nonsocial stimuli. Recent research with adults using adaptations of the traditional orienting task suggests that head or face cues may elicit a reflexive orienting response not traditionally found in response to nonsocial cues (Driver et al., 1999; Friesen & Kingstone, 1998; Langton & Bruce, 1999). There is also evidence of this tendency in infants in a task where targets are present in the visual field (Hood, Willen, & Driver, 1998). Given the

TABLE 6.1
Developmental Scheme of Gaze Following and Attentional Control

Level	*Age in Months*	*Gaze Following*	*Attentional Control*
1	1	None	Exogenous orienting
2	3	Follows head turn to target in visual field	Disengagement + exogenous orienting
3	9	Follows head turn to target out of visual field	Endogenous orienting

restricted range of evidence, however, it is difficult at this stage to make firm conclusions about infants' differential responses to social and nonsocial stimuli.

In the research reported in the following section, we attempt to establish whether the impairments in autism fit the general developmental scheme outlined in Table 6.1. Like the studies with infants, attentional orienting studies with older individuals with autism have also tended to use nonsocial rather than social stimuli.

Gaze Following and Attention in Children With Autism

We first set out to trace whether the impairments in autism would fit the developmental scheme in Table 6.1 by looking at the evidence from the attention literature in autism. First, is there evidence that individuals with autism reach the first level of development? Is it possible that children with autism who are developmentally delayed in gaze following are also delayed with respect to the simplest level of exogenous orienting? Research, mostly with older individuals, shows mixed evidence for nonresponsiveness or fluctuating responsiveness to visual or auditory stimuli, with some studies showing impairments while others show intact exogenous responding relative to mental-age-matched comparison groups (Burack & Iarocci, 1995; Courchesne, Lincoln, Kilman, & Galambos, 1985; Rincover & Ducharme, 1987; Wainwright & Bryson, 1996). More recent behavioral studies testing orienting to social stimuli as well as to nonsocial stimuli have found orienting difficulties in very young children with autism (Dawson, Meltzoff, Osterling, Rinaldi, & Brown, 1998; Swettenham et al., 1998). These difficulties seem to be particularly pronounced in response to social stimuli.

Second, is there evidence that individuals with autism reach level 2 of our scheme? Research on disengagement and shifting attention shows some evidence for difficulty although the research reported is with older individuals, using computerized displays. Individuals with autism appear to have problems with disengaging attention from a central to a peripheral stimulus (Wainwright-Sharp &

Bryson, 1993; Casey, Gordon, Mannheim, & Rumsey, 1993) and from one type of sensory stimulus to another (e.g., auditory to visual) (Courchesne et al., 1994). In these studies, it is difficult to separate the disengagement component from the predictive-cueing component because these tasks involve both a disengagement element and a cued-attention element. For example, the sensory modality of a target cues the predicted modality of the next target (Courchesne et al., 1994). Likewise, a central square or arrow cues the presentation of a peripheral stimulus (Wainwright-Sharp & Bryson, 1993; Casey et al., 1993). From the evidence available, it has been suggested that individuals with autism may be slower to shift attention as they may take more time to form expectations from an informational or "symbolic" cue (Burack, Enns, Stauder, Mottron, & Randolph, 1997). This suggests difficulty at level 3. Currently, however, there is little evidence on whether there is a specific deficit in the ability of the person with autism to use a symbolic cue rather than a problem disengaging and shifting. Our work aimed to explore this problem with relation to gaze following.

The working hypothesis was that children with autism might have difficulty at one or more levels of the developmental scheme outlined in Table 6.1. Their problems might be confined to the inability to understand the meaning of a head-turn cue, a problem we assume to be associated with endogenous orienting (level 3). This would show itself as a specific problem in following another person's head turn. Another possibility is that they might also have difficulty in disengaging their attention from a central stimulus (level 2) or in orienting to an exogenous event (level 1). Any one of these difficulties might apply to both social and nonsocial stimuli or might be confined to social stimuli. We explored these ideas in the series of studies described as follows.

What is the Nature of the Gaze Following Deficit in Autism?

We started with level 3 of the developmental scheme for gaze following—the ability to follow a head turn to a target outside of the visual field. Our first task was to ascertain the nature of this deficit. To what extent do children with autism show a lack of gaze-following behavior? Does their gaze-following ability take a developmental course that is similar to that of infants?

To investigate the nature of the gaze-following impairment, we used a gaze-following task based on work by Corkum and Moore (1998) with infants. In this part of the chapter, we describe the use of this task with typically developing infants and outline the developmental changes in response patterns at different ages. We then describe our research using the same task with children who have autism.

The setup for the task is shown in Fig. 6.1. The procedure was as follows. The child and experimenter sat opposite each other in the center of a cubicle. First the child's responses to a head turn were measured in the absence of targets. In these

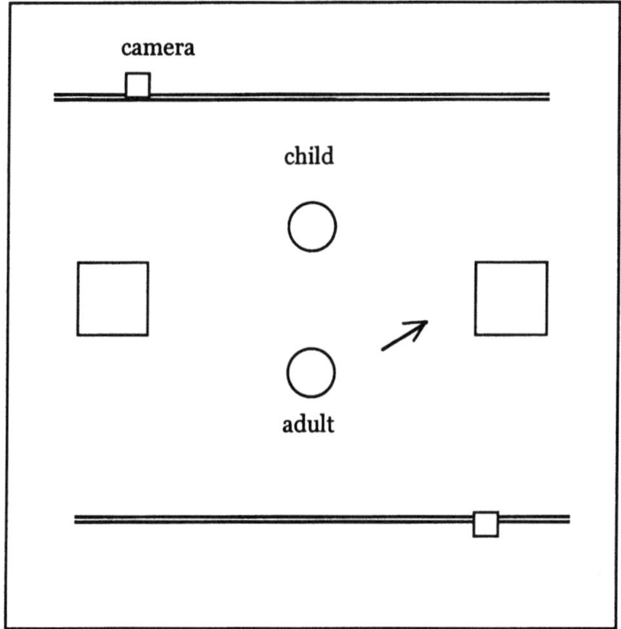

FIG. 6.1. Experimental setup for gaze following experiment.

baseline trials, the experimenter, seated opposite the child, attempted to gain eye contact. On obtaining mutual gaze, the experimenter turned her head left or right to each side of the cubicle. This initial baseline phase was followed by a training phase, in which the experimenter's head turn was followed by the activation of a remote controlled target object in the location to which the experimenter turned. Finally the training phase was followed by a test phase. In this phase, activation of the target object was contingent not simply on the experimenter's head turn but also on the child's head turn. This meant that during the test phase, the child had to follow the experimenter's head turn when there was no target in view and that the target was subsequently activated only if the child successfully turned in the correct location.

Gaze-Following Ability in Typically Developing Infants. When Corkum and Moore (1998) carried out their task with 6- to 12-month-old normal infants, they found that infants of 6 months followed the experimenter's head turn when the target was visible in the training phase, but showed very little gaze following when the target was out of sight during the baseline or test phase. In contrast, infants from about 9 months followed a head turn to targets outside of the visual field. Infants of 8 to 9 months did this mainly during the test phase whereas 10- to 12-month-olds reliably followed the experimenter's head turn both during the test phase and during the baseline phase. In a review of the evidence on gaze following, Moore (1999) suggested that at about 9 months, once infants discover that objects can potentially appear to the side in this procedure, they attempt to predict on which side the objects will appear using the head-turn cue to guide their response. Shortly thereafter the predictive meaning of cues, such as head turns, is so well established that infants 10 to 12 months old will follow gaze in the baseline phase, without any exposure to the target. These developmental changes suggest that by the end of the first year infants come to retain the meaning of a head turn as an indicator even when there are no target objects present.

Gaze-Following Ability in Children with Autism. How do children with autism compare with typically developing infants in regard to gaze-following ability? We investigated this in two separate studies. In the first study (Leekam, Hunnisett, & Moore, 1998), 17 school-aged children with autism, aged 5 years 6 months to 12 years 6 months, were individually matched with 17 typically developing children. The critical variable for individual matching was verbal mental age rather than chronological age, so the children in each group had the same mental ages but a range of chronological ages. Verbal mental ages ranged from 1 year 3 months to 10 years, with approximately half the children in each group having a mental age above 4 years and half having a mental age below 4 years. Children with autism were tested additionally for their nonverbal ability. They had nonverbal IQs ranging from 31 to 124 and nonverbal mental ages from 3 years to 9 years 7 months. Half had IQs above 80 and a nonverbal mental age above 5 years 6 months and half had IQs and mental ages that were below these levels.

The results of this study showed that the majority of children with autism performed like Corkum and Moore's oldest infants. That is, they followed gaze spontaneously in both the baseline and test phase. Although these results seemed to contradict previous studies with autistic populations, we assumed that this good performance was due to the older age of our sample.

However, when we split both the autism and comparison group into two subgroups—one with high verbal mental age (above 4 years) and one with low mental age—the results looked quite different. The children with autism performed very differently depending on their verbal mental age. One hundred percent of high-ability children followed gaze spontaneously (in baseline and test phases), whereas only one third of the low-ability children did so. Results based on nonverbal ability rather than verbal ability showed a similar pattern. The typically developing comparison group, in contrast, followed gaze spontaneously in the absence of targets regardless of whether they had high or low mental age.

In our second study, (Leekam, López, & Moore, 2000) we wanted to find out more about the developmental factors that might be affecting gaze-following ability and whether the same patterns would be found with younger preschool children with autism. In this study, we matched each child with autism with a nonautistic developmentally delayed child of the same age (e.g., mental retardation or language delay). For this study we tested 20 young children with autism and 20 children with developmental delays, language delays, or both, aged between 2 years 10 months and 5 years 10 months. This time the crucial variable for matching was nonverbal ability (IQ and MA) in order that we could hold these variables constant while looking separately at the independent effect of verbal ability. The sample was balanced so that approximately half the children with autism and the developmentally delayed children had IQs below 70 (20 to 58) and nonverbal MAs 10 months to 2 years 5 months. Half had IQs above 70 (74 to 134) and nonverbal MAs of 2 years 11 months to 7 years 2 months.

Results for this study showed a similar pattern to those of our previous study. For the developmentally delayed group, the results did not depend on whether children had high or low ability. The predominant response for developmentally delayed children whatever their ability level was to spontaneously follow gaze in baseline and test phase. In contrast, the results for children with autism were affected by ability level. Eighty-three percent of children with autism with high ability (IQ over 70 or MA over 2 years 11 months) reliably followed gaze, compared with only 25% of children with autism with low ability.

Children in the low-ability autism group (IQ below 70, MA below 2 years 6 months) were much worse at spontaneously following gaze than were their developmentally delayed counterparts. Seventy-five percent of these low-ability children with autism performed like Corkum and Moore's (1998) 6 to 7 month olds, following gaze only when there were targets to be seen. When the difference in verbal ability was taken into account, the results remained the same. In other words, the group differences between low-ability children with autism and developmentally delayed children remained significant even when adjustment was made for verbal ability.

The combined results of both studies show a distinctive pattern of developmental delay in autism. For children with autism, developmental level seems to affect the development of gaze following, whereas for the developmentally delayed children in our study, gaze following occurs spontaneously regardless of developmental level. It appears, therefore, that with increased mental age the meaning of the head-turn cue is consolidated for children with autism. Children with autism, however, may need many more years than is required by typically developing and developmentally delayed children in order to understand and generalize the meaning of a head-turn cue.

A striking finding from these studies was that a large number of young children with autism with low ability failed to follow the experimenter's head turn. Following the scheme on Table 6.1, could this point to the existence of a specific problem involving endogenous orienting (level 3)? According to the scheme, it is also possible that children might have difficulty in orienting to an exogenous event (level 1), especially if this involves disengaging from an object to which they are already attending (level 2). These difficulties might be confined to the social stimulus of another person's head turn or might involve a more general problem applicable to both people and objects. The experiment we discuss next concentrates on attentional orienting to nonsocial stimuli, while subsequent studies look at the effects of social and human stimuli.

A Problem of Attentional Orienting?

As mentioned earlier, arguments for a problem in disengaging attention in individuals with autism have been found in several sources. Courchesne and colleagues (1985, 1994) argue that a central problem is the difficulty in shifting attention between stimuli. Problems of disengagement and shifting cognitive set are also proposed as evidence for executive-functioning impairments in autism (Russell, 1996; Pennington & Ozonoff, 1996). Russell (1996, p. 269), for example, suggested that a test of attentional regulation such as that used by Atkinson et al. (1992) with infants might be used as a screening test for executive function impairments in the first year of life and that the results could be used to predict later joint-attention difficulties. We used this kind of test of attention regulation in our studies of preschool children described in the following section.

Our experiment (Leekam, López, & Moore, Experiment 3, 2000) was based on the design used by Hood and colleagues in their experiments with 1- to 3-month-old typically developing infants (Atkinson et al., 1992; Hood, 1995). The original 20 preschool children with autism and the original 20 matched comparison children from our earlier experiment took part in this study. For this experiment, we adapted the original setup (see Fig. 6.2). In place of the experimenter's chair, a third box, identical to those in the periphery, was positioned in front of the child. The box also contained a toy train. At the start of the experimental trial, the central train appeared out of the box, its side view visible to the child. For the overlap condition (half the trials), this central stimulus remained displayed while a peripheral target train appeared. For the non-overlap condition, the central stimulus disappeared into the box immediately before the peripheral target train appeared.

The prediction was that if children with autism have a general orienting impairment they might make more errors, be slower to respond, or both, when faced with both conditions. If they have a specific problem with disengagement, they should perform worse than the developmentally delayed comparison children on the overlapping trials only.

With respect to the first prediction, children with autism were not slower to respond in both conditions than were children in the comparison group. On the contrary, children with autism were faster at shifting toward the peripheral target than were the developmentally delayed children. The same result was independently found for the low-ability group when the groups were split according to either high or low IQ or high and low mental age. With respect to the second prediction, contrary to expectation again, children with autism were not slower than the nonautistic children in the overlap condition. Both groups were slightly slower in the overlap condition than the non-overlap condition, but the children with autism were

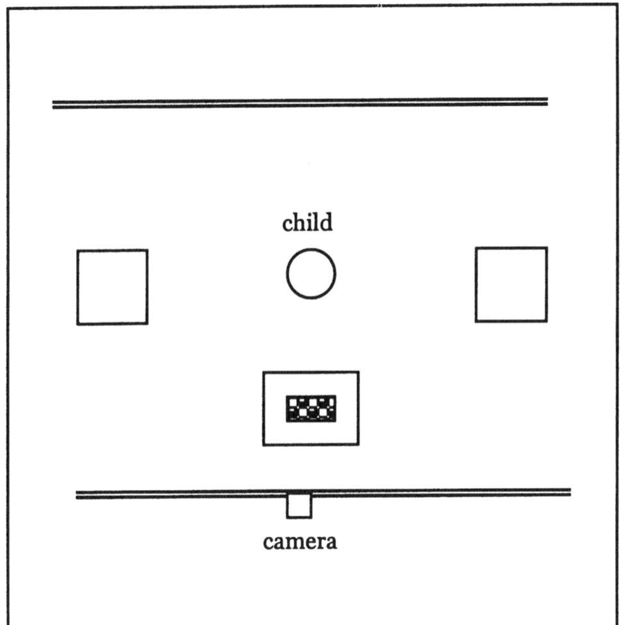

FIG. 6.2. Experimental setup for attention shifting experiment.

as accurate and as fast as comparison children in shifting attention to a peripheral target when a central stimulus overlapped and competed for attention. Indeed when the low-ability children with autism and developmental delay were compared, the children with autism were faster than the nonautistic children.

Children with autism, then, appear to have an intact ability to orient attention to stimuli even when this requires the disengagement of attention from something they are looking at. In terms of the developmental scheme in Table 6.1, levels 1 and 2 appear to present no difficulty for them. In contrast, the results for the gaze-following task show problems at level 3.

At first sight, this explanation seemed fairly clear. But it was obvious that these results did not represent the whole picture. First, our results were not entirely consistent with the literature on attention in adolescents and adults with autism. Related to this, it appeared that the study of gaze following might raise some particular difficulties for the traditional dichotomy between exogenous and endogenous orienting. Furthermore, the distinction between social versus nonsocial stimuli still needed to be tested. These issues are dealt with in the section that follows.

Exogenous Versus Endogenous Orienting

Comparisons between our own study and previous research studies of attentional orienting reveal a discrepancy. Wainwright-Sharp and Bryson (1993), for example, highlight the difficulties that individuals with autism have in processing symbolic information in attentional-orienting tasks. Their finding points to a deficit in endogenous orienting involving voluntary control of attention. In principle this conclusion is consistent with our findings for the gaze-following deficit. However, whereas Wainwright-Sharp and Bryson explained this finding in terms of a problem with the disengagement of attention, our own findings for the previously described attention-shifting task suggest that children with autism are not impaired in disengaging. How can this inconsistency be reconciled?

The difference between our study and traditional attention studies in terms of experimental task and subject population makes direct comparison difficult. In studies of cued attention, covert attention is typically measured with computer displays and decision tasks (computer key press on detection of target), whereas we have tested shifts of overt attention, measuring head-turn responses to moving mechanical objects. Subject populations for previous studies include older adolescents and adults, with typically developing age-matched comparison subjects, whereas our studies focus on preschool children and developmentally delayed comparison groups.

A different interpretation of the Wainwright-Sharp and Bryson studies is that the tasks involve not only the disengagement of attention, but also the ability to predict from a cue. A study by Courchesne et al. (1994) also involved a signal, in that the appearance of a target gave information about the predicted modality of the next target. Another interpretation of the results of these studies suggested by Burack et al. (1997), therefore, is that the problem may lie with the length of time it takes for the subject to form an expectation. Preliminary research using cues that did not give information about location (Burack & Iaarocci, 1995), showed no deficits in disengaging and shifting attention for individuals with autism. Their hypothesis is that "reading" or predicting information from a cue might create a problem. A finding that if symbolic cues, or those containing meaning or information, are particularly difficult for the child with autism to process or respond to would be consistent with the results we find for the gaze-following task.

Further research that directly tests between the disengagement hypothesis and the prediction hypothesis is needed. Nevertheless, the study we have carried out, even as it stands, may help to highlight a distinction between disengagement and prediction problems in attention tasks. It seems to be important to separate these two elements in order to better understand the problems people with autism have with executive-functioning tasks. Although impaired shifting of attention was previously considered as evidence of executive-functioning deficits in autism, the nature of this deficit may need to be specified in terms of a predictive as well as a disengaging element.

The traditional conceptual distinction between endogenous orienting (under voluntary control) and exogenous orienting (under stimulus control) seems, however, to become less clear when applied to gaze following. The distinction used in the adult attention literature assumes that endogenous attention makes use of informative central cues that are predictive. Exogenous orienting in contrast occurs whether or not the cue is predictive (Jonides, 1981). Exogenous orienting is also recognized by the fact that orienting to a stimulus is fast (Cheal & Lyon, 1991), persists for short duration (Müller & Rabbitt, 1989), is driven by physical characteristics of cues, and is impervious to cognitive influences (Posner, 1980). The traditional distinction between exogenous and endogenous orienting has recently been challenged, however. For example, Stolz (1996) recently found that exogenous cueing effects are influenced by higher order linguistic factors, a finding not predicted by the traditional distinction. Researchers also question whether the cue of eye direction in a human face induces endogenous or exogenous attention (Driver et al, 1999; Friesen & Kingstone, 1998; Langton & Bruce, 1999).

The distinction used in our studies rests upon individuals making a response based on the informational value or "meaning" of a cue when targets are not available in the visual field. A gaze-following task would therefore induce an endogenous response when targets are absent and an exogenous response when targets are present (Moore, 1999). This hypothesis is already suggested by the work of D'Entremont, Butterworth, and others who show that infants follow gaze when targets are present some months before being able to follow gaze in response to head turn alone. Further research with both infants and children with autism, however, will enable us to test this hypothesis more systematically.

Attentional Orienting to Objects and People

The studies reported so far confound developmental level of attention with type of attentional stimuli. We found that children with autism show intact (exogenous) orienting to objects and impaired (endogenous) orienting response to a social cue. It is important to separate the exogenous/endogenous distinction from the social/nonsocial distinction in order to determine their independent effects. Therefore, in two separate studies we tested the opposite pattern—children's orienting to a person and their response to an object cue.

To test children's responses to a nonhuman cue, we adapted our existing experimental paradigm and gave this new task to another group of preschool children with autism. The setup is shown in Fig. 6.3. The experimenter in the gaze-following task was replaced with a nonhuman cue—another toy train that rotated to face each of the peripheral targets before they were activated. We found that children with autism did not perform better in the nonhuman condition than in the human condition, although after some exposure to the link between nonhuman cue and target event across trials, they did eventually acquire a cue-following strategy.

To test children's orienting responses to a person, we conducted an analysis of the face-to-face interaction between the child and experimenter as they took part

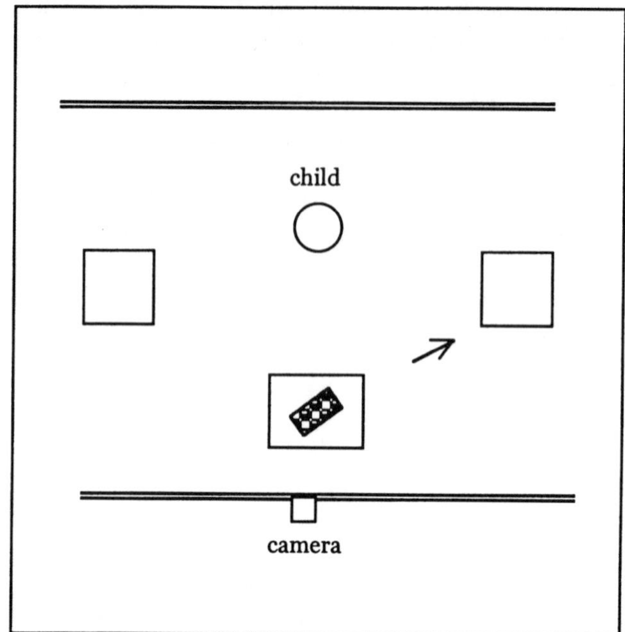

FIG. 6.3. Experimental setup for nonhuman cue experiment.

in the gaze-following experiment described earlier. To investigate this, a coder who was blind to the diagnosis of the children coded the videotape during the beginning of the experimental session, when the experimenter was trying to make eye contact with the child before she turned. During this period, the experimenter first tried to make eye contact by looking at the child. If this attempt did not succeed, she called his or her name and if that also failed, she called "Look at me." We were interested in whether the child would make an orienting response by looking at the experimenter when his or her name was called.

The results of this analysis showed that compared to developmentally delayed children, children with autism were much less responsive to the experimenter's attempts to gain their attention (e.g., response to name call). Children with autism responded to significantly fewer of the bids made. Further analysis showed that responding to attention bids was strongly related to gaze-following ability.

These results suggest that when social stimuli are considered, there may be a problem at level 1 of our developmental scheme as well as level 3 (see also Dawson et al., 1998). It remains to be tested whether social stimuli present a problem at level 2. Children's performance in the training phase of our gaze-following experiment suggests that they have no difficulty in shifting from looking at an adult to looking at a target object, but further research is needed to compare disengagement and shifting in both social and nonsocial conditions.

When nonsocial stimuli are considered, in contrast, there does not appear to be a problem in orienting at level 1 or 2 of the developmental scheme. The evidence for difficulties at level 3 is at present unclear. Our experiment using a nonhuman "symbolic" cue suggests that children with autism might be better than nonautistic children at learning to use this cue but that performance was not better with nonhuman than with human cues. Research with older individuals using traditional attention-orienting paradigms, on the other hand, does suggest specific difficulties with nonsocial symbolic cues relating to speed of processing (e.g., Wainwright-Sharp & Bryson, 1993; Courchesne et al., 1994). Further research is needed to establish the ability of both younger and older children to respond to nonsocial symbolic cues.

Table 6.2 gives an overview of the results from our studies. The difficulties shown in the right-hand column relate to difficulties experienced by the youngest and by those with the lowest ability among the children with autism. These difficulties are closely associated and show improvement as developmental levels increase. In subsequent research we discovered that once children engage in gaze following, they are also more likely to engage in initiating acts of joint attention such as pointing, showing, and giving (Leekam, Reddy, López, & Stan, 1999).

Summary

We started our research enterprise with a basic question, asking why children with autism should have difficulty with gaze following when nonhuman primates do not. Our initial argument was that gaze-following behaviors do not seem to necessarily involve either the understanding of other minds or "jointness" because an individual could simply track the directional movements of others to gain information about objects without engaging in face-to-face interaction with them or representing their attentional state. Having proposed an analysis of this problem—that children with autism might have a low-level attentional problem, we then set out to explore this hypothesis, using infant development as a model. What have we found out so far?

TABLE 6.2
Suggested Scheme of Developmental Impairments in Children with Autism

Level	*Attentional Control*	*To Objects*	*To People*
1	Exogenous orienting	√	×
2	Disengagement + exogenous orienting	√	?
3	Endogenous orienting	×?	×

Note. √ no difficulty, × difficulty

Our initial results suggest that preschool children with both high and low IQs were not impaired in low-level exogenous attentional orienting to objects. They were, however, impaired in following a head turn cue, suggesting that their problems could lie at the higher end of attentional processing involving voluntary endogenous control. However, when we looked at attentional orienting to a person (involving exogenous responding) we found a different picture. In an analysis of attentional orienting to a person's attention bid, we found impaired response by children with autism compared with nonautistic children and that this was strongly related to gaze-following ability. This result suggests that the problem for children with autism is not confined to the endogenous orienting of attention. It seems instead that human actions may fail to trigger a reflexive orienting response. This suggests that some very basic dyadic problems could underlie the triadic interaction difficulty between child, other, and object in joint attention.

Attention, Jointness, and Joint Attention

How do our findings fit the analysis presented at the beginning of this chapter? Our research aimed to investigate the "attentional" aspect of joint attention. The results seem to suggest that whereas the disengaging and orienting of attention to objects is not impaired for children with autism, they may have difficulty using cues to direct their action, especially if cues contain meaningful information. They seem to have difficulty specifically with meaningful social information, but it is not clear whether this difficulty is confined to social stimuli. There seems to be a developmental process involved related to age and general ability. Initially, it seems, children with autism do not follow cues, even when these are paired with targets. Like normally developing infants, however, they reach a stage where they can follow the head-turn cue, but this occurs years later than for typically developing infants. This developmental pattern suggests that it is something in the cue rather than the target that creates the developmental delay.

Our study of children's orienting to a person rather than to an object gave further insights into the possible basis for the child with autism's difficulty with head-turn cues. Initial analysis of gaze following suggested that the act of following another's head turn might not involve jointness. We argued that it might be possible to use another's head orientation alone to gain information about the world, without needing to engage in face-to-face gazing. However, the results of our studies suggest that it is not just the gaze-following response that is missing. Children also showed impairment in orienting to a person's attention bid. This suggests that jointness may well be implicated. Given the pattern of results we have found, this could be one of the more basic difficulties for children with autism and may be at the heart of their difficulty in reading the meaning of cues. If children with autism are not engaging with people, they may not be aware of either what another person is oriented to or the significance or meaning of this orientation.

According to the analysis presented here, the developing understanding of the meaning of a social cue is connected to the early development of attention. The process of this development emerges from a context of social engagement and social experience from the beginning of life. Our finding that children with autism orient less to the attention bid of another suggests that there is a specific failure in reflexively orienting to other people. Early difficulties at a dyadic level might underlie later difficulties with triadic joint attention, declarative acts, and the understanding of cues and signs. These difficulties may also affect higher level attentional orienting and the development of symbolic understanding. For example, if children with autism are limited to relying on the repeated and predictable links between target and cue (whether human or nonhuman) in order to learn the significance of signs and signals, this might account for their difficulties with invalid cues in spatial cueing tasks and their difficulty with gaze following, nonverbal gestures, and other communicative signs.

There is still much that we need to understand about the problems of attention and joint attention in autism. For example, we know that older and more able children do develop a gaze-following response (Leekam, Hunnisett, & Moore, 1998; Mundy, Sigman, & Kasari, 1994). Does this skill enable children to overcome other difficulties associated with autism or do fundamental problems still remain because of earlier missed experiences? For those children who do have joint-attention impairments, to what extent can this be traced specifically to an impairment in orienting to social stimuli? By what process will this problem eventually lead to other difficulties in reading the meaning of cues, conventions, and symbols? All of these questions invite speculation and await further investigation.

ACKNOWLEDGMENTS

The research reported in this chapter was carried out at the University of Kent and was supported by a Wellcome Trust grant (43022/94) to Sue Leekam. We are very grateful to the editors of the book for clarifying earlier versions of the manuscript. We also thank Peter Mundy and Vasu Reddy for helpful advice and comments on an earlier draft.

Address for correspondence: Dr. S. R. Leekam, Dept. of Psychology, University of Durham, Science Laboratories, South Road, Durham DH13LE, UK. E-mail: S.R.Leekam@durham.ac.uk.

REFERENCES

Aslin, R., & Salapatek, P. (1975). Saccadic localization of visual targets by the very young human infant. *Perception and Psychophysics, 17,* 293–302.

Atkinson, J., Hood, B., Wattam-Bell, J., & Braddick, O. (1992). Changes in infants' ability to switch visual attention in the first three months of life. *Perception, 21,* 643–653.

Bakeman, R., & Adamson, L. B. (1984). Coordinating attention of people and objects in mother–infant and peer–infant interaction. *Child Development, 55,* 1278–1289.

Baranek, G. T. (1999). Autism during infancy: A retrospective video analysis of sensory-motor and social behaviours at 9–12 months of age. *Journal of Autism and Developmental Disorders, 29, 3,* 213–224.

Baron-Cohen, S. (1989). Perceptual role taking and protodeclarative pointing in autism. *British Journal of Developmental Psychology, 7,* 113–127.

Baron-Cohen, S. (1995). *Mindblindness: An essay on autism and theory of mind.* Cambridge: Bradford/MIT Press.

Baron-Cohen, S., Cox, A., Baird, G., Swettenham, J., Nightingale, N., Morgan, K., Drew, A., & Charman, T. (1996). Psychological markers of autism at 18 months of age in a large population. *British Journal of Psychiatry,* 168, 158–63.

Baron-Cohen, S., Leslie, A. M., & Frith, U. (1985). Does the autistic child have a "theory of mind"? *Cognition, 4,* 37–46.

Bates, E., Camaioni, L., & Volterra, V. (1975). The acquisition of performatives prior to speech. *Merrill-Palmer Quarterly, 21,* 205–226.

Burack, J. A., Enns, J. T., Stauder, J. E. A., Mottron, L., & Randolph, B. (1997). Attention and autism: Behavioural and electrophysiological evidence. In D. J. Cohen & F. R. Volkmar (Eds.), *Handbook of autism and pervasive developmental disorders* (2nd ed.) (pp. 226–247). New York: Wiley.

Burack, J. A., & Iarocci, G. (1995). *Visual filtering and covert orienting in autism.* Paper presented at the meeting of the Society for Research in Child Development, Indianapolis, IN.

Butterworth, G. (1995). Origins of mind in perception and action. In C. Moore & P. Dunham (Eds.), *Joint attention: Its origins and role in development* (pp. 29–40). Hillsdale, NJ: Lawrence Erlbaum Associates.

Butterworth, G., & Cochran, E. (1980). Towards a mechanism of joint visual attention in human infancy. *International Journal of Behavioral Development, 3,* 253–272.

Butterworth, G. E., & Jarrett, N. (1991). What minds have in common is space: Spatial mechanisms serving joint attention in infancy. *British Journal of Developmental Psychology, 9,* 55–72.

Casey, B., Gordon, C., Mannheim, G., & Rumsey, J. (1993). Dysfunctional attention in autistic savants. *Journal of Clinical and Experimental Neuropsychology, 15,* 933–946.

Charman, T. (1998). Specifying the nature and course of the joint attention impairment in autism in the preschool years: Implications for diagnosis and intervention. *Autism: The International Journal of Research and Practice, 2,* 61–79.

Cheal, M. L., & Lyon, D. R. (1991). Central and peripheral precueing of forced-choice discrimination. *Quarterly Journal of Experimental Psychology, 43A,* 859–880.

Corkum, V., & Moore, C. (1998). The origin of joint visual attention in infants. *Developmental Psychology, 34,* 28–38.

Courchesne, E., Lincoln, A. J., Kilman, B. A., & Galambos, R. (1985). Event-related brain potential correlates of the processing of novel visual and auditory information in autism. *Journal of Autism and Developmental Disorders, 15,* 55–76.

Courchesne, E., Townsend J., Akshoomoff, N., Saitoh O., Yeung-Courchesne, R., Lincoln, A., James, H., Haas, R., Schriebman, L. A., & Lau, L. (1994). Impairment in shifting attention in autistic and cerebellar patients. *Behavioral Neuroscience, 108,* 848–865.

Cox, A., Klein, K., Charman, T., Baird, G., Baron-Cohen, S., Swettenham, J., Wheelwright, S., & Drew, A. (1998). The early diagnosis of autistic spectrum disorders: Use of the Autism Diagnostic Interview–Revised at 20 months and 42 months of age. Unpublished manuscript, University of London, UK.

Crawford, J. R. (1998). Introduction to the assessment of attention and executive functioning. *Neuropsychological Rehabilitation, 8, 3,* 209–211.

Curcio, F. (1978). Sensorimotor functioning and communication in mute autistic children. *Journal of Autism and Childhood Schizophrenia, 8,* 282–292.

Dawson, G., Meltzoff, A., Osterling, J., Rinaldi, J., & Brown, E. (1998). Children with autism fail to orient to naturally occurring social stimuli. *Journal of Autism and Developmental Disorders, 28,* 479–485.

D'Entremont, B., Hains, S. M. J., & Muir, D. (1997). A demonstration of gaze-following in 3-month-olds to 6-month-olds. *Infant Behaviour and Development, 20,* 567–572.

DiLavore, P., & Lord, C. (1995, April). Do you see what I see? Requesting and joint attention in young autistic children. Poster presentation at the Society of Research in Child Development, Indianapolis, IN.

Driver, J., Davis, G., Ricciardelli, P., Kidd, P., Maxwell, E., & Baron-Cohen, S. (1999). Gaze perception triggers reflexive visuospatial orienting. *Visual Cognition, 6,* 509–540.

Friesen, C. K., & Kingstone, A. (1998). The eyes have it: Reflexive orienting is triggered by nonpredictive gaze. *Psychonomic Bulletin and Review, 5,* 490–493.

Gilmore, R. O., & Johnson, M. H. (1995). Working memory in six-month-old infants revealed by versions of the oculomotor delayed response task. *Journal of Experimental Child Psychology, 59,* 397–418.

Griffith, E. M., Pennington, B. F., Wehner, E. A., & Rogers, S. J. (1999). Executive functions in young children with autism. *Child Development, 70, 4,* 817–832.

Harris, P., & MacFarlane, A. (1974). The growth of the effective visual field from birth to seven weeks. *Journal of Experimental Child Psychology, 18,* 340–348.

Hobson, P. (1993). *Autism and the development of mind.* Hove, UK: Lawrence Erlbaum Associates, Ltd.

Hood, B. (1995). Shifts of visual attention in the human infant: A neuroscientific approach. In C. Rover-Collier & L. Lipsett (Eds.), *Advances in infancy research* (pp. 63–216). Norwood, NJ: Ablex.

Hood, B., Willen, D., & Driver, J. (1998). Adult's eyes trigger shifts of visual attention in human infants. *Psychological Science, 9,* 131–134

Johnson, M., Posner, M., & Rothbart, M. (1994). Facilitation of saccades toward a covertly attended location in early infancy. *Psychological Science, 5,* 90–93.

Johnson, M. H. (1990). Cortical maturation and the development of visual attention in early infancy. *Journal of Cognitive Neuroscience, 2,* 81–95.

Jonides, J. (1981). Voluntary versus automatic control over the mind's eye's movement. In J. Long & A. Baddeley (Eds.), *Attention and Performance, 9,* 187–203. Hillsdale, NJ: Lawrence Erlbaum Associates.

Kasari, C., Sigman, M., Mundy, P., & Yirmiya, N. (1990). Affective sharing in the context of joint attention interactions of normal, autistic and mentally retarded children. *Journal of Autism and Developmental Disorders, 20,* 87–100.

Langton, S. R. H., & Bruce, V. (1999). Reflexive visual orienting in response to the social attention of others. *Visual Cognition, 1999, 6, (5),* 541–567.

Lauwereyns, J. (1998). Exogenous/endogenous control of space based/object-based attention: Four types of visual selection? *European Journal of Cognitive Psychology, 10 (1),* 41–74.

Leekam, S., Baron-Cohen, S., Perrett, D., Milders, M., & Brown, S. (1997). Eye-Direction Detection: A dissociation between geometric and joint attention skills in autism. *British Journal of Developmental Psychology, 15,* 77–95.

Leekam, S. R., Hunnisett, E., & Moore, C. (1998). Targets and cues: Gaze-following in children with autism. *Journal of Child Psychology and Psychiatry, 39,* 951–962.

Leekam, S. R., López, B., & Moore C. (2000). Attention and joint attention in preschool children with autism. *Developmental Psychology, 36, 2,* 261–273.

Leekam, S. R., Reddy, V., López, B., & Stan, P. (1999, April). Gaze-following and declarative joint attention in children with autism. Poster presented at Society for Research in Child Development, Albuquerque, NM.

Lord, C. (1995). Follow-up of two-year-olds referred for possible autism. *Journal of Child Psychology and Psychiatry, 36,* 1365–1382.

Loveland, K., & Landry, S. (1986). Joint attention and language in autism and developmental language delay. *Journal of Autism and Developmental Disorders, 16,* 335–349.

McEvoy, R., Rogers, S. J., & Pennington, B. F. (1993). Executive function and social communication deficits in young autistic children. *Journal of Child Psychology and Psychiatry, 34,* 563–578.

Moore, C. (1999). Gaze-following and the control of attention. In P. Rochat (Ed.), *Early social cognition.* Hillsdale, NJ: Lawrence Erlbaum Associates.

Moore, C., Angelopoulos, M., & Bennett, P. (1997). The role of movement in the development of joint visual attention. *Infant Behavior and Development, 20,* 83–92.

Müller, H. J., & Rabbit, P. M. A. (1989). Reflexive and voluntary orienting of spatial attention: Time course of activation and resistance to interruption. *Journal of Experimental Psychology: Human Perception and Performance, 15,* 315–330.

Mundy, P. (1995). Joint attention and social-emotional approach behavior in children with autism. *Development and Psychopathology, 7,* 63–82.

Mundy, P., Sigman, M., & Kasari, C. (1994). Joint attention, developmental level and symptom presentation in autism. *Development and Psychopathology, 6,* 389–401.

Mundy, P., Sigman, M., Ungerer J., & Sherman, T. (1986). Defining social deficits of autism: The contribution of non-verbal communication measures. *Journal of Child Psychology and Psychiatry, 27,* 657–659.

Osterling, J., & Dawson, G. (1994). Early recognition of children with autism: A study of first birthday home videotapes. *Journal of Autism and Developmental Disorders, 24,* 247–257.

Ozonoff, S., Strayer, D., McMahon, W., & Filloux, F. (1994). Executive function abilities in autism and Tourette syndrome: An information processing approach. *Journal of Child Psychology and Psychiatry, 35,* 1015–1032.

Pennington, B. F., & Ozonoff, S. (1996). Executive functions and developmental psychopathology. *Journal of Child Psychology and Psychiatry, 37,* 1, 51–87.

Posner, M. I. (1980). Orienting of attention. *Quarterly Journal of Experimental Psychology, 32,* 3–25.

Povinelli, D. J., & Eddy, T. J. (1997). Specificity of gaze-following in young chimpanzees. *British Journal of Developmental Psychology, 15,* 213–222.

Reddy, V. (1991). Playing with others' expectations: Teasing and mucking about in the first year. In A. Whiten (Ed.), *Natural theories of mind.* Oxford, UK: Blackwell.

Rincover, A., & Ducharme, J. M. (1987). Variables influencing stimulus over-selectivity and 'tunnel-vision' in developmentally delayed children. *American Journal of Mental Deficiency, 91,* 422–430.

Russell, J. (1996). *Agency. Its role in mental development.* Hove, UK: Erlbaum, Taylor & Francis Ltd.

Sigman, M., & Ruskin, E. (1999). Continuity and change in the social competence of children with autism, Down syndrome and developmental delay. *Monographs of the Society for Research in Child Development, 64,* 1–108.

Spence, C., & Driver, J. (1996). Audiovisual links in endogenous covert spatial attention. *Journal of Experimental Psychology: Human Perception and Performance, 22, 4,* 1005–1030

Stolz, J. A. (1996). Exogenous orienting does not reflect an encapsulated set of processes. *Journal of Experimental Psychology: Human Perception and Performanc,. 22, 1,* 187–201.

Swettenham, J., Baron-Cohen, S., Charman, T., Cox, A., Baird, G., Drew, A., & Rees, L. (1998). The frequency and distribution of spontaneous attention shifts between social and nonsocial stimuli in autistic, typically developing, and non-autistic developmentally delayed infants. *Journal of Child Psychology and Psychiatry, 39,* 747–753.

Tomasello, M., Kruger, A. C., & Ratner, H. H. (1993). Cultural learning. *Behavioural and Brain Sciences, 16,* 495–511.

Trevarthen, C., & Hubley, P. (1978). Secondary intersubjectivity: Confidence, confiding and acts of meaning in the first year. In A. Lock (Ed.), *Action, Gesture and Symbol* (pp. 183–229). London: Academic.

Wainwright, J. A., & Bryson, S. E. (1996). Visual-spatial orienting in autism. *Journal of Autism and Developmental Disorders, 26, 4,* 423–439.

Wainwright-Sharp, J. A., & Bryson, S. E. (1993). Visual orienting deficits in high-functioning people with autism. *Journal of Autism and Developmental Disorders, 23,* 1–13.

Wing, L. (1971). Perceptual and language development in autistic children: a comparative study. In M. Rutter (Ed.), *Infantile autism: Concepts, characteristics and treatment.* London: Churchill Livingstone.

7

Enhanced Perceptual Functioning in the Development of Autism

Laurent Mottron
Université de Montréal
Quebec, Canada
Jacob A. Burack
McGill University
Montreal, Quebec, Canada

Similar to most other behavioral disorders included in psychiatric diagnostic manuals, autism is defined clinically by both negative and positive symptoms that uniquely characterize individuals with the disorder. The negative symptoms refer to impairments in specific areas of functioning as compared with typically developing persons. These include problems in the social, communicative, and imaginative domains. Positive symptoms refer to the presence of behaviors that are not evident, at least to the same degree, among typically developing persons. For persons with autism, these include engagement in rituals and the preoccupation with perceptual features. In the study of most groups, both negative and positive symptoms are viewed within the context of generally impaired functioning or problematic behaviors that directly interfere with adaptive functioning. However, among persons with autism, the positive symptoms also include special abilities in certain areas of functioning. For example, a few savant persons with autism show absolute pitch (Mottron, Peretz, Belleville, & Rouleau, 1999c), the ability to reproduce 3-D displays (Mottron & Belleville, 1993), and the ability to recall long lists of words (Mottron, Belleville, Stip, & Morasse, 1998). Similarly, nonsavant persons with autism typically show relative strengths—levels of task performance that are higher than would be expected based on their overall level of development—in detecting simple patterns (Plaisted, O'Riordan, & Baron-Cohen, 1998a, 1998b; O'Riordan, 1998) as well as in completing geometric figures and in reproducing shapes (Mottron, Belleville, & Ménard, 1999b). These examples of enhanced performance are sufficiently common that they need to be included in the conceptualization of frameworks for understanding autism along with both the obviously maladaptive positive and negative symptoms.

The consideration of enhanced abilities necessitates the broadening of theoretical accounts of autism in order to consider these phenomena (see Charman & Swettenham, chap. 16, this volume). The initial attempt to explain the development of enhanced, but not necessarily savant, performance was forwarded by Frith and Happé (1994; Frith, 1989) within the context of weak central coherence (WCC) in information processing. Initial formulations of WCC were based on the premise that, among persons with autism, local processing is superior to the global integration of the whole as the latter process is impaired (Frith, 1989). Accordingly, a lower level of processing is not integrated into higher, or more central, processes. This formulation can be reframed within a cognitive neuropsychological conceptualization. Specifically, in sequential models of object processing, processes are ordered from simple to complex—from feature extraction to construction of perceptual representation to perceptual recognition to naming of the object, and finally, to increasingly complex processing in understanding the object's use (Ellis & Young, 1988). Similarly, with regard to the processing of faces, the base of this framework is characterized by the construction of face representations, followed by recognition, naming, and semantic processing of faces (Bruce & Young, 1986).

The lack of integration addressed by WCC can be viewed within the context of either vertical or horizontal relationships among processes. Vertical, or top-down, interpretations of WCC entail that low-level or perceptual processes are not integrated into higher order processes, and reflect an imbalance in the typical relation between higher and lower level processing. For example, the lower level phonological processing of words is virtually independent of higher level semantic interpretations for hyperlexic persons with autism who read at a higher level than they understand (Aram & Healy, 1988) and for the more general population of individuals with autism who typically decipher a word with diminished consideration of the context (Happé, 1997; Jolliffe & Baron-Cohen, 1999). In contrast, horizontal interpretations entail that the construction of perceptual representation of information is biased toward one aspect of processing rather than another, although the two are similar in terms of position on a primary versus associative hierarchical sequence of processing. For example, local and global processes are comparable with regard both to brain localization (the former requires the integrity of the left temporal lobe and the latter requires the integrity of the right temporal lobe), and to position on the "top-down" associative visual pathway in which peripheral occipital feature detection is at one end and higher order processes are at the other (Fink, et al., 1997; Mottron, Burack, Stauder, & Robaey, 1999a). Thus, among typically developing persons, the global and local processes occur with a certain hierarchy, or balance. The identification of a horizontal imbalance in this relationship is the focus of studies of differences between the global and local processing of hierarchical stimuli presented at short display intervals. Deviations in either vertical or horizontal cross-sectional frameworks are possible explanations of certain behaviors that are characteristic of autism. In this chapter, we examine examples of enhanced performance and their cognitive loci with regard to perseverative behaviors among persons with autism and to the relation between areas of impairments and enhanced behaviors.

Enhanced Perceptual Functioning (EPF) Within the Context of Developmental Psychopathology

We extend the premise of the discipline of developmental psychopathology that the studies of typical and atypical populations are mutually informative (Burack, 1997; Cicchetti, 1984) to suggest a similarly beneficial relationship between two or more atypical populations. Thus, we cite examples of persons with specific brain injury as "experiments of Nature" for the study of autism (Bronfenbrenner, 1979; Burack, 1997; Cicchetti, 1984), and address the implications of a processing imbalance within a sequential framework by examining the development and behaviors of nonautistic persons who are also considered atypical, specifically with regard to patterns of perceptual processing. Perception is a basic and early component of processing of all information, and therefore, early problems in this area may lead to a variety of atypical behaviors. However, we do not focus on perceptual impairments, but rather on perceptually oriented behaviors that are characteristic of certain nonautistic persons and that may be implicated in autistic symptomatology. In particular, we examine patterns of perceptual processing among persons with savant syndromes, blindness, visual agnosia, and frontotemporal dementia as models of a vertical imbalance that may be a source of enhanced abilities in general, and among persons with autism in particular. This strategy is consistent with and informed by the extensive literatures on theoretical and empirical attempts to explain enhanced performance among brain-injured patients and animals. Cases of markedly enhanced performance on specific tasks are evident in association with several types of brain injury and can provide frameworks for understanding their specific relevance to autism. In addition, this extensive literature on brain lesions provides a checklist of questions and even a vocabulary for the study of enhanced performance in individuals with autism.

We highlight three strategies that may be helpful in better understanding aspects of cognitive enhancement among persons with autism. One, we suggest certain neurological systems as loci of enhanced performance in cognition. Two, we highlight the relation between cognitive impairments and examples of enhanced performance in specific cases of persons with brain lesions or other anomalies in order to provide insights about enhanced perceptual functioning among persons with autism. Three, we provide a developmental framework for speculating about possible origins of enhanced perceptual functioning among persons with autism.

Brain Plasticity and Enhanced Perceptual Functioning

We suggest that the bias toward a low level of processing begins early in childhood and may be the consequence of the process of compensation for specific cognitive deficits by localized areas of the brain. This process, one aspect of brain plasticity, involves at least four mechanisms that are adaptive to some point, but may also include nonadaptive aspects and may not necessarily be successful in replicating the impaired function (Kapur, 1996). These mechanisms include i) neuronal sprouting, the growth of neural connections to optimize the neural network; ii) cortical rededication, use of the area of the brain normally involved in one purpose for another purpose; iii) suppression of inhibition, the failure of one process to limit the growth of another in a typical manner; and iv) functional persistence, the excessive development of basic processes due to the diminished growth of later, more evolved ones. At the behavioral level, neuronal sprouting is reciprocally related to the pervasive repetition of the same cognitive operation—this includes "overtraining" that arises when specific operations, such as calendar calculations, drawing, or reading, pervade daily activities. Cortical rededication is evidenced when the processing of a certain category of objects occurs according to the rules of another (Waterhouse, 1988). Thus, if faces that are typically processed holistically are processed like objects, the processing would be primarily locally biased—this would account for the phenomenon that people with autism are better than typically developing persons at recognizing inverted faces (Langdell, 1978; Schultz, Romanski, & Tsatsanis, 1999). Suppression of inhibition entails changes in typical brain functioning as a consequence of the undeterred growth of one function that is due to the failure of a second to suppress it. The outcome is evident among individuals with schizophrenia who, as compared with typically developing persons, are less likely to inhibit word associations. Accordingly, they produce irrelevant associations in everyday life, but superior semantic priming in experimental settings. Similarly, excessive functional persistence of a basic process is associated with enhanced functions, in this case more basic ones, at the expense of others that typically occur later in development (Johnson, 1997).

Organization of Processing of Perceptual Information: From Domain-Specificity to Domain-General Processing. Perception is the multicomponent cortical processing of sensory *dimensions*, such as movement, space, colors, and pitch, and *types of* *materials* such as language, objects, and faces. The bottom or initial rungs of vertical frameworks of processing are described as peripheral, or superficial, since they refer to processing by the senses. According to this perspective, the functions of the perceptual brain areas, the sites of this lower level processing, are the most localized and circumscribed in the brain. As these abilities are entrenched early and typically developed, they are likely to be utilized to compensate for impairments in other domains. This is in contrast to higher level processes of visual perception (e.g., object identification) and conscious, complex processes (e.g., theory of mind and problem solving) that entail the combination, manipulation, or both, of several chunks of information (Frye, Zelazo, & Burack 1999; Halford, Wilson, & Phillips, 1998; Zelazo, Burack, Boseovski, Jacques, & Frye, chap. 10, this volume). Accordingly, the higher order processes are not domain-specific in the sense that their functions can be attained via different paths. For example, semantic memory can be accessed auditorally or visually as both, the visual display of a bottle and the spoken word "bottle" are processed within the same semantic net (Ellis & Young, 1988).

The disparity between lower and higher level processing among persons with autism can be viewed within the context of a dichotomous groupings of processes—one group is brain localized, domain specific, and associated with enhanced performance, whereas the other is distributed across several areas in the brain, domain general, and associated with impaired performance. The veracity of this split is supported by evidence from fMRI studies of activation of regions typically used for processing objects in the processing of faces (Schultz et al., 2000) and enhanced primary associative and cortex activity on Embedded Figures tasks (Ring et al., 1999). Both are examples of enhanced activation in a clearly demarcated area of the brain dedicated to a function that is an area of strength.

The multiple subsystems of perception vary considerably with regard to the age of maturation, cortical versus subcortical processing, and the extent to which they are uniquely specialized and apparently hardwired—all contributing factors to the likelihood that they will compensate for other cognitive functions. Cortical subsystems that mature early—those that are based on subcortical activity—are more likely to compensate for others because their intended function is already acquired and, therefore, better suited to take on a new function. For example, within visual perception, the basic subsystems of perception of physical parameters, including movement, colors, feature extraction, and gaze, are especially effective in compensating for more sophisticated processes such as face and emotion perception. Once an intact function takes the place of an absent or impaired one, conditions are in place for the formation of a recurring loop in which increased training and enhanced development continue to perpetuate (Kapur, 1996). For example, Q.C., a savant young woman with autism and outstanding musical memory, who displays absolute pitch, spends most of her day engaged in music-related activities (Mottron, Peretz, & Ménard, 1999c).

Evidence From Brain-Lesioned Animals and Brain-Injured Humans. Based on a review of examples of cognitive performance among persons with brain injury and brain-lesioned animals, Kapur (1996) hypothesized that a deficit in one of two competing neurological systems can lead to enhanced development of the other. Examples of enhanced cognitive performance associated with brain pathology are evident across a range of animal and human populations and are addressed within the context of Paradoxical Functional Facilitation (PFF) (Kapur, 1996). PFF is seen among animals who are sensorily deprived, suffer from a general brain injury, or have specific brain lesions. For example, rats with hippocampal lesions show enhanced reversal learning of odor discriminations as they forget an initial odor distinction more quickly and are, therefore, better able to learn a second odor-reward association that is discrepant with the prior one. Among humans, the phenomenon is most cited among blind persons who can be considered brain-injured since their brain activity is affected by the absence of visual input (Kapur, 1996) and who show better than normal sound localization discrimination (Lessard et al., 1999), texture discrimination (Walker & Moylan, 1994), and odor perception (Murphy & Cain, 1986). Similarly, both persons with schizophrenia and those with amnesic deficit show enhanced priming—the ability to recognize words as a function of a previous encounter with a related word—that is likely due to diminished inhibition for irrelevant semantic associations.

The potential relevance of localized brain deficits to understanding the types of enhanced perceptual abilities seen among persons with autism is evidenced in the recent example of fronto-temporal dementia, a variant of pre-senile dementia in which the temporal lobe is destroyed (Miller et al., 1998). Persons with fronto-temporal dementia and those with autism present striking similarities with regard to domains of enhanced abilities. For example, several persons with fronto-temporal dementia show a temporary superiority in reproducing three-dimensional geometric figures (Miller et al., 1998), a skill displayed by E.C., a savant person with autism (Mottron & Belleville, 1993, 1995). Other examples of "special abilities" among persons with fronto-temporal dementia can be found in the areas of music and the solving of phonological and graphic word games (Miller et al., 1998), also domains of enhanced abilities among savant persons with autism (Mottron et al., 1999c; Hou et al., 2000). Similarly, both persons with fronto-temporal dementia and those with autism display restricted interests in the form of obsessive searching for simple objects with simple shapes (e.g., coins). Miller et al. (1998) suggest that these phenomena develop in persons with fronto-temporal dementia because "selective degeneration of the anterior temporal and orbital frontal cortex decreases inhibition of the more posteriorly located visual systems involved with perception, thereby enhancing these patients' artistic interests and abilities" (p. 981). Among persons with autism, lesions in the temporal regions are typically cited in preliminary postmortem studies (Bachevalier, 1994;

Bauman & Kemper, 1988; DeLong, 1999; Jambaqué, Mottron, Ponsot, & Chiron, 1998; Mottron et al., 1997; for a recent review, see Schultz, Romanski, & Tsatsanis, 1999).

The literatures on enhanced performance in atypical populations of animals and humans provide evidence for a notion of brain plasticity through which competing cognitive functions may evolve when one is impaired or eliminated. This entails the integration of neuronal bases and the training and eventual overtraining of skills that leads to enhanced performance on cognitive tasks. Thus, within the PFF framework, enhanced performance represents an extensive course of development and brain reorganization rather than the simple unfolding of "sleeping modules" that remain inactive among typically developing persons.

The Relation Between Perceptual Anomalies and Autism

Issues of perceptual functioning are relevant to the study of enhanced performance as peaks of abilities and savant skills among persons with autism are associated with low-level perceptual encoding (Mottron et al., 1999c; Mottron, Limoges, & Jelenic, in press, b) and atypical perceptual learning (Plaisted, chap. 8, this volume). In this section, we review perceptual phenomena and their association with examples of enhanced performance among persons with autism.

In our conceptualization of a vertical imbalance in autism, the relations between the higher and lower order processes appear disrupted. In a typical scenario, the abilities to see and recognize a bottle, a lower order process, and to think about a bottle, a higher order process, are mutually relevant. Thus, looking at the bottle does not prevent thinking about the bottle and, conversely, thinking about the bottle does not prevent looking at it. Although the direction of causality between deficits and enhanced functioning is likely reciprocal, certain behaviors of persons with autism suggest that overdeveloped lower processes can interfere with higher order operations—e.g., when the obsessive search for a certain shape interferes with the development of pretend play or other kinds of spontaneous activity. This is analogous to an increase in the importance of seeing the bottle rather than to thinking about it. A perceptual representation of an object permeates mental activity to the exclusion of functions and narratives that would otherwise provide context for its existence. Consistent with the notion of the relevance for lower processes, we contend that persons with autism may be overdependent on specific aspects of perceptual functioning that are excessively developed and, as a consequence, more difficult to control and more disruptive to the development of other behaviors and abilities. For example, the lower order perceptual function of movement perception interferes with the attainment of higher order processing when a child with autism stares for hours at a spinning fan instead of exploring the surroundings.

Classification of Perceptual Anomalies Among Persons With Autism. Within this framework, various examples of positive symptomatology in autism may be the sequelae of atypicalities in low-level perceptual processing. The perceptions of persons with autism appear to differ from those of typically developing persons in three general ways. One, persons with autism show functional dissociations, temporal dissociations, or both, (uneven profiles) among domains of functioning in relation to the perceptual properties of the processed information. For example, differences in the efficiency of processing between the perception of objects and that of faces and emotions are evident among persons with autism but not among typically developing persons (Schultz et al., 1999). The development of functioning in these domains appears complementary in the latter group. In contrast, adults with autism perceive objects as well as, or even better than, others do but show impairments in the processing of emotions and the perception of faces. We propose that this dissociation among specific aspects in the processing of faces versus objects is the consequence of increased dependence on low-level perceptual functions (e.g., feature extraction and discrimination of local cues) involved in the perception of objects but not of faces or emotions. Similarly, the synchronicity in the development of attention to noises and to voices observed among typically developing children is not seen among their peers with autism who show a delay in the socially relevant task of voice perception (Dawson, Meltzoff, Osterling, Rinaldi, & Brown, 1998).

A second example of the differences in perception, is that persons with autism, as compared with typically developing persons, show apparent overlap in the functions of various domains with one or more domains performing the functions of others. For example, among some persons with autism the perception of faces appears to activate regions of the brain used for object perception rather than those typically used for face perception (Schultz et al., 2000).

A third difference is that adults with autism display a general enhancement of low-level auditory and visual processing that is not evident among nonautistic persons. The level of performance of persons with autism on tasks of spatial orientation, phonological discrimination, word recognition, and simple geometrical patterns, is typically higher than their general level of development.

Examples of Enhanced Perceptual Functioning Among Persons With Autism

Atypicalities in the relations between lower and higher level processing may provide a framework for understanding two sets of findings in the visual modality; the evidence associated with WCC (Happé, 1999; chap. 12, this volume) and the evidence for enhanced basic visual processes (Plaisted, O'Riordan, & Baron-Cohen, 1998a, 1998b; Plaisted, Swettenham, & Rees, 1999). This perspective may also account for findings in the auditory modality of enhanced detection of local, or one-note, changes in melodies. In this framework, autism is characterized by the enhancement of several functions that share the properties of low-level processing not necessarily associated with an imbalance between local and global processing. Although the number of enhanced abilities for any individual are limited, the examples of peaks of abilities, as evidenced in both the clinical and empirical literatures, occur on a wider range of tasks than typically explained by WCC. For example, enhanced performance on spatial orientation is evident among persons with autism, but is not predicted by WCC since it does not entail local versus global processing. Thus, we suggest that WCC is consistent with many, but not all, cited examples of enhanced processing.

Examples of Enhanced Abilities in the Auditory Modality. As most evidence for WCC and enhanced modular processing is from studies of visual processing, examples from auditory performance are especially relevant to supporting a more general conceptualization of the phenomenon of enhanced performance. Mottron, Peretz, and Ménard (2000) examined the utility of hierarchical models in characterizing musical information processing among persons with autism with a task that consisted of same–different judgements between two melodies that differ on only one note. Differential local and global processing was assessed by manipulating the level of change—local changes involve one-note modifications that do not affect the melody contour (direction of intervals), whereas global changes involve one-note modifications that do affect the contour. Global changes were also assessed by examining ability to recognize transposed melodies. As compared with typically developing persons matched on CA, nonverbal IQ, laterality, and musical experience (none), adolescents and young adults with autism showed no deficit on two measures of global processing—increased ability to detect changes to musical stimuli in the condition with the changed contour as compared to that with preserved contour and ability to detect change in musical stimuli in the transposed melody condition. However, the persons with autism were better able to detect change in nontransposed, contour-preserved melodies that are used to assess local processing. These findings support the notion of a "local bias" in music perception among individuals with autism, but are discordant with the notion of a deficit in global music processing. In this domain, therefore, the enhanced local bias that is evident in the processing of elementary physical properties of auditory stimuli cannot be seen as compensation for deficient global processing, but rather as compensation for a deficit in higher level mental operations. Thus, consistent with a PFF framework, low-level auditory and visual functions are used to compensate for a higher order task.

The finding of enhanced phonological processing among adolescents with autism is another example of an enhanced low-level auditory function. Among high-functioning adolescents with autism the ability to retrieve words is similar with phonological and semantic cues, whereas this ability for adolescents without autism matched on CA, verbal IQ, and gender is superior with semantic cues as compared with phonological cues (Mottron, Morrasse, & Belleville, in press, a). This difference between the two groups is apparently due to the enhanced effect of the perceptual process of phonological cueing among the persons with autism, and not to an impairment in the higher order process effect of semantic cueing.

Evidence From Persons With Autism and Savant Skills

Persons with savant syndrome are able to perform some tasks in a restricted area of functioning (e.g., perspective drawing, proper-name memorization, music reproduction) at levels considerably higher than would be expected from their general level of functioning. This phenomenon always involves selected interests in a narrow domain and enhanced performance in detecting, remembering, reproducing, or manipulating information in that domain (Waterhouse, 1988). Although the continuity between savant and nonsavant autism is complex, there is some overlap between savant abilities and peaks of abilities found in nonsavant autism (Frith & Happé, 1994; Happé, 1997). For example, one of these rare capacities is *absolute pitch*, the ability to name or to produce pitches without referring to an external standard (Takeuchi & Hulse, 1993). Absolute pitch is seen in typically developing persons, but is more common among persons with autism and savant musical abilities (Young & Nettelbeck, 1995). Similarily, enhanced pitch perception and memory is also found among some persons with nonsavant autism (Heaton, Hermelin, & Pring, 1998; Mottron et al., 2000). Conversely, these domains of restricted interests and special abilities never include aspects of relative weakness among persons with autism, such as the recognition of emotions.

The Example of Absolute Pitch. Q.C. is a young adult with autism who displays several types of enhanced performance and hypersensitivity in musical and other aspects of auditory processing. She displays a lower than typical threshold for auditory stimuli, possesses absolute pitch in identification and production, and, as compared to MA- and CA-matched groups of persons with average intelligence, shows superior memory of sequences of notes and chords (Mottron et al., 1999c). Across a range of tasks, Q.C. displays no deficit in hierarchical perception in either the auditory or visual modality, although she displays deficits both in cognitive flexibility and planning for different tasks, two aspects of controlled, conscious, higher order tasks. Despite these examples of enhanced performance, Q.C. also displays maladaptive behaviors such as a considerable fear of the Larsen effect (circular reverberations that occur when a microphone and speaker are placed across from each other) that leads to a refusal to play the piano in front of a microphone, avoidance of places with microphones, and repetitive questioning about the presence of microphones in places she visits. Thus, within a PFF account, enhanced perception of basic properties of sound, resulting from compensation by basic auditory perceptual processes for an impairment in nonauditory, higher order processes (compensation among levels of processing), imposes both a restricted interest to music and aversive reaction to sounds. Similarly, enhanced auditory perception is also found among persons with congenital visual impairment, for whom detection of auditory features compensates for impairments in vision (Lessard, Pare, Lepore, & Lassonde, 1998).

The Example of Graphic Reproduction. Another savant capacity is the ability to graphically reproduce 3-D structures with exceptional accuracy and without corrections, whereas professional draughtspersons typically perform the task by trial and error. Despite the excellence of their drawings, savant draughtspersons with autism also display atypicalities in drawing strategies. For example, E.C., a savant autistic draughtsman, displays a local bias in graphic copy and the drawing from memory of 3-D drawings, because he begins his drawings with the internal components of figures rather than with their global ones as is typically done by professional draughtsmen (Mottron & Belleville, 1993). Although Mottron and Belleville (1993) initially interpreted E.C.'s abilities and strategies within a WCC-type framework, other aspects of his behavior do not fit well within such a framework. For example, E.C. is particularly adept at graphically completing shapes by rotating a 3-D object (Mottron & Belleville, 1995), a task that relies on a difficult manipulation of global (contour) aspects of the object.

E.C.'s quality of reproduction and manipulation of the 3-D aspects of objects reveals a capacity to manipulate visual properties, but also a selection of only certain restricted dimensions of perceptual processing. One, he persists in reproducing only what can be viewed and does not add interpretative aspects other than morphological transformations. Two, his drawing is superior in only a few aspects, including 3-D transformation and linear perspective, but is deficient in others, especially in color discrimination (Mottron & Belleville, 1993). Three, his abilities vary with regard to category of objects as he is adept at reproducing the geometrical properties of objects, but not at drawing faces. Thus, an alternative interpretation of E.C.'s performances might be that his selection of graphic feature is the result of a general enhanced ability for processing 3-D aspects of objects, based on processing lines, perceptual discontinuities, and their transformations according to rotation. In this scenario, local bias would be only a by-product of generally enhanced perceptual functioning.

The Contributions of the Savant Findings. These two examples of savant capabilities suggest that special abilities are evidence for a layer in cognition that is the site of low-level visual and auditory perception and that seems to be the location of considerable cognitive activity among persons with autism. The domains of enhanced functioning among persons with savant abilities and those with autism are, therefore, similar with regard to type and level of processing. Even if some areas of special abilities involve operations that are not solely perceptual (e.g., drawing or computation) and include several modalities, they are all pertinent to either perception of physical properties of stimuli (e.g., pitch processing) or simple operations (e.g., associating, combining, matching) on long-lasting tracks of perceptual aspects of visual or auditory stimuli.

Overdeveloped Basic Perceptual Processes and Behavioral Characteristics

Enhanced performance involves the automatic processing of some perceptual dimensions beyond the typical level and the resultant capture of attentional resources. Within our framework, laboratory-based examples of enhanced performance on experimental tasks of perceptual detection (Plaisted et al., 1998a, 1998b) are related to the observations from natural settings of behaviors indicative of obsessive and restricted interests and interest in objects containing a perceptual feature (Lord et al., 1994). The notion of apparently overdeveloped low-level perception may be cited as an alternative to more traditional explanations of the development of certain behaviors that are characteristic of persons with autism. For example, enhanced recognition of visual patterns, the obsessive search for these patterns, aversive reactions to unexpected changes in the environment, and hypersensitivity to sound are all typically understood within the context of an executive deficit (Hughes, chap. 13, this volume; Turner 1997), as persons with autism are less able to "escape" a prepotent stimulus in order to "switch" attention to another stimulus or idea. However, an alternative explanation is that the detection of visual and auditory patterns cannot be escaped because perceptual thresholds are lower than normal, because low-level perceptual information dominates the attentional resources, or for both reasons (Burack, 1994). The intrusion into consciousness of the automatic detection of noises or movements would produce the characteristic symptom of hypersensitivity to noise or automatic orienting toward fans. For example, persons with autism may be overdependent on their perceptions in the sense that pattern detection dictates behaviors such as the collection of and search for objects with specific physical characteristics.

The Enhanced Perceptual Functioning Framework and Development

The EPF model suggests that enhanced functioning of a cognitive operation *b* follows a developmental course that includes a specified sequence. The sequence involves an initial deficit of a related cognitive function *a* that is followed by compensatory functioning by *b,* overtraining of *b* due to increased demand, and an aggregation around *b* of related features that result in a category of objects for which the subject has a restricted interest. This is especially relevant for the late development of restricted interests, which according to our model are characterized by the obsessive research of anything semantically related to certain perceptual characteristics. For example, we infer this sequence in the case of 8-year-old I.E., born with both visual agnosia (due to prenatal destruction of temporo-occipital areas) and autism, but with intact perception of low-level visual features, such as lines and movement, and all aspects of audition. I.E. displays a restricted interest for planes, which he recognizes by the propellers, and for traffic intersections, which he recognizes by the crossed lines (Mottron et al., 1997). In the hypothesized sequence, the initial deficit in the recognition of complex patterns was followed by compensatory increases in aspects of functioning as evidenced by the obsessive search for lines and grids and the repetitive listening to music. Ultimately, this pattern resulted in the development of categories of restricted interest that included planes, intersections, and Greek music. Other examples of this developmental pattern are evident in our clinical work. One adolescent who displays a particular interest in electricity was, as a toddler, obsessively interested in ropes and wires, which are composed of elementary perceptual components (i.e., lines). Similarly, E.C., the accomplished draughtsperson, is interested in all information about boilers, which he is able to draw in detailed 3-D format with a focus on the basic geometrical properties of the pipes (Mottron & Belleville, 1993). This notion that an unusual interest in certain types of objects may lead to long-term behavioral and neurological changes is consistent with Schultz et al.'s (2000) finding that persons with autism exhibit a developmental displacement of their processing zone toward an "object" region.

Maladaptive Consequences of Paradoxical Functional Facilitation

An intriguing and somewhat counterintuitive aspect of enhanced functioning among persons with autism is that the sequelae are not necessarily positive and may even be maladaptive. Among other clinical groups where compensations are evident, such as persons with visual impairments who display increased sensitivity to sounds and odors, enhanced functioning is viewed as adaptive. However, the common outcome of this phenomenon among persons with autism is the emergence of restricted interests that may "pervade" daily activity. For example, the obsessive search displayed by a 10-year-old girl with autism and an IQ in low-normal range for a certain visual pattern, such as the one for the angle seen at the bottom-back part of a side-rear window of a car, cannot be considered adaptive! Similarly, increased detection of sounds can lead to detrimental emotional reactions like self-injurious behaviors, which cannot be seen as optimizing adaptation even if they result from an adaptive process.

These maladaptive outcomes may be seen as arising from one or more of the specific mechanisms of compensation that are generally useful, but are also problematic for persons with autism. For example, in the case of neuronal sprouting, the compensatory increased functioning of hardwired basic perceptual operations acts as a "blind" process, like nerve growth after amputation, with potentially damaging consequences for adaptation. This process may be genetically programmed to grow in response to deficits of neighboring functions, but may grow beyond a level of development optimal for adaptive purposes (Kapur, 1996). In the case of cortical rededication, a secondary compensatory mechanism—the region of the brain that takes on the function of another—imposes its own style of processing that might not be optimal for the processing of the specific stimuli. Thus, when the region of the brain used for processing objects is appropriated for the processing of faces, the latter function is impaired and appears to be more similar to the former (Schultz et al., 2000). Within our framework, this finding is associated with the impaired development of affect in one of at least two ways. One, the specific region for the perception of faces among children with autism may not develop or be may be underdeveloped due to lack of interest in emotions (Schultz et al., 1999). Two, the processing of faces as objects may interfere with the typical relation between face perception and affect. These examples of association between mechanism of compensation and maladaptive development point to the costs of brain plasticity in development.

The Temporal Course of Enhanced Perceptual Functioning. Consistent with the basic premise of developmental psychopathology that the presence, type, severity, and frequency of symptoms varies in relation to physiology, behavior, environment, and developmental level (Burack, 1997; Sroufe & Rutter, 1984), the notion that EPF involves an ongoing transaction among neurobiological impairments, neurobiological reactions, and alterations of behavioral changes dictates that the form or nature of its sequelae may change over time. Thus, patterns of developmental changes can be charted for each of the several processes and resultant behaviors associated with EPF. For example, at solely a behavioral level, hypersensitivity to sound and fixation on visual patterns appear in toddlerhood and diminish by ages 8 to 10 (Fecteau, Mottron, Berthiaume, & Burack, in preparation). As the EPF framework is enlarged to include brain processes as well as behaviors, the source and course of development is less obvious. For example, in the quest to understand the atypicalities in face processing among persons with autism, causal models can be forwarded in either direction between the behavioral phenomenon of diminished processing of faces and the physiological phenomenon of processing faces in the region typically used for processing objects. Alternatively, an uninterrupted transaction between them in which each is continuously influenced by the other, as well as possibly by other factors, may best explain the phenomenom.

CONCLUSION

Research on enhanced perceptual functioning is informative for understanding the long-term relations between two or more processes or aspects of functioning, especially between areas of enhanced and diminished cognitive functioning. In this chapter, we propose a EPF model of autism that we believe has several advantages over the WCC and other cognitive models of autism. The EPF model provides a neuro-cognitive-behavioral framework that can account for many of the characteristics of peaks of performance among persons with autism and that provides links between the developmental courses of cognitive operations and behaviors. Consistent with the EPF model, superior performances among persons with autism involves low-level processing, and examples of enhanced behavior can be found in most perceptual domain-specific systems, such as spatial perception and olfaction. Typically, only one peak or one special ability is found in any individual, which is consistent with the notion of a "blind" process that involves only one area of "overfunctioning" and the resultant areas of enhancement. For example, the search for patterns leads to ongoing obsessive repetitive search for specific patterns that prevents other higher order perceptually based repetitive behaviors from appearing. Within this model, and concordant with empirical evidence, a deficit in global processing is not inevitable. Our goal in delineating this model is consistent with the basic developmental principle of charting complex and continuously evolving relations across areas of functioning in both typically and atypically developing persons (Burack, 1992; Flavell, 1982; Hodapp & Burack, 1990).

ACKNOWLEDGMENTS

Laurent Mottron's work on this chapter was supported by a grant from the Medical Research Council of Canada and Jake Burack's by a Research Award from the Social Sciences and Humanities Research Council of Canada.

Please address correspondence to clinique spécialisée de l'autisme, hopital riviére des prairies, 7070 bvd Perras, Montréal(PQ) Canada, H1E1A4.

REFERENCES

Aram, D. M., & Healy, J. M. (1988). Hyperlexia: A review of extraordinary word recognition. In L. K. Obler & D. Fein (Eds.), *The exceptional brain: Neuropsychology of talent and special abilities* (pp. 70–102). New York: Guilford.

Bachevalier, J. (1994). Medial temporal lobe structures and autism: A review of clinical and experimental findings. *Neuropsychologia, 32,* 627–648.

Bauman, M. L., & Kemper, T. L. (1988). Limbic and cerebellar abnormalities: Consistent finding in early infantile autism. *Journal of Neuropathology and Experimental Neurology, 47,* 369.

Bronfenbrenner, U. (1979). *The ecology of human development: Experiments by nature and design.* Cambridge, MA: Harvard University Press.

Bruce, V., & Young, A. (1986). Understanding face recognition. *British Journal of Psychology, 77,* 305–327.

Burack, J. A. (1992). Debate and argument: Clarifying developmental issues in the study of autism. *Journal of Child Psychology & Psychiatry, 33,* 617–621.

Burack, J. A. (1994). Selective attention deficits in persons with autism: Preliminary evidence of an inefficient attentional lens. *Journal of Abnormal Psychology, 103,* 535–543.

Burack, J. A. (1997). The study of atypical and typical populations in developmental psychopathology: The quest for a common science. In S. S. Luthar, J. A. Burack, D. Cicchetti, & J. R. Weisz (Eds.), *Developmental psychopathology: Perspectives on adjustment, risk, and disorder* (pp. 139–165). New York: Cambridge University Press.

Cicchetti, D. (1984). The emergence of developmental psychopathology. *Child Development, 55,* 1–7.

Dawson G., Meltzoff, A. N., Osterling J., Rinaldi J., & Brown, E. (1998). Children with autism fail to orient to naturally occurring social stimuli. *Journal of Autism and Developmental Disorders, 28,* 479–485.

DeLong, G. R. (1999). Autism: New data suggest a new hypothesis. *Neurology, 52,* 911–916.

Ellis, A. W., & Young, A. W. (1988). *Human cognitive neuropsychology.* Hillsdale, NJ: Lawrence Erlbaum Associates.

Fecteau, S., Mottron, L., Berthiaume, C., & Burack, J. A. (in preparation). Developmental changes in autistic symptomatology.

Fink, G. R., Halligan, P. W., Marshall, J. C., Frith C. D., Frackowiak, R. S., & Dolan, R. J. (1997). Neural mechanisms involved in the processing of global and local aspects of hierarchically organized visual stimuli. *Brain, 120,* 1779–1791.

Flavell, J. (1982). Structures, stages, and sequences in cognitive development. In W. A. Collins (Ed.), *The concept of development: The Minnesota symposium on child psychology.* Hillsdale, NJ: Lawrence Erlbaum Associates.

Frith, U. (1989). Autism and "theory of mind." In C. Gillberg (Ed.), *Diagnosis and treatment of autism* (pp. 33–52). New York: Plenum.

Frith, U., & Happé, F. G. E. (1994). Autism: Beyond "theory of mind." *Cognition, 50,* 115–132.

Frye, D., Zelazo, P. D., & Burack, J. A. (1999). I. Cognitive complexity and control: Implications for theory of mind in typical and atypical development. *Current Directions in Psychological Science, 7,* 116–121.

Halford, G. S., Wilson, W. H., & Phillips, S. (1998). Processing capacity defined by relational complexity: Implications for comparative, developmental, and cognitive psychology. *Behavioral and Brain Sciences, 21,* 803–831.

Happé, F. G. E. (1997). Central coherence and theory of mind in autism: Reading homographs in context. *British Journal of Developmental Psychology, 15,* 1–12.

Happé, F. G. E. (1999). Autism: cognitive deficit or cognitive style. *Trends in Cognitive Sciences, 3,* 216–222.

Heaton, P., Hermelin, B., & Pring, L. (1998). Autism and pitch processing: A precursor for savant musical ability? *Music Perception, 15,* 291–305.

Hodapp, R. M., & Burack, J. A. (1990). What mental retardation teaches us about typical development: The examples of sequences, rates, and cross-domain relations. *Development and Psychopathology, 2,* 213–225.

Hou, C., Miller, B. L., Cummings, J. L., Goldberg, M., Mychack, P., Bottino, V., & Benson, D. F. (2000). Artistic savants. *Neuropsychiatry, Neuropsychology, and Behavioral Neurology, 13,* 29–38.

Jambaqué, I., Mottron, L., Ponsot, G., & Chiron, C. (1998). Autism and visual agnosia in a child with right occipital lobectomy. *Journal of Neurology, Neurosurgery, and Psychiatry, 65,* 555–560.

Johnson, M. H. (1997). *Developmental cognitive neuroscience*. Oxford, UK: Blackwell.

Jolliffe, T., & Baron-Cohen, S. (1999). A test of central coherence theory: Linguistic processing in high-functioning adults with autism or Asperger syndrome: Is local coherence impaired? *Cognition, 71,* 149–185.

Kapur, N. (1996). Paradoxical functional facilitation in brain-behaviour research. A critical review. *Brain, 119,* 1775–1790.

Langdell, T. (1978). Recognition of faces: An approach to the study of autism. *Journal of Child Psychology and Psychiatry, 19,* 255–268.

Lessard, N., Pare, M., Lepore, F., & Lassonde, M. (1998). Early-blind human subjects localize sound sources better than sighted subjects. *Nature, 395,* 278–280.

Lord, C., Rutter, M., & Le Couteur, A. (1994). Autism Diagnostic Interview-Revised: A revised version of diagnostic interview for caregivers of individuals with possible pervasive development disorders. *Journal of Autism and Developmental Disorders, 24,* 659–685.

Miller, B. L., Cummings, J., Mishkin, F., Boone, K., Prince, F., Ponton, M., & Cotman C. (1998). Emergence of artistic talent in frontotemporal dementia. *Neurology, 51,* 978–982.

Mottron, L., & Belleville, S. (1993). A study of perceptual analysis in a high-level autistic subject with exceptional graphic abilities. *Brain and Cognition, 23,* 279–309.

Mottron, L., & Belleville, S. (1995). Perspective production in a savant autistic draughtsman. *Psychological Medicine, 25,* 639–648.

Mottron, L., Belleville, S., & Ménard, E. (1999b). Local bias in autistic subjects as evidenced by graphic tasks: Perceptual hierarchization or working memory deficit. *Journal of Child Psychology and Psychiatry, 40,* 743–756.

Mottron, L., Belleville, S., Stip, E., & Morasse, K. (1998). Atypical memory performance in a autistic savant. *Memory, 6,* 593–607.

Mottron, L., Burack, J. A., Stauder, J. E., & Robaey, P. (1999a). Perceptual processing among high-functioning persons with autism. *Journal of Child Psychology and Psychiatry, 40,* 203–211.

Mottron, L., Limoges, E., & Jelenic, P. (in press, b). Can a cognitive deficit elicit an exceptional ability?: The case of Nadia. In C. Code, C. Wallesch, Y. Joanette, & A. R. Lecours (Eds.), *Classic Cases in Neuropsychology, vol II.*

Mottron, L., Mineau, S., Décarie, J. C., Jambaqué, I., Labrecque R., Pépin, J. P., & Aroichane, M. (1997). Visual agnosia with temporo-occipital brain lesions in an autistic child: A case study. *Developmental Medicine and Child Neurology, 39,* 699–705.

Mottron, L., Morasse, K., & Belleville, S. (in press, a). A study of memory functioning in individuals with autism. *Journal of Child Psychology and Psychiatry.*

Mottron, L., Peretz, I., Belleville, S., & Rouleau, N. (1999c). Absolute pitch in autism: A case study. *Neurocase, 5,* 485–502.

Mottron, L., Peretz, I., & Ménard, E. (2000). Local and global processing of music in high-functioning persons with autism: Beyond central coherence? *Journal of Child Psychology and Psychiatry, 41*, 1057–1065.

Murphy, C., & Cain, W. S. (1986). Odor identification: The blind are better. *Physiological Behavior, 37,* 177–180.

O'Riordan, M. (1998). Reduced perception of similarity in autism. Doctoral thesis, University of Cambridge, UK.

Plaisted, K., O'Riordan, M., & Baron-Cohen, S. (1998a). Enhanced discrimination of novel, highly similar stimuli by adults with autism during a perceptual learning task. *Journal of Child Psychology and Psychiatry, 39,* 765–775.

Plaisted, K., O'Riordan, M., & Baron-Cohen, S. (1998b). Enhanced visual search for a conjunctive target in autism: A research note. *Journal of Child Psychology and Psychiatry, 39,* 777–783.

Plaisted, K., Swettenham, J., & Rees, L. (1999). Children with autism show local precedence in a divided attention task and global precedence in a selective attention task. *Journal of Child Psychology and Psychiatry, 40,* 733–742.

Ring, H. A., Baron-Cohen, S., Wheelwright, S., Williams, S. C., Brammer, M., Andrew, C., & Bullmore, E. T. (1999). Cerebral correlates of preserved cognitive skills in autism: A functional MRI study of embedded figures task performance. *Brain, 122,* 1305–1315.

Schultz, R. T., Gauthier, I., Klin, A., Fulbright, R. K., Anderson, A. W., Volkmar, F. R., Skudlarski, P., Lacadie, C., Cohen, D. J., & Gore, J. C. (in press). Abnormal versus temporal cortical activity among individuals with autism and Asperger syndrome during face discrimination. *Archives of General Psychiatry.*

Schultz, R. T., Gauthier, I., Klin, A., Fulbright, R. K., Anderson, A. W., Volkmar, F. R., Skudlarski, P., Lacadie, C., Cohen, D. J., & Gore, J. C. (2000, April). Abnormal ventral temporal cortical activity during face discrimination among individuals with autism and Asperger syndrome. *Archives of General Psychiatry, 57(4),* 331–340.

Schultz, R. T., Romanski, L. M., & Tsatsanis, K. (1999). Neurofunctional models of autism and Asperger syndrome: Clues from neuroimaging. In A. Klin, F. R. Volkmar, & S. S. Sparrow (Eds.), *Asperger syndrome.* New York: Guilford.

Sroufe, L. A., & Rutter, M. (1984). The domain of developmental psychopathology. *Child Development, 55,* 17–29.

Takeuchi, A. H., & Hulse, S. H. (1993). Absolute pitch. *Psychological Bulletin, 113,* 345–361.

Turner, M. (1997). Towards an executive dysfunction account of repetitive behavior in autism. In J. Russell (Ed.), *Autism as an executive disorder* (pp. 57–100). Oxford, UK: Oxford University Press.

Walker, P., & Moylan, K. (1994). The enhanced representation of surface texture consequent on the loss of sight. *Neuropsychologia, 32,* 289–297.

Waterhouse, L. (1988). Extraordinary visual memory and pattern perception in an autistic boy. In L. K. Obler & D. Fein (Eds.), *The exceptional brain* (pp. 325–338). New York: Guilford.

Young, R. L., & Nettelbeck, T. (1995). The abilities of a musical savant and his family. *Journal of Autism and Development Disorders, 25,* 231–248.

8

Reduced Generalization in Autism: An Alternative to Weak Central Coherence

Kate C. Plaisted
Department of Experimental Psychology
University of Cambridge, England

It has long been observed that individuals with autism exhibit peculiar attentional and perceptual abnormalities. For example, individuals with autism frequently notice minor changes in their environments. In one of the earliest studies of autism, Kanner noted the following statement made by the mother of a child with autism: "On one of the bookshelves, we had three pieces in a certain arrangement. When this was changed, he always rearranged it in the old pattern" (Kanner, 1943; 1973, p. 9). This sort of behavior is consistent with many anecdotal and clinical reports that individuals with autism notice features about a situation or event that to others seem small and insignificant. Another example of this exquisite perception of detail has been observed when children with autism tackle jigsaw puzzles—the solution appears to be derived from the shapes of the pieces rather than the printed picture, so that the child with autism, unlike a normal child, could as easily complete a jigsaw puzzle with the picture facedown as when it is faceup (Frith & Hermelin, 1969). This ability to pick out individual features from some larger entity has also been observed using the Embedded Figures Task and the block design subtest of the Weschler intelligence scales. Several studies have established that both children and adults with autism show superior performance on these tasks compared with normal individuals and individuals with learning disabilities, matched for mental age (Shah & Frith, 1983; Shah & Frith, 1993; Jolliffe & Baron-Cohen, 1997).

This set of behaviors can be described as an acute ability to process fine detail, an ability that can surpass that of developmentally normal individuals. Over the past 10 years, the dominant explanation for these behaviors has been the weak central coherence hypothesis (Frith, 1989). In a general form, the hypothesis states that individuals with autism have a deficit in integrating disparate information in order to extract the "gist" of any situation. The hypothesis is flexible enough to allow predictions to be made at many stages of psychological processing—from perception and selective attention through to conception. Because weak central coherence could operate at any one (or all) of these levels, Frith initially thought that this integration deficit might explain both the superior perceptual and attentional abilities of individuals with autism and their deficits in conceptual-semantic domains of analysis, such as the pragmatic use of language and, indeed, the pervasive social deficits (Frith, 1989). However, this view has been abandoned in light of empirical investigations suggesting that weak central coherence and social deficits may be independent of one another (Happé, 1997; Frith & Happé, 1994). As a result, the weak central coherence hypothesis has become regarded as the explanation for the special abilities and savant skills observed in autism, leaving the theory of mind hypothesis (e.g. Baron-Cohen, Leslie, & Frith, 1985; Tager-Flusberg, chap. 9, this volume) and the executive dysfunction hypothesis (see Russell, 1997, and Hughes, this volume) to battle over the explanation of the co-occurrence of the characteristic triad of impairments in autism (Wing & Gould, 1979).

In this chapter, I argue that more recent evidence is highly suggestive of a causal link between the perceptual and attentional abnormalities in individuals with autism and their deficits in social processing. Given this, we should perhaps readopt the parsimonious position that many aspects of autism stem from one underlying deficit. The question then becomes whether this deficit is indeed a weakening of central-coherence mechanisms, or whether weak central coherence "effects" may be better explained by alternative mechanisms. This question is answered, in part, by reviewing some of the studies that have assessed the weak central coherence hypothesis at the level of perception and selective attention. On the whole, the evidence is not in its favor, although the same cannot be said of studies that assess the weak central coherence hypothesis at the level of conception. My argument is that there is an alternative explanation of the perceptual and attentional abnormalities in autism to weak central coherence that pivots on the notion that individuals with autism are unable to draw pieces of information together because of an inability to recognize the similarities between stimuli or situations. However, the challenge is to assess whether this alternative can also explain weak central coherence effects at the conceptual level. I draw on some recent insights concerning perceptual and conceptual processes in developmentally normal individuals (Goldstone & Barsalou, 1998) to offer possible ways in which a reduced ability to process similarity at the perceptual and attentional level of the kind observed in autism can lead to abnormalities at the conceptual level.

Weak Central Coherence and Social Information Processing

Historically, research in autism has attempted to find an explanation that could account for the entire set of autistic symptoms. In fact, two of the most dominant theories, the theory of mind deficit (e.g. Baron-Cohen, et al., 1985) and the executive dysfunction theory (see Russell, 1997) focus on finding a single underlying cause for the triad of impairments (Frith, 1989; Wing & Gould, 1979), rather than on the perceptual and attentional profile in autism. What is so exciting about the weak central coherence hypothesis is that it stands alone as a potential explanation of both the triad of impairments and the perceptual and attentional abnormalities. In her original formulation of the hypothesis, Frith (1989) described how the inability to draw together into a meaningful pattern disparate and complex pieces of information typical of a social interaction could easily give rise to a mentalizing deficit. Similarly, she explained that being unable to extract the "gist" from a speech stream would prevent an individual from understanding the "deeper intentional aspects of communication" (Frith, 1989, p. 124). She also applied the hypothesis to the presence of repetitive behaviors—automatically elicited behaviors that are normally inhibited by the operation of those central control processes that are responsible for bringing coherence to experience. Thus, in these three areas, weak central coherence will give rise to deficits in behavior compared with that of nonautistic individuals. On the other hand, where task success lies in being able to ignore gist or meaning in order to focus on details and parts of objects, weak central coherence will give rise to superior performance, such as in the case of the Embedded Figures Task and the block design task. In this way, the weak central coherence hypothesis elegantly captures both the strengths and weaknesses of the autistic disorder.

However, on the basis of studies conducted by Happé (1991; 1997), Frith has abandoned the idea that weak central coherence is the single underlying deficit in autism (Frith & Happé, 1994). Happé (1991; 1997) compared different groups of individuals with autism—individuals who showed no ability to pass theory-of-mind tasks, individuals who passed first-order theory-of-mind tasks, and individuals who passed second-order theory-of-mind tasks—with developmentally normal children on the ability to correctly pronounce homographs embedded within sentence contexts. Her prediction was that if weak central coherence underlies theory-of-mind deficits, then those individuals with autism who were unable to pass theory-of-mind tasks would show a deficit in the homograph task, whereas those who showed good theory-of-mind task performance would show a level of performance comparable with that of the normal children. Because all of the individuals with autism, regardless of their ability to solve theory-of-mind tasks, showed deficits on the homograph task, Happé (Happé, 1997; 1994) concluded that central coherence and theory-of-mind skills were underpinned by independent mechanisms and that individuals with autism suffered deficits in both.

One possibility, then, is that weak central coherence underlies the perceptual and attentional abnormalities in autism, whereas theory-of-mind deficits and executive dysfunction underlie aspects of the triad of impairments. The question then becomes one of how these three mechanisms are related, a question addressed by others in this volume. However, there is another line of inquiry that raises another possibility. This research suggests, contrary to Frith and Happé's conclusions, that central coherence and theory-of-mind performance are, in fact, causally linked. If this is so, then we return to the possibility that the various aspects of autism may stem from the same underlying psychological mechanism.

Some of this research has been conducted by Baron-Cohen and his colleagues (Baron-Cohen & Hammer, 1997; Baron-Cohen, Jolliffe, Mortimore, & Robertson, 1997). Each of these studies compared two populations (for example, female and male adults, or parents of children with Asperger's syndrome and parents of developmentally normal children, or individuals with and without autism and those with Asperger's syndrome) on the Embedded Figures Task as the test for central coherence and the "Mind in the Eyes" task as the test for mentalizing. In the Mind in the Eyes task, participants were presented with a pair of photographic images, each displaying the eye region of a face and asked which of the pair indicates a particular mental state, such as "sympathetic" or "concerned" or "playful." In each population of participants, he found an inverse relationship between performance on the Embedded Figures Task and the Mind in the Eyes task, strongly suggesting a link between central coherence and mentalizing skills.

A similar conclusion was drawn by Jarrold, Butler, Cottington, and Jimenez, (2000), who argued that Happé's (1997) study provides no direct evidence against the hypothesis of a causal link between weak central coherence and poor theory-of-mind skills, because those individuals who were able to solve second-order theory-of-mind skills were likely to have developed this ability later than developmentally normal children. This late development may well have been caused by weak central coherence. Accordingly, Jarrold et al. (2000) examined the relationship between weak central coherence and theory-of-mind performance in individuals with autism on tests of mentalizing in the form of a battery of theory-of-mind tasks that required belief inference and the Embedded Figures Task. Significant inverse correlations between the two were found when verbal mental age and verbal mental age plus chronological age were partialled out.

Evaluating Perceptual Weak Central Coherence

These studies resurrect the potential importance of the weak central coherence hypothesis as an explanation of the major characteristics of autism. Thus, the central issue becomes what are the mechanisms of weak central coherence? Only by addressing this can we discover how weak central coherence explains the various symptoms of autism. The difficulty, however, is that the weak central coherence hypothesis is a rather unformulated notion. Frith's use of the word "central" refers to processes that are marshaled in order to extract the overall meaning from a range of informational inputs (Frith, 1989). If these processes are truly "central," then weak central coherence might be expected to affect many levels of processing, from perception (often referred to as weak central coherence at "lower" levels) to conception (often referred to as weak central coherence at "higher" levels). The problem is knowing what the central processes are. For example, they could be those processes responsible for building a mental model or schema (Johnson-Laird, 1983). Or they could be attentional control processes, which select from a range of input that which is goal-relevant and inhibit that which is not. However, it is not at all clear how deficits in these sorts of processes would give rise to weak central coherence at the level of perception. Perceptual weak central coherence may be more likely the result of abnormal or weakened gestalt processes, responsible for the integration of the component parts of a stimulus into a global whole. And, if this is the case, the word "central" becomes redundant, because gestalt processes are usually thought of as innate principles of perceptual organization.

Most researchers who have tested weak central coherence in autism at the perceptual level have adopted the idea that weak central coherence derives from a deficit in perceptual integration processes, which weakens the ability to perceive a gestalt. Hierarchical stimuli, in which a larger figure such as a letter *h* is composed of a number of other smaller figures, such as the letter *s*, were used in at least four studies (Mottron & Belleville, 1993; Mottron, Burack, Stauder, & Robaey, 1999; Ozonoff, Strayer, McMahon, & Filloux, 1994; Plaisted, Swettenham, & Rees, 1999). In such tasks, the participant is required to respond to either the larger global figure or to the smaller local figures. Typically, (although not always) developmentally normal individuals respond faster and more accurately to the global than to the local level of the stimulus (Navon, 1977). And, contrary to the expectations of the weak central coherence hypothesis, the same has been found for individuals with autism. If the weak central coherence hypothesis is interpreted in its strictest sense, as a deficit in the integration of stimulus input resulting in an inability to perceive gestalt wholes, these results can be seen as staunch evidence against it.

Frith probably did not have this in mind, as she stated that weak central coherence comes about because individuals with autism cannot see the *need* to draw separate pieces of information (or at the perceptual level, parts of a stimulus or scene) together (Frith, 1989). This implies that individuals with autism should be able to *perceive* a gestalt, but have a tendency to *attend* to the local parts of the stimulus. And, on the whole, these studies primed participants to attend to either the global or the local level prior to a block of trials, by telling them to identify the large (global) letter or the small (local) letter. Thus, according to the idea that individuals with autism do not ordinarily see the need to attend to the global whole, it is not surprising that when they are explicitly informed of the need to attend to the global level, they process the gestalt figure in the normal way. However, we (Plaisted, et al., 1999) also included a task that required participants to inspect both the local level and global level of the stimulus on each trial, a procedure that prevented priming attention to one or another level by instruction. Under these conditions, individuals with autism exhibited a weak-central-coherence effect by responding more accurately to the target figure at the local than the global level.

This finding can be seen as consistent with Frith's version of the weak central coherence hypothesis, that in the absence of a drive for global meaning, individuals with autism have a tendency to attend to the local level. However, the important fact is that the weak central coherence theory does not tell us why such an effect should come about—it simply describes the effect. We (Plaisted et al., 1999) suggested that one reason may lie in the relative levels of activity in the two visual channels responsible for high- and low-spatial-frequency processing. The faster and more accurate responding to the global level of a hierarchical stimulus in developmentally normal adults may relate to the relatively higher levels of activity in low-spatial-frequency channels (Badcock, Whitworth, Badcock, & Lovegrove, 1990). When adults are adapted to a low-spatial-frequency grating, preferential global processing reverses to preferential local processing. If this balance is reversed in autism, the local level should be processed prior to the global. Furthermore, the relative levels of activity in these visual channels do not appear to be fixed, but can be modulated by attentional processing, possibly mediated by parietal mechanisms (Robertson & Lamb, 1991). When adults search for a target that is more likely to appear at the local than the global level, they show faster and more accurate performance at the local compared with the global level (Kinchla, Solis-Macias, & Hoffman, 1983). Thus, the level of the stimulus that should be attended to can be primed, and this appears to override, in developmentally normal individuals, any "default" setting of activity levels within the spatial-frequency channels. The normal performance of individuals with autism on hierarchical stimulus tasks in which target levels are primed suggests that this is also the case in autism.

A similar analysis could be applied to the finding that individuals with autism do not succumb to all visual illusions. Happé (1996) assessed children with autism on their propensity to succumb to six visual illusions. Although a similar percentage of children with autism and children with learning disabilities matched for mental age succumbed to one of the illusions (the Muller-Lyer), a rather lower percentage of children with autism succumbed to the remaining five (the Ponzo, Kanisza, Titchener, Hering, and Poggendorf illusions). This might be explained by enhanced levels of activity in high-spatial-frequency visual channels, thereby providing sufficiently more information about the local parts of the illusory figures to prevent the illusion that is derived only from low-spatial-frequency information concerning the global level. If global processing operates normally in autism when primed by instruction, then this effect should disappear when children with autism are asked a question about the illusion that refers to the global level. Some consistent evidence is available from a study in progress that is being conducted by Scott, Brosnan, and Wheelwright (submitted). They wondered whether the participants with autism in Happé's study (1996) interpreted the questions asked (e.g., "Are these two lines the same length?" in the Ponzo illusion) in a literal way. They therefore asked their participants two questions about each illusion, one of which referred to the actual form of the stimulus (e.g., "Is there a triangle?" in the case of the Kanisza triangle illusion) and another that referred to the appearance of the stimulus (e.g., "Does it look like there is a triangle?"). They found that individuals with autism can see the actual form of the stimulus and the illusion. The appearance question could therefore prime the individual with autism to attend to the global level of the stimulus, thus overriding otherwise enhanced local processing.

There are very few other convincing demonstrations of perceptual weak central coherence. Jarrold and Russell (1997) attempted to test the hypothesis by asking children to count dot stimuli, which were presented either in canonical form (i.e., like the arrangement of dots on dice) or in a distributed form, where the dots appeared randomly arranged with several other distracters (small squares). They suggested that, according to the weak central coherence hypothesis, children with autism should show no benefit for dots arranged canonically, whereas developmentally normal children and children with learning disabilities would find counting easier in the canonical condition than in the distributed condition. Although there were no differences between groups for counting in the two conditions when there were only three and four dots, the two groups without autism showed more benefit from having stimuli presented in canonical form than in distributed form when there were five and six dots to count. However, Jarrold and Russell (1997) note that some children within the group with autism showed as much benefit from canonical presentations as the other groups, and the proportion of these "global" counters did not differ significantly from the proportion of global counters in the group of children with learning disabilities.

In one study that is frequently cited in favor of perceptual weak central coherence, Shah and Frith (1993) compared developmentally normal individuals and individuals with autism on a "pre-segmented" form of the block-design task. They argued that if individuals with autism fail to perceive the overall gestalt of the pattern, they should, unlike developmentally normal individuals and individuals with learning disabilities, show no benefit from the presentation of the pattern to be copied in a segmented form compared with their performance when it was presented in its complete form. Shah and Frith (1993) also compared groups on patterns presented rotated versus nonrotated and patterns with and without oblique lines. They found an interaction between groups only in the segmented versus nonsegmented condition. Thus, nonautistic groups appeared to benefit no more than individuals with autism by nonrotated and non-oblique line patterns but were facilitated by segmentation.

There are, however, reasons to be cautious about this result. When separate analyses were conducted on the data, Shah and Frith (1993) found that the interaction between the older normal and high-IQ persons with autism was not statistically significant at the 0.05 probability level. One way of salvaging the weak central coherence hypothesis in the light of this nonsignificant result might be to say that if the block-design task marshals the same processes as the Embedded Figures Task, then, given that performance on the Embedded Figures Task improves with age, so may performance improve on the block-design task. Thus, by the age of 16 years, developmentally normal individuals may perform to the level of individuals with autism on both segmented and unsegmented forms of the task. However, the weak central coherence hypothesis fares less well from this explanation for the comparison between younger normal and low-IQ persons with autism, which yielded a significant interaction. If developmentally normal individuals' performance improves with age, then superior performance would be expected from a group of 18-year-old individuals with autism compared to 10-year-old developmentally normal children, regardless of the difference between groups in diagnosis. But why, then, did the older individuals with autism show superior performance compared with the other groups only on the unsegmented form? This brings us to the final problem with the data from this study. In both groups of individuals with autism, there were improvements in performance when patterns were presented in segmented form. This strongly suggests that segmentation facilitated all groups, regardless of diagnosis. Although these improvements in the groups with autism were presumably nonsignificant (simple effects were unfortunately not reported), this is some indication that performance in the groups with autism was at ceiling in the segmented version. Thus, if the patterns had been more difficult, individuals with autism may have shown superior performance on both the unsegmented and segmented patterns compared with the other groups, a result that would require some other explanation than weak central coherence.

The evaluation of the weak central coherence hypothesis so far may seem overly harsh. After all, those studies that ostensibly provide evidence against the weak central coherence hypothesis do so by presenting nonsignificant differences between groups with and without autism (Mottron & Belleville, 1993; Ozonoff et al., 1994; Plaisted et al., 1999) and null results can be argued either way. The argument against the weak central coherence hypothesis might seem more compelling if a group with autism performed on a task in the opposite way to that predicted by weak central coherence. Such a result was found when performance on conjunctive visual search tasks was compared between children with autism and developmentally normal children (Plaisted, O'Riordan, & Baron-Cohen, 1998a). These tasks require participants to search for a target that shares its features with two or more simultaneously presented sets of distracters, such as a green X target among green T and red X distracters. Because the detection of this target among such distracters requires integration of the color feature green and the shape feature X, the weak central coherence hypothesis predicts that children with autism should perform significantly worse compared with developmentally normal children. In direct contradiction, we found that children with autism were significantly faster. This result is hardly amenable to the idea that priming a gestalt target by instruction (the children were told to look for a green X), boosts the otherwise weak central coherence processes, because this merely predicts that the performances of the two groups would not differ. The finding of superior performance in the opposite direction to that predicted by weak central coherence requires an entirely different explanation. The explanation I shall offer later not only accounts for this superior performance, but also suggests an alternative explanation for the other demonstrations of superior performance in perceptual-attentional tasks that have generally been regarded as weak central coherence effects.

Evaluating Conceptual Weak Central Coherence

In contrast to perceptual weak central coherence, conceptual weak central coherence has received relatively little direct empirical testing. However, there are phenomena within the literature that are certainly consistent with the idea that children with autism are less able to extract meaning from a given array of information. For example, Hermelin and O'Connor (1967) found that children with autism were less able than developmentally delayed children to chunk items according to categories from a word sequence that exceeded memory span. Similarly, Tager-Flusberg (1991) found that children with autism, unlike developmentally normal and learning disabled children, were not facilitated in immediate free recall by the semantic similarity in a list of nouns.

The better known studies that are cited in support of conceptual weak central coherence have assessed the ability of individuals with autism to correctly pronounce homographs within the context of sentences. Frith & Snowling (1983) found that children with autism read fewer homographs correctly in context compared with developmentally normal and dyslexic children. This is consistent with the idea that individuals with autism are less able to extract the "gist," which might normally determine the correct pronunciation. Unfortunately, this study did not determine whether or not this effect is specific to autism, since the developmentally normal children, although significantly better at homograph pronunciation than children with autism, were significantly poorer than the children with dyslexia, raising the possibility that these group differences emerged because of differences in general mental functioning. Although IQ scores were not reported for the developmentally normal children, it is possible that they were of lower average IQ than the group of children with dyslexia (the upper IQ limit in that group was over two standard deviations above the mean) and of higher average IQ than the children with autism (the lower IQ limit in the group of children with autism was over three standard deviations below the mean).

The specificity of the homograph pronunciation effect to autism was further challenged by Snowling and Frith (1986), who assessed children with autism, children with learning disabilities and developmentally normal children on the homograph task. Half of each group of children were of high verbal ability and the other half were of low verbal ability. Regardless of diagnosis, children of high verbal ability scored higher than children of low verbal ability. Furthermore, there were no differences in performance between the three groups of children of low verbal ability. These findings appear to confirm the impression given by Frith and Snowling's data (1983) that using context to disambiguate homograph pronunciation has less to do with weak central coherence in autism than with low general mental functioning.

Two further studies need be taken into account before accepting this conclusion. In Happé's (1997) study (discussed previously), the group of individuals with autism who passed second-order theory-of-mind tasks had a full-scale IQ of less than one standard deviation below the mean and, unlike the developmentally normal group (whose IQ data were not reported), showed no facilitation in performance when the homograph was presented toward the end of the sentence—i.e., after the context had been supplied. And, in a rigorously controlled study with respect to IQ matching, Jolliffe (1997) compared high-functioning adults with autism and developmentally normal adults, matched on full-scale IQ, on the homograph task, and again found facilitation in the normal group when the homograph was presented after the sentence context and no facilitation in the group with autism.

It is not clear how the results of these later studies can be reconciled with Snowling and Frith's (1986) data, which showed that homograph disambiguation by sentence context is related to general mental functioning. The most useful approach is to adopt the stance that when nonautistic individuals with low IQ produce patterns of performance that are similar to those of individuals with autism, they may do so for entirely different reasons. Thus, when studies reveal null results between these two groups, it is not sufficient to conclude that performance is determined only by nonspecific low mental functioning. What is required in these cases is further testing to decide the case one way or another.

Enhanced Discrimination and Reduced Generalization in Autism

If, as I have tried to argue, the evidence for weak central coherence at the level of perception is not in its favor, it makes sense to consider alternative explanations for the kinds of perceptual and attentional abnormalities observed in the behavior of individuals with autism and their superior performance on tasks like embedded figures. The alternative that I have been considering is that many of the attentional and perceptual abnormalities in autism are phenomena of reduced generalization, or a reduced processing of the similarities that hold between stimuli and between situations. Specifically, I have drawn from elemental theories of generalization, which state that one stimulus will be responded to in a similar way to another if they share sufficient features or elements in common (e.g., Estes, 1950; Pearce, 1987; Thompson, 1965). If they share few features in common, they will be regarded as different stimuli. And, if individuals with autism process similarities between stimuli and situations poorly compared with normal individuals, then they will tend to view even similar stimuli as quite different.

In order to see how this suggestion relates to the performance of individuals with autism on the Embedded Figures Task, it is useful to draw an analogy between this task and a camouflaged detection task. When, for example, a moth is camouflaged against a piece of bark, it is very difficult to detect because many of its features are precisely those of the bark background. Discriminating the moth from its background therefore requires processing those features that are unique to the moth and not shared in common with the bark (Plaisted & Mackintosh, 1995; Plaisted, 1997). Similarly, in the Embedded Figures Task, the target contains some features or elements in common with the overall picture and some unique features that define it. Detection of the target will therefore be enhanced if those unique features are processed well and those features held in common with features contained in the rest of the picture are processed poorly. In the case of the block-design task, again the final solution will be assisted if an individual is able to process well those features that uniquely define the required block face and to ignore those features that are held in common with other faces that may be required for another part of the design.

Acute processing of unique features hinders rather than helps in other situations—such as when trying to transfer learning from one situation to another—especially when the two situations share few common features. Poor transfer, or generalization, is often observed in autism (e.g. Swettenham, 1996; Ozonoff & Miller, 1995). Any simple elemental model of generalization predicts that successful transfer under these conditions will occur if those few features that are held in common between the two situations are processed rather than those features unique to each stimulus and that transfer will be hindered if those common features are processed poorly.

The hypothesis that individuals with autism process features unique to a situation or stimulus relatively well and features held in common between situations or stimuli rather poorly, makes two complementary predictions. First, individuals with autism should show superior performance on a difficult discrimination task—i.e., one where stimuli to be discriminated hold many elements in common and each possesses very few unique elements. Second, individuals with autism should show inferior performance on a task that requires categorization of two sets of stimuli.

Support for the first prediction was found in a perceptual-learning task (Plaisted, O'Riordan, & Baron-Cohen, 1998b). Perceptual learning describes the phenomenon whereby two very similar stimuli, which at first appear indistinguishable, become discriminable following a period of simple exposure. As a result of exposure to the stimuli, elements held in common (and which initially prevent discrimination) become less salient and the unique elements of each stimulus become relatively more salient (see McLaren, Kaye, & Mackintosh, 1989, for a model of the mechanisms underlying perceptual learning). If, however, individuals with autism process the unique elements of stimuli well and the common elements poorly, they should not require exposure to the stimuli in order to discriminate them. In our experiment (Plaisted et al., 1998b), we compared high-functioning adults with autism and normal adults on their ability to perform two discriminations. One discrimination involved two highly similar stimuli that had been preexposed, the other involved two entirely novel similar stimuli. The group of normal adults showed the classic perceptual learning effect; they solved the discrimination between the two preexposed stimuli significantly better than the discrimination between the two novel, non-preexposed stimuli. The group of adults with autism, however, performed significantly better on the novel discrimination problem compared with the normal adults. They also did not show the perceptual learning effect: they performed as well on the discrimination involving novel stimuli as on the discrimination involving the preexposed stimuli. This is consistent with the idea that unique features are processed well and common features processed poorly by individuals with autism and relates to the nature of the stimuli employed in this task. The stimuli that were preexposed contained only some features in common to those presented during the test phase. Furthermore, these features were also held in common between the two stimuli in the test discrimination, and were therefore the features to be ignored when trying to solve the discrimination. Thus, benefiting from preexposure in this procedure required participants to process those features of the test stimuli that were held in common with the preexposure stimuli as familiar. This would therefore facilitate the test discrimination. However, if individuals with autism do not process common features well—whether those held between two concurrently experienced stimuli or those held between the current experience and a prior experience—such facilitation would not occur.

Support for the second prediction, that individuals with autism should show a deficit in categorization, was found using a prototype abstraction task (Plaisted, O'Riordan, Aitken, & Killcross, submitted). When typical adults are first trained to categorize two sets of exemplars, they are subsequently able to categorize the prototype of each set more accurately than other nonprototypical exemplars, even though they have never experienced the prototypes before. Any explanation of this prototype effect appeals to a mechanism of estimating the similarity between exemplars. Because the prototype is the central tendency of the set of training exemplars, its similarity to the trained set will be higher than that of any other novel but nonprototypical exemplar and it will therefore be categorized more accurately. Categorization and prototype abstraction are, therefore, phenomena of generalization between the common features of a set of exemplars. According to the reduced generalization hypothesis, individuals with autism should show a deficit in category learning in the initial categorization phase of a prototype experiment and a reduced prototype effect in comparison to normal subjects. Both predictions were supported.

The hypothesis also provides an explanation of their superior performance on the aforementioned conjunctive visual search task (Plaisted, et al.,1998a). The conjunctive visual search task is difficult for developmentally normal individuals precisely because there is a high similarity between the target and the distracters (Duncan & Humphries, 1989). However, if this similarity is processed less well by individuals with autism, the target effectively "pops out" from the other items in the array. We tested this further by administering to high-functioning children with autism and developmentally normal children conjunctive search tasks that varied target-distracter similarity. Increasing the similarity between targets and distracters impeded the performance of the developmentally normal children, but not the children with autism (O'Riordan & Plaisted, in press).

Thus, the hypothesis of reduced generalization appears to provide an alternative account for the kinds of phenomena often described as perceptual weak central coherence and has generated novel predictions that are supported in a variety of tasks. One remaining important question is how well this hypothesis can account for the phenomena described as conceptual weak central coherence. My argument is that it is often the unique features of a situation that are the least important when trying to make sense of an experience—understanding is much more easily derived from assimilating current experience with what one already knows. But assimilation can be successful only if one recognizes that there are features of the current situation that have been encountered in previous situations—i.e., are held in common with those past experiences. Any reduction in the processing of common features will cause a deficit in this process of bringing prior experiences to bear on new experiences. In effect, this amounts to a deficit in extracting the meaning or gist of a current experience. Furthermore, the proposal that individuals with autism process unique features somewhat better than developmentally normal individuals can account for why individuals with autism notice features that seem obscure or irrelevant—these are likely to be the unique features, which are generally rejected by the normal individual as irrelevant because they are unable to contribute to the process of assimilation.

Possible Mechanisms Underlying Reduced Generalization

The hypothesis that individuals with autism process unique features well and common features poorly compared with nonautistic individuals is based on theories that state that any stimulus is represented as a set of elements (e.g., Estes, 1950; McLaren et al., 1989). These elemental theories of stimulus representation provide a foundation from which speculations may be made about why individuals with autism show reduced generalization between stimuli that hold features in common. These theories assume that generalization from one stimulus to another normally occurs to the degree to which the elements of one are able to excite the elements of the other, by *associative excitation*. Theories differ with respect to what causes that associative excitation. For example, the activation of one stimulus representation may excite another by virtue of the representation of an outcome with which both stimuli have been equally paired in the past. Such an effect is known as *acquired equivalence* (Hall, 1992). Alternatively, associations could be formed between each and every element of one stimulus during exposure to that stimulus (so that the individual need only sample a small proportion of the total set in order for the full representation to be activated). The consequence of that process is generalization to another stimulus by virtue of the elements shared in common: that is, the activated common elements of the first stimulus will retrieve, by associative excitation, not only its own remaining set of elements, but also the remaining elements of the second stimulus that share the activated common elements (McLaren et al., 1989).

But any such theory needs also to account for the perceptual learning phenomenon—the reduction of generalization over time between stimuli that share elements in common. Any reduction in generalization effectively comes down to a reduction in the salience of the elements held in common. There are two learning mechanisms known to reduce salience: latent inhibition and habituation. *Latent inhibition* is the phenomenon whereby mere exposure to a stimulus retards the propensity of that stimulus to enter into association with any other stimulus at a later occasion. McLaren et al. (1989) proposed that latent inhibition is the primary process that reduces generalization between two stimuli to produce perceptual learning (i.e., enhanced discrimination). They assume that during exposure to the two stimuli, each element of each stimulus gradually becomes latently inhibited. However, because the elements common to both stimuli, are, in effect, presented twice as often as the unique elements, they will become twice as latently inhibited as the unique elements. Thus, by the end of preexposure, the common elements are relatively less salient than the unique elements, and therefore the unique elements are better able to enter into new associations with the discriminative response. This leads to better discrimination, or reduced generalization. Is it possible, then, that mechanisms of latent inhibition operate with greater efficiency in autism? Possibly—but this would not explain our finding that individuals with autism show enhanced discrimination between highly similar stimuli. Enhanced latent inhibition would affect common *and* unique elements equally, and if the unique elements were very much less salient for the individual with autism compared with other individuals, one might even expect the opposite result.

Differences in the processes of habituation, however, could well account for the reduced generalization we have observed in autism. Killcross and Hall (in preparation) propose that perceptual learning (or reduced generalization) in any individual is the result of differential habituation (rather than latent inhibition) of common and unique elements. *Habituation* is a nonassociative learning process in which repeatedly presented stimuli lose their capacity to elicit a response. Like McLaren et al., (1989), Killcross and Hall propose that common elements will lose salience at a faster rate than unique elements because they are presented twice as often as unique elements, but through habituation rather than latent inhibition. However, they additionally propose that in the case of similar stimuli, common elements will, at the outset, be more salient per se than unique elements. They will therefore receive greater processing of the sort that leads to habituation than will unique elements. Thus, during preexposure, the common elements will be more than twice reduced in salience compared with the unique elements. If processes underlying the habituation of stimulus elements are enhanced in autism, common elements would be preferentially influenced over unique elements. This possibility simultaneously predicts our empirical results of more rapid discrimination performance and poorer prototype abstraction in categorization tasks.

This analysis of reduced generalization is based on learning mechanisms that may reduce associative excitation between encoded elements of two or more stimuli. However, a reduction in associative excitation could be the outcome of differences in even more fundamental processes, such as perception. For example, Gustafsson (1997) proposed that the excellent discrimination skills that have been observed among persons with autism could be caused by excessive lateral inhibition between neurons. This, he argues, would impact the development of cortical maps, which respond to a range of stimuli that share certain common properties (Kohonen, 1984). Furthermore, since lateral inhibition is a general mechanism that operates throughout the central nervous system, excessive lateral inhibition could affect processing at any level, including perception. This kind of suggestion raises the possibility that perception in autism is altered such that stimuli are perceived with greater acuity and thus with greater differentiation, allowing small and seemingly irrelevant stimuli to be perceived as important and salient features.

This might account not only for the superior performance of individuals with autism on the Embedded Figures Task but also other effects such as enhanced local processing on variants of the Navon task that do not prime participants to attend to the global level. Kimchi (1992) argued that the local parts of a hierarchical stimulus are only perceived when the elements are large and few in number. When they are small and densely spaced, they are perceived instead simply as the texture of the overall figure (Kimchi & Palmer, 1982). Perceiving local parts of a whole therefore depends on the extent to which the elements are perceived as differentiated. The suggestion that perception in autism operates to enhance the differentiation of perceptual elements, therefore, predicts that individuals with autism will perceive the elements as local parts in hierarchical stimuli in which normal individuals perceive elements as texture. But why should this lead to enhanced local processing in autism? According to Kimchi (1992), the dominance of global processing over local processing in developmentally normal individuals occurs only when the elements are perceived as texture. However, when the elements are larger and more sparse, developmentally normal individuals show dominance of local processing (Kinchla & Wolfe, 1979; McLean, 1979). Making elements larger and more sparse effectively increases the differentiation between them, so that they are perceived as forms rather than simply as texture (Julesz, 1981). Thus, if the elements of a particular hierarchical stimulus are more greatly differentiated for an individual with autism than for a developmentally normal individual, they may show enhanced local processing compared with that of an individual without autism.

Conception and Categorization in Autism

The proposal that perception operates differently in autism to allow for finer registration of the available stimuli has important implications for concept formation and category structure in autism and for whether individuals with autism can or cannot categorize. Frith (1989) argued from the weak central coherence hypothesis that individuals with autism have the capacity to categorize, but may not see the need to. Although children with autism do not categorize as well as developmentally normal children, they rarely show deficits compared with mentally handicapped children matched for mental age (e.g., Tager-Flusberg, 1985; Ungerer & Sigman, 1987). I argued elsewhere, however, (Plaisted, 2000) that the capacity of children with autism to form categories is rarely assessed; more often, children's preexisting knowledge of concepts such as vegetables, furniture, or vehicles is the focus of study. Furthermore, researchers typically use sorting or matching-to-sample procedures, which assess simple simultaneous matching processes rather than categorization processes. In one exception, Klinger and Dawson (1995) compared typically developing children, children with learning disabilities, and children with autism on a prototype abstraction task. They found that the performance of children with autism was no worse than that of children with learning disabilities, although they showed poor prototype abstraction compared with typically developing children. However, our finding of high-functioning adults with no associated mental handicap who show a deficit in prototype abstraction (Plaisted et al., submitted) strongly suggests that deficits in categorization in autism arise for different reasons than the deficits seen in individuals with learning disabilities. One strong candidate is a difference in perception that leads to poor processing of elements or features held in common among stimuli. I suggest that this impinges on all levels of psychological processing.

The most likely response to this is that such differences in perceptual processing would lead only to a deficit in categorization tasks based on perceptual similarity. Such an objection is based on the long-held and traditional view that there is a dissociation between perceptual similarity on the one hand and abstract, rule-based classification on the other. This traditional view holds that cognitive processes operate entirely independently of perceptual processes and that concepts are formed on the basis of either perceptual similarities or amodal symbols.

More recent views have vigorously challenged this traditional dissociation between perception and abstract conception (Goldstone & Barsalou, 1998; Barsalou & Prinz, 1997; Mackintosh, 2000). In their article, Goldstone and Barsalou (1998) mount a persuasive case that conceptual processing is dependent on and derives from perception, not only with respect to perceptual similarity but also to abstract rules. More specifically, they argue that "mechanisms that represent shape, colour and location in perception, also represent shape, colour and location in concepts" (p. 232). In support of their argument, they note the following findings: that categorization according to an abstract rule is preceded by categorizing exemplars according to perceptual similarity (Allen & Brooks, 1991); that many symbolic concepts derive from perceptual representations (Stigler, 1984; Barwise & Etchemendy, 1991); and that individuals perceptually simulate the referents of concepts (Wu, 1995; Soloman, 1997). They also highlight the link between perceptually and conceptually based selective attention processes. For example, negative priming (in which a target stimulus on a second trial is responded to more slowly if it had previously occupied the role of an irrelevant distracter on the first trial) is observed using both physically identical stimuli and semantically identical stimuli (Tipper, 1985). Goldstone and Barsalou (1998) point out that such studies reveal that perceptually and conceptually based conception share processes of selective attention and inhibition.

If conception, or abstract thought, derives from perception, and perception is different in individuals with autism in the ways I suggest, then it follows that the structure and content of concepts will be quite different in autism. Specifically, the idea that perception in autism enhances the discriminability of stimuli predicts that category boundaries will be sharper and category content much narrower in autism than in typically developing individuals. Furthermore, these qualities of concepts will serve to restrict further development and enrichment of categories and concepts. If categories have sharper boundaries, then it is less likely that novel unusual exemplars (i.e., those that might lie at the category boundary for the developmentally normal individual) will be recognized and encoded as part of an existing category. Such exemplars might therefore be considered meaningless and ignored as a consequence. It is clear what this might mean to understanding emotional expressions: It is well known that emotional expressions undergo categorization during early infancy (e.g., Kestenbaum & Nelson, 1990). However, the child with autism might be expected to encode a highly restricted set of expressions within an emotion concept compared with what a typically developing child might encode and thus ignore, or be unable to understand, an unusual facial configuration as an exemplar of a particular emotion. It is also clear how this might relate to the fact that individuals with autism develop highly restricted interests. These interests tend to be characterized by very specific exemplars, so that a child with autism might be fascinated by a certain make of car, but entirely uninterested in other makes, let alone other forms of transport. Young typically developing children similarly become fascinated with particular categories of stimuli. However, unlike the child with autism, these categories broaden so that one interest leads onto another.

Narrower concepts and sharper category boundaries also have important implications for *semantic processing*, or extracting meaning, because these qualities would reduce the likelihood of activation by associative excitation of concepts that could be brought to bear on making sense of the current array of stimuli. Indeed, a reduction in associative excitation could account for conceptual weak central coherence effects, such as performance on the homograph task. According to several theories of word recognition, an initial lexical-access stage involves the activation of several meanings of the fixated word and the appropriate meaning is subsequently selected given the context provided by the sentence (Onifer & Swinney, 1981; Seidenberg, Tanenhaus, Leiman, & Bienkowski, 1982; Rayner & Frazier, 1989). However, in autism, reduced associative excitation predicts that fewer meanings may be initially activated, resulting in an impoverished input on which selection processes can operate.

There are other implications of a reduction in associative excitation as a result of narrower concepts and sharper category boundaries. For example, associative excitation is at the heart of generativity. It is a common experience that one thought sparks or generates another and, in reflecting on a thought sequence, one can recognize the features or elements of one thought that gave rise to the next and so on. But a reduction in associative excitation, as a result of the kinds of processes I have outlined, would lead to generativity deficits, deficits that are well documented in autism (Jarrold, Boucher, & Smith, 1996).

Finally, I should consider how this analysis might be brought to bear on social information processing in autism. It is a popular view that the social world is enormously complex and highly variable. No doubt this is true—but it would be extreme to propose that there are no regularities that occur across social situations. Development of social cognition could therefore be conceived (at least in part) as the abstraction of widely applicable social rules by generalization across these regularities, and effective social behavior in any particular situation can be seen as the utilization of the relevant social rules. And what determine and activate the relevant set of rules, of course, are those features of the current social situation that have been reliably present in previous similar social situations. But a deficit in the ability to process those common features, as observed in our experiments with individuals with autism, will result in a deficit in the abstraction of social rules, and the consequent reduction in associative excitation will result in poor social interaction and social understanding in any one situation. It may therefore be that the superior processing of those features that are unique to a situation and the poor processing of those features held in common among situations substantially contribute to the profound deficits in the social domain observed among persons with autism.

REFERENCES

Allen, S. W., & Brooks, L. R. (1991). Specializing the operation of an explicit rule. *Journal of Experimental Psychology: General, 120,* 3–19.

Badcock, J. C., Whitworth, F. A., Badcock, D. R., & Lovegrove, W. J. (1990). Low-frequency filtering and the processing of local-global stimuli. *Perception, 19,* 617–629.

Baron-Cohen, S., & Hammer, J. (1997). Parents of children with Asperger syndrome: What is the cognitive phenotype? *Journal of Cognitive Neuroscience, 9,* 548–554.

Baron-Cohen, S., Jolliffe, T., Mortimore, C., & Robertson, M. (1997). Another advanced test of theory of mind: Evidence from very high functioning adults with autism or Asperger syndrome. *Journal of Child Psychology and Psychiatry, 38,* 813–822.

Baron-Cohen, S., Leslie, A., & Frith, U. (1985). Does the autistic child have a 'theory of mind'? *Cognition, 21,* 37–46.

Barsalou, L. W., & Prinz, J. J. (1997). Mundane creativity in perceptual symbol systems. In T. B. Ward, S. M. Smith, & J. Vaid (Eds.), *Creative thought: An investigation of conceptual structures and processes* (pp. 267–307). Washington, DC: American Psychological Association.

Barwise, J., Etchemendy, J. (1991). Visual information and valid reasoning. In W. Zimmerman & S. Cunningham (Eds.), *Visualization in Mathematics* (pp. 9–24). Washington DC: Mathematical Association of America.

Duncan, J., & Humphreys, G. (1989). Visual search and stimulus similarity. *Psychological Review, 96,* 433–458.

Estes, W. K. (1950). Towards a statistical theory of learning. *Psychological Review, 57,* 94–107.

Frith, U. (1989). *Autism: Explaining the enigma.* Oxford, UK: Blackwell.

Frith, U., & Happé, F. G. E. (1994). Autism: Beyond "theory of mind". *Cognition, 50,* 115–132.

Frith, U., & Hermelin, B. (1969). The role of visual and motor cues for normal, subnormal and autistic children. *Journal of Child Psychology and Psychiatry, 10,* 153–163.

Frith, U., & Snowling, M. (1983). Reading for meaning and reading for sound in autistic and dyslexic children. *British Journal of Developmental Psychology, 1,* 329–342.

Goldstone, R. L., & Barsalou, L. W. (1998). Reuniting perception and conception. *Cognition, 65,* 231–262.

Gustafsson, L. (1997). Inadequate cortical feature maps: A neural circuit theory of autism. *Biological Psychiatry, 42,* 1138–1147.

Hall, G. (1992). *Perceptual and associative learning.* Oxford, UK: Clarendon Press.

Happé, F. G. E. (1991). *Theory of mind and communication in autism.* Unpublished PhD thesis, University of London.

Happé, F. G. E. (1994). *Autism: An introduction to psychological theory.* London: UCL Press.

Happé, F. G. E. (1996). Studying weak central coherence at low levels: Children with autism do not succumb to visual illusions. A research note. *Journal of Child Psychology and Psychiatry, 37,* 873–877.

Happé, F. G. E. (1997). Central coherence and theory of mind in autism: Reading homographs in context. *British Journal of Developmental Psychology, 15,* 1–12.

Hermelin, B., & O'Connor, N. (1967). Remembering of words by psychotic and subnormal children. *British Journal of Developmental Psychology, 58,* 213–218.

Jarrold, C., Boucher, J., & Smith, P. (1996). Generativity deficits in pretend play in autism. *British Journal of Developmental Psychology, 14,* 275–300.

Jarrold, C., Butler, D. W., Coltington, E. M., & Jimenez, F. (2000). Linking theory of mind and central coherence bias in autism and the general population. *Developmental Psychology, 36,* 126–138.

Jarrold, C., & Russell, J. (1997). Counting abilities in autism: Possible implications for central coherence theory. *Journal of Autism and Developmental Disorders, 27,* 25–37.

Johnson-Laird, P. (1983). *Mental models.* Cambridge, UK: Cambridge University Press.

Jolliffe, T. (1997) Weak central coherence in autistic spectrum disorder. Unpublished PhD thesis, University of Cambridge, UK.

Jolliffe, T., & Baron-Cohen, S. (1997). Are people with autism and Asperger's Syndrome faster than normal on the embedded figures test? *Journal of Child Psychology and Psychiatry, 38,* 527–534.

Julesz, B. (1981). Textons, the elements of texture perception and their interactions. *Nature, 290,* 91–97.

Kanner, L. (1943). Autistic disturbance of affective contact, *Nervous Child, 2,* 217–250. Reprinted in L. Kanner (1973), *Childhood psychosis: Initial studies and new insights.* New York: Wiley.

Kestenbaum, R., & Nelson, C. A. (1990). The recognition and categorization of upright and inverted emotional expressions by 7-month-old infants. *Infant Behavior and Development, 13,* 497–511.

Killcross, A. S., & Hall, G. (in preparation). Stimulus differentiation and discrimination: A model for perceptual learning.

Kimchi, R. (1992). Primacy of wholistic processing and global/local paradigm: A critical review. *Psychological Bulletin, 112,* 24–38.

Kimchi, R., & Palmer, S. E. (1982). Form and texture in hierarchically constructed patterns. *Journal of Experimental Psychology: Human Perception and Performance, 8,* 521–535.

Kinchla, R. A, Solis-Macias, V., & Hoffman, J. (1983). Attending to different levels of structure in a visual image. *Perception and Psychophysics, 33,* 1–10.

Kinchla, R. A., & Wolfe, J. M. (1979). The order of visual processing: "Top down," "bottom up," or "middle out." *Perception and Psychophysics, 25,* 225–231.

Klinger, L. G., & Dawson, G. (1995). A fresh look at categorisation abilities in persons with autism. In E. Schopler & G. B. Mesibov (Eds.), *Learning and cognition in autism* (pp. 119–136). New York: Plenum.

Kohonen, T. (1984). *Self-organizing maps.* Berlin, Germany: Springer-Verlag.

Mackintosh, N. J. (2000). Abstraction and discrimination. In C. M. Heyes and L. Huber (Eds.), *Evolution of cognition* (pp. 123–141). Cambridge, MA: MIT Press.

McLaren, I. P. L., Kaye, H., & Mackintosh, N. J. (1989). An associative theory of the representation of stimuli: Applications to perceptual learning and latent inhibition. In R. G. M. Morris (Ed.), *Parallel distributed processing: Implications for psychology and neurobiology* (pp. 102–130). Oxford, UK: Clarenden Press.

McLean, J. D. (1979). Perspectives on the forest and trees: The precedence of parts and whole in visual processing. Doctoral dissertation, University of Oregon.

Mottron, L., & Belleville, S. (1993). A study of perceptual analysis in a high-level autistic subject with exceptional graphic abilities. *Brain and Cognition, 23,* 279–309.

Mottron, L., Burack, J. A., Stauder, J. E. A., & Robaey, P. (1999). Perceptual processing among high-functioning persons with autism. *Journal of Child Psychology and Psychiatry, 40,* 203–211.

Navon, D. (1977). Forest before trees: The precedence of global features in visual perception. *Cognitive Psychology, 9,* 353–383.

Onifer, W., & Swinney, D. A. (1981). Accessing lexical ambiguities during sentence comprehension: Effects of frequency of meaning and contextual bias. *Memory and Cognition, 9,* 443–448.

O'Riordan, M. A. F., & Plaisted, K. C. (in press). Enhanced discrimination in autism. *Quarterly Journal of Experimental Psychology* (Section A).

Ozonoff, S., & Miller, J. N. (1995). Teaching theory of mind—A new approach in social skills training for individuals with autism. *Journal of Autism and Developmental Disorders, 25,* 415–433.

Ozonoff, S., Strayer, D. L., McMahon, W. M., & Filloux, F. (1994). Executive function abilities in autism and Tourette syndrome: An information processing approach. *Journal of Child Psychology and Psychiatry, 35,* 1015–1032.

Pearce, J. (1987). A model for stimulus generalisation in Pavlovian conditioning. *Psychological Review, 94,* 61–73.

Plaisted, K. C. (1997). The effect of inter-stimulus interval on the discrimination of cryptic targets. *Journal of Experimental Psychology: Animal Behavior Processes, 23,* 248–259.

Plaisted, K. C. (2000). Aspects of autism that theory of mind cannot explain. In S. Baron-Cohen, H. Tager-Flusberg, & D. J. Dohen (Eds.), *Understanding other minds: Perspectives from developmental cognitive neuroscience* (2nd ed., pp. 222–250). Oxford, UK: Oxford University Press.

Plaisted, K. C., & Mackintosh, N. J. (1995). Visual search for cryptic prey in the pigeon: Implications for the search image and search rate hypotheses. *Animal Behavior, 50,* 1219–1232.

Plaisted, K. C., O'Riordan, M. A. F., & Baron-Cohen, S. (1998a). Enhanced discrimination of novel, highly similar stimuli by adults with autism during a perceptual learning task. *Journal of Child Psychology and Psychiatry, 39,* 765–775.

Plaisted, K. C., O'Riordan, M. A. F., & Baron-Cohen, S. (1998b). Enhanced visual search for a conjunctive target in autism: a research note. *Journal of Child Psychology and Psychiatry, 39,* 777–783.

Plaisted, K. C., O'Riordan, M. A. F., Aitken, M. R. F., & Killcross, A. S. (submitted). Categorisation in autism: Evidence of a reduced prototype effect.

Plaisted, K. C., Swettenham, J., & Rees, E. (1999). Children with autism show local precedence in a divided attention task and global precedence in a selective attention task. *Journal of Child Psychology and Psychiatry, 40,* 733–742.

Rayner, K., & Frazier, L. (1989). Selection mechanisms in reading lexically ambiguous words. *Journal of Experimental Psychology, 15,* 779–790.

Robertson, L. C., & Lamb, M. R. (1991). Neuropsychological contributions to theories of part/whole organization. *Cognitive Psychology, 23,* 299–330.

Russell, J. (1997). *Autism as an executive disorder.* Oxford, UK: Oxford University Press.

Scott, F., Brosnan, M., & Wheelwright, S. (Submitted). Perception of illusions by people with autism: Is there a low-level central coherence deficit?

Seidenberg, M. S., Tanenhaus, M. K., Leiman, J. M., & Bienkowski, M. (1982). Automatic access of the meanings of ambiguous words in context: Some limitations of knowledge-based processing. *Cognitive Psychology, 14,* 489–537.

Shah, A., & Frith, U. (1983). An islet of ability in autistic children: A research note. *Journal of Child Psychology and Psychiatry, 24,* 613–620.

Shah, A., & Frith, U. (1993). Why do autistic individuals show superior performance on the block design task? *Journal of Child Psychology and Psychiatry, 34,* 1351–1364.

Snowling, M., & Frith, U. (1986). Comprehension in "hyperlexic" readers. *Journal of Experimental Child Psychology, 42,* 392–415.

Soloman, K. O. (1997). *The spontaneous use of perceptual representations during conceptual processing.* Doctoral dissertation, University of Chicago.

Stigler, J. W. (1984). 'Mental abacus': The effect of abacus training on Chinese children's mental calculation. *Cognitive Psychology, 16,* 145–176.

Swettenham, J. G. (1996). Can children with autism be taught to understand false belief using computers? *Journal of Child Psychology and Psychiatry, 37,* 157–165.

Tager-Flusberg, H. (1985). Basic level and superordinate level categorization by autistic, mentally retarded and normal children. *Journal of Experimental Child Psychology, 40,* 450–469.

Tager-Flusberg, H. (1991). Semantic processing in the free recall of autistic children: Further evidence for a cognitive deficit. *British Journal of Developmental Psychology, 9,* 417–430.

Thompson, R. F. (1965). The neural basis of stimulus generalisation. In D. I. Mostofsky (Ed.), *Stimulus generalisation* (pp. 154–178). San Francisco: Stanford University Press.

Tipper, S. P. (1985). The negative priming effect: Inhibitory priming by ignored objects. *Quarterly Journal of Experimental Psychology, 37,* 571–590.

Ungerer, J. A., & Sigman, M. (1987). Categorization skills and receptive language development in autistic children. *Journal of Autism and Developmental Disorders, 17,* 3–16.

Wing, L., & Gould, J. (1979). Severe impairments of social interaction and associated abnormalities in children: epidemiology and classification. *Journal of Autism and Developmental Disorders, 9,* 11–30.

Wu, L. (1995). *Perceptual representation in conceptual combination.* Doctoral dissertation, University of Chicago.

III

Cognition, Theory of Mind, and Executive Functioning

9

A Reexamination of the Theory of Mind Hypothesis of Autism

Helen Tager-Flusberg
University of Massachusetts and Eunice Kennedy Shriver Center, Waltham, Massachusetts

The Theory of Mind Hypothesis of Autism

In 1985 a group of British researchers published a seminal paper titled *Does the autistic child have a theory of mind?* (Baron-Cohen, Leslie, & Frith, 1985), igniting a new era of research on autism. Baron-Cohen and his colleagues found that the majority of children with autism failed a classic theory-of-mind test, in contrast to normally developing preschoolers and children with Down syndrome. Follow-up studies provided further support for their hypothesis that children with autism do not have a theory of mind: They fail to understand stories that involve deception and do not use mental-state terms such as *think* and *know* in their retelling of these kinds of stories (Baron-Cohen, Leslie, & Frith, 1986). The significance of the theory of mind hypothesis of autism, as it came to be known in the literature (Baron-Cohen, Tager-Flusberg, & Cohen, 1993), was that it not only explained the failure of children with autism on tasks tapping theory-of-mind abilities, but also provided a unified explanation for the primary diagnostic impairments in pretend play, social functioning, and communication (Baron-Cohen, 1988; Frith, 1989; Leslie, 1987). Yet over the past decade much of the excitement originally generated by work on theory of mind in autism has been dispelled. Several researchers are now skeptical about its significance as a theory that explains the primary symptoms that define this complex neurodevelopmental disorder. In this chapter I review this history, critically examining the issues that led to the current status of the theory of mind hypothesis of autism.

Early studies on theory of mind in autism were guided by ongoing work in cognitive science. Following commentary by the philosopher Dennett (1978) and others on studies of theory of mind in chimpanzees (Premack & Woodruff, 1978), much of the focus of developmental research initially addressed when typically developing children first understand false-belief and related concepts of mind. Studies by Perner, Wellman, Flavell, and their colleagues (e.g., Flavell, Flavell, & Green, 1983; Perner, Leekam, & Wimmer, 1987; Wellman & Estes, 1986; Wellman & Bartsch, 1988; Wimmer & Perner, 1983) provided the major measures that became the standards in the field. Theories emphasized the child's acquisition of a representational understanding of mind, especially knowledge that a person's mind is *opaque*—its contents are not a direct reflection of reality and are not available to the minds of others. Research with false-belief tasks demonstrated repeatedly that beginning around the age of 4, normally developing children exhibit this understanding. Although modifications in the procedural administration of such tasks may push the developmental timing down a few months (e.g., Mitchell & Lacohée, 1991; Moses & Flavell, 1990; Sullivan & Winner, 1993; Zaitchik, 1991), the dramatic change in performance on these kinds of tasks at about the age of 4 is one of the most robust findings in child development literature (Wellman, Cross, & Watson, 1999).

Research on theory of mind in children with autism reflected this emphasis on the acquisition of a representational understanding of mind by exploring their difficulties using a range of different tasks (Baron-Cohen, 2000a). Other studies were conducted within this conceptual framework that focused on language, communication, and pretend play (e.g., Baron-Cohen, 1987; Happé, 1993, 1994a; Tager-Flusberg, 1992, 1993). In these studies, the primary emphasis was on the child with autism's failure to appreciate mental states in his or herself or others and the implications of this failure for everyday social and communicative functioning (Frith, Happé, & Siddons, 1994). Nevertheless, the primary emphasis in the literature on theory of mind in autism is on the cognitive developments associated with a representational understanding of mind (Baron-Cohen, 2000a).

Challenges to the Theory of Mind Hypothesis

After a brief honeymoon period, during which many researchers came to view the theory of mind hypothesis of autism as an important approach for understanding this enigmatic syndrome, criticisms began to surface. Questions were raised on a number of fronts:

- Are deficits on theory-of-mind tasks universal among individuals with autism?
- Are deficits on theory-of-mind tasks unique to individuals with autism?

- How can the theory of mind hypothesis explain the impairments that are evident in infants with autism, long before the emergence of a representational theory of mind?
- How can the theory of mind hypothesis explain some of the other features of autism, such as repetitive behaviors and interests or savant abilities?
- Can failure on theory-of-mind tasks be interpreted in terms of other constructs, such as executive functions or language?

Thus, despite its wide-ranging appeal, the theory of mind hypothesis came under attack in ways that could not easily be dismissed. From the earliest study (Baron-Cohen et al., 1985), it was clear that a minority of individuals with autism were able to pass classic theory-of-mind tasks. The number who passed varied from one study to the next, but even a small percentage must be accounted for in any theory. If autism involves a failure to develop a theory of mind, how could these well-defined research participants with autism pass the tasks? One straightforward explanation was that theory-of-mind deficits are not universal among people with this disorder, thus calling into question the specificity of this hypothesis.

Studies also began to emerge questioning the selectivity or uniqueness of theory-of-mind impairments in autism. It is now clear that nonautistic children and adolescents with mental retardation fail standard theory-of-mind tasks at a higher rate than would be expected given their age and developmental level (Benson, Abbeduto, Short, Bibler-Nuccio, & Maas, 1993; Yirmiya, Erel, Shaked, & Solomonica-Levi, 1998; Zelazo, Burack, Benedetto, & Frye, 1996). The same is true for oral deaf children (de Villiers, 2000; Gale, de Villiers, de Villiers, & Pyers, 1996; Peterson & Siegal, 1995; 1998; Russell et al., 1998), blind children (Brown, Hobson, Lee, & Stevenson, 1997), children with specific language impairment (Cassidy & Ballaraman, 1997; Miller, 2000), and people with schizophrenia (Corcoran, 2000). If all these populations also have difficulty on theory-of-mind tasks, can theory-of-mind be interpreted as the unique deficit in autism?

Another concern with the theory of mind hypothesis of autism is the age at which autism symptoms are first identified. As noted earlier, much of the research on theory of mind in autism focuses on performance on tasks that normally developing children pass at around the age of 4. Yet, clearly, autism is apparent much earlier than this. Indeed, onset prior to the age of 3 is required in the current diagnostic criteria, according to DSM–IV (APA, 1994). Symptoms often are noted during infancy, which is long before the emergence of a representational theory of mind. Anecdotal evidence as well as empirical studies suggest that infants and toddlers with autism exhibit deficits in social responsiveness, empathy, play, joint attention, and imitation (e.g., Dawson & Adams, 1984; Gillberg et al., 1990; Mundy & Sigman, 1989; Ornitz, Guthrie, & Farley, 1977; Volkmar et. al., 1987). Clearly not all the early-appearing deficits in autism entail an appreciation of others' minds. For example, social responsiveness and primary intersubjectivity depend simply on appreciating and responding contingently to another person's presence or behavior (Klin & Volkmar, 1993), and their absence is not easily interpreted in terms of a deficit in a representational understanding of mind.

Not only do some symptoms of autism appear prior to the age at which children's theory of mind may be expected to develop, but other symptoms of the disorder—some of which develop later—are not so clearly interpreted in terms of a primary impairment in theory of mind. Diagnostic criteria for autism include three distinct areas of impairment: social and communicative impairments—which have been interpreted within a theory-of-mind framework (cf. Baron-Cohen, 1988; Tager-Flusberg, 2000)—and repetitive behaviors and interests. It is not obvious how one might understand the relationship between a theory-of-mind deficit and this kind of limited behavioral repertoire, or obsessional interest in a narrow area such as train timetables or washing machines (for a different view, see Baron-Cohen, 1989). Furthermore, there are other features of autism that frequently are apparent, even though they are not part of the DSM–IV criteria. These include savant abilities (such as outstanding memory for facts, calendrical calculating ability, or artistic talent), deficits in emotional expression, inability to generalize, exceptionally good visual perceptual skills, and atypical sensory sensitivities. Impairments in theory of mind also do not explain these features of the disorder (Happé, 1999, chap. 12, this volume; Plaisted, chap. 8, this volume).

Finally, recent evidence suggests that theory-of-mind deficits may not be the primary underlying impairment in autism and may not provide an explanation for surface symptoms such as deficits in communication and social functioning (cf. Baron-Cohen, 1988; Happé, 1994b; Pennington, 1999; Tager-Flusberg, 1999). According to some researchers, failure on tasks that tap theory-of-mind abilities may be more directly interpreted in terms of more fundamental deficits in either executive functions or language. For example, Russell (1997) argued that theory-of-mind tasks entail executive functions, such as action monitoring or self-regulation, which may explain why children with autism fail on these tasks. As an alternative explanation for the syndrome, executive-function impairments—especially in set shifting and planning—may account for a range of both social and nonsocial problems, including the repetitive behaviors and interests as well as play deficits that define autism (Jarrold, 1997).

Other researchers (e.g., de Villiers, 2000; Tager-Flusberg, 2000) argue that deficits in language ability may be at the root of the problems that children with autism have in performing theory-of-mind tasks. Language ability, as measured on standardized tests of vocabulary or grammar, is closely related to theory-of-mind performance in children with autism (e.g., Dahlgren & Trillingsgaard, 1996; Happé, 1995; Sparrevohn & Howie, 1995; Tager-Flusberg & Sullivan, 1994). Some researchers suggest that this connection between language ability and theory-of-mind performance results from the nature of language needed to understand the tasks and test questions (e.g., Bruner & Feldman, 1993). Others claim that there is a deeper connection between language and theory of mind, especially a representational theory of mind. For example, de Villiers (2000; de Villiers & de Villiers, 2000; see also Tager-Flusberg, 1997) argues that the cognitive architecture required to represent propositional attitudes, in which the content of the proposition could be marked true or false, is isomorphic to the linguistic representations needed for sentential complement constructions, in which one clause is embedded in a matrix sentence (e.g., Bobby *thought/forgot/knew/said/whispered* that the cake was in the cupboard). Studies of children with autism find a close relationship between knowledge of the semantics and syntax of sentential complements and theory-of-mind performance (Tager-Flusberg, 1997; 2000). Perhaps deficits on theory-of-mind tasks are the result of limitations and impairments in the linguistic knowledge of children with autism.

Taken together, this set of arguments seems to provide a compelling case against the theory of mind hypothesis of autism. Is it really viable at this point to claim that autism involves primary impairments in theory of mind? In the remainder of this chapter, I argue that, despite these criticisms, the theory of mind hypothesis of autism provides a coherent view of many of the phenomenological features of autism that are not easily captured by alternative perspectives. Nevertheless, the challenges summarized here need to be taken seriously; in particular, they provide a guide for how we might conceptualize the place of theory-of-mind impairments in a more comprehensive account of the autistic syndrome.

A Developmental Perspective on Theory of Mind

As noted previously , much of the early work on theory of mind focused on the transition that takes place between the ages of 3 and 4 in normally developing children.[1] The primary change at this stage is from a nonrepresentational understanding of mind to a representational understanding, for which false-belief tasks are an excellent measure. This narrow emphasis, however, failed to provide a developmental framework for theory of mind in the field of cognitive development, and this failure carried over to research on theory of mind in autism. The problem is compounded by the fact that false-belief and other related tasks are scored as either passing or failing. We are led to believe that theory of mind is something one does or does not have—it emerges spontaneously at a single point in time. Autism research was especially influenced by this narrowly defined approach to theory of mind (for a similar critique, see also Charman, 2000; Bowler, chap. 11, this volume). Thus, the literature on autism often equates

[1]In fact, from the earliest conference and published volumes in this field, there was an interest in a developmental perspective on theory of mind—with studies looking at mental-state understanding in children younger than 4 and later developments taking place in middle childhood (see Astington, Harris, & Olson, 1988; Wellman, 1990). This broader perspective was soon eclipsed by the intense focus on the changes occurring at the age of 4.

performance on a false-belief task to the presence or absence of a theory of mind, reducing what should be a rich, complex, unfolding mentalistic conception of people to a categorical capacity. This absence of a developmental perspective may be partially responsible for the criticisms of the theory of mind hypothesis discussed earlier. If so, we may be able to rescue this hypothesis by exploring the development of theory of mind and its impairment in autism.

The past few years witnessed a significant increase in studies on both early and later developments in theory of mind. False-belief understanding is now viewed as just one developmental milestone along a pathway that can be traced back to the emergence of infants' interpretation of intentional action, continuing with the older child's ability to integrate concepts of intention, knowledge, mind, and action to interpret morality, human personality, and nonliteral language (Flavell, 1999; Wellman & Lagattuta, 2000). For some current cognitive theorists, theory of mind begins at birth with the newborn's ability to imitate facial expressions and orient to social stimuli including both faces and voices (e.g., Gopnik, Capps, & Meltzoff, 2000).[2] These innate capacities are viewed as the groundwork on which theory of mind develops over the course of infancy. By the age of 5 or 6 months, infants demonstrate that they interpret human actions (e.g., a moving hand) as goal-directed (i.e., as reaching for an object) or intentional (Woodward, 1996). In the second year of life, older infants have a more sophisticated conceptual view of people as having subjective experiences. For example, Repacholi (1998) showed that 14-month-olds differentiate between objects based on the emotional expressions directed to them by someone else. Baldwin's (1993) studies of early word learning also demonstrate that older infants use the direction of eye gaze to interpret referential intent. These early abilities to interpret other people's behavior as intentional are complemented by the infant's own intentional actions, including communicative pointing, early language, and social referencing. The foundation of an early theory of mind—the capacity to impute mental states to others and to interpret action within a mentalistic causal framework—is in place by the second year of life.

The later toddler years are referred to as the "dark ages" of theory-of-mind development (Meltzoff, Gopnik, & Repacholi, 1999) because little research is done on children at this stage. But the gaps are beginning to be filled in (see, for example, Gopnik et al., 2000; Lewis & Mitchell, 1994; Meltzoff et al., 1999; Wellman & Lagattuta, 2000) with studies showing that the ability to interpret

[2]There are, of course, a number of different rival theoretical accounts of theory of mind in the literature. These theories, the most prominent of which include nativism (e.g., Fodor, 1992; Leslie & Roth, 1993), the "theory theory" (e.g., Gopnik & Wellman, 1994), and simulation theory (e.g., Harris, 1992; Gordon, 1986), offer different perspectives on the development of theory of mind. These theoretical controversies are not directly relevant to the main arguments in this chapter, so I have chosen to emphasize the empirical studies that illustrate the broad range of phenomena encompassed by theory of mind.

desire, emotion, and perception emerge at around 2 to 3 years of age, before the understanding of belief or other epistemic states. Parallel changes occur in language and communicative competence as young children become increasingly good conversationalists and demonstrate sensitivity to their listener's needs (e.g., Bloom, Rocissano, & Hood, 1976; Shatz & Gelman, 1977; Shatz & O'Reilly, 1990). This line of research highlights the growth in the toddler's appreciation of other people with an expanding understanding of their mental worlds (Shatz, 1994).

This brief overview of early development serves to illustrate that the acquisition of a representational understanding of mind is simply one more step on a developmental pathway to a rich understanding of mind. It is also not the end point; children at age 4 who pass false-belief tests still have much to learn about the mind and the mental life of themselves and other people. Studies on later developments in theory of mind have explored a range of tasks tapping a more advanced understanding of mind within the broader context of social cognition and metacognitive ability (Perner, 1988).

During middle childhood, children come to a deeper appreciation of ambiguity (e.g., Gopnik & Rosati, 1997; Pillow, 1991) and a more mature understanding of the mind as an interpreter of knowledge (e.g., Flavell, Green, & Flavell, 1998). They develop a more sophisticated conception of the enduring nature of personality traits and how trait information may be important for interpreting the intentional nature of people's actions (Heyman & Dweck, 1998; Yuill, 1993, 1997). The central place of intentionality in making moral judgments and attributions also develops during this period (Mant & Perner, 1989). In addition, higher order theory-of-mind abilities are important in explaining developmental changes in communication during middle childhood. For example, children's understanding of various forms of nonliteral language such as irony or bluffing depends on this kind of knowledge (Sullivan, Winner, & Hopfield, 1995), and changes in performance on referential communication tasks are partially attributed to more sophisticated theory-of-mind abilities (e.g., Bonitatibus, 1988). At the same time, adolescents continue to develop the capacity to read cues from people's faces about their internal states, especially cues to more subtle emotional and cognitive mental states (Baron-Cohen, Jolliffe, Mortimore, & Robertson, 1997).

This brief overview, covering the full developmental range from birth to adolescence, serves as a reminder that the development of theory of mind cannot be reduced to a single period in the life span. When viewed from this developmental stance, the focus of the theory of mind hypothesis of autism needs to be more clearly conceptualized as being on impairments that cover the wider developmental scope, from the earliest emergence of social-intentional knowledge to the more complex social cognitive constructs that develop during later childhood and adolescence. Furthermore, the definition of *impairment* in this domain suggests that there is diminished capacity, rather than the complete absence of the capacity to interpret or to view people as mental beings. Deficits in theory of mind in autism need to be defined as differences in the rate of developmental change in this domain, both in comparison to other populations and within the child with autism in comparison to other cognitive domains. Finally, more emphasis should be placed on individual differences in the degree of impairment among persons with autism and on the underlying cognitive processes and mechanisms that mediate theory-of-mind processing in this population.

A New Model of Theory of Mind

The developmental perspective summarized here underscores the general consensus that theory of mind encompasses more than just a representational concept of mind. Reflecting this broader perspective, terms such as *social intelligence* or *mentalizing ability* (cf. Frith, Morton, & Leslie, 1991) are sometimes used as synonyms for theory of mind to refer to the capacity for viewing human behavior within a mentalistic framework. Yet as this conceptual domain expands to encompass early emerging capacities in infants as well as more advanced social reasoning in adolescents and adults, it seems likely that theory of mind is composed of several interacting components—each associated with distinct underlying mechanisms for processing different aspects of social information. Thus, in this view, theory of mind is similar to other cognitive systems, such as memory or language, that are analyzed into their component subsystems (e.g., episodic vs. semantic memory; syntax vs. pragmatics).[3]

As a first step toward formulating a developmental model of theory of mind, I propose that there is an important distinction between basic *social-perceptual* and *social-cognitive* components (see also Tager-Flusberg & Sullivan, 2000). The perceptual component refers to the online immediate judgment of a person's mental state, based on information available in faces, voices, and body posture and movement. The cognitive component refers to our capacity to make more complex cognitive inferences, requiring the integration of information across time and events, about the content of mental states. Support for this model may be taken from a variety of sources, including developmental and neurobiological research, as outlined in this section.

The social-perceptual component of theory of mind builds on the innate preferences of infants to attend to human social stimuli, especially faces and voices (e.g., Fernald, 1989, 1993; Gopnik et al., 2000; Johnson & Morton, 1991; Mehler & Dupoux, 1994). The route to interpreting mental-state information from these stimuli lies in the interaction of innately specified mechanisms with social information in the world, which is obtained through continued interactions with

[3]Although numerous alternative theories of theory of mind have been proposed (for a review see Carruthers & Smith, 1996), including one account of the component modules that make up a theory of mind (e.g., Baron-Cohen, 1995), none of these theories have taken a strong developmental perspective.

people. The social preferences of infants that promote continued interactions with people may be driven by affective motives—the intrinsic reward of social stimuli. By the latter half of the first year of life, infants use information from faces and voices to interpret the emotional state of other people; they may also use more subtle cues such as eye gaze to judge what another person is attending to (cf. Baldwin, 1993; Baron-Cohen, 1994; Repacholi, 1998). Thus, the perceptual component of theory of mind emerges first in development and is available to infants for making a range of mental-state judgments about other people. However, these online perceptual capacities continue to develop as children become more adept at using facial and prosodic information as cues to mental state, culminating, for example, in the ability of adults to make very sophisticated judgments from just the eye region of the face (cf. Baron-Cohen et al., 1997). The social-perceptual component of theory of mind is probably not related to other cognitive systems, including language, although this speculation has not been systematically investigated.

The development of the social-cognitive component of theory of mind builds on the earlier emerging perceptual component. This component is involved in making mental-state inferences that depend on integrating information not only from perceptual cues, but also from sequences of events over time. The social-cognitive component of theory of mind is more closely linked to other cognitive or information-processing systems, such as working memory (needed for integrating information) and language. The development of the cognitive component of theory of mind begins during the early preschool years when children begin to talk and reason about epistemic states (Bartsch & Wellman, 1995). It is firmly in place by 4 years of age, when young children are able to pass false-belief and other related tasks. Other cognitive systems, especially language, may play an especially significant role in the development of this component of theory of mind (de Villiers, 2000; Hale & Tager-Flusberg, 1999). More advanced social-cognitive knowledge continues to develop in middle childhood and early adolescence, as described earlier. These later developments involve the integration of constructs such as belief and intention and entail more complex social reasoning and inferencing skills.

Thus, in this model, there are two distinct components to a theory-of-mind—each with its own developmental time course, each dependent on different underlying cognitive mechanisms. In everyday life, the social-perceptual and social-cognitive capacities described here function in a complex interconnected way such that our mental-state judgments, inferences, and reasoning entail both components. At the same time, traditional theory-of-mind tasks tap into the social-cognitive component more exclusively, by eliminating online social cues to mental state. More recently, new experimental theory-of-mind paradigms that depend on dynamic stimuli (e.g., Repacholi & Gopnik, 1997) or at the least real faces (e.g., Baron-Cohen et al., 1997), also provide some measure of the social-perceptual component.

Converging evidence for this componential model of theory of mind comes from studies of brain function. Support for this model of theory of mind may be drawn from research on the neurobiological substrate of what Leslie Brothers (1990) refers to as the "social brain." The primary areas of the brain that are involved in making social-perceptual judgments include the amygdala and associated regions of the medial temporal cortex. The amygdala is central to the processing of emotion (e.g., Adolphs, Tranel, Damasio, & Damasio, 1994; Adolphs, Tranel, & Damasio, 1998) and other complex social stimuli (Brothers, Ring, & Kling, 1990; Perrett et al., 1990). Functional brain-imaging studies show that the amygdala and associated areas of the medial temporal cortex are activated in tasks tapping the recognition of facial expressions of emotions and other mental states (Baron-Cohen et al., 1999; Breiter et al., 1996) and the perception of biological or intentional motion (Bonda, Petrides, Ostry, & Evans, 1996). The brain areas that subserve the social-cognitive component of theory of mind include regions in the prefrontal cortex. The orbito-frontal cortex is involved in reasoning about the social appropriateness of action (Eslinger & Damasio, 1985) and in making lexical judgments about cognitive mental-state terms (Baron-Cohen et al., 1994). Areas in the medial frontal cortex are closely associated with other theory-of-mind abilities, especially tasks tapping advanced social-cognitive capacities (Fletcher et al., 1995; Goel, Grafman, Sadato, & Hallett, 1995). In summary, there is preliminary evidence that different neural substrates underlie the components of theory of mind described here (see also Frith & Frith, 1999). These brain regions form a unified neural system for processing a range of social information from basic perception of intentional motion to inferring the contents of other people's minds.

Autism and the Componential Model of Theory of Mind

In the final sections of this chapter I return to reevaluate the theory of mind hypothesis of autism in light of this new model of theory of mind. The combination of both a componential and developmental framework provides a set of counterarguments to many of the criticisms with the theory-of-mind hypothesis of autism as it was initially articulated (Baron-Cohen et al., 1993) and summarized at the beginning of this chapter.

Within the componential model, the theory of mind hypothesis of autism clearly encompasses a significantly broader range of phenomena than the original metarepresentational theories (cf. Leslie & Roth, 1993; Perner, 1993). The roots of the impairments in autism may be seen in the social-orienting deficits that are evident in infants (Dawson, Meltzoff, Osterling, Rinaldi, & Brown, 1998; Klin, 1991; Osterling & Dawson, 1994), which are the foundation of the social-perceptual aspects of theory of mind. These deficits are correlated with their failure to perceive behavior in others as intentional or to appreciate others' perspectives, as exemplified in the joint-attention deficits that are among the hallmark symptoms of the disorder (Mundy & Sigman, 1989; Mundy, Sigman, & Kasari, 1990, 1993; Travis & Sigman, chap. 14, this volume). Thus, children with autism below the age of 3 demonstrate significant impairment in the range of behaviors that are among the early developments in the social-perceptual component of theory of mind (cf. Klin & Volkmar, 1993). Autism involves fundamental deficits in these aspects of theory of mind. Even older high-functioning people with autism or Asperger syndrome perform poorly on tasks that measure the ability to read mental states from the eye region of the face (Baron-Cohen et al., 1997) or the attribution of intentional and social significance to ambiguous visual stimuli (Klin, Schultz, & Cohen, 2000).

The majority of children with autism are also impaired on social-cognitive measures of theory of mind, as evidenced by their failure to pass false-belief tasks (cf. Baron-Cohen, 2000a; Baron-Cohen et al., 1985), or to explain human behavior using mental-state terms (Tager-Flusberg & Sullivan, 1994). From a developmental framework, these deficits in the cognitive aspects of theory of mind grow out of the earlier deficits in social-perception because these components are closely interconnected, with cognition building on social perception. At the same time, as noted earlier, false-belief measures of theory of mind, along with other experimental tasks, are limited in that they necessitate the grading of performance in an all-or-none or categorical way. There are other ways of tapping the cognitive components of theory of mind using continuous variables, thus emphasizing the kind of developmental perspective that is so important to this theory. For example, measures of discourse skills or other pragmatic abilities that depend on understanding other minds provide more sensitive measures of individual differences among children with autism (Tager-Flusberg, 1993). Tager-Flusberg and Anderson (1991) found that the ability to maintain a topic of conversation and to add new information to the ongoing discourse varied among children with autism, but that overall children with autism were significantly impaired in these abilities compared to matched controls with Down syndrome. Capps, Kehres, and Sigman (1998) demonstrated that this aspect of communicative competence is significantly correlated with false-belief performance in children with autism.

These kinds of noncategorical measures of theory of mind are also useful for exploring within population *developmental asynchronies* between theory-of-mind and other cognitive domains. This approach, referred to as the "fine-cuts approach" (Happé & Frith, 1996), provides additional evidence that cognitive aspects of theory of mind are specifically impaired in autism, in that the developmental patterns for this domain differ from other aspects of cognitive development. Thus, in our study of communicative competence in children with autism (Tager-Flusberg & Anderson, 1991), we found that communicative competence showed a different developmental trajectory compared with other aspects of language development, as measured by mean length of utterance (MLU). Specifically, while MLU showed continuing growth over the course of the study, the ability to add new information to a conversational topic showed no developmental changes after an initial period of growth (Tager-Flusberg & Anderson, 1991). In other studies of language-related aspects of theory of mind in autism, we found similar kinds of unique developmental asynchronies. For example, there are asynchronies between the development of form and function for several linguistic constructions, including personal pronouns and questions (Tager-Flusberg, 1994). Even among different functional uses of particular forms—such as negation, questions, and modal verbs—my data show that there are developmental asynchronies between those functions that do entail an understanding of other minds and those that do not (Tager-Flusberg, 1997). These language asynchronies are only found in children with autism and not in other populations, suggesting that this evidence provides strong support for the theory of mind hypothesis of autism.

Experimental studies also illustrate the fine-cuts approach to theory of mind in autism (cf. Happé, 1999). For example, children with autism are impaired in understanding minds as representational, but are unimpaired in their understanding of photographs as representations (Charman & Baron-Cohen, 1992; Leekam & Perner, 1991; Leslie & Thaiss, 1991). More broadly, Baron-Cohen (2000b) argued that while theory of mind (or folk psychology) is impaired in autism, folk physics (understanding the physical causes of events) is not. Taken together, this work showing that in autism we find uniquely asynchronous patterns of development in different cognitive domains is among the strongest evidence for the theory of mind hypothesis of autism.

At the same time, recall that one criticism of the theory of mind hypothesis is that there are some individuals with autism who do pass the cognitive tasks that tap a representational understanding of mind. How might we explain this on the model presented here? The cognitive component of theory of mind develops not only by building on the social-perceptual capacities that begin to emerge during infancy, but also in close interaction with other cognitive systems and information-processing capacities. One possibility is that those children with autism who pass false-belief tasks have acquired this cognitive capacity to interpret the contents of other minds via a different developmental pathway. Instead of building on earlier social-perceptual knowledge about the mental life of people, they rely exclusively on language (Tager-Flusberg, 1997, 2000) or on more general logical reasoning skills to "hack" out a solution to cognitively based theory-of-mind tasks (Happé et al., 1996; Leslie & Roth, 1993).

Support for the idea that children with autism may not develop theory-of-mind abilities in the same way as other children comes from several sources. Language ability, especially knowledge of sentential complements, is the single best predictor of false-belief performance for children with autism (Tager-Flusberg, 2000). Earlier, I discussed the hypothesis that failure on false-belief tasks may be the result of poor language rather than of impaired theory of mind. On the contrary, only those children with autism who have the requisite linguistic knowledge can pass these tasks because, more than other children, they are especially dependent on language for providing the bootstrap into theory of mind. Further evidence that people with autism who pass theory-of-mind tasks do so using nonsocial cognitive and linguistic mechanisms comes from brain-imaging studies. Happé and her colleagues found that adults with Asperger syndrome did not activate areas in the medial frontal cortex when listening to theory-of-mind stories, in contrast to normal adults (Happé et al., 1996). In these patients, theory of mind was associated with activation in frontal regions that are typically involved in general cognitive processing, located close to language-related areas in the left hemisphere.

I have outlined one proposal for how theory of mind develops in children with autism, within the framework of the componential model. On this model, autism is viewed as a disorder that is defined by fundamental impairments to the neurocognitive system that serves the social-perceptual component of theory of mind. The impairments are present during infancy, thus impeding the development of the ability to make online judgments of intentionality. In those individuals who have additional cognitive and linguistic deficits, the development of the social-cognitive component of theory of mind is also severely compromised. At the same time, children who have relatively good language and general cognitive and information-processing skills can acquire the capacity to pass tasks assessing a representational understanding of mind via these nonsocial cognitive routes.

Deficits in theory of mind are not unique to autism. As noted earlier, numerous populations have significant problems on false-belief tasks. How might we interpret these deficits in other populations, especially in comparison to children with autism? Although other groups of children are developmentally delayed on false-belief tasks, it appears that in autism the delays are more severe. For example, Happé (1995) found that children with autism were not likely to pass false-belief tasks until they reached at least a verbal mental age of 8 or 9 years, compared to age 4 for normally developing children. Children with mental retardation are also delayed (Yirmiya et al., 1998), but the mental age at which they pass these tasks is around 6 years (Tager-Flusberg, Sullivan, Joseph, & Joffre, 1999). Oral deaf children begin to pass false-belief tasks when they are about 7 years old (Gale et al., 1996). Although the research is fairly limited, it appears that there are differences in the rates of development in the social-cognitive component of theory of mind across different populations.

From a developmental perspective, I would argue that these differences in rate reflect differences in the developmental pathway. Thus, delays in passing false-belief tests are linked to different kinds of deficits in the various groups of children that have been tested. For example, in mental retardation, it may be that the areas of deficit that most delay the development of theory of mind are general cognitive and language skills. In oral deaf children, it is the lack of access to language, which primarily influences the social-cognitive component of theory of mind. And in blind children, the lack of access to facial information very early on affects the development of the social-perceptual component of theory of mind. These speculations lead to testable hypotheses that are based on the componential model of theory of mind.

Conclusions and Future Directions

Autism involves fundamental impairments in theory of mind. These impairments are evident early in development and are broad in scope. Reflecting back on the criticisms of the theory of mind hypothesis discussed earlier in this chapter, most were addressed in light of the componential model of theory of mind. Within this model we can explain many of the very early characteristics of autism that are evident long before the development of a representational understanding of mind. Furthermore, deficits in the online perception of mental states in other people are viewed as central and universal among people with autism across a wide age-range (Klin et al., 2000; Tager-Flusberg & Sullivan, 2000). While theory-of-mind deficits are not unique to autism, the etiology and developmental history of these deficits may be. Although performance on false-belief tasks may well be interpreted as being closely related to other cognitive systems, especially language or executive functions, these other domains cannot explain the full range of theory-of-mind problems that are evident even in toddlers with autism.

At the same time it is also clear that autism involves more than deficits in theory of mind, even within this broader componential framework. There are other features found in many people with autism that cannot be encompassed by the theory of mind hypothesis (cf. Happé, 1999; Plaisted, 2000). These include repetitive behaviors and obsessive interests in narrowly defined topics, excellent visual-spatial skills, savant abilities, and impaired language. Autism is a complex and heterogeneous disorder that should not be reduced to a single underlying cognitive impairment. From a genetic perspective we now know that several interacting independent genes cause autism. One current hypothesis is that each of these genes (which may vary from one individual to another) contributes to different components of the autism phenotype (Bailey, Phillips, & Rutter, 1996; Santangelo & Folstein, 1999; Szatmari, 1999). Thus we could not expect that there is a single underlying psychological deficit in a disorder caused by several different genes.

The complexity and heterogeneity of autism pose a significant challenge for our theoretical models. We must appreciate the variability of the many different features that together make up the syndrome of autism, and most especially to view them all within a developmental framework. Our future research exploring the development of theory-of-mind impairments in this population should be undertaken with a clearer understanding of the other characteristics that define the disorder. In turn, research on theory-of-mind in autism will continue to provide important insights into the underlying neurocognitive architecture for this specialized domain of human cognition.

ACKNOWLEDGMENTS

Preparation of this chapter was supported by grants from the National Institute on Deafness and Other Communication Disorders (RO1 DC 01234; PO1 DC 03610) and the National Institute on Neurological Diseases and Stroke (RO1 NS 38668).

Address for correspondence: Center for Research on Developmental Disorders, Eunice Kennedy Shriver Center, 200 Trapelo Road, Waltham, MA 02452. E-mail: htagerf@shriver.org.

REFERENCES

American Psychiatric Association. (1994). *DSM–IV: Diagnostic and statistic manual of mental disorders.* (4th ed.). Washington, DC: Author.

Adolphs, R., Tranel, D., Damasio, H., & Damasio, A. (1994). Impaired recognition of emotion in facial expressions following bilateral damage to the human amygdala. *Nature, 372,* 669–672.

Adolphs, R., Tranel, D., & Damasio, A. R. (1998). The human amygdala in social judgment. *Nature, 393,* 470–473.

Astington, J., Harris, P. L., & Olson, D. (Eds.). (1988). *Developing theories of mind.* Cambridge, UK: Cambridge University Press.

Bailey, A., Phillips W., & Rutter M. (1996). Autism: towards an integration of clinical, genetic, neuropsychological, and neurobiological perspectives. *Journal of Child Psychology and Psychiatry, 37,* 89–126.

Baldwin, D. (1993). Infants' ability to consult the speaker for clues to word reference. *Journal of Child Language, 20,* 395–418.

Baron-Cohen, S. (1987). Autism and symbolic play. *British Journal of Developmental Psychology, 5,* 139–148.

Baron-Cohen, S. (1988). Social and pragmatic deficits in autism: Cognitive or affective? *Journal of Autism and Developmental Disorders, 18,* 379–402.

Baron-Cohen, S. (1989). Do autistic children have obsessions and compulsions? *British Journal of Clinical Psychology, 28,* 193–200.

Baron-Cohen, S. (1994). How to build a baby that can read minds: Cognitive mechanisms in mindreading. *Cahiers de Psychologie Cognitive [Current Psychology of Cognition], 13,* 513–552.

Baron-Cohen, S. (1995). *Mindblindness: An essay on autism and theory of mind.* Cambridge, MA: MIT Press.

Baron-Cohen, S. (2000a). Theory of mind and autism: A fifteen year review. In S. Baron-Cohen, H. Tager-Flusberg, & D. J. Cohen (Eds.), *Understanding other minds: Perspectives from developmental cognitive neuroscience* (pp. 3–20). Oxford, UK: Oxford University Press.

Baron-Cohen, S. (2000b). Autism: Deficits in folk psychology exist alongside superiority in folk physics. In S. Baron-Cohen, H. Tager-Flusberg, & D. J. Cohen (Eds.), *Understanding other minds: Perspectives from developmental cognitive neuroscience* (pp. 73–82). Oxford, UK: Oxford University Press.

Baron-Cohen, S., Leslie, A. M., & Frith, U. (1985). Does the autistic child have a "theory of mind?" *Cognition, 21,* 37–46.

Baron-Cohen, S., Leslie, A. M., & Frith, U. (1986). Mechanical, behavioral, and intentional understanding of picture stories in autistic children. *British Journal of Developmental Psychology, 4,* 113–125.

Baron-Cohen, S., Tager-Flusberg, H., & Cohen, D. J. (Eds.). (1993). *Understanding other minds: Perspectives from autism.* Oxford, UK: Oxford University Press.

Baron-Cohen, S., Jolliffe, T., Mortimore, C., & Robertson, M. (1997). Another advanced test of theory of mind: Evidence from very high functioning adults with autism or Asperger Syndrome. *Journal of Child Psychology and Psychiatry, 38,* 813–822.

Baron-Cohen, S., Ring, H., Moriarty, J., Shmitz, P., Costa, D., & Ell, P. (1994). Recognition of mental state terms: A clinical study of autism, and a functional neuroimaging study of normal adults. *British Journal of Psychiatry, 165,* 640–649.

Baron-Cohen, S., Ring, H., Wheelwright, S., Bullmore, E. T., Brammer, M. J., Simons, A., & Williams, S. (1999). Social intelligence in the normal and autistic brain: An fMRI study. *European Journal of Neuroscience, 11,* 1891–1898.

Bartsch, K., & Wellman, H. (1995). *Children talk about the mind.* Oxford, UK: Oxford University Press.

Benson, G., Abbeduto, L., Short, K., Bibler-Nuccio, J., & Maas, F. (1993). Development of theory of mind in individuals with MR. *American Journal on Mental Retardation, 98,* 427–433.

Bloom, L., Rocissano, L., & Hood, L. (1976). Adult-child discourse: Developmental interaction between information processing and linguistic knowledge. *Cognitive Psychology, 8,* 521–552.

Bonda, E., Petrides, M., Ostry, D., & Evans, A. (1996). Specific involvement of human parietal systems and the amygdala in the perception of biological motion. *Journal of Neuroscience, 15,* 3737–3744.

Bonitatibus, G. (1988). What is said and what is meant in referential communication. In J. Astington, P. L. Harris, & D. Olson (Eds.), *Developing theories of mind* (pp. 326–338). Cambridge, UK: Cambridge University Press.

Breiter, H. C., Etcoff, N. L., Whalem, P. J., Kennedy, W. A., Rauch, S. L., Buckner, R. L., Strauss, M. M., Hyman, S. E., & Rosen, B. R. (1996). Response and habituation of the human amygdala during visual processing of facial expression. *Neuron, 17,* 875–887.

Brothers, L. (1990). The social brain: A project for integrating primate behaviour and neurophysiology in a new domain. *Concepts in Neuroscience, 1,* 27–51.

Brothers, L., Ring, B., & Kling, A. (1990). Responses of neurons in the macaque amygdala to complex social stimuli. *Behavioral Brain Research, 41,* 199–213.

Brown, R., Hobson, P., Lee, A., & Stevenson, J. (1997). Are there 'autistic-like' features in congenitally blind children? *Journal of Child Psychology and Psychiatry, 38,* 693–704.

Bruner, J., & Feldman, C. (1993). Theories of mind and the problem of autism. In S. Baron-Cohen, H. Tager-Flusberg, & D. J. Cohen (Eds.), *Understanding other minds: Perspectives from autism.* Oxford, UK: Oxford University Press.

Capps, L., Kehres, J., & Sigman, M. (1998). Conversational abilities among children with autism and children with developmental delays. *Autism, 2,* 325–344.

Carruthers, P., & Smith, P.K. (Eds.). (1996). Theories of theories of mind. Cambridge, UK: Cambridge University Press.

Cassidy, K., & Ballaraman, G. R. (1997). *Theory of mind ability in language delayed children.* Biennial Meeting of the Society for Research in Child Development, Washington, DC.

Charman, T. (2000). Theory of mind and the early diagnosis of autism. In S. Baron-Cohen, H. Tager-Flusberg, & D. Cohen (Eds.), *Understanding other minds: Perspectives from developmental cognitive neuroscience,* (2nd ed.) (pp. 422–441). Oxford, UK: Oxford University Press.

Charman, T., & Baron-Cohen, S. (1992). Understanding beliefs and drawings: A further test of the metarepresentation theory of autism. *Journal of Child Psychology and Psychiatry, 33,* 1105–1112.

Corcoran, R. (2000). Theory of mind in other clinical samples: Is a selective theory of mind deficit exclusive to autism? In S. Baron-Cohen, H. Tager-Flusberg, & D. J. Cohen (Eds.). *Understanding other minds: Perspectives from developmental cognitive neuroscience* (2nd ed.) (pp. 391–421). Oxford, UK: Oxford University Press.

Dahlgren, S., & Trillingsgaard, A. (1996). Theory of mind in non-retarded children with autism and Asperger's syndrome. A research note. *Journal of Child Psychology and Psychiatry, 37,* 759–763.

Dawson, G., & Adams, A. (1984). Imitation and social responsiveness in autistic children. *Journal of Abnormal Child Psychology, 12,* 209–226.

Dawson, G., Meltzoff, A. N., Osterling, J., Rinaldi, J., & Brown, E. (1998). Children with autism fail to orient to naturally occurring social stimuli. *Journal of Autism and Developmental Disorders, 28,* 479–485.

de Villiers, J. (2000). Language and theory of mind: What are the developmental relationships? In S. Baron-Cohen, H. Tager-Flusberg, & D. Cohen (Eds.), *Understanding other minds: Perspectives from developmental cognitive neuroscience,* (2nd ed.) (pp. 83–123). Oxford, UK: Oxford University Press.

de Villiers, J., & de Villiers, P. (2000). Linguistic determinism and false belief. In P. Mitchell & K. Riggs (Eds.), *Children's reasoning and the mind.* Hove, UK: Psychology Press.

Dennett, D. C. (1978). Beliefs about beliefs. *Behavioral and Brain Sciences, 1,* 568-570.

Eslinger, P., & Damasio, A. (1985). Severe disturbance of higher cognition after bilateral frontal lobe ablation: Patient EVR. *Neurology, 35,* 1731–41.

Fernald, A. (1989). Intonation and communicative intent in mothers' speech to infants: Is the melody the message? *Child Development, 60,* 1497–1510.

Fernald, A. (1993). Approval and disapproval: Infant responsiveness to vocal affect in familiar and unfamiliar languages. *Child Development, 64,* 657–674.

Flavell, J. H. (1999). Cognitive development: Children's knowledge about the mind. *Annual Review of Psychology, 50,* 21–45.

Flavell, J. H., Flavell, E. R., & Green, F. L. (1983). Development of the appearance–reality distinction. *Cognitive Psychology, 15,* 95–120.

Flavell, J. H., Green, F. L., & Flavell, E. R. (1998). The mind has a mind of its own: Developing knowledge about mental uncontrollability. *Cognitive Development, 13,* 127–138.

Fletcher, P. C., Happé, F., Frith, U., Baker, S. C., Dolan, R. J., Frackowiak, R. S. J., & Frith, C. D. (1995). Other minds in the brain: A functional imaging study of "theory of mind" in story comprehension. *Cognition, 57,* 109–128.

Fodor, J. A. (1992). A theory of the child's theory of mind. *Cognition, 44,* 283–296.

Frith, U. (1989). *Autism: Explaining the enigma.* Oxford, UK: Blackwell.

Frith, C. D., & Frith, U. (1999). Interacting minds: A biological basis. *Science, 286,* 1692–1695.

Frith, U., Happé, F., & Siddons, F. (1994). Autism and theory of mind in everyday life. *Social Development, 3,* 108–124.

Frith, U., Morton, J., & Leslie, A. M. (1991). The cognitive basis of a biological disorder: Autism. *Trends in Neurosciences, 14,* 433–438.

Gale, E., de Villiers, P., de Villiers, J., & Pyers, J. (1996). Language and theory of mind in oral deaf children. In A. Stringfellow, D. Cahana-Amitay, E. Hughes, & A. Zukowski (Eds.), *Proceedings of the 20th Annual Boston University Conference on Language Development, Vol. 1.* Somerville MA: Cascadilla Press.

Gillberg, C., Ehlers, S., Schaumann, H., Jakobsson, G., Dahlgren, S. O., Lindblom, R., Bagenholm, A., Tjuus, T., & Blinder, E. (1990). Autism under age 3 years: A clinical study of 28 cases referred for autistic symptoms in infancy. *Journal of Child Psychology and Psychiatry, 31,* 921–934.

Goel, V., Grafman, J., Sadato, N., & Hallett, M. (1995). Modeling other minds. *Neuroreport, 6,* 1741–1746.

Gopnik, A., & Wellman, H. (1994). The theory theory. In L. A. Hirschfeld & S. Gelman (Eds.), *Mapping the mind: Domain specificity in cognition and culture* (pp. 257–293). New York: Cambridge University Press.

Gopnik, A., Capps, L., & Meltzoff, A. (2000). Early theories of mind: What the theory theory can tell us about autism. In S. Baron-Cohen, H. Tager-Flusberg, & D. J. Cohen (Eds.), *Understanding other minds: Perspectives from developmental cognitive neuroscience* (2nd ed.) (pp. 50–72). Oxford, UK: Oxford University Press.

Gopnik, A., & Rosati, A. (1997). *Perception, cognition, and young children's reversal of ambiguous figures.* Biennial Meeting of the Society for Research in Child Development, Washington, DC.

Gordon, R. (1986). Folk psychology as simulation. *Mind and Language, 1,* 158–171.

Hale, C. M., & Tager-Flusberg, H. (1999). The influence of language on theory of mind: A training study. Manuscript under review.

Happé, F. (1993). Communicative competence and theory of mind in autism: A test of relevance theory. *Cognition, 48,* 101–119.

Happé, F. (1994a). An advanced test of theory of mind: Understanding of story characters' thoughts and feelings by able autistic, mentally handicapped, and normal children and adults. *Journal of Autism and Developmental Disorders, 24,* 129–154.

Happé, F. (1994b). *Autism: An introduction to psychological theory.* London: University College London Press.

Happé, F. (1995). The role of age and verbal ability in the theory of mind task performance of subjects with autism. *Child Development, 66,* 843–855.

Happé, F. (1999). Autism: Cognitive deficit or cognitive style? *Trends in Cognitive Sciences, 3,* 216–222.

Happé, F., & Frith, U. (1996). The neuropsychology of autism. *Brain, 119,* 1377–1400.

Happé, F., Ehlers, S., Fletcher, P., Frith, U., Johansson, M., Gillberg, C., Dolan, R., Frackowiak, R., & Frith, C. (1996). "Theory of mind" in the brain. Evidence from a PET scan study of Asperger Syndrome. *NeuroReport, 8,* 197–201.

Harris, P. L. (1992). From simulation to folk psychology: The case for development. *Mind and Language, 7,* 120–144.

Heyman, G., & Dweck, C. (1998). Children's thinking about traits: Implications for judgments of self and others. *Child Development, 69,* 391–403.

Jarrold, C. (1997). Pretend play in autism: Executive explanations. In J. Russell (Ed.), *Autism as an executive disorder* (pp. 101–140). Oxford, UK: Oxford University Press.

Johnson, M. H., & Morton, J. (1991). *Biology and cognitive development: The case of face recognition.* Oxford, UK: Blackwell.

Klin, A. (1991). Young autistic children's listening preferences in regard to speech: A possible characterization of the symptom of social withdrawal. *Journal of Autism and Developmental Disorders, 21,* 29–42.

Klin, A., & Volkmar, F. (1993). The development of individuals with autism: Implications for the theory of mind hypothesis. In S. Baron-Cohen, H. Tager-Flusberg, & D. J. Cohen (Eds.), *Understanding other minds: Perspectives from autism* (pp. 317–331). Oxford, UK: Oxford University Press.

Klin, A., Schultz, R., & Cohen, D. J. (2000). Theory of mind in action: Developmental perspectives on social neuroscience. In S. Baron-Cohen, H. Tager-Flusberg, & D. J. Cohen (Eds.), *Understanding other minds: Perspectives from developmental cognitive neuroscience* (2nd ed.) (pp. 357-388). Oxford, UK: Oxford University Press.

Leekam, S., & Perner, J. (1991). Does the autistic child have a metarepresentational deficit? *Cognition, 40,* 203–218.

Leslie, A. M. (1987). Pretense and representation: The origins of "theory of mind." *Psychological Review, 94,* 412–426.

Leslie, A. M., & Roth, D. (1993). What autism teaches us about metarepresentation. In S. Baron-Cohen, H. Tager-Flusberg, & D. J. Cohen (Eds.), *Understanding other minds: Perspectives from autism* (pp. 83–111). Oxford, UK: Oxford University Press.

Leslie, A. M., & Thaiss, L. (1992). Domain specificity in conceptual development: Evidence from autism. *Cognition, 43,* 225–251.

Lewis, C., & Mitchell, P. (Eds.). (1994). *Children's early understanding of mind: Origins and development.* Hillsdale, NJ: Lawrence Erlbaum Associates.

Mant, C., & Perner, J. (1989). The child's understanding of commitment. *Developmental Psychology, 24,* 343–351.

Mehler, J., & Dupoux, E. (1994). *What infants know: The new cognitive science of early development.* Oxford, UK: Blackwell.

Meltzoff, A., Gopnik, A., & Repacholi, B. (1999). Toddlers' understanding of intentions, desires, and emotions: Explorations of the dark ages. In P. Zelazo, J. Astington, & D. Olson (Eds.), *Developing theories of intention: Social understanding and self-control* (pp.17–41). Mahwah, NJ: Lawrence Erlbaum Associates.

Miller, C. (2000). False belief understanding in children with specific language impairment. *Journal of Communication Disorders.*

Mitchell, P., & Lacohée, H. (1991). Children's early understanding of false belief. *Cognition, 39,* 107–127.

Moses, L., & Flavell, J. (1990). Inferring false beliefs from actions and reactions. *Child Development, 61,* 929–945.

Mundy, P., & Sigman, M. (1989). Specifying the nature of the social impairment in autism. In G. Dawson (Ed.), *Autism: Nature, diagnosis and treatment.* New York: Guilford.

Mundy, P., Sigman, M., & Kasari, C. (1990). A longitudinal study of joint attention and language development in autistic children. *Journal of Autism and Developmental Disorders, 20,* 115–123.

Mundy, P., Sigman, M., & Kasari, C. (1993). The theory of mind and joint-attention deficits in autism. In S. Baron-Cohen, H. Tager-Flusberg, & D. J. Cohen (Eds.), *Understanding other minds: Perspectives from autism* (pp. 181–203). Oxford, UK: Oxford University Press.

Ornitz, E., Guthrie, D., & Farley, A. (1977). Early development of autistic children. *Journal of Autism and Childhood Schizophrenia, 7,* 207–229.

Osterling, J., & Dawson, G. (1994). Early recognition of children with autism: A study of first birthday home videotapes. *Journal of Autism and Developmental Disorders, 24,* 247–257.

Pennington, B. (1999). Dyslexia as a neurodevelopmental disorder. In H. Tager-Flusberg (Ed.), *Neurodevelopmental disorders* (pp. 307–330). Cambridge, MA: MIT Press.

Perner, J. (1988). Higher-order beliefs and intentions in children's understanding of social interaction. In J. Astington, P. L. Harris, & D. Olson (Eds.), *Developing theories of mind* (pp. 271–294). Cambridge, UK: Cambridge University Press.

Perner, J. (1993). The theory of mind deficit in autism: Rethinking the metarepresentation theory. In S. Baron-Cohen, H. Tager-Flusberg, & D. J. Cohen (Eds.), *Understanding other minds: Perspectives from autism* (pp. 112–137). Oxford, UK: Oxford University Press

Perner, J., Leekam, S., & Wimmer, H., (1987). Three-year-olds' difficulty with false belief. *British Journal of Developmental Psychology, 5,* 125–137.

Perrett, D., Harries, M., Mistlin, A., Hietanen, J., Benson, P., Bevan, R., Thomas, S., Oram, M., Ortega, J., & Brierley, K. (1990). Social signals analyzed at the single cell level: Someone is looking at me, something touched me, something moved! *International Journal of Comparative Psychology, 4,* 25–55.

Peterson, C., & Siegal, M. (1995). Deafness, conversation and theory of mind. *Journal of Child Psychology and Psychiatry, 36,* 459–474.

Peterson, C., & Siegal, M. (1998). Changing focus on the representational mind: Deaf, autistic and normal children's concepts of false photos, false drawings and false beliefs. *British Journal of Developmental Psychology, 16,* 301–320.

Pillow, B. H. (1991). Children's understanding of biased social cognition. *Developmental Psychology, 27,* 539–551.

Plaisted, K. (2000). Aspects of autism that theory of mind cannot easily explain. In S. Baron-Cohen, H. Tager-Flusberg, & D. J. Cohen (Eds.), *Understanding other minds: Perspectives from developmental cognitive neuroscience* (2nd Ed.) (pp. 222–250). Oxford, UK: Oxford University Press.

Premack, D., & Woodruff, G. (1978). Does the chimpanzee have a "theory of mind?" *Behavioral and Brain Sciences, 1,* 515–526.

Repacholi, B. (1998). Infants' use of attentional cues to identify the referent of another person's emotional expression. *Developmental Psychology, 34,* 1017–1025.

Repacholi, B., & Gopnik, A. (1997). Early reasoning about desires: Evidence from 14- and 18-month-olds. *Developmental Psychology, 33,* 12–21.

Russell, J. (1997). How executive disorders can bring about an inadequate 'theory of mind.' In J. Russell (Ed.), *Autism as an executive disorder* (pp. 256–304). Oxford, UK: Oxford University Press.

Russell, P., Hosie, J. A., Gray, C., Scott, C., Hunter, N., Banks, J., & Macaulay, M. (1998). The development of theory of mind in deaf children. *Journal of Child Psychology and Psychiatry, 39,* 903–910.

Santangelo, S., & Folstein S. E. (1999). Autism: A genetic perspective. In H. Tager-Flusberg (Ed.), *Neurodevelopmental disorders* (pp. 431–447). Cambridge, MA: MIT Press.

Shatz, M. (1994). *A toddler's life: Becoming a person.* New York: Oxford University Press.

Shatz, M., & Gelman, R. (1977). Beyond syntax: The influence of conversational constraints on speech modifications. In C. E. Snow & C. A. Ferguson (Eds.), *Talking to children* (pp. 189–198). Cambridge, UK: Cambridge University Press.

Shatz, M., & O'Reilly, A. (1990). Conversational or communicative skill? A reassessment of two-year-olds' behavior in miscommunication episodes. *Journal of Child Language, 17,* 131–146.

Sparrevohn, R., & Howie, P. (1995). Theory of mind children with autistic disorder: Evidence of developmental progression and the role of verbal ability. *Journal of Child Psychology and Psychiatry, 36,* 249–263.

Sullivan, K., & Winner, E. (1993). Three-year-olds' understanding of mental states: The influence of trickery. *Journal of Experimental Child Psychology, 56,* 135–148.

Sullivan, K., Winner, E., & Hopfield, N. (1995). How children tell a joke from a lie: The role of second-order mental state attributions. *British Journal of Developmental Psychology, 13,* 191–204.

Szatmari, P. (1999). Heterogeneity and the genetics of autism. *Journal of Psychiatry and Neuroscience, 24,* 159–165.

Tager-Flusberg, H. (1992). Autistic children's talk about psychological states: Deficits in the early acquisition of a theory of mind. *Child Development, 63,* 161–172.

Tager-Flusberg, H. (1993). What language reveals about the understanding of minds in children with autism. In S. Baron-Cohen, H. Tager-Flusberg, & D. J. Cohen (Eds.), *Understanding other minds: Perspectives from autism.* Oxford, UK: Oxford University Press.

Tager-Flusberg, H. (1994). Dissociations in form and function in the acquisition of language by autistic children. In H. Tager-Flusberg (Ed.), *Constraints on language acquisition: Studies of atypical children* (pp. 175–194). Hillsdale, NJ: Lawrence Erlbaum Associates.

Tager-Flusberg, H. (1997). The role of theory of mind in language acquisition: Contributions from the study of autism. In L. Adamson & M. A. Romski (Eds.), *Communication and language acquisition: Discoveries from atypical development* (pp. 133–158). Baltimore, MD: Paul Brookes Publishing.

Tager-Flusberg, H. (1999). A psychological approach to understanding the social and language impairments in autism. *International Review of Psychiatry, 11,* 325–334.

Tager-Flusberg, H. (2000). Language and understanding minds: Connections in autism. In S. Baron-Cohen, H. Tager-Flusberg, & D. J. Cohen (Eds.), *Understanding other minds: Perspectives from developmental cognitive neuroscience* (2nd ed.) (pp. 124–149). Oxford, UK: Oxford University Press.

Tager-Flusberg, H., & Anderson, M. (1991). The development of contingent discourse ability in autistic children. *Journal of Child Psychology and Psychiatry, 32,* 1123–1134.

Tager-Flusberg, H., & Sullivan, K. (1994). Predicting and explaining behavior: A comparison of autistic, mentally retarded, and normal children. *Journal of Child Psychology and Psychiatry, 35,* 1059–1075.

Tager-Flusberg, H., & Sullivan, K. (2000). A componential view of theory of mind: Evidence from Williams syndrome. *Cognition, 76,* 59–89.

Tager-Flusberg, H., Sullivan, K., Joseph, R., & Joffre, K. (1999). False belief understanding in individuals with mental retardation. Unpublished manuscript, Eunice Kennedy Shriver Center.

Volkmar, F., Sparrow, S., Goudreau, D., Cicchetti, D. V., Paul, R., & Cohen, D. J. (1987). Social deficits in autism: An operational approach using the Vineland Adaptive Behavior Scales. *Journal of the American Academy of Child Psychiatry, 26,* 156–161.

Wellman, H. (1990). *The child's theory of mind.* Cambridge, MA: MIT Press.

Wellman, H., & Estes, D. (1986). Early understanding of mental entities: A reexamination of childhood realism. *Child Development, 57,* 910–923.

Wellman, H., & Bartsch, K. (1988). Young children's reasoning about beliefs. *Cognition, 30,* 239–277.

Wellman, H., Cross, D., & Watson, J. K. (1999, April). *A meta-analysis of theory of mind development: The truth about false-belief.* Biennial Meeting of the Society for Research in Child Development, Albuquerque, NM.

Wellman, H., & Lagattuta, K. H. (2000). Developing understandings of mind. In S. Baron-Cohen, H. Tager-Flusberg, & D. J. Cohen (Eds.), *Understanding other minds: Perspectives from developmental cognitive neuroscience* (2nd ed.) (pp. 21–49). Oxford, UK: Oxford University Press.

Wimmer, H., & Perner, J. (1983). Beliefs about beliefs: Representation and constraining function of wrong beliefs in young children's understanding of deception. *Cognition, 13,* 103–128.

Woodward, A. (1996). *Infants' reasoning about the goals of a human actor.* International Society for Infant Studies, Providence, RI.

Yirmiya, N., Erel, O., Shaked, M., & Solomonica-Levi, D. (1998). Meta-analyses comparing theory of mind abilities of individuals with autism, individuals with mental retardation, and normally developing individuals. *Psychological Bulletin, 124,* 283–307.

Yuill, N. (1993). Understanding of personality and dispositions. In M. Bennett (Ed.), *The development of social cognition: The child as psychologist* (pp. 87–110). New York: Guilford.

Yuill, N. (1997). Children's understanding of traits. In S. Hala (Ed.), *The development of social cognition* (pp. 273–295). Hove, UK: Psychology Press.

Zaitchik, D. (1991). Is only seeing really believing? Sources of true belief in the false belief task. *Cognitive Development, 6,* 91–103.

Zelazo, P., Burack, J., Benedetto, E., & Frye, D. (1996). Theory of mind and rule use in individuals with Down's syndrome: A test of the uniqueness and specificity claims. *Journal of Child Psychology and Psychiatry, 37,* 479–484.

10

A Cognitive Complexity and Control Framework for the Study of Autism

Philip David Zelazo
University of Toronto, Ontario, Canada
Jacob A. Burack
McGill University, Montreal, Quebec, Canada
Janet J. Boseovski
Queen's University, Kingston, Ontario, Canada
Sophie Jacques
University of Toronto, Ontario, Canada
Douglas Frye
University of Pennsylvania, Philadelphia

Introduction: Autism and Theory of Mind

Typical development serves as a standard that can be used to assess the occurrence and severity of deviance and delay in various atypical populations. In turn, the study of atypical development informs our understanding of typical development—for example, by allowing researchers to identify necessary relations among cognitive structures (Cicchetti, 1984; Hodapp & Burack, 1990). One area that well illustrates the mutually beneficial nature of the typical–atypical relation is research on *theory of mind*—the ability to attribute mental states to oneself and to others (e.g., Astington, 1993). In a seminal article, Baron-Cohen, Leslie, and Frith (1985) reported that high-functioning individuals with autism performed worse than did mental-age-matched individuals with Down Syndrome on a test of theory of mind. A subsequent study (Baron-Cohen, Leslie, & Frith, 1986) reported that the same individuals with autism were impaired on theory-of-mind tasks but not on other types of task, such as a mechanical (physical) causality task in which reasoning about mental states was not required.

Based on these and other findings (see Baron-Cohen, 2000, for a review), two claims have been made regarding the nature of autism (e.g., by Baron-Cohen, 1995; Frith, Morton, & Leslie, 1991). The first claim, referred to as the Specificity Claim, is that autism involves a domain-specific deficit in theory of mind. The second claim, called the Uniqueness Claim, is that this deficit is unique to individuals with autism and hence is able to account for the social and communicative impairments associated with autism. These claims are important because they offer a characterization of autism that points toward a particular etiology. That is, if true, they imply that the symptoms of autism result from a failure to develop a theory of mind. In addition, these claims have broad implications regarding the general nature of human cognitive architecture and its development. For example, they imply that under normal circumstances, theory of mind is a domain-specific and potentially dissociable (i.e., independent) cognitive function. Moreover, because autism appears to be a neurological disorder with a genetic basis (e.g., Bailey et al., 1995), these claims suggest that theory of mind is innate and has a dedicated neurological locus. Thus, the Specificity and Uniqueness claims, if true, provide prima facie support for the modularity approach to theory of mind (e.g., Baron-Cohen, 1995; Leslie, 1991), and for modularity theory (e.g., Fodor, 1983), more generally.

According to Fodor (1983), some aspects of human cognitive architecture are modular—that is, some cognitive functions are accomplished by mental modules. A *mental module* is an information-processing device that accepts a specific type of information as its input and processes this information in isolation from the rest of the cognitive system. The visual system provides a good example; its modularity is indicated by optical illusions, which tend to be unaffected by general knowledge (e.g., knowledge that a particular illusion is an illusion). Fodor argues that mental modules are characterized by domain specificity, informational encapsulation, obligatory firing, shallow outputs, rapid speed, inaccessibility to consciousness, a characteristic ontogenetic course, a dedicated neural architecture, and a characteristic pattern of breakdown. Baron-Cohen (1994) argues that theory of mind exhibits six of these criteria (domain specificity, obligatory firing, rapid speed, a characteristic ontogenetic course, a dedicated neural architecture, and a characteristic pattern of breakdown), and suggests that the remaining criteria are really neither necessary nor sufficient for modularity.

Perhaps emboldened by evidence that seems to support the Specificity and Uniqueness Claims, researchers have since postulated the existence of numerous other cognitive modules in addition to a theory-of-mind module. Baron-Cohen (1994; 1995), for example, describes an Intentionality Detector (ID) that reads stimuli in terms of volition, an Eye-Direction Detector (EDD) that detects the presence of eyes, and a Shared Attention Mechanism (SAM) that identifies joint-attention behavior. Similarly, Leslie (1994) suggests that children's understanding of physical causality has its basis in the growth of a Theory of Body mechanism (ToBY), and Blair (1995) proposes that individuals who are psychopathic fail to inhibit violence because they have defective Violence Inhibition Mechanisms (VIMs). As Tooby and Cosmides note in their introduction to Baron-Cohen's (1995) book, "On this view, our cognitive architecture resembles a confederation of hundreds or thousands of functionally dedicated computers (often called modules) designed to solve adaptive problems endemic to our hunter gatherer ancestors. Each of these devices has its own agenda and imposes its own exotic organization on different fragments of the world" (p. xiv).

The idea of modularity as proposed by Fodor (1983) and employed (in modified form) by Baron-Cohen (1994) stands in sharp contrast to traditional developmental theories, which describe the acquisition (and refinement) of cognitive structures that operate across broad domains of knowledge (e.g., Piaget, 1970; Werner, 1957). However, most contemporary cognitive developmental theories (e.g., Case & Okamoto, 1996; Elman, Bates, Johnson, Karmiloff-Smith, & Plunkett, 1996; Halford, Wilson, & Phillips, 1998; Fischer, 1980; Frye, Zelazo, & Burack, 1998; Zelazo & Frye, 1998) represent some degree of synthesis between traditional domain-general accounts of development and the idea of modularity. These theories tend to emphasize complex developmental interactions between relatively general cognitive skills (such as reasoning and problem solving) and the acquisition of knowledge about particular topics. In contrast to the broad developmental reorganizations predicted by traditional theories or the cross-domain variability predicted by modularity theory, these theories predict coherence across different domains of knowledge along with developmental unevenness.

A number of these interactionist approaches to cognitive development have been used to explain the development of theory of mind, and several other proposed accounts of theory of mind are generally consistent with the interactionist perspective. For example, Russell, Hughes, and colleagues (e.g., Hughes & Russell, 1993; Russell, Mauthner, Sharpe, & Tidswell, 1991) proposed that theory of mind (or at least performance on theory-of-mind tasks) depends in part on inhibitory control, or the ability to disengage from salient aspects of a situation. Pennington, Ozonoff, and colleagues (e.g., Bennetto, Pennington, & Rogers, 1996; Ozonoff, 1997; Ozonoff, Pennington, & Rogers, 1991; Pennington, 1994; Pennington et al., 1997) offered similar proposals, although they have emphasized the importance of memory (especially working memory) as opposed to inhibition. Working memory also figures prominently in Olson's (Gordon & Olson, 1998; Olson, 1993) and Halford's (Halford, Wilson, & Phillips, 1998) accounts of theory of mind, both of which view the growth of memory as a prerequisite for the ability to consider multiple representations or relations simultaneously (see also Flavell, 1988).

Clearly, the picture of human cognitive architecture and its development that is provided by these interactionist theories differs markedly from that provided by modularity theory. The two types of theory also provide markedly different characterizations of autism—characterizations with important implications for etiology and, perhaps, intervention. Thus, in addition to providing an important test case that allows us to distinguish between these two approaches, a careful consideration of the evidence for the Specificity and Uniqueness claims about theory of mind in autism will constrain speculation regarding the etiology of autism and related disorders.

In this chapter, we review and evaluate arguments for modularity in the context of neuropsychological theory and the broader field of developmental psychopathology, and assess evidence for the Specificity and Uniqueness claims regarding theory of mind and autism. Because evidence for the Specificity and Uniqueness claims is found to be wanting, we review evidence for domain-general cognitive impairments in autism (in particular, executive-function impairments) and describe an alternative framework for conceptualizing typical and atypical development—the Cognitive Complexity and Control (CCC) theory (e.g., Frye et al., 1998; Frye, Zelazo, & Palfai, 1995; Zelazo, P. D., & Frye, 1997, 1998).

Arguments Used in Support of Modularity

Although Fodor (1983) argued that modules are key components of human cognitive architecture, he maintained that they are not the only ones. Indeed, he claimed that if modules exist, then there must also be central processes that operate across these modules. Normally, then, these central processes correspond to higher level cognitive functions. Not all higher level cognitive functions are accomplished by central processes, however. For example, Fodor (1992) expects that theory of mind " ... is, essentially, an innate, modularized database" (p. 284). The proposal that modularity might characterize higher level cognitive processes is certainly plausible, but in the end, it is an empirical claim. We now turn to a brief consideration of relevant empirical findings from neuropsychology and developmental psychopathology.

Neuropsychological Evidence.

Semantic memory is a prime example of a higher level function, and research on the consequences of focal brain lesions has revealed numerous domain-specific cognitive impairments in semantic memory (e.g., Schechter, 1953; Warrington, 1975; Warrington & Shallice, 1984). For example, Shelton, Fouch, and Caramazza (1998) reported a case study of a woman with neurological damage who had preserved ability to comprehend and produce names of body parts despite widespread impairments in the naming and comprehension of other semantic categories. The presence of domain-specific impairments (animal words vs. tool words; body parts vs. other categories) clearly indicates that certain very similar skills are dissociable in human adults, and it appears to indicate that these skills are organized according to content domains—at both the psychological and the neurological levels. These impairments are thought to suggest that the skills in question correspond to domain-specific, modular functions (e.g., Caramazza & Shelton, 1998). Thus, different, independent neurological mechanisms are inferred to be prededicated to processing information about the different content domains.

However, this inference is problematic in the absence of additional evidence for modularity. Goldberg (1995) notes that some category-specific effects may arise from damage to graded, distributed representations (cf. Munakata, McClelland, Johnson, & Seigler, 1997). Representations of items from some categories are likely to be more multimodal than items from other categories, and consequently more robust in the face of neurological insult. For example, because function is the defining dimension of artifacts (such as tools), people's representations of artifacts likely involve somatosensory and motor information in addition to visual information. Representations of natural kinds, on the other hand, are less likely to include somatosensory and motor information. Goldberg suggests that the relatively multimodal nature of artifact representations may explain why names of natural kinds such as animate objects are relatively vulnerable to disruption in anomias or agnosias (e.g., Warrington & Shallice, 1984).

Goldberg (1995) also notes that some degree of neurocognitive localization may be an emergent property of an interactive self-organizing functional system—in other words, it may correspond to emergent modularization rather than to modularity (cf. Johnson, 1999; Karmiloff-Smith, 1992; Moscovitch & Ulmita, 1990). Elman et al. (1996) suggest that neural plasticity during brain development supports this possibility. In nonhuman animals, changing the sensory input to specialized areas of the brain early in development can change the eventual specialization of those areas. Similarly, in human beings, significant recovery of function can occur after cortical damage, especially when the trauma occurs early in life. This plasticity is difficult to explain if the functions are innate and their neurological localization is predetermined. Elman et al. also review demonstrations from connectionist modeling showing that it is possible for specialized processing to emerge from initially undifferentiated networks. These demonstrations, together with the evidence regarding plasticity, show that emergent modularization rather than modularity could be responsible for specialized and localized processing in adult cognition.

To the extent that particular functions are located in similar brain areas under normal circumstances (i.e., in cases of typical development), it is reasonable to conclude that certain developmental outcomes are more likely than others. However, instead of being inevitable, these outcomes may simply be the likely consequences of interactions between environmental input and constraints imposed by the developing organism itself (Johnson, 1999). Indeed, according to Goldberg (1995), the notion of an interactive self-organizing functional cortical system makes sense both neuroanatomically and evolutionarily. Goldberg (1995) writes:

> Throughout evolution, the emphasis has shifted from the brain invested with rigid, fixed functions (thalamus) to the brain capable of flexible adaptation (cortex). The advent of neocortex may have represented an evolutionary repudiation of strong

> modularity as the dominant principle of neural organization, and a shift toward a more interactive principle of neural organization dominated by emergent properties (p. 203).

In any case, however, evidence of psychological and neurological specialization in adults does not imply modularity—does not imply the existence of innate neurological structures dedicated to the processing of information about particular topics.

Unevenness in Atypical Development. Prima facie support for modularity also comes from research on atypical populations, which are often characterized by uneven profiles of cognitive strengths and weaknesses (e.g., Burack, 1997; Hodapp & Burack, 1990). For example, people with Williams syndrome exhibit better performance on tests of language processing than they do on tests of other skills, such as nonverbal cognition (e.g., Bellugi, Wang, & Jernigan, 1994; though see Karmiloff-Smith et al., 1998, for limitations of syntactic skill in Williams syndrome). Because these profiles reveal differences in performance across different areas of functioning, they might be taken as evidence of the existence of modules.

Such patterns can also be considered within the context of an organismic developmental framework, however. For example, Cicchetti and his colleagues (e.g., Cicchetti & Pogge-Hesse, 1982; Cicchetti & Sroufe, 1978) suggested that the uneven patterns of development evident in atypical populations reveal the limits to which certain developmental links might be stretched, but still be maintained, within an organized developing system. From this perspective, different areas of functioning can be interrelated even when developmental profiles are uneven, because the variability across areas is still subject to the organizational principles of the overarching developmental system (Burack, 1997; Cicchetti & Pogge-Hesse, 1982).

Both the principles that link different areas of function and the areas themselves may be different from those that are typically identified in contemporary developmental research. For example, Hodapp and colleagues (e.g., Hodapp & Zigler, 1995) describe local homologies of shared origin (Bates, Benigni, Bretherton, Camaioni, & Volterra, 1979), which involve two or more behaviors that share a single underlying scheme or cognitive function and, consequently, are subject to developmental changes that occur relatively synchronously. Consistent with this framework, the development of means–end behaviors with objects is related to early intentional communication in typically developing children as well as in children with autism and children with mental retardation (Hodapp & Zigler, 1995). Similarly, changes in level of early language (one-word sentences to multiword utterances) are associated with changes in symbolic play (single-schemed play to multischemed play) in all three groups (Hodapp & Zigler, 1995).

Within this framework, domain-general deficits that occur early in life can result in severe disturbances in apparently distinct aspects of behavior years later. Sometimes this outcome occurs because simple skills become hierarchically integrated into more complex skills. For example, problems in attention in early childhood are related to later impairments in social skills such as the ability to modulate behaviors with regard to peers' activities and adult demands (Coldren & Corradetti, 1997). However, all skills, regardless of complexity, are assumed to interrelate in complicated ways during the course of development, with the consequence that level of impairment at one point in time may not be proportional to level of impairment at a later point in time.

This framework, according to which (a) development is constrained by organizational principles, (b) there are interactions among many influences on development, and (c) there are complex interactions in development among different aspects of psychological function, allows us to understand how difficulty in one area of function can lead not only to difficulty in other areas, but also, occasionally, to strengths (Happé, 1996, 1999, chap. 12, this volume; Mottron & Burack, chap. 7, this volume).

Two General Questions Concerning Modular Human Cognitive Architecture

Modules are by definition domain specific because they respond only to a certain class of inputs and not to other types of input (e.g., Fodor, 1983). However, there is currently no consensus regarding the definition of a domain (Hirschfeld & Gelman, 1994), and it is often unclear how to establish the domain specificity of a putative module. For example, Maratsos (1992) suggests that " ... a domain means any organized content area in which one might imagine or propose there being innate, specific distinctive mechanisms of ideas" (p. 4). In contrast, Hirschfeld and Gelman (1994) define a domain as "a body of knowledge that identifies and interprets a class of phenomena assumed to share certain properties and to be of a distinct and general type" (p. 21). According to the latter definition, a domain corresponds to knowledge, whereas according to the former definition, it corresponds to an object of knowledge (a "content area"). These definitions are pretheoretical—referring as they do to a content area that one "might imagine" to have certain properties and to knowledge that one "assumes" to share such properties—and they leave several questions unanswered. For example, how many domains exist? And, are there domains within domains? (e.g., Is syntax a separate domain within the domain of language? Is physical causation a domain within the domain of causal phenomena?).

In the absence of answers, modularity theory would appear to be stopped at the start by an inability to provide a precise definition of its subject matter. Taking an evolutionary perspective promises to shed light on this problem by grounding definitions of domains in specific adaptive problems (Cosmides & Tooby, 1994). However, a good deal of uncertainty is likely to remain. For example, in a list of domain-specific adaptive problems that human beings allegedly faced in the course of evolution, Cosmides and Tooby (1994) include "allocating effort between activities." In what sense is this domain specific?

Even in cases where domains can be reasonably well specified, however, researchers often fail to establish that information about that domain is processed by a module. For example, Baron-Cohen (1994, 1995) attempts to show that ID and EDD (both components of a larger modular "mindreading" system) meet the criteria for modularity, but in attempting to do so, he conflates the specificity of a domain with the domain specificity of his mechanism. Thus, as evidence that his putative modules exhibit domain specificity, Baron-Cohen (1994) writes that "stimuli with direction, and self-propelling stimuli, appear to be a reasonably well-defined domain" (sect. 1.1) and that, "Eye-like stimuli certainly constitute a well-defined domain" (sect. 2.1). Quite apart from the fact that such assertions are pretheoretical in the sense just described, they are completely inadequate to establish the domain specificity of a mechanism. As Jacques and Zelazo (1994) point out, the ease of defining a particular domain is irrelevant to whether that domain is processed by a specific or general mechanism. Instead, it is necessary to establish whether or not a mechanism responds exclusively to a specific class of input, and this is far more difficult to do.

Modularity and Theory of Mind: A Critical Look at the Evidence for the Specificity and Uniqueness Claims

Leaving aside the theoretical difficulties surrounding claims about modularity in general, and bearing in mind the fact there is little direct evidence for the modularity of higher level cognitive processes, we now turn to the empirical evidence for the Specificity and Uniqueness claims regarding theory of mind and autism. This evidence is the basis of arguments for the modularity of theory of mind in autism.

Baron-Cohen et al. (1985) found that, unlike typically developing 5-year-old children and children with Down syndrome, relatively high-functioning individuals with autism failed to attribute a false belief to a protagonist. Similarly, Baron-Cohen et al. (1986) determined that these individuals with autism performed as well as, or better than, individuals with Down syndrome and normal preschoolers on causal mechanical or behavioral picture-sequencing tasks, but worse on sequences in which they were required to ascribe intentional states to a protagonist. More recently, Scott and Baron-Cohen (1996) reported that children with autism performed comparably to typically developing children and children with mental retardation on tests of transitive inference and analogical reasoning, but performed significantly worse on a false-belief task. Scott, Baron-Cohen, and

Leslie (1999) extended these findings to include a test of counterfactual reasoning, with and without prompts to pretend, and found that in the absence of pretense prompts, individuals with autism performed well relative to control participants. Finally, Leekam and Perner (1991) established that children with autism, but not typically developing children, performed worse on a false-belief task than on a false-photograph task, which requires reasoning about outdated physical representations, but not mental representations. This basic pattern was also found by Leslie and Thaiss (1992) and by Charman and Baron-Cohen (1992, 1995).

At first glance, these findings appear to provide support for both the Specificity and the Uniqueness claims, and consequently, for the hypothesis that individuals with autism have an impaired theory-of-mind module. However, this interpretation can be questioned for several reasons. For example, Baron-Cohen et al. (1985) only assessed theory of mind, so the group differences may be attributed to more general cognitive deficits that lead to difficulty on theory of mind. In other words, this finding on its own does not provide evidence of specificity, although it does speak to the issue of uniqueness insofar as there was no difference between the individuals with Down syndrome and the typically developing children (see Charman & Lynggaard, 1998, for discussion). However, this latter aspect of the results was not supported in subsequent studies. Consistent with the results of a comprehensive meta-analysis (Yirmiya, Erel, Shaked, & Solomonica-Levi, 1998), children with mental retardation also exhibit deficits in theory of mind relative to their mental age (e.g., Benson, Abbeduto, Short, Nuccio, & Mass, 1993; Charman & Lynggaard, 1998; Yirmiya, Solomonica-Levi, Shulman, & Pilowsky, 1996; Zelazo, Burack, Benedetto, & Frye, 1996), although these deficits appear to be less severe than among individuals with autism (Yirmiya et al., 1998).

The claim that deficits in theory of mind are domain specific (Baron-Cohen et al., 1986) also has not been supported by subsequent empirical research. Oswald and Ollendick (1989) found no differences in the Baron-Cohen et al. (1986) picture-sequencing task when they compared a relatively low-functioning group of individuals with autism to an age- and nonverbal-IQ-matched group of mentally retarded adolescents. Similarly, Ozonoff et al. (1991) found no group differences on the intentional subtest (i.e., the theory-of-mind items) in a study with a relatively large group of high-functioning individuals with autism who were compared to a well-matched clinical control group. However, the comparison group performed better on each of the mechanical subtests (i.e., the physical causality items) and on one of the two behavioral subtests.

A primary premise in the assessment of claims regarding cross-domain differences in performance is that the tasks test different abilities but are of the same underlying complexity. Failure to meet this assumption is problematic because performance on complex tasks may be more sensitive to disruption for several reasons. At a minimum, these reasons include the fact that simpler behaviors are more likely to be automatized, complex behaviors comprise multiple simple behaviors and consequently provide more opportunities for performance to break down, and complex or difficult tasks are more likely to elicit overwhelming stress (perhaps especially in individuals with autism; see Rogers, Zelazo, Mendelson, & Rotsztein, 1998). Thus, the failure to account explicitly for complexity across tasks in various studies cited in support of specific deficits in mental-state understanding (Baron-Cohen et al., 1986; Russell, Saltmarsh, & Hill, 1999; Scott & Baron-Cohen, 1996; Scott et al., 1999) considerably weakens any arguments for domain specificity and modularity (for a more complete review of these issues, see P. D. Zelazo, Burack, Frye, Boseovski, & Jacques, 2000). Moreover, there is a growing corpus of positive evidence—both from typically developing and autistic individuals—that performance across domains relies on shared psychological processes.

Evidence for Domain-General Cognitive Impairments in Autism: Toward a Characterization of Executive Function and its Cognitive Basis

Individuals with autism show marked impairments (relative to mental age and to various comparison groups) on a wide variety of measures of executive function (e.g., Ozonoff et al., 1991; Prior, 1984; Prior & Hoffman, 1990; Rumsey, 1985; see Ozonoff, 1997, for a review). For example, Ozonoff et al. (1991) found that people with autism performed worse than a clinical comparison group on the Tower of Hanoi and the Wisconsin Card Sorting Test (WCST) (Grant & Berg, 1948). Additionally, performance on these measures was correlated with performance on several measures of theory of mind. Russell et al. (1991) also found correlations between performance on a theory-of-mind task and performance on a deception task that could be construed as a measure of executive function (see Hughes & Russell, 1993, and Hughes, chap.13, this volume, for similar findings). Russell et al. (1991) suggested that the behavior of the children with autism on this task and on measures of theory of mind could be explained by a failure to inhibit prepotent response tendencies.

Tests of executive function typically involve competition among different underlying processes, one of which is correct and one of which is prepotent, so that failures of executive function at all ages are often manifested as perseveration. Perseveration appears to provide an informative window on executive function, but there is debate concerning what difficulties in executive function are implicated. At first glance, it may seem that perseveration must result from a lack of inhibition. Perseveration simply means that a behavior is emitted that should have been inhibited, so in one sense this is true. However, when invoking inhibition, researchers usually also mean that a person is unable to suppress prepotent response tendencies or otherwise resist interference because of an immature, inefficient, or damaged inhibition *mechanism* (presumably the person tries to inhibit, but fails; his or her inhibition mechanism is too weak). That is, poor inhibitory control is attributed to a weak inhibitory control mechanism.

On its own, however, and without substantial specification, the construct of inhibition is too simple to account for perseveration in different situations at different ages. For example, why do 3-year-olds perseverate in Russell et al.'s (1991) windows task but not in the A-not-B task? Is it because the former requires more inhibition? Obviously, such a suggestion lacks predictive utility. Additionally, the construct of inhibition seems too simple to capture the full range of executive-function phenomena (Stuss, Eskes, & Foster, 1994). In contrast to the construct of inhibition, however, many definitions of executive function are perhaps too complex; these definitions often amount to partially overlapping lists of tasks that appear to be sensitive to damage of prefrontal cortex.

In our own attempt to make sense of the construct (P. D. Zelazo, Carter, Reznick, & Frye, 1997), we took seriously the suggestion (from Luria) that executive function is a function, the outcome of which is deliberate problem solving. The term "function" is used here to refer to a complex, hierarchically organized activity with a constant outcome. In the case of executive function, the outcome is deliberate problem solving, so we can identify temporally and functionally distinct phases of problem solving and show how they contribute to that outcome (see Fig. 10.1).

For example, in the WCST, participants are shown four target cards that vary along three dimensions (color, shape, and number), and participants are required to discover how to sort test cards that vary along the same three dimensions. On

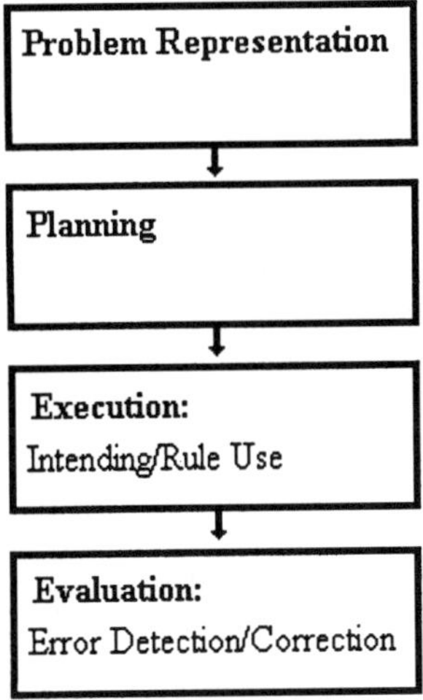

FIG. 10.1. A problem-solving framework that identifies four temporally distinct phases of executive function.

each trial, participants are informed whether or not they sorted correctly. After correctly sorting 10 cards, the sorting rule is changed. In this task, one must first construct a representation of the problem space, which includes identifying the relevant dimensions. Then, one must choose a promising plan—for example, sorting according to shape. After selecting a plan, one must (a) keep the plan in mind long enough for it to guide one's thought or action, and (b) actually carry out the prescribed behavior. Keeping a plan in mind to control behavior is referred to as *intending*; translating a plan into action is *rule use*. Finally, after acting, one must evaluate one's behavior, which includes both error detection and error correction.

According to this framework, inflexibility can occur at each phase so there are several possible explanations of perseverative performance on the WCST—and on global executive-function tasks more generally. For example, perseveration could occur after a rule change in the WCST either because a new plan was not formed or because the plan was formed but not carried out. Although the framework does not explain executive function, it does allow us to ask more precisely when in the process of problem solving performance breaks down. In addition, the framework accomplishes the following: (a) it clarifies the way in which diverse aspects of executive function work together to fulfil the higher order function of problem solving, (b) it avoids conceptualizing executive function as a homuncular ability, (c) it suggests relatively well-defined measures of executive function (e.g., measures of rule use for which problem representation, planning, and evaluation are not required), and (d) it permits the formulation of specific hypotheses regarding the role of basic cognitive processes (e.g., working memory) in different aspects of executive function.

Of course, knowledge is also required to solve any particular problem. If a problem pertains to physical causality, then some knowledge about mechanics may be needed. Similarly, if a problem pertains to human behavior (e.g., if one wants to determine where someone will look for an object), then mental state concepts will perhaps be useful. Nonetheless, the actual use of mental state concepts to solve a problem about human behavior just is executive function qua problem solving. Thus, an adequate explication of theory of mind will depend on an adequate explication of executive function, and a developmental theory of the former topic will require a developmental theory of the latter.

In our research, we have studied the circumstances in which children at different ages are susceptible to perseveration and we have designed tasks in reference to the problem-solving framework. This approach has allowed us to chart the development of executive function and to begin to reveal the way in which basic cognitive processes are normally orchestrated in order to fulfill the higher order function of problem solving. The results of our research suggest that this orchestration is made possible in part by age-related changes in awareness and in the complexity of children's plans. This work, in turn, has informed our thinking about the cognitive impairments associated with autism.

Cognitive Complexity and Control Theory

According to the Cognitive Complexity and Control (CCC) theory (Frye et al., 1995; Zelazo & Frye, 1997), a number of major developmental transitions are evident in the complexity of children's conscious plans. Children's plans, which are necessarily conditional (P. D. Zelazo & Jacques, 1996), are assumed to correspond literally to rules, in potentially silent self-directed speech, linking antecedent conditions to consequences, as when we tell ourselves, "If I see a mailbox, then I need to mail this letter." Age-related changes in rule complexity can, in turn, be attributed to age-related changes in the degree to which children can reflect on the contents of consciousness (e.g., see Zelazo, 1999; Zelazo & Zelazo, 1998). Thus, when children reflect on the rules they represent, they are able to consider them in contradistinction to other rules and embed them under higher order rules. This accomplishment can be compared to saying, "If it is before 5 p.m., then if I see a mailbox, I need to mail this letter (otherwise, I'll have to go directly to the post office)." A simple conditional statement regarding the mailbox is made dependent on the satisfaction of yet another condition (namely, the time).

The tree-structure in Fig. 10.2 illustrates the way in which one rule can be embedded under another and controlled by it. A rule such as A, which indicates that consequent *1* (c_1) should follow antecedent *1* (a_1) is incompatible with rule C, which connects a_1 to c_2. Rule A is embedded under, and controlled by, a higher order rule (rule E) that can be used to select rules A and B, as opposed to rules C and D. To deliberate between rules C and D, on the one hand, and rules A and B, on the other, children need to be aware of the fact that they know both pairs of rules. Thus, increases in self reflection on lower order rules are logically required for increases in embedding to occur. These increases in embedding provide a metric for measuring the degree of complexity of the entire rule system that needs to be kept in mind to perform particular tasks.

For each developmental transition, a general process is recapitulated. Specifically, a conscious rule at a particular level of complexity is acquired, and this rule permits children to exercise a new degree of control over their environment and behavior. However, the use of this rule is subject to limitations that cannot be overcome until yet another level of complexity is achieved.

The limitations, and their implications for the development of executive function, can be seen in a wide range of situations, but they are perhaps most clearly illustrated by typically developing 3-year-olds' performance on the dimensional change card sort (DCCS; see Fig. 10.3). In the DCCS, children are shown two target cards, each of which is affixed to a sorting tray, and they are asked to sort a series of test cards into the trays according to one dimension (e.g., for color, they are told, "Put the blue ones here; put the red ones there."). Then, after sorting several cards, they are told to stop playing the first game and switch to another game (e.g., shape, for which they are told, "Put the flowers here; put the boats there.").

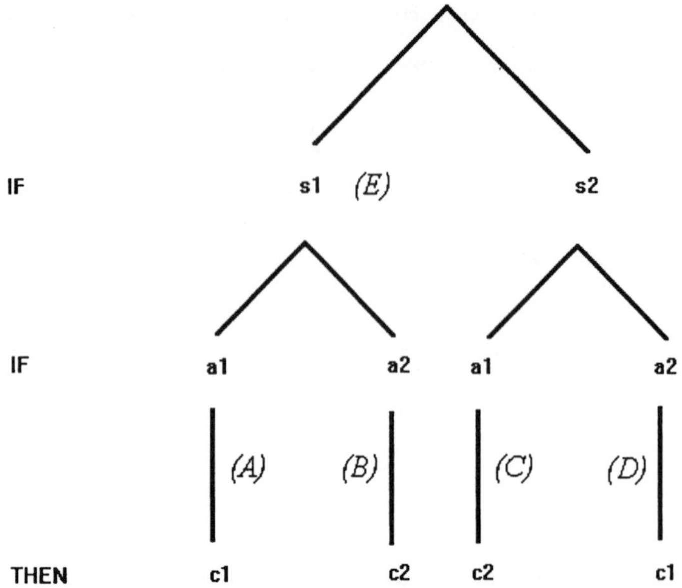

FIG. 10.2. Hierarchical tree structure depicting formal relations among rules. (Note: s_1 and s_2 = setting conditions; a_1 and a_2 = antecedent conditions; c_1 and c_2 = consequences).

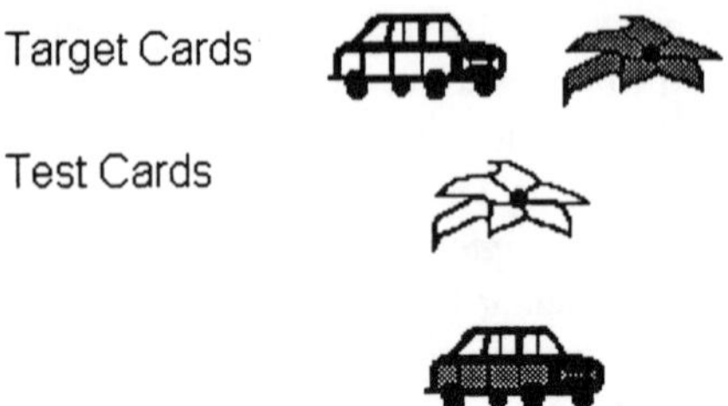

FIG. 10.3. Stimuli from the dimensional change card sort in which children are first told to sort test cards with target cards according to one dimension (e.g., color) and then told to sort test cards according to the other dimension (e.g., shape).

Regardless of which dimension is presented first, 3-year-olds typically continue to sort the cards by that dimension despite being told the new rules on every trial and despite having sorted cards by the new dimension on other occasions (e.g., Frye et al., 1995).

In terms of the tree structure in Fig. 10.2, rule A might be, "If it's red, put it here," and rule B might be, "If blue ... there." To sort by color, children would need to reflect on rule A and contrast it with rule B. According to the CCC theory, 2-year-olds only represent a single rule at a time (e.g., "If red ... here"). By 3 years, children can easily consider a pair of rules simultaneously ("If red ... here; if blue ... there"). However, it is not until 5 years of age that children typically represent a higher order rule (such as E) that allows them to select between two different pairs of rules ("If we're playing color, then if red ... here, if blue ... there, but if we're playing shape, then if boats ... here, if flowers ... there").

Zelazo, Frye, and Rapus (1996) asked 3-year-olds who had been sorting by one dimension to switch and start sorting by the other dimension. As usual, the majority of children perseverated and continued to sort by the first dimension. These children were then asked questions to determine whether they understood what they were supposed to be doing. For example, children who were supposed to be sorting by shape were asked, "Where do the boats go in the shape game? And where do the rabbits go?" Almost invariably, children answered these knowledge questions correctly, pointing to the correct box. Nonetheless, when the children were told to go ahead and sort the cards according to these rules ("Okay, good, now play the shape game: Where does this rabbit go?"), nearly all of them perseverated, sorting by color. The children answered an explicit question about the new rules, showing that they knew these rules, but then they immediately persisted in using the old ones.

According to the CCC theory, these kinds of abulic dissociations—that is, dissociations between having knowledge and actually using that knowledge—occur until incompatible pieces of knowledge are integrated into a single-rule system via their subordination to a new higher order structure. Three-year-olds know the first pair of rules, and they know the second pair of rules, but they have difficulty "stepping back" from their knowledge and reflecting on the rule pairs and their relation (Zelazo & Frye, 1997). As a result, the pair that they select is determined by relatively local considerations, such as the way in which the question is asked or the way in which they have approached the situation in the past.

Because the CCC framework provides a metric for comparing performance on tasks from different domains of function, it can be applied in a straightforward manner to theory of mind. To succeed on the theory-of-mind tasks that 3-year-olds find difficult, children must reason from two different, incompatible perspectives. For example, in a representational-change task (Gopnik & Astington, 1988), children must be able to reason flexibly about their own past knowledge vis-a-vis their appraisal of the current situation. To do so, they must say something like: "There are sticks in the box, not crayons, but I'm being asked about before I saw that, so the answer is crayons, not sticks." That is, children must formulate rules in natural language (based on both their knowledge and the task demands) that allow them to access and focus on particular pieces of knowledge at the time of responding. In contrast to typically developing 5-year-olds, 3-year-olds and children with autism may perform poorly on these theory-of-mind tasks because they are unable to integrate the incompatible perspectives into a higher order rule that allows them to select the appropriate perspective from which to reason.

If the CCC theory is correct, then one would expect performance on theory of mind to be related to performance on a comparable measure of rule use that did not involve reasoning about mental states. To test this prediction, Frye et al. (1995, Exp. 2) compared 3- to 5-year-olds' performance on the DCCS with their performance on several measures of theory of mind. As predicted, individual children's performance on the two tasks was related even when age was partialled out. Subsequent research has replicated and extended this finding (see Perner & Lang, 1999, for review).

Applying CCC Theory to Atypical Populations. The CCC theory also provides a useful way for thinking about the cognitive difficulties associated with autism and other developmental disabilities. Together with the Levels of Consciousness model (e.g., Zelazo & Zelazo, 1998), CCC theory identifies three key dimensions of cognitive development: consciousness, rule complexity, and behavioral control. Age-related changes in reflective consciousness permit the formulation and use of increasingly complex rule structures, which in turn permit increased behavioral flexibility and control. These dimensions of development are equally important in cases of typical and atypical development, and they serve as an important index of developmental level. Autism is likely a neurological disorder with a (complex) genetic basis (e.g., Bailey et al., 1995; Szatmari, Jones, Zwaigenbaum, & MacLean, 1998), and it is clearly different from other developmental disorders. Nonetheless, from the perspective of CCC theory, any developmental disorder (i.e., any perturbation of the epigenetic process) will likely lead to disturbances along each of the three key developmental dimensions.

Characterizing the phenotypic commonalities among developmental disorders is just as important as determining what makes different disorders unique. From the perspective of CCC theory, many different developmental disorders, including mental retardation, will lead to disturbances in consciousness, rule complexity, and behavioral control. By most estimates, about 75% of individuals with autism have IQs below 70 (e.g., DeMyer et al., 1974). Moreover, among individuals with autism, verbal IQ is a strong predictor of level of function (e.g., Happé, 1995) and prognosis (e.g., Gillberg, 1991). However, as Bailey et al. (1995) note, most psychological theories of autism have ignored this association with mental retardation on the assumption that "because mental retardation is not specific to autism, it does not require explanation" (p. 92). Although it is possible that mental retardation is an independent consequence of whatever insult causes autism, it is also possible that mental retardation is intrinsic to the disorder.These disturbances will, in turn, lead to deficits in executive function and lowered IQ. Indeed, autism may cause a normal distribution of IQ to be shifted downward, with the result that about 75% of the distribution falls below the cutoff for retardation (i.e., below an IQ score of 70). If this is the case, then an adequate characterization of autism must include an account of the consequences of autism for general intelligence, as well as an account of the way in which low IQ interacts with other aspects of autism. In any event, however, one cannot simply ignore the large majority of individuals with autism who have IQs below 70.

Although characterizing the phenotypic commonalities among developmental disorders is important, CCC theory also proves useful in determining what makes different disorders unique; because differences among developmental disorders can be considered within the problem-solving framework of executive function rather than in terms of a global construct of executive function. From this perspective, different disorders may be associated with difficulties in different basic cognitive processes (e.g., working memory, attention), and consequently associated with different patterns of strengths and weaknesses in specific phases of executive function.

Finally, because CCC theory provides a metric for comparing performance on tasks from different domains, it allows for a legitimate test of the Specificity and Uniqueness claims regarding autism and theory of mind. For example, Zelazo, Burack et al. (1996) assessed performance on theory of mind, and performance on the DCCS among groups of typically developing 5-year-olds and low-functioning adults with Down syndrome matched on mental age (mean MA was 5.1 years). Whereas the majority of 5-year-olds passed both sets of tasks, participants with Down syndrome were only able to sort correctly on the first dimension in the DCCS, and the majority of them also failed the theory-of-mind tasks. Moreover, performance on the two types of tasks was highly correlated. These findings are important for two reasons. First, as noted earlier, these findings contradict the Uniqueness Claim because people with Down syndrome clearly had difficulty on the theory-of-mind tasks. Second, these findings contradict the hypothesis that performance in these different domains is independent (i.e., the Specificity Claim).

Recently, P. D. Zelazo, Jacques, Burack, & Frye (2000) conducted a similar study with individuals with autism. A battery of tasks, including (among other tasks) two rule-use tasks (the DCCS and a ramp task), and two standard theory-of-mind tasks (an explicit false-belief task and an unexpected contents false-belief task), was administered to high- and low-functioning people with autism. The low-functioning group performed near floor on most tasks, so not surprisingly, their performance on the theory-of-mind tasks was not related to performance on the rule-use tasks when verbal mental age was partialled out. However, among high-functioning individuals, the correlation between rule use and theory of mind was very high ($r = .76$). This finding challenges the notion of a domain-specific impairment in theory of mind in people with autism. Instead, poor performance on theory-of-mind and other tasks of similar structure can be attributed to a more general difficulty—such as a difficulty using higher order rules in order to integrate two incompatible perspectives into one rule system.

These studies provide evidence for the suggestion that domain-general mechanisms underlie the development of a theory of mind, and that these mechanisms are impaired in at least two different kinds of developmental disorder. These results suggest that the impairment of theory of mind is neither unique nor specific to people with autism. When tasks of equivalent levels of complexity are compared, people with autism display multifaceted deficits in reasoning and problem solving (see also Yirmiya & Shulman, 1996; Yirmiya et al., 1996). Mental-state reasoning, as well as causal reasoning and executive function more generally, are likely to emerge within a broader context in which individuals come to use higher order rules in order to integrate incompatible perspectives into a complex rule system. Failure to succeed on all of these tasks, as seen in young preschoolers and some people with atypical development, may result from an inability to represent a higher order rule that allows individuals to select the appropriate condition from which to reason. In general, this approach moves us away from the simplicity of modularity theory and considers cognitive development as a complex epigenetic process. In this respect, it has much in common with the organismic approaches to developmental psychopathology described earlier (e.g., Cicchetti & Pogge-Hesse, 1982; Zigler, 1969).

Conclusion

We question theoretical arguments for the modularity of higher level cognitive processes, and for the modularity of theory of mind in individuals with autism. Support for the Specificity and Uniqueness claims regarding autism and theory of mind is inconclusive at best. People with autism experience difficulties in numerous areas besides theory of mind, including (among others) rule use on the DCCS (Zelazo et al., 2000), reasoning about physical causality (Zelazo et al., 2000), seriation and conservation (Yirmiya & Shulman, 1996), and executive function more generally (Ozonoff et al., 1991). Moreover, other atypical populations, such as people with Down syndrome and mental retardation, also show deficits in theory of mind (e.g., Yirmiya et al., 1998).

We propose that deficits in theory of mind in people with autism can be best understood in terms of a (relatively) domain-general developmental framework that identifies three key dimensions of cognitive development: consciousness, rule complexity, and behavioral control. These dimensions of development are equally important in cases of typical and atypical development, and they serve as an important index of developmental level. According to this approach, success on tests of false belief requires the ability to use rule systems at a particular level of complexity. Support for this proposal is evidenced among typically developing children, individuals with Down syndrome, and high-functioning individuals with autism. Cognitive Complexity and Control theory is also useful in identifying differences among developmental disorders as they can be considered within the problem-solving framework of executive function, rather than in terms of a global construct of executive function. Thus, different disorders may be associated with difficulties in different basic cognitive processes, and consequently associated with different patterns of strengths and weaknesses in specific phases of executive function.

From this perspective, interventions for a variety of disorders might be based on techniques that foster the development of executive function, and more precisely, the development of self-reflection and rule complexity. Preliminary work with typically developing preschoolers (Dowsett & Livesay, 2000) has yielded positive results and encourages further research with clinical groups.

ACKNOWLEDGMENTS

The preparation of this chapter was supported in part by a grant from NSERC of Canada to Phil Zelazo and a grant from SSHRC to Jake Burack. We thank Stuart Marcovitch and Ulrich Mueller for providing helpful comments on an earlier draft of this manuscript.

REFERENCES

Astington, J. W. (1993). *The child's discovery of the mind.* Cambridge, MA: Harvard University Press.

Bailey, A., Le Couteur, A., Gottesman, I., Bolton, P., Simonoff, E., Yuzda, E., & Rutter, M. (1995). Autism as a strongly genetic disorder: Evidence from a British twin study. *Psychological Medicine, 25,* 63–77.

Baron-Cohen, S. (1994). How to build a baby that can read minds: Cognitive mechanisms in mindreading. *Cahiers de Psychologie Cognitive [Current Psychology of Cognition], 13,* 513–552.

Baron-Cohen, S. (1995). *Mindblindness.* Cambridge, MA: MIT Press.

Baron-Cohen, S. (2000). Autism: Deficits in folk psychology exist alongside superiority in folk physics. In S. Baron-Cohen, H. Tager-Flusberg, & D. J. Cohen (Eds.), *Understanding other minds: Perspectives from developmental cognitive neuroscience* (pp. 73–82). Oxford, UK: Oxford University Press.

Baron-Cohen, S., Leslie, A. M., & Frith, U. (1985). Does the autistic child have a "theory of mind"? *Cognition, 21,* 37–46.

Baron-Cohen, S., Leslie, A. M., & Frith, U. (1986). Mechanical, behavioural, and intentional understanding of picture stories in autistic children. *British Journal of Developmental Psychology, 4,* 113–125.

Bates, E., Benigni, L., Bretherton, I., Camaioni, I., & Volterra, V. (1979). *The emergence of symbols: Cognition and communication in infancy.* New York: Academic Press.

Bellugi, U., Wang, P. P., & Jernigan, T. L. (1994). In S. H. Broman & J. Grafman (Eds.), *Atypical cognitive deficits in developmental disorders: Implications for brain function* (pp. 23–56). Hillsdale, NJ: Lawrence Erlbaum Associates.

Bennetto, L., Pennington, B. F., & Rogers, S. J. (1996). Intact and impaired memory functions in autism. *Child Development, 67,* 1816–1835.

Benson, G., Abbeduto, L., Short, K., Nuccio, J. B., & Maas, F. (1993). Development of a theory of mind in individuals with mental retardation. *American Journal on Mental Retardation, 98,* 427–433.

Blair, R. J. R. (1995). A cognitive developmental approach to morality: Investigating the psychopath. *Cognition, 57,* 1–29.

Burack, J. A. (1997). The study of atypical and typical populations: Lessons from developmental psychopathology. In S. S. Luthar, J. A. Burack, D. Cicchetti, & J. R. Weisz (Eds.), *Developmental psychopathology: Perspectives on adjustment, risk, and disorder* (pp. 139–165). New York: Cambridge University Press.

Caramazza, A., & Shelton, J. R. (1998). Domain-specific knowledge systems in the brain the animate-inanimate distinction. *Journal of Cognitive Neuroscience, 10,* 1–34.

Case, R., & Okamoto, Y. (1996). The role of central conceptual structures in the development of children's thought. *Monographs of the Society for Research in Child Development, 61(1–2),* v-265.

Charman, T., & Baron-Cohen, S. (1992). Understanding drawings and beliefs: A further test of the metarepresentation theory of autism: A research note. *Journal of Child Psychology and Psychiatry, 33,* 1105–1112.

Charman, T., & Baron-Cohen, S. (1995). Understanding photos, models, and beliefs: A test of the modularity thesis of theory of mind. *Cognitive Development, 10,* 287–298.

Charman, T., & Lynggaard, H. (1998). Does a photographic cue facilitate false belief performance in subjects with autism? *Journal of Autism and Developmental Disorders, 28,* 33–42.

Cicchetti, D. (1984). The emergence of developmental psychopathology. *Child Development, 55,* 1–7.

Cicchetti, D., & Pogge-Hesse, P. (1982). Possible contributions of the study of organically retarded persons to developmental theory. In E. Zigler & D. Balla (Eds.), *Mental retardation: The developmental-difference controversy* (pp. 277–318). Hillsdale, NJ: Lawrence Erlbaum Associates.

Cicchetti, D., & Sroufe, L. A. (1978). An organizational view of affect: Illustrations from the study of Down's syndrome infants. In M. Lewis & L. Rosenblum (Eds.), *The development of affect* (pp. 309–350). New York: Plenum.

Coldren, J. T., & Corradetti, K. (1997). Conceptual relations between attention processes in infants and children with attention-deficit/hyperactivity disorder: A problem-solving approach. In J. A. Burack & J. T. Enns (Eds.), *Attention, development, and psychopathology* (pp. 147–167). New York: Guilford.

Cosmides, L., & Tooby, J. (1994). Origins of domain specificity: The evolution of functional organization. In L. A. Hirschfeld & S. A. Gelman (Eds.), *Mapping the mind: Domain specificity in cognition and culture* (pp. 85–116). New York: Cambridge University Press.

DeMyer, M. K., Barton, S., Alpern, G., Kimberlin, C., Allen, J., Yang, E., & Steele, R. (1974). The measured intelligence of autistic children. *Journal of Autism and Childhood Schizophrenia, 2,* 264–287.

Dowsett, S. M., & Livesay, D. J. (2000). The development of inhibitory control in preschool children: Effects of "executive skills" training. *Developmental Psychobiology, 36,* 161–174.

Elman, J. L., Bates, E. A., Johnson, M. H., Karmiloff-Smith, A., & Plunkett, K. (1996). *Rethinking innateness: A connectionist perspective on development.* Cambridge, MA: MIT Press.

Fischer, K. W. (1980). A theory of cognitive development: The control and construction of hierarchies of skills. *Psychological Review, 87,* 477–531.

Flavell, J. H. (1988). The development of children's knowledge about the mind: From cognitive connections to mental representations. In J. W. Astington, P. L. Harris, & D. R. Olson (Eds.), *Developing theories of mind* (pp. 244–267). Cambridge, UK: Cambridge University Press.

Fodor (1983). *Modularity of mind.* Cambridge, MA: MIT Press.

Fodor (1992). A theory of the child's theory of mind. *Cognition, 44,* 283–296.

Frith, U., Morton, J., & Leslie, A. (1991). The cognitive basis of a biological disorder: Autism. *Trends in Neurosciences, 14,* 433–438.

Frye, D., Zelazo, P. D., & Burack, J. A. (1998). I. Cognitive complexity and control: Implications for theory of mind in typical and atypical development. *Current Directions in Psychological Science, 7,* 116–121.

Frye, D., Zelazo, P. D., & Palfai, T. (1995). Theory of mind and rule-based reasoning. *Cognitive Development, 10,* 483–527.

Gillberg, C. (1991). Outcome in autism and autistic-like conditions. *Journal of the American Academy of Child and Adolescent Psychiatry, 30,* 375–382.

Goldberg, E. (1995). Rise and fall of modular orthodoxy. *Journal of Clinical and Experimental Neuropsychology, 17,* 193–208.

Gopnik, A., & Astington, J. W. (1988). Children's understanding of representational change and its relation to the understanding of false belief and the appearance–reality distinction. *Child Development, 59,* 26–37.

Gordon, A., & Olson, D. (1998). The relation between acquisition of a theory of mind and information processing capacity. *Journal of Experimental Child Psychology, 68,* 70–83.

Grant, D. A., & Berg, E. A. (1948). A behavioral analysis of degree of reinforcement and ease of shifting to new responses in a Weigl-type card-sorting problem. *Journal of Experimental Psychology, 38,* 404–411.

Halford, G., Wilson, W. H., & Phillips, S. (1998). Processing capacity defined by relational complexity: Implications for comparative, developmental, and cognitive psychology. *Behavioral and Brain Sciences, 21,* 803–864.

Happé, F. G. E. (1995). The role of age and verbal ability in the theory of mind task performance of subjects with autism. *Child Development, 66,* 843–855.

Happé, F. G. E. (1996). Studying weak central coherence at low levels: Children with autism do not succumb to visual illusions: A research note. *Journal of Child Psychology and Psychiatry, 37,* 873–877.

Happé, F. G. E. (1999) Autism: Cognitive deficit or cognitive style? *Trends in Cognitive Sciences, 3,* 216–222.

Hirschfeld, L. A., & Gelman, S. A. (1994). *Mapping the mind: Domain specificity in cognition and culture.* New York: Cambridge University Press.

Hodapp, R. M., & Burack, J. A. (1990). What mental retardation teaches us about typical development: The examples of sequences, rates, and cross-domain relations. *Development and Psychopathology, 2,* 213–225.

Hodapp, R. M., & Zigler, E. (1995). Past, present, and future issues in the developmental approach to mental retardation and developmental disabilities. In D. Cicchetti & D. Cohen (Eds.), *Developmental psychopathology: Risk, disorder, and adaptation* (pp. 299–331). New York: Wiley.

Hughes, C., & Russell, J. (1993). Autistic children's difficulty with mental disengagement from an object: Its implication for theories of autism. *Developmental Psychology, 29,* 498–510.

Jacques, S., & Zelazo, P. D. (1994). Several strictures on specificity. *Cahiers de Psychologie Cognitive [Current Psychology of Cognition], 13,* 623–629.

Johnson, M. H. (1999). Cortical plasticity in normal and abnormal cognitive development: Evidence and working hypotheses. *Development and Psychopathology, 11,* 419–437.

Karmiloff-Smith, A. (1992). *Beyond modularity: A developmental perspective on cognitive science.* Cambridge, MA: MIT Press.

Karmiloff-Smith, A., Tyler, L. K., Voice, K., Sims, K., Udwin, O., Howlin, P., & Davies, M. (1998). Linguistic dissociations in Williams syndrome: Evaluating receptive syntax in on-line and off-line tasks. *Neuropsychologia, 36,* 343–351.

Leekam, S. R., & Perner, J. (1991). Does the autistic child have a metarepresentational deficit? *Cognition, 40,* 203–218.

Leslie, A. (1991). The theory of mind impairment in autism: Evidence for a modular mechanism of development? In A. Whiten (Ed.), *Natural theories of mind* (pp. 63–78). Oxford, UK: Blackwell.

Leslie, A. (1994). ToMM, ToBy, and Agency: Core architecture and domain specificity. In L. A. Hirschfeld & S. A. Gelman (Eds.), *Mapping the mind: Domain specificity in cognition and culture* (pp. 119–148). New York: Cambridge University Press.

Leslie, A. M., & Thaiss, L. (1992). Domain specificity in conceptual development: Neuropsychological evidence from autism. *Cognition, 43,* 225–251.

Maratsos, M. (1992). Constraints, modules, and domain specificity: An introduction. In M. R. Gunnar & M. Maratsos (Eds.), *Modularity and constraints in language and cognition: The Minnesota symposia on child psychology, Vol. 25,* (pp. 1–23). Hillsdale, NJ: Lawrence Erlbaum Associates.

Moscovitch, M., & Umilta, C. (1990). Modularity and neuropsychology: Modules and central processes in attention and memory. In M. F. Schawartz (Ed.), *Modular deficits in Alzheimer's disease* (pp. 1–59). Cambridge, MA: MIT Press.

Munakata, Y., McClelland, J. L., Johnson, M. H., & Seigler, R. (1997). Rethinking infant knowledge: Toward an adaptive process account of successes and failures in object permanence tasks. *Psychological Review, 104,* 686–713.

Olson, D. R. (1993). The development of representations: The origins of mental life. *Canadian Psychology, 34,* 293–304.

Oswald, D. P., & Ollendick, T. H. (1989). Role taking and social competence in autism and mental retardation. *Journal of Autism and Developmental Disorders, 19,* 119–1270.

Ozonoff, S. (1997). Components of executive function in autism and other disorders. In J. Russell (Ed.), *Autism as an executive disorder* (pp. 179–211). New York: Oxford University Press.

Ozonoff, S., Pennington, B. F., & Rogers, S. J. (1991). Executive function deficits in high-functioning autistic individuals: Relationship to theory of mind. *Journal of Child Psychology and Psychiatry, 32,* 1081–1105.

Pennington, B. F. (1994). The working memory function of the prefrontal cortices: Implications for developmental and individual differences in cognition. In M. M. Haith, J. B. Benson, R. Roberts, & B. F. Pennington (Eds.), *The development of future-oriented processes* (pp. 243–289). Chicago: The University of Chicago Press.

Pennington, B. F., Rogers, S. J., Bennetto, L., Griffith, E., M., Reed, D. T., & Shyu, V. (1997). Validity tests of the executive dysfunction hypothesis of autism. In J. Russell (Ed.), *Autism as an executive disorder* (pp. 143–178). Oxford, UK: Oxford University Press.

Perner, J., & Lang, B. (1999). Development of theory of mind and executive control. *Trends in Cognitive Sciences, 3,* 337–344.

Piaget, J. (1970). Piaget's theory. In P. H. Mussen (Ed.), *Carmichael's manual of child psychology* Vol. 1. New York: Wiley.

Prior, M. (1984). Developing concepts of childhood autism: The influence of experimental cognitive research. *Journal of Consulting and Clinical Psychology, 52,* 4–16.

Prior, M., & Hoffman, W. (1990). Brief report: Neuropsychological testing of autistic children through an exploration with frontal lobe tests. *Journal of Autism and Developmental Disorders, 20,* 581–590.

Rogers, C. -L., Zelazo, P. R., Mendelson, M., & Rotsztein, B. (1998). Behavioral, affective and attentional responses of developmentally-delayed and nondelayed pre-schoolers to task difficulty. *Infant Behavior and Development, 21 (Special ICIS Issue).*

Rumsey, J. (1985). Conceptual problem-solving in highly verbal, nonretarded autistic men. *Journal of Autism and Developmental Disorders, 15,* 23–36.

Russell, J., Mauthner, N., Sharpe, S., & Tidswell, T. (1991). The "windows task" as a measure of strategic deception in preschoolers and autistic subjects. *British Journal of Developmental Psychology, 9,* 331–349.

Russell, J., Saltmarsh, R., & Hill, E. (1999). What do executive factors contribute to the failure on false belief tasks by children with autism? *Journal of Child Psychology and Psychiatry and Allied Disciplines, 40,* 859–868.

Schechter, M. D. (1953). Visual agnosia for animate objects. *Journal of Nervous and Mental Disease, 117,* 341–344.

Scott, F. J., & Baron-Cohen, S. (1996). Logical, analogical, and psychological reasoning in autism: A test of Cosmides [sic] theory. *Development and Psychopathology, 8,* 235–245.

Scott, F. J., Baron-Cohen, S., & Leslie, A. (1999). 'If pigs could fly': A test of counterfactual reasoning and pretence in children with autism. *British Journal of Developmental Psychology, 17,* 349–362.

Shelton, J. R., Fouch, E., & Caramazza, A. (1998). The selective sparing of body part knowledge: A case study. *Neurocase: Case Studies in Neuropsychology, Neuropsychiatry, and Behavioural Neurology, 4,* 339–351.

Stuss, D. T., Eskes, G. A., & Foster, J. K. (1994). Experimental neuropsychological studies of frontal lobe functions. In F. Boller, & J. Grafman (Eds.), *Handbook of Neuropsychology, Vol. 9,* (pp. 149–185). Amsterdam: Elsevier.

Szatmari, P., Jones, M. B., Zwaigenbaum, L., & MacLean, J. E. (1998). Genetics of autism: Overview and new directions. *Journal of Autism and Developmental Disorders, 28,* 351–368.

Tooby, J., & Cosmides, L. (1995). Foreword to *Mindblindness.* Cambridge, MA: MIT Press.

Warrington, E. K. (1975). The selective impairment of semantic memory. *Quarterly Journal of Experimental Psychology, 27,* 635–657.

Warrington, E. K., & Shallice, T. (1984). Category specific naming impairments. *Brain, 107,* 829–853.

Werner (1957). The concept of development from a comparative and organismic point of view. In D. Harris (Ed.), *The concept of development.* Minneapolis, MN: University of Minnesota.

Yirmiya, N., Erel, O., Shaked, M., & Solomonica-Levi, D. (1998). Meta-analyses comparing theory of mind abilities of individuals with autism, individuals with mental retardation, and normally developing individuals. *Psychological Bulletin, 124,* 283–307.

Yirmiya, N., & Shulman, C. (1996). Seriation, conservation, and theory of mind abilities in individuals with autism, individuals with mental retardation, and normally developing children. *Child Development, 67,* 2045–2059.

Yirmiya, N., Solomonica-Levi, D., Shulman, C., & Pilowsky, T. (1996). Theory of mind abilities in individuals with autism, Down syndrome, and mental retardation of unknown etiology. *Journal of Child Psychology and Psychiatry, 37,* 1003–1014.

Zelazo, P. D. (1999). Language, levels of consciousness, and the development of intentional action. In P. D. Zelazo, J. W. Astington, & D. R. Olson (Eds.), *Developing theories of intention: Social understanding and self-control* (pp. 95–117). Mahwah, NJ: Lawrence Erlbaum Associates.

Zelazo, P. D., Burack, J., Benedetto, E., & Frye, D. (1996). Theory of mind and rule use in individuals with Down syndrome: A test of the uniqueness and specificity claims. *Journal of Child Psychology and Psychiatry, 37,* 479–484.

Zelazo, P. D., Burack, J., Frye, D., Boseovski, J., & Jacques, S. (2000). Theory of mind and autism: Arguments against modularity. Manuscript in preparation.

Zelazo, P. D., Carter, A., Reznick, J. S., & Frye, D. (1997). Early development of executive function: A problem-solving framework. *Review of General Psychology, 1,* 198–226.

Zelazo, P. D., & Frye, D. (1997). Cognitive complexity and control: A theory of the development of deliberate reasoning and intentional action. In M. Stamenov (Ed.), *Language structure, discourse, and the access to consciousness* (pp. 113–153). Amsterdam & Philadelphia: John Benjamins.

Zelazo, P. D., & Frye, D. (1998). II. Cognitive complexity and control: The development of executive function. *Current Directions in Psychological Science, 7,* 121–126.

Zelazo, P. D., Frye, D., & Rapus, T. (1996). An age-related dissociation between knowing rules and using them. *Cognitive Development, 11,* 37–63.

Zelazo, P. D., & Jacques, S. (1996). Children's rule use: Representation, reflection and cognitive control. In R. Vasta (Ed.), *Annals of child development, Vol. 12,* (pp. 119–176). London: Jessica Kingsley.

Zelazo, P. D., Jacques, S., Burack, J., & Frye, D. (2000). The relation between theory of mind and rule use in autism. Manuscript under review.

Zelazo, P. R., & Zelazo, P. D. (1998). The emergence of consciousness. In H. H. Jasper, L. Descarries, V. F. Castellucci, & S. Rossignol (Eds.), *Consciousness: At the frontiers of neuroscience, Advances in Neurology, Vol. 77* (pp. 149–165). New York: Lippincott-Raven Press.

Zigler, E. (1969). Developmental versus difference theories of mental retardation and the problem of motivation. *American Journal of Mental Defficiency, 73,* 536–556.

11

Autism: Specific Cognitive Deficit or Emergent End Point of Multiple Interacting Systems?

Dermot M. Bowler
Department of Psychology
City University, London, England

In keeping with the characterization of autism as a developmental disorder, psychologists attempting to explain the condition have drawn increasingly on models from the psychology of typical development. Foremost among such accounts has been its identification as a specific deficit in the understanding of others—a deficit in "theory of mind" (see Baron-Cohen, Tager-Flusberg, and Cohen, 2000). The success of this approach in generating research into the psychology of autism is evident from the burgeoning literature of the field. Yet despite its undoubted effect in furthering research into autism, the theory-of-mind deficit approach, at least in its strongest form, has particular features that make it an interesting case study of the ways in which aspects of a theory may hinder rather than help our understanding of the phenomenon we are trying to explain. Conceptualizing the problem of autism as being limited specifically to mental states risks marginalizing other, similarly disabling difficulties faced by individuals with the condition. Moreover, encapsulating the problem within a dedicated psychological or neuropsychological system risks playing down developmental considerations whereby different patterns of adaptation emerge over time. It is possible to take another perspective on the behavioral-adaptive end point we call autism by viewing it as an emergent result of a range of psychological processes, none of which is specific to either mental state understanding or to autism. Such an account need not reject the obvious truth that individuals with autism experience difficulties with the socially constructed world. But it has the potential advantage of offering explanations of their difficulties that go beyond social understanding.

Over the past 50 or so years, a range of theoretical perspectives have been brought to bear on the explanation of autistic spectrum disorders, each tending to reflect the prevailing scientific zeitgeist. Within the theoretical framework of behaviorist psychology, autism was conceptualized in terms of faulty conditioning (Ferster, 1961), and therapeutic efforts were directed toward the learning of more adaptive responses (Lovaas, 1987; Lovaas, Koegel, Simmons, & Long, 1973). Central to this approach was the idea that the trajectory and final end point of behavioral development were entirely a function of environmental contingencies of the organism's behavior acting on a structure that was common to all members of a given species. With the rise of cognitive psychology from the late 1950s (see Gardner, 1985), it became increasingly respectable to speak of internal processes, and greater interest was taken in the way in which individuals with autism process information. The seminal work on autism in this area is that of Hermelin & O'Connor (1970), who concluded that autism is a failure to "encode information meaningfully" (p. 129). The general philosophical orientation of such work was that the human mind was the mirror of Nature and that autism was, metaphorically, a distorted reflection.

The tradition of O'Connor and Hermelin's work on autism was taken up in the theoretical work of Leslie (1987) and the empirical work of Baron-Cohen, Leslie, & Frith (1985). By adopting a procedure and theoretical framework from the psychology of typical development, the approach of Baron-Cohen and colleagues represented one of the first psychological accounts of autism to incorporate an explicitly developmental perspective. In their seminal study, they showed that children with autism had difficulty in understanding false beliefs. Baron-Cohen et al. demonstrated this using their now almost canonical adaptation of Wimmer and Perner's (1983) false-belief task. In Baron-Cohen et al.'s task a protagonist (Sally) hides a marble in one of two locations and then leaves the scene. During her absence, another character, Anne, moves the marble to another location. On Sally's return, children participating in the study are asked where Sally will look for her marble. Children with autism characteristically fail this task, unlike children with typical development who are over 4 years of age or children with retardation whose mental ages are equivalent to those of the children with autism. This set of findings has formed the basis of an account of autism usually known as the "theory-of-mind-deficit account." From this perspective, much of the abnormal behavior seen in individuals with autism is due to a failure to engage with the social world, resulting from a deficient system specifically dedicated to the understanding of mental states such as "believe," "pretend," and so forth. As well as being cast within a cognitivist, information-processing, "software-specification" world view, such research has also adopted the metaphors of a Fodorian view of mind (Fodor, 1983). This sees human mental functioning as operating by means of a series of processing units or modules, each of which is dedicated to the treatment of a specific type of information (i.e., is domain specific) and which operate automatically in the presence of such information. The operation of these modules is cognitively impenetrable—i.e., is not amenable to introspection and is independent of the operation of other modules—which means that an individual module can be impaired without affecting the functioning of other modules in the system.

From the perspectives of both research and practice, the theory-of-mind-deficit account of autism can be thought of as having evolved along a continuum ranging from "strong" to "weak" forms. This terminology is borrowed from Cromer's (1974) review of the relationship between cognitive and language development. "Strong" forms of developmental theory argue for strict relationships of necessity between variables. So, for example, in language development, a strong form of the cognition hypothesis would argue that children must have object permanence before they can develop vocabularies. In principle, the existence of a single child who possesses some words but who does not reliably show evidence of object permanence refutes the theory. "Weak" forms are more accommodating of noisy relationships among variables as long as theory-consistent patterns are broadly maintained. Although scientists operating within the theory-of-mind-deficit framework of autism have typically not explicitly acknowledged the distinction between strong and weak forms of the theory, such approaches can readily be discerned (see Baron-Cohen, 1995, for a strong account and Sigman, 1998, for a weaker one). However, the theory as originally formulated lends itself to a strong interpretation and it is around such formulations that the critique presented here is centered.

In terms both of its impact on research into the fundamental nature of autism and into the development of potential remediation strategies, all forms of the theory-of-mind-deficit account of autism have been highly influential. Their major strengths are twofold. First, they have redescribed autism in a way that helps to make parsimonious sense of some previously hard to understand aspects of the condition, such as why individuals with autism often behave in embarrassing or insensitive ways. Second, they have provided a framework within which hypotheses can be systematically tested. But the strongest manifestations of the account contain assumptions that can sometimes occlude more fruitful perspectives on the problems they purport to explain. It should be emphasized that it is not the intention here to call into question the notion that children with autism (especially children who resemble those described by Kanner, 1943) are likely to fail false-belief tasks, or that such individuals are impaired in their capacity to engage in reciprocal social interactions; the data on these points make a very convincing case. Rather, the intention is to argue for a change in emphasis in the interpretation of the findings in order to develop a clearer understanding of their cause and thus better elucidate their developmental implications.

Assumptions Underlying a Strong Theory-of-Mind-Deficit Approach to Autism

In an essay on the philosophy of scientific enquiry, Harré (1972) discusses the question of corpuscularianism. This mode of explanation, which scientists have inherited from ancient Greek philosophy, proposes that the diversity of the phenomenal world can be accounted for by interactions between a small number of fundamental particles whose properties have no necessary similarity to those of the phenomenon they purport to explain. Harré (1972) argues that chemistry—in which a small set of entities (the hundred or so elements) coupled with a small number of principles (the laws of valence, bonding theory, etc.) were sufficient to explain both the diversity of materials found in the real world and the possible interactions and transformations among them—is the best example of this approach. In this respect, chemistry represents an advance over its predecessor, alchemy, in that it distances the properties of its fundamental particles from those of the phenomena to be explained and bridges the gap between the relatively small number of fundamental particles and the wide diversity of the phenomenal world by an appeal to interparticle processes and emergent properties.

The corpuscularian approach to scientific explanation has been adopted more or less successfully by virtually all the natural sciences, including psychology. Much of the psychological research into autism has attempted to explain delays or deficiencies of function in one or more domains of functioning in terms of deficient underlying structures. So, as we have seen, theory-of-mind-oriented research starts from the observation that individuals with autism show social impairment that is operationalized in terms of their continuing to fail false-belief tasks at a verbal mental age at which one would expect them to pass. This evidence is then used to construct an account cast in terms of a deficiency of certain structures (cognitive architectures—the corpuscles of this analysis) that are necessary to understand certain observed aspects of the real world. However, not only are the proposed mechanisms conceptually rather close to the phenomenon to be explained, investigators also make a further link from specific underlying cognitive mechanisms to specific underlying neurological structures. For example, several researchers have used Positron Emission Tomography (PET) and functional Magnetic Resonance Imaging (fMRI) scanning in an attempt to identify the physical locus of the supposed modular architectures thought to underpin mental-state understanding (see Frith & Frith, 2000, for a review). Such approaches could be said to be closer to Harré's concept of alchemy than to chemistry in that they could be thought of as overidentifying underlying structure with surface process and thereby diminishing the potential explanatory power of the former.

A more fruitful approach to the quest to localize theory of mind in the brain would be to consider the level of analysis at which phenomena are conceptualized. Sapsford (1984) has proposed that psychological phenomena can be approached from societal, interpersonal, and intrapersonal levels of analysis. Individuals with autism are maladaptive at all three of these levels. They experience difficulties in becoming fully functioning members of society, problems that stem from impairments of reciprocal social interaction seemingly related to modes of understanding that disrupt such interactions and that appear to be related to neurological impairment. The conceptual issue, however, lies in the degree to which units of analysis at one level can be unequivocally mapped onto categories at another. Although Fodor (1975) has argued that attempts to look for direct correspondences between cognition and biology were unlikely to be helpful, all levels of analysis should nevertheless ultimately be reconcilable with one another, even if not in a manner that involves strict one-to-one correspondence. For example, although convincing arguments can be made for the case that adaptive social functioning necessitates an understanding of other people's minds as conceptualized in false-belief tasks (see Baron-Cohen, 1995), the conclusion that there is therefore a set of cognitive structures or mechanisms specifically dedicated to the understanding of mind and, ipso facto, to adaptive social functioning may still not be justified.

Before we can conclude that there are one-to-one correspondences between particular deficits and specific cognitive mechanisms, we need to attend to the ways in which we gain access to the constructs we use (at whatever level of analysis) to explain the phenomenon under investigation. Adaptive functioning of an organism can be thought of in terms of the more or less effective congruence between aspects of an "external reality" and the internal structure of the individual. Since we know that typical development does not usually take place in the absence of a certain minimal level of environmental input, we can legitimately conclude that the process of increasingly effective adaptation with age is not merely a predetermined maturational process. Yet, in cases of atypical development (autism, in particular), even quite heavily enriched environments rarely if ever yield a typical end point, suggesting that there is something about the organism rather than the environment that is dysfunctional. It is this set of assumptions about the relationship between adaptive behavior and underlying mechanisms that has led theorists working within the paradigms described earlier to identify missing or dysfunctional components.

But such approaches tend to obscure the relationship between adaptive behavioral ability and the tests used to operationalize them and to assume an equivalent relation between the phenomenon and its operationalization across diagnostic groups or levels of developmental delay. The capacity for reciprocal social interaction is assumed to rest on the possession of a theory of mind that can be operationalized, however imperfectly, by false-belief tasks. The relationship between the test and the underlying capacity is assumed to be reasonably unequivocal, that is to say, individuals who can interact in a socially reciprocal manner should pass the test, and those who cannot, should not pass. Concentrating narrowly on the passing or failing of one of a number of false-belief tasks, such as the unexpected-transfer

(Wimmer & Perner, 1983) or representational-change (Perner, Leekam, & Wimmer, 1987) paradigms may yield an internally consistent picture, but when the focus is widened, problems begin to emerge. For example, older and more able individuals from the autistic spectrum can pass even quite complex, second-order false-belief tasks, despite remaining autistically socially impaired (Bowler, 1992) and despite showing impairments in symbolic and imaginative activities that according to Leslie (1987) are prerequisites for false-belief understanding. And whereas performance on a test of pragmatic understanding was found to be the best predictor of passing false-belief tests in children with autism (Eisenmajer & Prior, 1991), this was not found for typically developing children (Bowler & Norris, 1993). Findings such as these suggest that the simple, linear account inherent in the strong form of the theory-of-mind-deficit account—that of a deficient module that (directly or indirectly) mediates the understanding of false belief and, by extension, social understanding—may need some revision.

Furthermore, it follows from the strong form of the theory-of-mind-deficit account that interventions aimed at improving performance on one capacity should improve performance on others, and that this should hold across diagnostic groups. Yet the evidence on interventions presents a mixed picture. Researchers who did demonstrate improved performance on false-belief tasks often did not assess the effects of this training on everyday social functioning (Bowler & Strom, 1998; Charman & Lynggaard, 1998) or, if they did so, reported either poor generalization (McGregor, Whiten, & Blackburn, 1999) or inconsistent effects across different tasks (Bowler & Briskman, 2000). All of these findings call into question a simple model that assumes everyday functioning is based on underlying cognitive mechanisms that can be measured by controlled assessment procedures, which if found to be deficient will imply impaired everyday functioning. Furthermore, such a formulation risks becoming tautologous, since the everyday behavior is used to infer the underlying structure, which is then asserted as the reason for the everyday behavior. Looser or weaker forms of the theory-of-mind-deficit account, in Cromer's (1974) terms, are less problematic in these respects.

The conceptual difficulties outlined in the foregoing sections contribute directly to another weakness in strong theory-of-mind-deficit accounts of autism, namely, their lack of a truly developmental dimension. The last sentence may seem outrageous to many readers, especially given that the theory-of-mind paradigm had its origins in the study of typical development (see Perner, 1991; Wimmer & Perner, 1983). Moreover, considerable advances have been made in describing the development of theory-of-mind-related behaviors in autism over time. For example, Baron-Cohen and his colleagues have demonstrated that absence of behaviors such as symbolic play and joint-referencing behaviors in infancy is strongly predictive of the subsequent development of autistic pathology (Baird et al., 2000). And Sigman and her colleagues (Sigman, 1998; Sigman & Ruskin, 1999) have provided exceptionally sensitive and rigorously controlled observations of the developmental trajectories of children with autism. But the use of the language of a given theoretical perspective in descriptions of developmental phenomena does not necessarily imply adherence to all the implications inherent in that perspective. In either case, the adequacy of any position presented as a developmental account must be evaluated.

Strictly modularist theories have little to say about development beyond a maturationist account in which children move from a stage where particular modules are not switched on to one in which they are. In the case of autism, certain modules never become activated, or arrive so late on the scene as to compromise any chance of typical functioning. The challenge to nonmodularist accounts is to offer a convincing explanation for the observed developmental transitions. In either case, it is important to avoid either starting from one's conclusion—that is, assuming that those capacities that need to develop for mature adaptive functioning are already in place ("[presupposing] what it is we are trying to explain" as Thelen and Smith (1994, p. 43) put it)—or retreating to a naive form of biological determinism in which everything is predetermined in the genetic blueprint.

To summarize so far, strong forms of the theory-of-mind-deficit account of autism have inherent characteristics that render them problematic both as adequate scientific explanations and as candidates for a truly developmental account of the condition. They risk being tautological in the way they establish an isomorphism between surface behavior (as defined by patterns of performance on particular tests) and underlying structures. And in modularist form, they risk embodying a crudely maturationist account of development. Looser or weaker forms of the theory that have the more modest aim of charting developmental changes in particular behaviors face the equally demanding challenge of explaining why these changes come about in the way that they do.

Ways Around the Problems

It is one thing to survey a field of scientific endeavor and identify weak points. It is quite another to come up with alternative (and possibly equally problematic!) courses of action. However, across the natural sciences, a number of conceptual orientations could be applied to the question of appropriate underlying explanatory structures and their organization into an adequate developmental framework. Such approaches can help to reconceptualize existing findings in ways that can advance understanding. Cosmologists have long been aware of the need to explain current diversity in the physical world in terms not only of the interactions of a small number of fundamental particles and forces, but also of how such complexity arose, without a plan, from the events of the big bang (see Hawking, 1993, for a popular treatment of these topics). Developmental biologists have long known that the final form of the organism is not completely specified in the genome, and from Darcy Thompson (Thompson, 1968) onward, attempts have been made to account for changes in form over time in response to environmental and genetic constraints, rather than prescriptions of the end point. In the context of genetics, Monod (1972) invokes the notion of teleonomy to explain how certain molecular systems such as those involved in protein synthesis self-organize without containing within them an exact blueprint of the final outcome state.

In the domain of developmental psychology, Thelen and Smith (1994) identify what they call the "crisis in cognitive development" (pp. 21–44). Starting from a distinction between views of development "from above," where we see large-scale regularities in development (children's memory gets better, they move from an inability to an ability to pass conservation tasks, etc.), and "from below," where there are marked individual differences and where the same transitions are not always found across tasks. They go on to develop the thesis that accounts of developmental change that focus solely on, for example, innately specified constraints on information-processing capacity, or modularity, will miss the point of explaining the "how" of development and will produce compendia of facts about children's capacities on different tasks at different ages without specifying ways in which observed changes come about. This problem has also been identified by Van Geert (1998), who described much of developmental psychology as a "sociology of age groups,"—that is to say, that the discipline is quite good at cataloguing the characteristics of children at different phases of development but not so good at providing convincing explanations either of why the entries in the catalogue should look like they do or be organized in the way we observe them to be.

As an alternative, Thelen and Smith (1994) center their approach on *nonlinear dynamic systems theory* (NDST), which is an approach to modeling change over time in complex systems that does not have recourse either to prespecified blueprints for end state complexity or for prior knowledge of the end point to specify pathways to it from less complex beginnings. The NDST approach involves the investigation not only of behavioral stability (such as whether a child reliably passes or fails a false-belief task), but also of variability, e.g., what manipulations will shift a child from failing to passing or vice versa, and how such manipulations operate differentially over time or across diagnostic groups. Thelen and Smith argue that such an approach can be applied to available data and can also suggest more fruitful pathways for future research. For example, explanations of the disappearance of the neonatal "stepping reflex" at about 2 months of age have typically referred to maturational processes or to hierarchical control mechanisms such as central pattern generators (Forssberg, 1985) to account for the patterning of developmental pathways. Explanations like these typically make two kinds of assertion. In one, neonatal stepping is subcortically mediated but becomes inhibited by increasing cortical activity prior to the cortex taking control of the stepping (and, ultimately, walking) process. The second approach posits *central pattern generators*—spinal mechanisms that render the elements of stepping possible. These then come under increasing control by higher brain centers. In both these accounts responsibility for the developmental trajectory lies in the biological substrate—much as advocates of the modularist theory-of-mind position argue for the specific localization of such mechanisms in the brain. But Thelen and Smith argue that this reductionism is the result of fallacious reasoning, in that researchers such as Gesell (1939) and McGraw (1945) infer a singular process from an equifinal outcome (Thelen & Smith, 1994, p. 7). The hierarchical-control accounts also fall foul of this criticism, albeit at one level of remove.

Thelen and Smith, using their own and other researchers' observations of locomotor behavior under varying conditions, such as level of arousal of the baby in babies with different rates of weight gain or when immersed in water, noted that the transitions were not as clear as was typically thought. Such observations led Thelen and Smith to conclude that developmental changes in this ability are not unitary but made up of a range of components (e.g., ability to step in a coordinated fashion, ability to use leg movements intentionally, capacity to stand unaided), each of which showed a different developmental trajectory and which was affected differentially by varying environmental contexts. The implications of this analysis are that there is no essence of locomotor development residing in specific locations, mechanisms, or both, in the brain; there are only the co-occurrence of certain action patterns (which in all likelihood, have neural correlates) constrained by specific anatomical and environmental contexts. At any given point in development, stepping behavior in a particular context will be the emergent property of a number of factors operating together. Identification of these factors and their patterns of co-occurrence requires a research program that systematically explores the effects of manipulation of parameters on performance both cross-sectionally and longitudinally.

The Specific Case of Autism

A number of research possibilities follow from the theoretical positions just outlined. For instance, rather than jumping to the conclusion that failure to perform a specific task represents a specific impairment in a module dedicated to that task, as in accounts that explain failure on the false-belief task in terms of a deficient theory-of-mind module or precursor module (Baron-Cohen, 1995; Leslie, 1994), we should ask ourselves questions about what a child has to do in order to pass such a false-belief task or how systematic variations of parameters of the task affect performance. Such an approach will tell us whether these tasks are uniquely tests of mental-state understanding, or whether they tap capacities that, although necessary for mental-state understanding, are not in themselves particular to this domain.

There are now several strands of research that suggest that procedures such as the Sally–Anne false-belief task are not necessarily tests of mental-state understanding. Bowler, Briskman, and Gurvidi (submitted) point out that the scenario of the Sally–Anne task can be conceptualized as requiring the child to understand that the behavior of an agent (Sally) toward a goal (the hidden object) can be mediated by a signal (Sally's belief) that can stand in true or false relation to the goal. On the basis of this analysis, they developed a scenario, illustrated in Fig. 11.1, in which a plane (the goal) could land on one of either a yellow or a blue landing pad. An automatic (driverless) train (the agent) transported goods from the plane to the airport. Because there was no driver to see where the train should go, the system contained a signal light to indicate to the train which route to take. When the plane landed on the one of the pads, the signal light changed the color of that pad and the train went toward the pad with the plane. When children had demonstrated that they understood the operation of the mechanism, they were given a test trial in which the color of the pad with the plane and the signal light were different. When asked to predict where the train would go, it was found that children who passed the Sally–Anne false-belief task overwhelmingly predicted that the train would obey the color of the light. Children who failed the

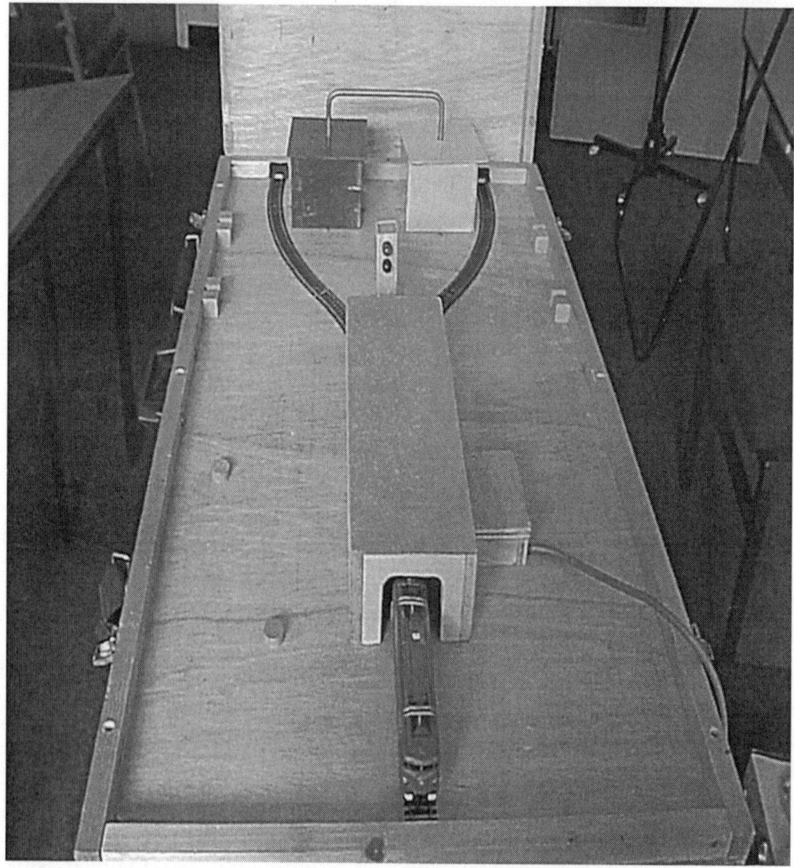

FIG. 11.1. Nonsocial analogue of the false-belief task.

Sally–Anne task, by contrast, overwhelmingly indicated that the train would head toward the actual location of the plane. Moreover, this pattern of results was found for children with typical development, retardation, or autism, even when verbal mental age was partialled out. And for all three groups of children, both tasks were of equal difficulty, suggesting that arguments that explained false-belief understanding in terms of the prior necessity of mechanical understanding or vice versa are untenable.

The most parsimonious interpretation of these findings is that both the train and Sally–Anne tasks tap some common psychological process or set of processes that are not specific to the understanding of mental states. What these common processes are cannot be determined from Bowler et al.'s (submitted) results, but a number of speculations can be made. One possibility is to opt for a weak form of theory of mind by enlarging its domain of operation to more general cases of signal-dependent behavior. However, apart from being uncomfortably post hoc, this vitiates the whole notion of mental-state specificity inherent in the theory-of-mind-deficit account of autism. A second possibility stems from a theoretical analysis of psychological tasks in terms of the number of elements that need to be processed simultaneously for successful solution of the task (Halford, Wilson, & Phillips, 1998). Halford et al. argue that false-belief tasks require three elements to be manipulated and thus present problems up until a specific point in development. A related and more empirically supported analysis of false-belief tasks is that expressed in terms of embedded conditional rules and first formulated by Zelazo, Frye, and their colleagues (see Frye, Zelazo, & Burack, 1998 and Zelazo & Frye, 1998). According to this account, younger children have difficulty with embedded conditional rules, so, in the case of the Sally–Anne task, the statements forming the two rules are "Sally knows where marble is" and "I (the child) know where marble is." The problem, according to Frye and Zelazo, is that younger children have difficulty hierarchizing these statements into a structure whereby one acts as a setting condition for the other, a difficulty that is not restricted to situations involving mental-state reasoning. In a series of experimental studies, Frye, Zelazo, and their colleagues have reported significant correlations between performance on embedded-conditional-rule tasks and false-belief performance (Zelazo, Burack, Boseovski, Jacques, & Frye, chap. 10, this volume).

From the perspective of NDST, these findings could be taken further by exploring the effects of manipulations of sets of variables thought to improve or diminish performance on such tasks. For example, the performance of children with typical development on Sally–Anne tests of false belief can be improved by embedding the scenario in a narrative context (Lewis, Freeman, Hagestadt, & Douglas, 1994) or by using a capricious agent (Bowler, Briskman, & Grice, 1999; see also McGarrigle & Donaldson, 1975). If children with autism and children with typical development are using similar mechanisms when solving false-belief tasks, then such interventions should operate similarly for both groups. Likewise, if the Sally–Anne and train tasks tap common mechanisms, then they should benefit from similar interventions. Differences in response to interventions either across groups, over developmental time, or across tasks imply different underlying processes and would warrant further investigation.

To return to Bowler et al.'s (submitted) train task findings, understanding complex, embedded rules or signal-dependent behavior cannot be the whole story, since typical children who fail these tasks are not autistic, and children with autism who pass them remain so. To account for these observations, they argue that both the Sally–Anne task and their train task require an understanding of the behavior of agents in relation to goals. The question of agents' behavior in relation to objects is an important part of Leslie's account of the development of an understanding of pretense and other mental states (Leslie, 1987). He argues that infants develop agent-centered representations of objects that enable them to grasp the idea that, say, a block of wood can also be represented—in pretense—as another object, such as a car. This ability develops shortly after children begin to engage in *protodeclarative pointing* (Bates, Camaioni, & Volterra, 1975), where they point to an object and alternate their gaze between the object and another person. It can be argued that both these abilities require what Bakeman and Adamson (1984) have called *triadic deployment of attention*, in which the child has to coordinate its attention between him or herself, an object, and another person. Impairments in protodeclarative pointing are well documented in children with autism (Mundy, Sigman, Ungerer, & Sherman, 1986), and there is some evidence that related impairments persist in the older child with autism. For example, a study by Bowler & Thommen (2000) has shown that when asked to describe a short, animated cartoon sequence developed by Heider and Simmel (1944), children with autism are delayed in the extent to which they describe events depicting the action of an animate agent on an inanimate object. Moreover, they are deficient (i.e., they are delayed even in relation to mental-age and IQ-matched controls) in the extent to which they describe chase scenes, which involve the coordinated action at a distance of two animate characters. This is a capability that has been shown by Rochat, Morgan, and Carpenter (1997) to be discriminable by infants at 3 months of age, i.e., *before* they engage in the joint-attention behaviors that are notably absent from the development of children with autism.

The findings of both Bowler et al.'s (submitted) train study and those of Bowler and Thommen (2000) could both be considered under a common rubric of generation of new information from a consideration of the covariation of at least two other spatially, temporally, or in both ways disparate sources of information. Such an account would almost certainly invoke certain kinds of executive processes such as the switching of attention, which are known to be impaired in autism (see Burack, Enns, Stauder, Mottron, and Randolph, 1997; Leekam and Moore, chap. 6, this volume; Travis and Sigman, chap. 14, this volume). But an identification of putative general mechanisms is only a first step. In order to understand fully the phenomenon of autism, both in terms of its difference from typical development and from other forms of developmental psychopathology, we need to follow Thelen and Smith's (1994) prescriptions and establish developmental trajectories for this group across a range of tasks that represent systematic variations of a canonical paradigm, i.e., to study variability as well as stability of performance. This approach would allow us to tease out developmental contingencies and relations of necessity and sufficiency among tasks over time, thus better identifying those processes and sets of processes that are important determinants of a particular developmental pathway.

Longitudinal programs of research would also help to shed light on some of the anomalies documented earlier on in the patterning of developmental contingencies over time in the field of theory-of-mind research in autism, such as Bowler's (1992) observation that individuals with Asperger's syndrome could pass first- and second-order false-belief tasks despite being impaired on their supposed precursor, pretend play (Leslie, 1987). Such findings reinforce the point mentioned earlier that a mechanism's being common to two processes does not imply that it is limited to them; it may be that the two processes are but a subset of a wider set of potential impairments. These findings force us to argue post hoc either that there is more than one way to pass such tests or that some individuals with autism are delayed on such measures and eventually catch up. The only way to settle questions like these is to see what happens in samples of children with and without autism observed over time.

At least two consequences would flow from the course of action just advocated. The first would require us to cease considering development as a linear progression to a fixed end point, with individuals with autism somehow fallen by the wayside or stuck at traffic lights. The second would force us to be more open-minded about relationships of necessity and sufficiency among measures. Such an approach would have the advantage of seeing autism as a different form of adaptation, which may be less suited to certain contexts. Rather than positing a distorted reflection of nature or a blindness to certain aspects of it, the account presented here echoes earlier behavioral accounts by arguing for a different epigenesis leading to a different adaptational end point. It differs from the behaviorist accounts in assuming neither a common organismic structure across individuals or functional independence among behaviors. But most important, it aims to take account of how interactions among processes over time combine to produce adaptational end points across a large range of domains of functioning. In this respect it can encompass the whole range of autistic symptomatology, not just those aspects relating to social impairment.

From Harré's corpuscularian analysis of science, the nature of the fundamental particles in the approach advocated here will depend on the level of analysis at which we wish to operate. So, for example, it may make sense to speak of relations between children's performance on false-belief or appearance-reality tasks (Flavell, Green, & Flavell, 1986) and adaptive social functioning. But we need not feel constrained to carry these units of analysis directly to the level of brain function, or to consider them equivalent at different points in the developmental trajectory. To do either of these things, a careful analysis is needed of structures at other levels (both singly and in combination) that are thought to contribute to the particular phenomenon under investigation. Due consideration should also be given to how the interaction between phenomena at different levels changes over time. Chemists readily understand that the physical properties of compounds described in the high-level language of carboxyl groups or aromatic rings bear a highly indirect relation to the physical properties of equally complex compounds that are their precursors in a chain of synthesis or to those of the carbon, hydrogen, and oxygen that compose them. Like the chemist, the developmental psychologist should not assume simple commensurability between psychological functions at different levels of analysis or at different points in a developmental trajectory.

Autism is a developmental disorder with a wide-ranging symptom profile. Attempts to conceptualize the condition in a way that transcends descriptions at fixed points in time or concentration on specific clusters of symptoms need to do a number of things. They need to recognize that the relation between the properties of underlying systems and those of the phenomena to be explained may not be straightforward. They must also adopt a developmental perspective that not only acknowledges that behavior changes over time but that such changes are lawful, and that these laws can be elucidated. Such elucidation should eventually give clues to underlying structures and their interactions that will inform the whole of autistic symptomatology and not just a part of it.

ACKNOWLEDGMENTS

This paper was written while the author was on sabbatical leave at the Department of Educational and Counseling Psychology, McGill University, and l'Hôpital Rivière des Prairies, Université de Montréal. Sincere thanks are due to Jake Burack, Laurent Mottron, Charles Legg, and Donald Peterson for discussions, to the editors for helpful feedback, and to the British Council and the Wellcome Trust for financial assistance during the writing of the paper.

REFERENCES

Baird, G., Charman, T., Baron-Cohen, S., Cox, A., Swettenham, J., Wheelwright, S., Drew, A. & Kemal, S. (2000). A screening instrument for autism at 18 months of age: A six-year follow-up study. *Journal of the American Academy of Child and Adolescent Psychiatry, 39,* 694–702.

Bakeman, R., & Adamson, L. (1984). Co-ordinating attention to people and objects in mother-infant and peer-infant interaction. *Child Development, 55,* 1278–1289.

Baron-Cohen, S. (1995). *Mindblindness: An essay on autism and theory of mind.* Cambridge, MA: MIT Press.

Baron-Cohen, S., Leslie, A., and Frith, U. (1985). Does the autistic child have a 'theory of mind'? *Cognition, 21,* 37–46.

Baron-Cohen, S., Tager-Flusberg, H., & Cohen, D. J. (Eds.). (2000). *Understanding other minds: Perspectives from cognitive science* (2nd ed.). Oxford, UK: Oxford University Press.

Bates, E., Camaioni, L., & Volterra, V. (1975). The acquisition of performatives prior to speech. *Merrill-Palmer Quarterly, 21,* 205–226.

Bowler, D. M. (1992). 'Theory of Mind' in Asperger's syndrome. *Journal of Child Psychology and Psychiatry, 33,* 877–893.

Bowler, D. M., & Briskman, J. (2000). Photographic cues do not always facilitate performance on false belief tasks in children with autism. *Journal of Autism and Developmental Disorders, 30,* 295–304.

Bowler, D. M., Briskman, J., & Grice, S. (1999). Experimenter effects on children's understanding of false drawings and false beliefs. *Journal of Genetic Psychology, 160,* 443–460.

Bowler, D. M., Briskman, J., & Gurvidi, N. (submitted). Understanding the mind or predicting signal-dependent action?: Performance of children with and without autism on analogues of the false belief task.

Bowler, D. M., & Norris, M. (1993). Predictors of success on false belief tasks in pre-school children. In G. Rudinger, C. Rietz, U. Kleimas, & T. Meiser (Eds.), *Developmental psychology in a changing Europe*. Bonn, Germany: Pace.

Bowler, D. M., & Strom, E. (1998). Elicitation of first-order 'theory of mind' in children with autism and non-autistic children. *Autism, 2,* 33–44.

Bowler, D. M., & Thommen, E. (2000). Attribution of mechanical and social causality to animated displays by children with autism. *Autism, 4,* 147–171.

Burack, J. A., Enns, J. T., Stauder, J. E. A., Mottron, L., & Randolph, B. (1997). Attention and autism: Behavioral and electrophysiological evidence. In D. J. Cohen & F. R. Volkmar (Eds.), *Handbook of autism and pervasive developmental disorders* (pp. 226–247). New York: Wiley.

Charman, T., & Lynggaard, H. (1998). Does a photographic cue facilitate false belief performance in children with autism. *Journal of Autism and Developmental Disorders, 18,* 33–42.

Cromer, R. (1974). The development of language and cognition: The cognition hypothesis. In B. Foss (Ed.), *New Perspectives in Child Development* (pp. 184–252). Harmondsworth, UK: Penguin.

Eisenmajer, R., & Prior, M. (1991). Cognitive linguistic correlates of 'theory of mind' ability in autistic children. *British Journal of Developmental Psychology, 9,* 351–364.

Ferster, C. B., (1961). Positive reinforcement and behavioral deficits of autistic children. *Child Development, 32,* 437–456.

Flavell, J. H., Green, F. L. & Flavell, E. R. (1986). Development of knowledge about the appearance–reality distinction. *Monographs of the Society for Research in Child Development, 51,* (Serial No. 212).

Fodor, J. A. (1975). *The language of thought.* New York: Crowell.

Fodor, J. A. (1983). *The modularity of mind.* Cambridge, MA: MIT Press.

Forssberg, H. (1985). Ontogeny of human locomotor control. I. Infant stepping, supported locomotion and transition to independent locomotion. *Experimental Brain Research, 57,* 480–493.

Frith, C., & Frith, U. (2000). The physiological basis of theory of mind: Functional neuroimaging studies. In. S. Baron-Cohen, H. Tager-Flusberg, & D. J. Cohen (Eds.), *Understanding other minds: Perspectives from cognitive neuroscience* (pp. 334–356). Oxford, UK: Oxford University Press.

Frye, D., Zelazo, P. D., & Burack, J. A. (1998). Cognitive complexity and control. I. Theory of mind in typical and atypical development. *Current Directions in Psychological Science, 7,* 116–121.

Gardner, H. (1985). *The mind's new science: a history of the cognitive revolution.* New York: Basic Books.

Gesell, A. (1939). Reciprocal interweaving in neuromotor development. *Journal of Comparative Neurology, 70,* 161–180.

Halford, G. S., Wilson, W. S., & Phillips, S. (1998). Processing capacity defined by relational complexity: Implications for comparative, developmental and cognitive psychology. *Behavioral and Brain Sciences, 21,* 803–864.

Harré, R. (1972). *The philosophies of science: An introductory survey.* Oxford, UK: Oxford University Press.

Hawking, S. (1993). *Black holes and baby universes and other essays.* London: Bantam Press.

Heider, F., & Simmel, M. (1944). An experimental study of apparent behavior. *American Journal of Psychology, 57,* 243–249.

Hermelin, B., & O'Connor, N. (1970). *Psychological experiments with autistic children.* Oxford, UK: Pergamon.

Kanner, L. (1943). Autistic disturbances of affective contact. *Nervous Child, 2,* 217–250.

Leslie, A. M. (1994). ToMM, ToBY and Agency: Core architecture and domain specificity. In L. Hirschfeld & S. Gelman (Eds.), *Mapping the mind: Domain specificity in cognition and culture.* Cambridge, UK: Cambridge University Press.

Leslie, A. M. (1987). Pretence and representation: The origins of "theory of mind." *Psychological Review, 94,* 412–426.

Lewis, C., Freeman, N., Hagestadt, C., & Douglas, H. (1994). Narrative access and production in preschoolers' false belief reasoning. *Cognitive Development, 9,* 397–424.

Lovaas, O. I. (1987). Behavioral treatment and normal educational and intellectual functioning in young autistic children. *Journal of Abnormal Child Psychology, 20,* 555–566.

Lovaas, O. I., Koegel, R., Simmons, J., & Long, J. S. (1973). Some generalization and follow-up measures on autistic children in behavior therapy. *Journal of Applied Behavior Analysis, 6,* 131–166.

McGarrigle, J., & Donaldson, M. (1975). Conservation accidents. *Cognition, 3,* 341–350.

McGraw, M. B. (1945). *The neuromuscular maturation of the human infant.* New York: Columbia University Press.

McGregor, E., Whiten, A., & Blackburn, P. (1998). Teaching theory of mind by highlighting intention and illustrating thoughts: A comparison of their effectiveness with three-year-olds and autistic subjects. *British Journal of Developmental Psychology, 16,* 281–300.

Monod, J. (1972). *Chance and necessity.* London: Collins.

Mundy, P., Sigman, M., Ungerer, J., & Sherman, T. (1986). Defining the social deficits of autism: The contribution of non-verbal communication measures. *Journal of Child Psychology and Psychiatry, 27,* 657–669.

Perner, J. (1991). *Understanding the representational mind.* London: MIT Press.

Perner, J., Leekam, S., & Wimmer, H. (1987). Two-year-olds' difficulty with false belief—the case for a conceptual deficit. *British Journal of Developmental Psychology, 5,* 125–137.

Rochat, P., Morgan, R., & Carpenter, M. (1997). Young infants' sensitivity to movement information specifying social causality. *Cognitive Development, 12,* 441–465.

Sapsford, R. (1984). Levels of analysis. In R. Stevens (Ed.), *Metablock: Social psychology, development, experience and behavior in a social world.* Buckingham, UK: Open University Press.

Sigman, M. (1998). Change and continuity in the development of children with autism. *Journal of Child Psychology and Psychiatry, 39,* 817-828.

Sigman, M., & Ruskin, E. (1999). Continuity and change in the social competence of children with autism, Down syndrome, and developmental delays. *Monographs of the Society for Research in Child Development, 64,* 131–139.

Thelen, E., & Smith, L. B. (1994). *A dynamic systems approach to the development of cognition and action.* Cambridge, MA: MIT Press.

Thompson, D. W. (1968). *On growth and form* (2nd ed.). Cambridge, UK: Cambridge University Press.

Van Geert, P. (1998). We almost had a great future behind us: The contribution of non-linear dynamics to developmental-science-in-the-making. *Developmental Science, 1,* 143–159.

Wimmer, H., & Perner, J. (1983). Beliefs about beliefs: Representation and constraining function of wrong beliefs in young children's understanding of deception. *Cognition, 13,* 103–128.

Zelazo, P. D., & Frye, D. (1998). Cognitive complexity and control: II. The development of executive control in childhood. *Current Directions in Psychological Science, 47,* 121–126.

12

Social and Nonsocial Development in Autism: Where Are the Links?

Francesca Happé
Social, Genetic and Developmental Psychiatry Research Centre
Institute of Psychiatry, King's College, London, England

INTRODUCTION

Autism is characterized by an array of specific social and nonsocial abnormalities. Not surprisingly, attention and theoretical speculation have tended to show a pendulum swing to and fro between the handicapping social and communication difficulties and the puzzling repetitive behaviors and fascinating special interests exhibited by people with autism. Current psychological theories of autism can be divided into those that posit a primary social impairment and those that suggest a primary nonsocial impairment. At present these two camps also divide along a different dimension: Social theories suggest a domain-specific difficulty (processing a certain stimulus class), whereas nonsocial theories implicate domain-general processes (which apply a certain process to many different types of content). The aim of the present chapter is to explore possible links between domain-specific social impairment and domain-general nonsocial abnormalities. Is it possible to trace a developmental path from a primary social deficit to the nonsocial features of autism, or vice versa? Of course there are alternatives to this sort of, perhaps unrealistic, parsimony. Autism may very well be the result of multiple primary deficits. Alternatively, the array of social and nonsocial features seen may result from a biological coincidence—disturbance to proximal but functionally unrelated brain substrates (Pennington et al., 1997). This chapter, however, explores possible links between social and nonsocial features of autism at the cognitive level.

The Challenge. Broadly speaking, social and nonsocial accounts of autism face different challenges. Social theories explain well why certain behaviors and skills should be intact in autism; for example, why inferring a false belief may be hard but inferring the content of an out-of-date photo may be easy; why pointing to direct another's attention may be absent but pointing to direct another's behavior does emerge (see chapters in Baron-Cohen, Tager-Flusberg, & Cohen, 2000). However, they face a challenge in trying to account for the nonsocial features, such as repetitive behaviors and stereotypies, failure to generalize skills, and the characteristic uneven IQ profile. Note that it is as yet unclear which of these features are specific, universal, or both, in autism. While the diagnostic criterion of "repetitive and restricted interests and activities" (DSM–IV; APA, 1994) must by definition apply in every case, it may not be specific to autism—individuals with other forms of mental handicap show similar behaviors (e.g., Tan, Salgado, & Fahn, 1997), and it remains to be seen whether repetitive behaviors in autism are distinct in quality or quantity (see Charman & Swettenham, chap. 16, this volume, for discussion). Similarly, although savant skills (specific areas of talent in music, art, memory, or calculation that are out of line with general level of functioning) are at least 10 times more common in people with autism than in other handicapped groups, they do occur in people without autism (Rimland & Hill, 1984; see Mottron & Burack, chap. 7, this volume). Theories of autism are not entirely absolved of explaining features also seen in other groups, but it will certainly be important to know which features are specific and universal when attempting to trace developmental causal links.

Nonsocial accounts have, in general, developed with just such aspects of autism in mind, but are often at risk of explaining too much. They face the challenge of accounting for social difficulties of a remarkably specific sort; for example, children with autism generally fail to use or understand deception, but can use sabotage: Similarly, they understand "seeing" but not "knowing." These "fine cuts" suggest that autism is not a disorder of sociability, but is characterized instead by deficits in a specific social ability, "theory of mind" (see chapters in Baron-Cohen, Tager-Flusberg, & Cohen, 2000, for details; see Frith & Happé, 1994, for discussion of the fine-cuts approach). To derive such a specific profile from a domain-general deficit is no small challenge.

In this chapter three current accounts of autism are discussed as examples of social and nonsocial theories of autism. The first is the influential hypothesis that autism is the result of deficits in "theory of mind"— the ability to attribute mental states, an example of a domain-specific social account (see Tager-Flusberg, chap. 9, this volume). The second is the more recent notion that autism is a dysexecutive syndrome (see Hughes, chap. 13, this volume). The third is the proposal that autism is characterized by a cognitive style—weak central coherence—which biases processing in favor of local features at the expense of global, context-dependent meaning or gestalt (see Happé, 1999; for an alternative but related view, see Plaisted, chap. 8, this volume). These latter two accounts suggest domain-general, rather than specifically social, deficits. Other theories are mentioned briefly to illustrate general points. It is hoped that, whatever the lasting merits of these specific accounts, at least some of the general points concerning the relation between social and nonsocial accounts will have enduring relevance.

ESTABLISHING CAUSAL LINKS

Developmental Versus Online Cause

This chapter is primarily concerned with discussing possible developmental causal links between social and nonsocial features of autism. Such developmental causes are logically distinct from online causes, and it may be worth saying a word here about the latter to help keep this distinction clear. There are two ways, for example, that executive deficits might "cause" theory-of-mind impairment (as reflected, for example, in false-belief task failure): Executive functions may be necessary to the development of metarepresentational skill, and/or executive control may be necessary online for metarepresentation or some other component of task success (see Perner, Stummer, & Lang, 1999, for fuller discussion). The necessity for online executive control in theory of mind tasks has been argued extensively in the literature, with, for example, the suggestion of "reality masking" (due to impaired inhibitory control) underlying false-belief task failure (Robinson & Mitchell, 1995; Hughes & Russell, 1993). The same is true for links between theory of mind and central coherence; while some tests of theory of mind may require context-dependent processing (e.g., story comprehension, Happé, 1994a), this online relation is distinct from possible developmental links between metarepresentation and coherence. It is quite possible, in principle, for such online effects to operate without positing any developmental link between the ability to represent mental states and executive control or coherence. For this reason, online associations and dissociations between social and nonsocial ability may not tell us about developmental links.

So, for example, Ozonoff, Rogers, and Pennington (1991) showed that some individuals on the autism spectrum do poorly on executive-function tests while passing theory-of-mind tasks—and concluded that executive dysfunction is the more fundamental deficit. Leaving aside the problem of equating these different tasks for difficulty and sensitivity, this finding cannot tell us about developmental causes. It may well be, for example, that those individuals with autism who now pass the theory-of-mind tests did not possess this competence at the stage in development when it really counted (e.g., preschool years). In this case theory-of-mind problems (at least delay) may be universal and may be the developmental cause of executive dysfunction. Equally, although the data may appear to show that poor executive functions are not the cause of theory-of-mind failure (since individuals with significant executive impairments passed theory-of-mind tasks), we cannot assess this question without knowing about intact development of theory of mind and impaired development of executive functions. So while Ozonoff et al.'s very interesting study provides evidence that good executive function is not necessary online for theory-of-mind task success, it is silent on the question of developmental cause.

The importance of having information about the development of cognitive abilities is highlighted by recent work showing the fluidity of executive skills in development. Griffith, Pennington, Wehner, and Rogers (1999) found no differences between age- and MA-matched autism and mental handicap groups of children at 3 or 4 years in performance on certain executive-function tasks (e.g., working memory)—differences that do reach significance at age $5^1/_2$ (McEvoy, Rogers, & Pennington, 1993; see also Bennetto, Pennington, & Rogers, 1996). At the biological level, too, snapshots of brain functioning at one age may miss transient but developmentally important anomalies; Zilbovicius et al. (1995) found transient hypoperfusion of frontal regions in 5 children with autism at 3 to 4 years but not at 6 to 7 years. Thus we cannot conclude that the pattern of deficits we see at one age necessarily represents the pattern of deficits (or relations between deficits) at previous ages. Clearly, longitudinal studies tracking children with autism from the earliest possible age are needed.

Types Of Evidence For Developmental Causal Relations

How can we set about establishing developmental causal relations between areas of psychological functioning in autism? If we posit that impairment in function A causes developmental disruption in function(s) B, several sorts of data could, in principle, provide strong evidence for or against.

What Comes First in Normal Development, and What Impairment Manifests First in Autism? Our theory predicts that, if deficits in A cause dysfunction in B, A will precede B in normal development, and dysfunction in A will be evident before dysfunction in B (see Angold & Hay, 1993, for a discussion of precursor issues in normal and abnormal development; see Gómez, Sarriá, & Tamarit, 1993, for discussion of these issues in autism). What evidence do we have concerning the normal developmental precedence of the key social and nonsocial abilities implicated in autism? Executive functions are widely defined and cover a number of more or less sophisticated abilities. While the frontal lobes have traditionally been considered to mature only in middle or late childhood, it is clear that much younger children have already started on a developmental trajectory in abilities such as inhibition, attention switching, and planning (e.g., Diamond & Taylor, 1996; Hughes, chap. 13, this volume). Russell (1996, 1997) proposes that normal theory-of-mind development rests upon a "pretheoretical" form of self-awareness, which in turn requires the ability to monitor one's own actions—the infant's experience of "self as agent" is crucial. This would appear to be a very early emerging competence in typically-developing children—certainly in place well before false-belief test success at age 3 or 4 years. However, theory of mind, or its social precursors, can also be traced to infancy (see Charman, 2000, for discussion). Baron-Cohen (1995) has pointed to gaze following and joint attention as the first signs of the social mechanism that becomes theory of mind—abilities in place in typically-developing children by age 18 months. By 18 months the infant also demonstrates ability to track intentions in an imitation task (Meltzoff, 1995). Meltzoff and Gopnick (1993) have discussed an even earlier ability, namely neonatal imitation, as a key competence for later social ability—although there is as yet no evidence to suggest that absence of neonatal imitation would have later deleterious consequences, nor that such imitation is in fact missing in autism. Central coherence has not been explored in young children, but signs of global processing are present in infants. Bhatt, Rovee-Collier, and Shyi (1994), for example, showed that 6-month-olds transferred learning (kicking to make a mobile move) across contexts (crib-liners) that differed in features but shared configural (pattern) characteristics. It is unclear at present, then, whether theory of mind, executive function, or central coherence emerges first in normal development—in part because of the uncertain status of precursor behaviors for these functions.

Which area of functioning is first to show deficits in autism? Answering this question has been difficult because autism is rarely diagnosed before the age of 3 years. So, for example, we do not know about neonatal imitation in children with autism and are left extrapolating (with questionable justification) from studies of older children. Recent work by Baron-Cohen and his colleagues has pushed back this boundary, finding reliable signs of autism at 18 months—namely lack of gaze following, protoimperative pointing, and pretend play (Baron-Cohen et al., 1996). Charman et al. (1998) studied these children at 20 months and found clear impairments in joint attention and imitation—impairments that were also seen, however, in children with developmental delay but without autism. Studies of early home videos of children later diagnosed as having autism may show abnormalities in the first year of life (e.g., less orientation to others), although to date it is not clear which are specific to autism (Adrien et al., 1993; Osterling & Dawson, 1994). Some parents of children with autism report that their children appeared entirely normal until age $1^1/_2$ or 2 years (Volkmar & Cohen, 1989), which might argue against primary deficits in a process as fundamental as action monitoring or "agency." However, it is possible that if we knew what to look for we might find signs pre-18 months betraying lack of this very early executive control—perhaps passivity? The same holds for early signs of weak coherence: We have anecdotal reports of toddlers with autism being fascinated with details and parts of objects, but perhaps there are even earlier signs of weak coherence (e.g., featural versus configural object recognition) if only we knew what exactly to look for.

What Predicts What, Longitudinally? If A causes B, deficits in A and B should covary. Depending on the nature of the causal effect, degree of ability or impairment in A may predict degree of ability or impairment in B. Alternatively, a threshold effect may occur, where a critical level of A is necessary for B to develop, but degree of A over this threshold is not reflected in the degree of B. What evidence is there for predictive relation between social and nonsocial competencies in normal development? A number of studies have demonstrated significant correlations between tasks involving executive skills (e.g., inhibiting prepotent response, conditional rules, attentional flexibility, working memory) and theory-of-mind tests at 3 to 4 years—and in most cases such correlations remain significant with age and verbal ability partialled out (see Perner et al., 1999, for full review and discussion; see Hughes, chap. 13, this volume). That such correlations are not merely the result of shared methodological demands (e.g., requirement to inhibit reference to reality in standard false-belief tasks) is nicely demonstrated by Hughes (1998), who found equally strong correlations between attentional flexibility and false-belief prediction, and flexibility and false-belief explanation tasks (the latter having no obvious executive demand; Perner et al., 1999). Rather fewer studies have moved beyond correlation to attempt to establish causal direction—which would in principle be revealed by asymmetries in the contingencies of passing or failing tasks. Bischof-Kohler (1998; cited in Perner et al., 1999) has shown that among 3- and 4-year-olds, theory-of-mind test competence appears to be necessary but not sufficient for good performance on a simple planning test—suggesting that awareness of one's own mental states aids executive control rather than vice versa. Perner, Lang, and Stummer (1998) examined the relation between an intention attribution task (discriminating whether a knee-jerk reflex was intentional) and standard theory-of-mind and executive tasks. They found that the knee-jerk task explained a significant amount of variance of performance on false belief, even if entered into a regression analysis after executive tasks, but that the opposite was not true—that is, executive tasks no longer explained a significant proportion of variance on false belief once knee-jerk performance was entered. They argue from this that the conceptual advance demonstrated in the standard and knee-jerk theory-of-mind tests cannot be due to advances in executive control. Such asymmetries are in principle informative. However, it remains possible to argue that the problem of equating tests of theory of mind and executive functioning for difficulty (and hence discriminant power) weakens such evidence.

Hughes and others are exploring the developmental causal links between theory of mind and executive functions in longitudinal studies of normally developing children. She has tracked children over one year from age 3 years 6 months and found that executive-function performance predicts theory of mind (even with theory of mind at time 1 partialled out), but that the reverse is not true (Hughes, 1998). It may be, however, that there are even earlier effects of theory of mind on executive functions—and Hughes highlights the importance of testing with relevant tasks at different developmental stages. There are no longitudinal studies of central coherence as yet, and it remains to be seen whether coherence is, as seems implied, a persistent trait or whether it shows a developmental trajectory. Early individual differences have been measured in processes that may relate to coherence. Colombo, Freeseman, Coldren, and Frick (1995), for example, have shown concurrent relations in 4-month-olds between preference for global versus local stimulus characteristics and short versus long looking time (itself predictive of cognitive level). Whether such infant measures show a predictive relation to executive function or theory of mind has not been assessed.

What evidence is there for the predictive status of social or nonsocial abnormalities in autism? Again, there is little evidence from the first 2 years, because of timing of diagnosis. Sigman and colleagues have followed up a group of 70 children with autism from age 5 or earlier over 1 year and a subsample of the cohort over 8 to 12 years (Sigman & Ruskin, 1999). They found that early levels of nonverbal communication, representational play, and emotional responsiveness predicted later degree of peer engagement at school. In addition, responsiveness to joint attention at time 1 predicted language gains 1 year later and 8 to 9 years later. What predictive relation exists between these social capacities and later nonsocial features of autism remains unclear.

Clinically, development of useful language before age 5 has been taken as a sign of good prognosis (Gillberg, 1991)—the latter, presumably reflecting in part level of competence in executive control (e.g., inhibition of inappropriate actions, planning, and monitoring of appropriate behavior). Although we are far from understanding what determines which children do develop language, the role of social understanding and intention-tracking/joint attention is becoming increasingly clear from research on normal word learning (e.g., Tomasello, 1992; Baldwin, 1995). General intelligence, or IQ, is also a prognostic indicator—although it is not clear whether this should be interpreted as suggesting that domain-general cognitive capacity somehow determines development of social understanding in autism, or whether high IQ allows some compensation for nonetheless impaired social understanding. Later in life, nonsocial measures related to executive functions have been found to predict progress: Berger, van Spaendonck, and Horstinck (1993) found that cognitive shifting predicted social understanding in high-functioning people with autism (aged 16 to 25 years) at 2-year follow-up. Whether such relations exist in early development is an interesting question for future research.

To test this causal link we might look to intervention studies; our hypothesis suggests that if we intervene to preserve or restore A we will preserve or restore B. Early intervention is underway, focusing on social deficits in young children with autism, and it will be informative to see the effects of such therapy on nonsocial aspects such as executive function and central coherence.

Do All Children Showing Deficit A, Go on to Show Deficit B?

Note that the opposite prediction is not valid; not all children showing abnormal B need have reached this point due to deficits in A, since other functions may also be necessary for normal development of B. Associations and dissociations in current functioning of A and B provide interesting, but inconclusive, evidence regarding developmental causal connections (see preceding section).

Do all children with theory-of-mind problems show executive deficits or weak coherence? On the face of it, the answer would appear to be "no." Here the question is clouded by the fact that any test is at best an indirect probe of an underlying cognitive ability. The evidence is that some people who do not have autism, such as children with general developmental delay (Yirmiya, Erel, Shaked, & Solomonica-Levi, 1998) and deaf children not exposed to early signing (Peterson & Siegal, 1995), may fail theory-of-mind tests. These groups have not been reported to show specific executive dysfunction or anomalies of coherence, although these have not been systematically investigated. However, whether such individuals really lack the ability to attribute mental states is up for question; in autism, theory-of-mind task failure is validated by everyday life "mind-blindness," which does not appear to be the case in these other groups (e.g., Frith, Happé, & Siddons, 1994).

The existence of executive-function deficits in a wide array of developmental disorders not accompanied by qualitative social impairment (e.g., ADHD, Williams syndrome, Tourettes) appears to argue against a causal link from executive to social skills. However, the term "executive function" covers a wide range of somewhat fractionable abilities (including planning, monitoring, inhibition, generativity), and autism may be unique in its particular profile of dysfunctions (Pennington & Ozonoff, 1996). Ozonoff and her colleagues have speculated that autism is characterized by deficits in shifting set, in contrast to, say, ADHD in which deficits on tests of inhibitory control are notable. Another possible dimension of difference is in the developmental timing and trajectory of executive functions—the point in development at which executive dysfunctions emerge may determine their secondary effects and long-term impact.

In considering relations between coherence and other functions, the only data available so far relate to online relations. There is evidence that some people with autism who pass false-belief tests still show weak central coherence. For example, theory-of-mind task performance is related to performance on the Comprehension subtest of the Wechsler scales (commonly thought to require pragmatic and social skill), but not to performance on the Block Design subtest (Happé, 1994b); good performance on Block Design has been taken as a marker of weak central coherence. Weak coherence seems to characterize people with autism regardless of their theory-of-mind ability in studies using perceptual (e.g., visual illusions, Happé, 1996), and verbal tasks (e.g., homograph reading, Happé, 1997). Jarrold, Butler, Cottington, and Jimenez (2000), however, have evidence of an inverse relation between ability to ascribe mental states to faces (interpreted as tapping theory of mind) and segmentation ability (interpreted as evidence of weak coherence, Shah & Frith, 1983; or good "folk physics," Baron-Cohen & Hammer, 1997). They found that performance on Baron-Cohen's "Eyes task" and speed on the Embedded Figures Test (EFT) were significantly negatively correlated in a sample of undergraduates. In addition, in a group of children with autism, false-belief task performance was negatively correlated with EFT performance, with the correlation reaching significance once verbal mental age was partialled out. Longitudinal studies would be necessary, however, to establish possible developmental causal relations between coherence and theory of mind.

POSSIBLE MODES OF DEVELOPMENTAL EFFECT BETWEEN SOCIAL AND NONSOCIAL ABNORMALITIES

Is it possible, in principle, to derive the very specific pattern of intact and impaired social abilities in autism from a primary nonsocial deficit? This is quite a challenge, perhaps more than for the opposite causal direction if only because so much research in the last 10 years has been focused on refining the precise nature of the social impairment. It is hard to see how some domain-general accounts could lead to this pattern. For example, is it plausible that a general deficit in switching attention rapidly (Courchesne et al., 1994) would affect only those social abilities requiring mentalizing? Such a claim appears to be based on an implicit (sometimes explicit) assumption that the social world constitutes the most complex set of stimuli we process, and hence any domain-general difficulty (such as attention switching) will be most dramatically evident in social disability. This claim, though intuitively appealing, requires empirical test, and as yet we lack a metric for comparing the challenge posed by social and nonsocial information processing (but see Zelazo, Burack, Boseovski, Jacques, & Frye, chap. 10, this volume). Indeed, given the likelihood that we have evolved cognitive capacities precisely to handle certain types of problem, even a formal computational analysis of social and nonsocial problems may not reflect the degree of challenge to the human cognitive system. For example, 3-D object recognition is challenging to artificial intelligence, while multiplication is not; yet intellectually impaired children have no difficulty with the former but often fail to master the latter.

Can a developmental causal link be sketched from executive dysfunction to the specific social deficits in autism? The link between executive-function deficits and theory of mind has been discussed elsewhere at length and with greater expertise than this author could attempt (see e.g., Russell, 1996; Hughes, chap. 13, this volume). Russell (1997) has suggested that autism constitutes a primary deficit in agency, due to executive deficits in recognizing one's own actions as one's own, and that this deficit in agency leads to later problems in understanding minds. Rogers and Pennington (1991), on the other hand, suggest that early prefrontal abnormalities affect neonatal imitation through which, they postulate, normal theory of mind develops. For illustration, Fig. 12.1 shows some of the possible links between executive function and theory of mind, using different arrow types to attempt to distinguish online and developmental effects.

Central coherence was at first proposed to account for the theory-of-mind deficit as well as for nonsocial assets and deficits (Frith, 1989). Deficits in theory of mind were conceptualized as just one consequence of weak central coherence: Understanding social interaction and extracting the higher level representation of thoughts underlying behavior, was seen as the pinnacle of coherent processing and gist extraction. Thus, on this account, people with autism were socially

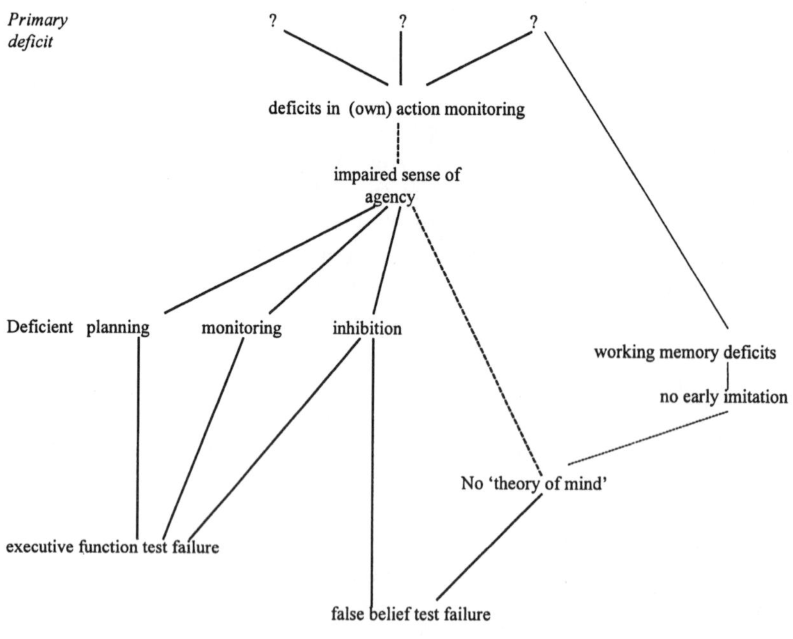

FIG. 12.1. Could a primary nonsocial deficit in executive functions result in secondary social features?

impaired because they were unable to derive the high-level meaning necessary for development and use of theory of mind. Subsequently, Frith and Happé (1994) modified this view and proposed as a working hypothesis that the two aspects of autism—weak central coherence and impaired theory of mind—were independent (though interacting) facets of the disorder (for discussion see Happé, 2000). Could it be, however, that weak coherence is the developmental cause of mind-blindness? The finding that even people with autism who pass theory-of-mind tests show weak coherence does not rule out such a developmental relationship. Figure 12.2 shows an attempt to derive social abnormalities from weak coherence. In this highly speculative model, autism is characterized by exemplar-based encoding that preferences detail information and fails to extract invariances across stimuli for higher level meaning. One result is that an exact stimulus-stimulus match might be required for recognition ("insistence on sameness") or, alternatively, recognition might depend on the presence of a (to us, minor) detail of the original presentation (leading to limited and idiosyncratic generalization; Rincover & Koegel, 1975). Featural processing may lead directly to talents such as absolute pitch (Heaton, Hermelin, & Pring, 1998; Takeuchi & Hulse, 1993) and, where accompanied by conducive environmental or personality factors, to the development of musical, artistic, or numeric talents. Featural processing of faces (as reflected in, for example, decreased inversion decrement) may be an online effect of weak coherence, but might impair the development of emotion recognition (McKelvie, 1995) and hence impact on theory of mind developmentally. As the child develops, exemplar encoding and detail focus will lead to the development of an idiosyncratic network of semantic associations, and a calculation of relevance that is out of line with the norm. This in itself may hamper the establishment of joint attention online, since this relies on sharing a common focus of interest as well as the ability to follow line of sight (Happé, 1994c). In this model, problems in theory of mind might derive developmentally from difficulties processing facial emotion and deficits in joint-attention. This latter will feedback; children with idiosyncratic interests will not have their interests shaped by others if they fail to develop joint-attention skills. It is conceivable that, in addition, integrative processing of stimuli in context provides the inputs necessary for the maturation of the theory of mind mechanism.

Is it possible to derive the puzzling nonsocial assets and deficits from a primary social impairment? Figure 12.3 shows an example of a causal model attempting to do this. The starting point may be one or more primary deficits in social processes such as joint attention that result, developmentally, in lack of theory of mind. Alternatively, there may be a primary deficit in an innately predisposed metarepresentational (theory of mind) mechanism. In either case, failure to recognize the intentions of others, leads online to failure of socially-directed attention. Without directive processes such as social referencing and joint attention, word learning and learning by imitation will be delayed or absent (Bloom, 1997). Developmentally, interests will not be socially shaped and

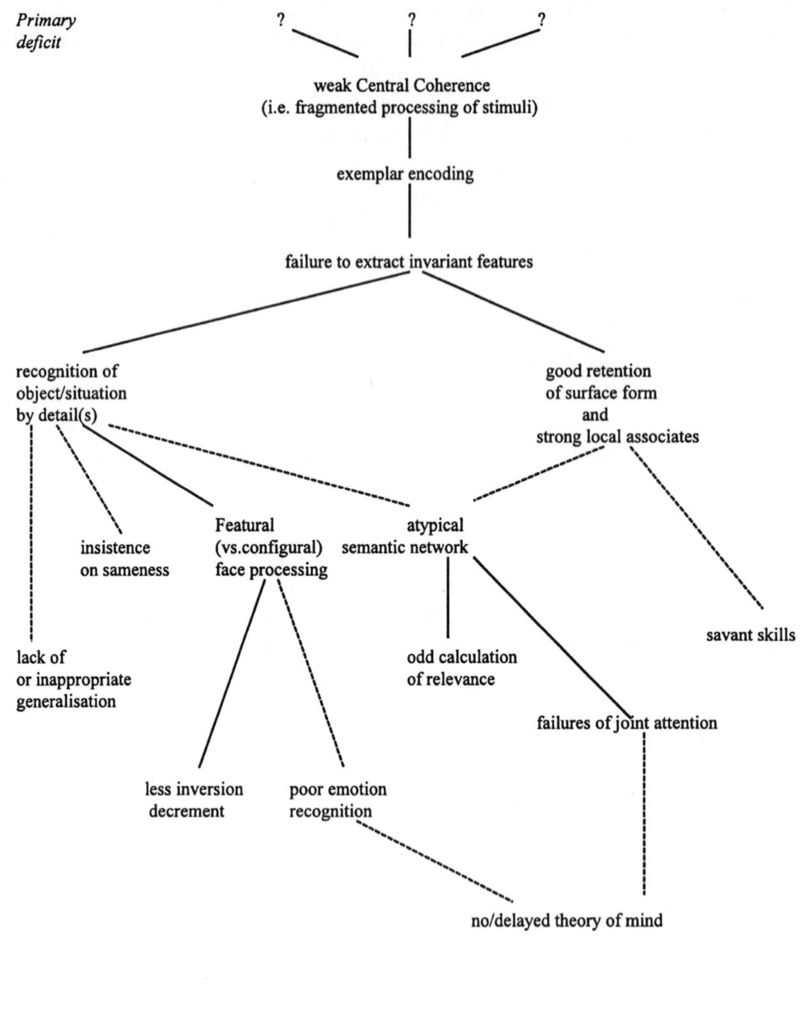

FIG. 12.2. Could a primary nonsocial abnormality in central coherence result in secondary social features?

will be idiosyncratic. Might this path be sufficient to account for weak coherence and detail focus? To argue this one would need to assume that without social direction our cognitive systems would default to local processing. This seems implausible at first glance. However, it is worth noting that even some apparently

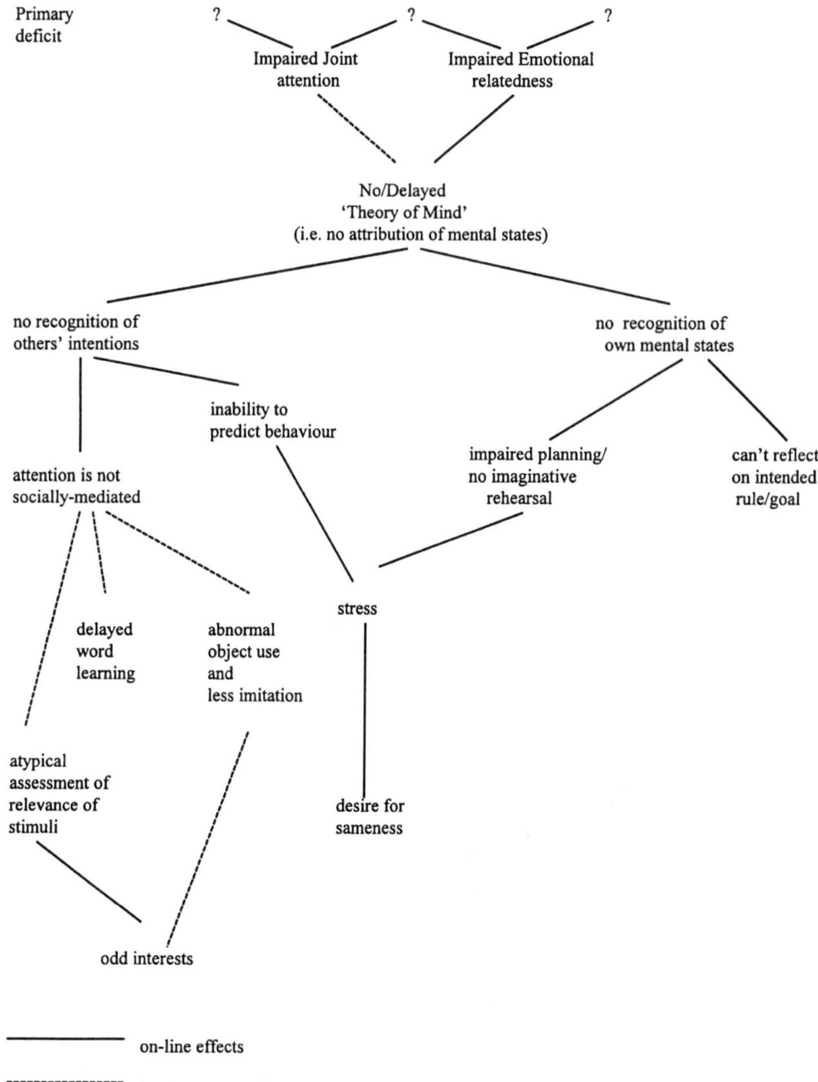

FIG. 12.3. Could a primary social deficit result in secondary nonsocial features?

low-level perceptual processes that in ordinary children and adults show global bias may reflect higher level influences. For example, Fagot & Deruelle (1997) found that baboons do not show the global-precedence effect seen in humans viewing hierarchical figures, despite very similar low-level visual systems. Coren and Enns (1993) found that object category (e.g., human face versus dog) affected the degree of distortion in the Titchener circles illusion: a top-down effect on apparently low-level perceptual processing. It is conceivable, then, that our tendency for extraction of higher level meaning is socially mediated, although apparently global processing in nonhuman animals (e.g., Jitsumori & Matsuzawa, 1991) and infants (e.g., Bhatt et al., 1994) renders this less likely.

Without the ability to reflect on his or her own mental states, the child with autism may be impaired in planning (imaginative rehearsal), monitoring (of intentions—normally possible without external feedback), and holding rules in mind. Perner et al. (1999) and Carruthers (1996) have discussed in detail how such executive-function impairments might result from an inability to represent (own) mental states. Also shown in the model is an attempt to derive desire for sameness from social deficits, through the intermediate variable of stress. This link is rendered less likely by the finding that stereotypies and desire for sameness characterize high-functioning as well as low-functioning people with autism (see Turner, 1997), those who pass as well as those who fail theory-of-mind tests (Frith et al., 1994), and may be more prominent in situations of understimulation than overstimulation (Dadds, Schwartz, Adams, & Rose, 1988).

Conclusions

Autism is a complex disorder and is likely to reflect dysfunction or difference in a number of systems. Whether a primary core deficit in a single domain-specific or domain-general function can be responsible for all these impairments, through a cascade effect in development, is unclear. Improved early diagnosis, however, makes it likely that in the future we will be able to gather the necessary evidence to untangle cause and effect among the various features of autism. This will bring us a clearer understanding of how social and nonsocial development interact in the normal and abnormal case, with consequences for possible intervention to reroute the developmental process.

ACKNOWLEDGMENTS

I would like to thank the editors for their helpful comments on earlier drafts of this chapter. Special thanks go to all the individuals with autism, their parents and teachers, who gave their help and support to our research.

REFERENCES

Adrien, J. L., Lenoir, P., Martineau, J., Perrot, A., Hameury, L., Larmande, C., & Sauvage, D. (1993). Blind ratings of early symptoms of autism based upon family home movies. *Journal of the American Academy of Child & Adolescent Psychiatry, 32,* 617–626.

American Psychiatric Association. (1994). *Diagnostic and statistical manual of mental disorders,* (4th ed.) (DSM–IV). Washington, DC: Author.

Angold, A., & Hay, D. F. (Eds.). (1993). *Precursors and causes in development and psychopathology.* London: Wiley.

Baldwin, D. A. (1995). Understanding the link between joint attention and language acquisition. In C. Moore & P. Dunham (Eds.), *Joint Attention: its origins and role in development.* Hillsdale, NJ: Lawrence Erlbaum Associates.

Baron-Cohen, S. (1995). *Mindblindness: An essay on autism and theory of mind.* Cambridge, MA: MIT Press.

Baron-Cohen, S., Cox, A., Baird, G., Swettenham, J., Nightingale, N., Morgan, K., Drew, A., & Charman, T. (1996). Psychological markers in the detection of autism in infancy in a large population. *British Journal of Psychiatry, 168,* 158–163.

Baron-Cohen, S., & Hammer, J. (1997). Is autism an extreme form of the male brain? *Advances in Infancy Research, 11,* 193–217.

Baron-Cohen, S., Tager-Flusberg, H., & Cohen, D. J. (Eds.). (2000). *Understanding other minds: Perspectives from autism and developmental cognitive neuroscience* (2nd ed.). Oxford, UK: Oxford University Press.

Bennetto, L., Pennington, B. F., & Rogers, S. J. (1996). Intact and impaired memory functions in autism. *Child Development, 67,* 1816–1835.

Berger, H. J. C., van Spaendonck, K. P. M., & Horstinck, M. W. I. M. (1993). Cognitive shifting as a predictor of progress in social understanding in high-functioning adolescents with autism: A prospective study. *Journal of Autism and Developmental Disorders, 23,* 341–359.

Bhatt, R. S., Rovee-Collier, C., & Shyi, G. C. W. (1994). Global and local processing of incidental information and memory retrieval at 6 months. *Journal of Experimental Child Psychology, 57,* 141–162.

Bloom, P. (1997). Intentionality and word learning. *Trends in Cognitive Sciences, 1,* 9–12.

Carruthers, P. (1996). Simulation and self-knowledge: A defence of theory-theory. In P. Carruthers & P. K. Smith (Eds.), *Theories of theories of mind* (pp. 22–38). Cambridge, UK: Cambridge University Press.

Charman, T. (2000). Theory of mind and the early diagnosis of autism. In S. Baron-Cohen, H. Tager-Flusberg, & D. Cohen (Eds.), *Understanding other minds: Perspectives from autism and developmental cognitive neuroscience* (2nd Ed.). Oxford: OUP.

Charman, T., Swettenham, J., Baron-Cohen, S., Cox, A., Baird, G., & Drew, A. (1998). An experimental investigation of social-cognitive abilities in infants with autism: Clinical implications. *Infant Mental Health Journal, 19,* 260–275.

Colombo, J., Freeseman, L. J., Coldren, J. T., & Frick, J. E. (1995). Individual differences in infant fixation duration: Dominance of global versus local stimulus properties. *Cognitive Development, 10,* 271–285.

Coren, S., & Enns, J. T. (1993). Size contrast as a function of conceptual similarity between test and inducers. *Perception and Psychophysics, 54,* 579–588.

Courchesne, E., Townsend, J., Akshoomoff, N. A., Saitoh, O., Yeung-Courchesne, R., Lincoln, A. J., James, H. E., Haas, R. H., Schreibman, L., & Lau, L. (1994). Impairment in shifting attention in autistic and cerebellar patients. *Behavioral Neuroscience, 108,* 848–865.

Dadds, M. R., Schwartz, S., Adams, T., & Rose, S. (1988). The effects of social context and verbal skill on the stereotypic and task-involved behavior of autistic children. *Journal of Child Psychology and Psychiatry, 29,* 669–676.

Diamond, A., & Taylor, C. (1996). Development of an aspect of executive control: Development of the abilities to remember what I said and to "Do as I say, not as I do." *Developmental Psychobiology, 29,* 315–334.

Fagot, J., & Deruelle, C. (1997). Processing of global and local visual information and hemispheric specialization in humans (*Homo sapiens*) and baboons (*Papio papio*). *Journal of Experimental Psychology: Human Perception and Performance, 23,* 429–442.

Frith, U. (1989). *Autism: Explaining the enigma.* Oxford, UK: Basil Blackwell.

Frith, U., & Happé, F. (1994). Autism: Beyond "theory of mind." *Cognition, 50,* 115–132.

Frith, U., Happé, F., & Siddons, F. (1994). Autism and theory of mind in everyday life. *Social Development, 3,* 108–124.

Gillberg, C. (1991) Outcome in autism and autistic-like conditions. *Journal of the American Academy of Child & Adolescent Psychiatry, 30,* 375–382.

Gómez, J. C., Sarriá, E., & Tamarit, J. (1993). The comparative study of early communication and theories of mind: Ontogeny, phylogeny, and pathology. In S. Baron-Cohen, H. Tager-Flusberg, & D. Cohen (Eds.), *Understanding other minds: Perspectives from autism* (pp. 397–426). Oxford, UK: Oxford University Press.

Griffith, E. M., Pennington, B. F., Wehner, E. A., & Rogers, S. J. (1999). Executive functions in young children with autism. *Child Development, 70,* 817–832.

Happé, F. G. E. (1994a). An advanced test of theory of mind: Understanding of story characters' thoughts and feelings by able autistic, mentally handicapped and normal children and adults. *Journal of Autism and Developmental Disorders, 24,* 129–154.

Happé, F. G. E. (1994b). Wechsler IQ profile and theory of mind in autism: A research note. *Journal of Child Psychology and Psychiatry, 35,* 1461–1471.

Happé, F. G. E. (1994c). Reading minds through a glass darkly. Commentary. *Cahiers de Psychologie Cognitive [Current Psychology of Cognition], 13,* 599–606.

Happé, F. G. E. (1996). Studying weak central coherence at low levels: Children with autism do not succumb to visual illusions. A research note. *Journal of Child Psychology and Psychiatry, 37,* 873–877.

Happé, F. G. E. (1997). Central coherence and theory of mind in autism: Reading homographs in context. *British Journal of Developmental Psychology, 15,* 1–12.

Happé, F. G. E. (1999). Autism: Cognitive deficit or cognitive style? *Trends in Cognitive Sciences, 3,* 216–222.

Happé, F. G. E. (2000). Parts and wholes, meaning and minds: Central coherence and its relation to theory of mind. In S. Baron-Cohen, H. Tager-Flusberg, & D. Cohen (Eds.), *Understanding other minds: Perspectives from autism and developmental cognitive neuroscience* (2nd Ed.) (pp. 203–221). Oxford, UK: Oxford University Press.

Heaton, P., Hermelin, B., & Pring, L. (1998). Autism and pitch processing: A precursor for savant musical ability. *Music Perception, 15,* 291–305.

Hughes, C. (1998). Finding your marbles: Does preschoolers' strategic behavior predict later understanding of mind? *Developmental Psychology, 34,* 1326–1339.

Hughes, C., & Russell, J. (1993). Autistic children's difficulty with mental disengagement from an object: Its implications for theories of autism. *Developmental Psychology, 29,* 498–510.

Jarrold, C, Butler, D. W., Cottington, E. M., & Jimenez, F. (2000). Linking theories of mind and central coherence bias in autism and in the general population. *Developmental Psychology, 36,* pp. 126–138.

Jitsumori, M., & Matsuzawa, T. (1991). Picture perception in monkeys and pigeons: Transfer of right-side-up versus upside-down discrimination of photographic objects across conceptual categories. *Primates, 32,* 473–482.

McEvoy, R. E., Rogers, S. J., & Pennington, B. F. (1993). Executive function and social communication deficits in young autistic children. *Journal of Child Psychology & Psychiatry, 34,* 563–578.

McKelvie, S. J. (1995). Emotional expression in upside-down faces: Evidence for configurational and componential processing. *British Journal of Social Psychology, 34,* 325–334.

Meltzoff, A. N. (1995). Understanding the intentions of others: Re-enactment of intended acts by 18-month-old children. *Developmental Psychology, 31,* 838–850.

Meltzoff, A. N., & Gopnik, A. (1993). The role of imitation in understanding persons and developing a theory of mind. In S. Baron-Cohen, H. Tager-Flusberg, & D. Cohen (Eds.), *Understanding other minds: Perspectives from autism* (pp. 335–366). Oxford, UK: Oxford University Press.

Osterling, J., & Dawson, G. (1994). Early recognition of children with autism: A study of first birthday home videotapes. *Journal of Autism and Developmental Disorders, 24,* 247–259.

Ozonoff, S., Rogers, S. J., & Pennington, B. (1991). Asperger's syndrome: Evidence of an empirical distinction from high-functioning autism. *Journal of Child Psychology and Psychiatry, 32,* 1107–1122.

Pennington, B. F., & Ozonoff, S. (1996). Executive functions and developmental psychopathology. *Journal of Child Psychology & Psychiatry, 37,* 51–87.

Pennington, B. F., Rogers, S. J., Bennetto, L., Griffith, E. M., Reed, D. T., & Shyu, V. (1997). Validity tests of the executive dysfunction hypothesis of autism. In J. Russell (Ed.), *Autism as an executive disorder* (pp. 143–178). New York: Oxford University Press.

Perner, J., Long, B., & Stummer, S. (1998). Theory of mind and executive function: Which depends on which? Unpublished manuscript, University of Salzburg, Salzburg, Austria.

Perner, J., Stummer, S., & Lang, B. (1999). Executive functions and theory of mind: Cognitive complexity or functional dependence? In P. D. Zelazo, J. W. Astington, & D. R. Olson (Eds.), *Developing theories of intention: Social understanding and self control* (pp. 133–152). Hillsdale, NJ: Lawrence Erlbaum Associates.

Peterson, C. C., & Siegal, M. (1995). Deafness, conversation and theory of mind. *Journal of Child Psychology & Psychiatry, 36,* 459–474.

Rimland, B., & Hill, A. L. (1984). Idiot savants. In Wortis, J. (Ed.), *Mental Retardation and Developmental Disabilities, Vol. 13* (pp. 155–169). New York: Plenum.

Rincover, A., & Koegel, R. L. (1975). Setting generality and stimulus control in autistic children. *Journal of Applied Behavior Analysis, 8,* pp. 235–246.

Robinson, E. J., & Mitchell, P. (1995). Masking of children's early understanding of the representational mind: Backwards explanation versus prediction. *Child Development, 66,* 1022–1039.

Rogers, S. J., & Pennington, B. F. (1991). A theoretical approach to the deficits in infantile autism. *Development and Psychopathology, 3,* 137–162.

Russell, J. (1996). *Agency: Its role in mental development.* Hove, UK: Lawrence Erlbaum Associates.

Russell, J. (Ed.). (1997). *Autism as an executive disorder.* New York: Oxford University Press.

Shah, A., & Frith, U. (1983). An islet of ability in autistic children: A research note. *Journal of Child Psychology and Psychiatry, 24,* 613–620.

Sigman, M., & Ruskin, E. (1999). Continuity and change in the social competence of children with autism, Down syndrome, and developmental delays. *Monographs of the Society for Research in Child Development, 64,* v–114.

Takeuchi, A. H., & Hulse, S. H. (1993). Absolute pitch. *Psychological Bulletin, 113,* 345–361.

Tan, A., Salgado, M., & Fahn, S. (1997). The characterization and outcome of stereotypical movements in nonautistic children. *Movement Disorders, 12,* 47–52.

Tomasello, M. (1992). The social bases of language acquisition. *Social Development, 1,* 67–87.

Turner, M. (1997). Towards an executive dysfunction account of repetitive behavior in autism. In J. Russel, (Ed.), *Autism as an executive disorder* (pp. 57–100). New York: Oxford University Press.

Volkmar, F. R., & Cohen, D. J. (1989). Disintegrative disorder or "late onset" autism. *Journal of Child Psychology and Psychiatry, 30,* 717–724.

Yirmiya, N., Erel, O., Shaked, M., & Solomonica-Levi, D. (1998). Meta-analyses comparing theory of mind abilities of individuals with autism, individuals with mental retardation, and normally developing individuals. *Psychological Bulletin, 124,* 283–307.

Zilbovicius, M., Garreau, B., Samson, Y., Remy, P., Barthelemy, C., Syrota, A., & LeLord, G. (1995). Delayed maturation of the frontal cortex in childhood autism. *American Journal of Psychiatry, 152,* 248–252.

13

Executive Dysfunction in Autism: Its Nature and Implications for the Everyday Problems Experienced By Individuals With Autism

Claire Hughes
Institute of Psychiatry
London, England

The term *executive function* encompasses the processes (e.g., planning, inhibitory control, attentional set-shifting, working memory) that underlie flexible goal-directed behavior (Duncan, 1986). Predicted consequences of executive dysfunction include a marked difficulty in novel or ambiguous situations coupled with intact performance on routine or well-learned tasks. These predictions fit well with many of the behavioral characteristics of autism—an observation that motivated numerous independent investigations of executive dysfunction in autism. Such studies demonstrate that executive dysfunctions in autism are typically severe, persistent, and universal (see Bishop, 1993; Ozonoff, 1995, 1997; Pennington & Ozonoff, 1996). However, several questions remain unresolved: Do executive impairments in autism have a primary etiological significance, or are they merely secondary consequences of neurological damage? How should executive impairments in autism be characterized? What are the real-life implications of executive dysfunction in autism? The aim of this chapter is to address these three questions, focusing in particular on some speculative suggestions as to the relevance of executive impairments for everyday behavior in autism.

Evidence from neuroimaging and neuroanatomical studies suggests that executive function (EF) processes are typically associated with the prefrontal cortex (e.g., Rakic, Bourgeois, Zecevic, Eckenhoff, & Goldman-Rakic, 1986). This association has had a guiding influence on research. For example, until recently it was thought that the prefrontal cortex becomes functional relatively late in development (Golden, 1981). As a result, standard EF tests such as the Wisconsin Card Sorting Test (WCST: Grant & Berg, 1948) were designed for adult populations, and so are typically complex and multicomponential. In consequence, similar levels of poor performance may arise from quite different impairments. That is, standard EF tasks offer good sensitivity but poor specificity when used to identify EF impairments that are characteristic of particular disorders.

The problem of discriminant validity prompted researchers to adopt a finer grain of analysis using information-processing techniques (e.g., Hughes, Russell, & Robbins, 1994; Ozonoff, 1997). Such studies suggest that distinct aspects of EF are independently impaired in specific disorders. Both neuroanatomical findings of parallel and segregated fronto-striatal circuits (Alexander, Delong, & Strick, 1986; Robbins, 1996) and clinical findings of weak across-task correlations in performance (e.g., Hughes et al., 1994) support this model of EF as a multicomponential system. Further support comes from investigations with typically developing children. For example, Hughes (1998a) showed that distinct EF factors could be identified as early as preschool, while Luciana and Nelson (1998) and Welsh, Pennington, and Grossier (1991) demonstrated that separate EF factors have contrasting developmental trajectories. The final argument for examining distinct EF processes is philosophical: Although less parsimonious, the metaphor of a multicomponential "toolbox" avoids the "ghost in the machine" criticism leveled at earlier models of executive control (Shallice, 1982). In this chapter, then, EF does not refer to a unitary system, but is used as a kind of shorthand for the set of component processes that have in common an involvement in flexible goal-directed activity.

Are Impairments in EF Just a Secondary Consequence of Neurological Damage?

An early criticism of EF accounts of autism was that executive impairments have little discriminative validity, because they appear in several developmental disorders with quite different symptomatologies, including attention deficit hyperactivity disorder (ADHD) (Grodzinsky & Diamond, 1992); Tourette syndrome (Baron-Cohen, Cross, Crowson, & Robertson, 1994), and Conduct Disorder (Chelune, Ferguson, Koon, & Dickey, 1986). However, reviews of the literature (Ozonoff, 1997; Pennington & Ozonoff, 1996) and direct investigation (Ozonoff, 1995) both indicate that problems of discriminant validity for the EF model may be more apparent than real. By adopting an information-processing approach (in which comparisons are based on specific rather than global measures of performance), both quantitative and qualitative distinctions between EF impairments in different clinical groups can be established. For example, the EF impairments associated with ADHD are characterized as reflecting low-level problems of motor inhibition (Barkley, 1997), while those associated with autism are characteristically high-level (i.e., cognitive) and nonspatial (Hughes et al., 1994; Minshew, Goldstein, & Siegal, 1997; Ozonoff, 1995; Ozonoff & Jensen, 1999). The association of different profiles of executive dysfunction with different disorders argues against the view that problems of EF are simply a general consequence of neurological insult.

A second argument against the etiological significance of EF in autism concerns the timing of impairments. In particular, we do not yet know whether significant problems in EF exist at the very onset of autism or whether these impairments emerge later in development, and so may be consequences rather than causes of autism. Findings from a recent large-scale prospective study of autism support this skeptical view (Cox et al., 1999). In particular, Cox et al. identified social and communicative impairments in 18-month-olds with autism, but could not identify symptoms that might reflect EF impairment (e.g., stereotypes and repetitive behaviors) until around 30 months. However, research into early-emerging EF is still in its infancy, with developmentally appropriate tasks appearing only very recently in the literature (Diamond & Taylor, 1996; Hughes, 1998a; Kochanska, Murray, Jacques, Koenig, & Vandegeest, 1996; Zelazo, Frye, & Rapus, 1996). Recent neuropsychological studies show that preschool-aged children with autism perform poorly on tests that require flexibility in thought (McEvoy, Rogers, & Pennington, 1993; but see Wehner & Rogers, 1994) or attention (Bryson, Landry, & Wainwright, 1997). These results suggest that with appropriate tasks, detecting EF impairments in even younger children with autism may become possible in the future.

Alternatively, EF impairments may be genuinely primary, but appear slightly later than other autistic deficits—alongside associated behavioral problems of stereotypies. This suggestion is consistent with the view that autism is underpinned by a constellation of deficits rather than by any single impairment (Bailey, Palferman, Heavey, & Le Couteur, 1998; Goodman, 1994; Pickles et al., 1995). If autism involves a constellation of deficits, separate impairments may come to the fore at different periods of development. Information other than timing is therefore needed to establish whether particular abnormalities have a primary role in the etiology of autism. One alternative strategy for identifying primary impairments in autism is to investigate close relatives of individuals with autism. The rationale for this approach comes from the evidence provided by family and twin studies for strong genetic influences on the etiology of autism (see Bailey et al.). In addition, the growing consensus is that many complex disorders are multifactorial, involving normal variation of several genetically influenced traits (Rutter et al., 1997). In fact, autism is unlikely to be caused by a single mutation or abnormal gene. Instead, recent family studies of autism adopt a "broader phenotype" approach by examining autistic characteristics that appear in a more subtle form among otherwise unaffected close relatives (Rutter, 1991). These characteristics are unlikely to be secondary consequences of neurological damage and so are good candidates for the etiology of autism.

Until recently, family studies focused on abnormalities in sociability and communication among relatives, since these appear to be the cardinal symptoms of autism. However, peculiarities in sociability and communication that are genuine subclinical markers of autism are difficult to disentangle from those caused by the strain of caring for an autistic child. In particular, the impact of an autistic child on family members is known to be profound, even in comparison with the impact of caring for children with other developmental disabilities (Bouma & Schweitzer, 1990). This problem is less of an issue for basic cognitive characteristics such as attentional set-shifting or planning ability, because such processes are less likely to be differentially affected by living with an autistic child. It is therefore significant that four studies recently reported elevated incidences of EF impairments among both parents (Hughes, Leboyer, & Bouvard, 1997a; Piven & Palmer, 1997) and siblings (Hughes, Plumet, & Leboyer, 1999; Ozonoff, Rogers, Farnham, & Pennington, 1993) of children with autism. In addition, problems of repetitive stereotyped behavior (that appear strongly linked with executive dysfunction, see Turner, 1997) are more frequent among relatives of individuals with autism than among relatives of children with other developmental disorders (Bolton et al., 1994). These studies provide convergent evidence that impairments of EF should be included in the broader autism phenotype. Research with family members therefore provides independent evidence that problems of EF carry a primary significance for the etiology of autism.

How Should Executive Impairments in Autism Be Characterized?

What is the nature of EF impairments in autism? Is it possible to identify characteristics of executive dysfunction that are universal in autism? Or does it make more sense to explore within-group heterogeneities associated with factors such as age or ability level?

The defining character of executive dysfunction in autism has yet to be fully agreed on. One reason for this is that since the overall construct of EF is so broad, separate research groups adopted rather different theoretical frameworks in which different aspects of EF are emphasized (e.g., see chapters in Russell, 1997). However, across studies a number of findings converge. For instance, EF impairments in autism are characteristically high-level and non-spatial (see the following section for examples) (Hughes et al., 1994; Minshew et al., 1997; Ozonoff, 1995). These characteristics also apply to the EF impairments observed among relatives of individuals with autism, suggesting close ties between the broader autism phenotype and autism itself. In particular, individuals with autism and their close relatives show a consistent uneven cognitive profile.

The strategy of examining EF deficits alongside intact cognitive processes may refine our understanding of the exact nature of executive dysfunction in autism by providing useful insights into how an underlying impairment has a differential impact on performance on different types of task. For instance, a study by Bennetto, Pennington, and Rogers (1996) reported significant working-memory impairments in autism, yet other studies of individuals with autism (e.g., Russell, Jarrold, & Henry, 1996) or their relatives (Hughes et al., 1997a; 1999) show no such impairment. This apparent inconsistency may reflect the spatial nature of the tasks used in the latter studies, since spatial ability in autism is often superior to that in other groups (see Happé & Frith, 1996), and this superiority could mask deficits in working memory.

Future studies should therefore adopt a broader neuropsychological profiling approach to enable the mechanisms underlying task performances to be identified with greater precision. There are at least two advantages to this broad approach. First, as previously noted, identifying intact cognitive processes enables certain factors (e.g., spatial ability) to be eliminated from interpretations of performance deficits. Second, investigating between-task correlations may also be illuminating. For example, Hughes et al. (1997a, 1999) found that relatives of people with autism showed a qualitatively distinct profile of associations in task performances, suggesting that these individuals adopted unusual strategies to solve the EF tasks (perhaps as a result of differences in levels of functioning). This possibility needs to be addressed systematically in future research.

Despite encouraging consistencies across studies, attempts to identify universal characteristics of executive dysfunction associated with autism may be limited by inherent heterogeneity among individuals. For example, as Turner (1997) argued, low-ability and high-functioning individuals with autism show contrasting types of repetitive stereotypies coupled with distinct patterns of EF impairment. In particular, repetitive motor stereotypies were associated with perseveration in set-shifting; these difficulties were especially characteristic of low-functioning individuals with autism. In contrast, restricted interests were associated with impoverished generativity ability; these difficulties were more characteristic of the high-functioning group. Heterogeneity in the nature of EF impairments may therefore prove valuable in accounting for specific symptoms associated with autism, rather than just an inconvenient limit on the generalizability of findings. This heterogeneity highlights the importance of ensuring that between-study comparisons involve samples with similar ability levels.

Age may also prove important for within-group variability in EF performance. In particular, work with typically developing children suggests contrasting developmental trajectories for different aspects of EF (Luciana & Nelson, 1998; Welsh et al., 1991). For example, typically developing children do not appear to develop high-level (extradimensional) attentional switching before the age of 6 years (Luciana & Nelson, 1998). Impairments in high-level attentional switching are therefore unlikely to be observed among young children with autism, although they are apparent in the majority of school-aged children with autism (Hughes et al., 1994; Ozonoff, Pennington, & Rogers, 1991). These findings from typically developing populations highlight the danger of extrapolating downwards from adult-oriented EF tasks to investigate early EF impairments in autism. Instead, more research with young typically developing children is needed to establish the ages at which specific aspects of EF become developmentally salient before investigating the onset of EF impairments in autism.

What Are the Real-Life Implications of Executive Dysfunction in Autism?

Accounts of autism can be judged not only by the specificity and universality of proposed deficits, but also by their explanatory value (i.e., the extent to which the degree and kind of proposed deficit relates to the symptomatology of autism). A new direction for cognitive research is therefore a shift away from documenting group differences in task performance toward considering the relevance of posited deficits for the everyday problems experienced by individuals with autism. For example, in several studies involving individuals with autism, theory-of-mind performance was significantly associated with real-life adaptive social and communicative behaviors (Fombonne, Siddons, Archard, Frith, & Happé, 1994; Frith, Happé, & Siddons, 1994; Hughes, Soares-Boucaud, Hochmann, & Frith, 1997b). In contrast, the case for theory-of-mind involvement in the third area of impairment identified in DSM–IV (American Psychiatric Association, 1994) (restricted, repetitive, and stereotyped patterns of behavior, interests, and activities) is weaker (Happé & Frith, 1996). In the following section, the question of links between executive dysfunction and real-life impairment is therefore divided in two parts.

Links Between Executive Function and Sociocommunicative Ability

Problems of sociability and communication are universal among individuals with autism; even the talented minority who pass advanced theory-of-mind tasks display clear impairments in their everyday social and communicative interactions (Happé & Frith, 1996). Deficits in theory of mind therefore cannot entirely explain the social and communicative peculiarities that characterize autism. In this section the impact of EF impairments on the social and communicative impairments of individuals with autism is considered.

The earliest suggestion of a link in autism between problems in sociability and cognitive flexibility is due to Kanner's (1961) emphasis on "aloneness" and "preservation of sameness" as the two cardinal symptoms for the diagnosis of autism. Support for this view comes from Wing and Gould's (1979) seminal finding that restricted interests and repetitive activities always accompany social impairment, and are significantly associated with degree and type of social deficit. With the development of operational diagnostic criteria for autism, this co-occurrence of impairments in sociability, communication, and flexibility in thought and behavior became a defining feature of autism. The implication from this criterion of co-occurrence is that at the level of etiology, the mechanisms underlying impairments in sociocommunicative ability, and executive control are closely linked. In the following section, evidence for associations between these two domains in autism is reviewed, together with a brief outline of competing accounts as to the nature of this association.

Joint Attention. Several different theoretical accounts place joint attention as the cornerstone of social development (e.g., Baron-Cohen, 1994; Mundy, Sigman, & Kasari, 1994); the absence of joint attention is often the first sign of social impairment among young children with autism. From around 6 months, typically developing infants show an array of joint attention behaviors including gaze following, tracking in response to pointing gestures, bringing, or pointing to an object of interest. Early accounts of why these behaviors are absent among children with autism center on affective abnormalities (Hobson, 1993; Kasari, Sigman, Mundy, & Yirmiya, 1990; Mundy & Sigman, 1989) or deficits in metarepresentation (Baron-Cohen, 1995). Recent findings suggest difficulties in rapid shifting of attentional focus may contribute to autistic problems of joint attention (Burack, 1994; Courchesne, Townsend, Akshoomoff, & Saitoh, 1994; Townsend, Harris, & Courchesne, 1996). Three types of evidence support this view. First, the frequency of joint-attention behaviors in young children with autism is significantly associated with performance on a simple test of cognitive flexibility (McEvoy et al., 1993). Second, in developmentally normal infants, developmental improvements in joint attention parallel the development of behavioral flexibility, as indexed by a reduction in perseverative actions (Butterworth & Grover, 1988; Corkum & Moore, 1998). Third, as noted earlier, the neural substrate for EF is generally considered to be the prefrontal cortex, and in young children with brain lesions, impairments of joint-attention behaviors relate specifically to the extent of damage to the prefrontal cortex (Caplan et al., 1993). However, in a recent test of this "attentional set-shifting" account of joint-attention impairments in autism, Swettenham et al. (1998) found that infants with autism have more difficulty shifting attention between people than between objects, suggesting an abnormality in social orientation rather than in attentional set-shifting per se. In addition, Dawson, Meltzoff, Osterling, and Rinaldi (1998) recently reported that the severity of autistic impairments in social attention is strongly correlated with performance on a medial temporal lobe task, but not with performance on a dorsolateral prefrontal task. The extent to which executive dysfunction contributes to impairments in joint attention in autism therefore remains open to debate.

Imitation. Another early social behavior that is markedly lacking in young children with autism is imitation, in particular, social imitative play. Although the importance of imitation is highlighted in several accounts of early social behavior, accounts differ in the interpretation of why children with autism rarely spontaneously imitate others. In one view, lack of imitation is an early reflection of autistic deficits in metarepresentation and mental-state awareness (Baron-Cohen, 1988). However, others suggest that problems in theory of mind arise from a core impairment in imitation and interpersonal coordination (Meltzoff, 1995; Rogers & Pennington, 1991). Findings from several studies suggest that poor imitation in autism reflects either general dyspraxia or impaired executive control of action (Jones & Prior, 1985; Smith & Bryson, 1994). According to this view, social imitation is particularly affected in autism because social gestures require the cognitive flexibility to extract invariant information from different contexts. In other words, "an essentially nonsocial deficit could have a disproportionate effect on socially mediated behavior" (Smith & Bryson, 1994).

Pretend Play. A marked absence of spontaneous pretend play is a third early feature of sociocommunicative impairments in autism. Pretend play is closely associated with mental-state awareness, at the level of both cognition (Leslie, 1987) and behavior (Hughes & Dunn, 1997; Taylor & Carlson, 1997; Youngblade & Dunn, 1995). However, it is also clear that an understanding of mind is neither necessary nor sufficient for pretend play. First, as Harris (1993) and Perner (1991) argued, children can engage in pretend play without attributing specific mental representations to themselves or others. For example, at 3 years of age, my godchild would relish games of pretend cooking, but became quite alarmed if I appeared to eat the Play-Doh—and was clearly unsure as to whether I had understood the pretend nature of the game. Second, despite a marked lack of spontaneous pretense the comprehension of pretend play appears relatively intact in autism (Jarrold, Boucher, & Smith, 1994). Clearly then, children's engagement in pretense depends on more than a formal understanding of mental states. In fact, naturalistic observations reveal that for children with autism pretend play is typically replaced by stereotypic behaviors elicited by the simple physical properties of toys (e.g., sniffing or eating Play-Doh or spinning round objects). In addition, where pretend play is found in autism it is generally repetitive, limited in repertoire, and stereotyped or fragmentary in form (Wing & Gould, 1979). These observational findings suggest that impaired imaginative activity might reflect a lack of executive control, a proposal that is supported by the report of significant improvements in imaginative play when the demands for spontaneity and flexibility are reduced (Lewis & Boucher, 1988).

Communication. Social impairments in autism also include marked problems of communication. The most widespread of these is a lack of spontaneous speech (Schopler & Mesibov, 1985). This is manifest in various forms: by the total lack of speech or elective mutism typical of younger children, and by the repetitive echolalia or monosyllabic speech characteristic of more able children. Lack of spontaneous speech is also common to patients with damage to the dorsolateral prefrontal cortex (Alexander, Benson, & Stuss, 1989), an area mentioned earlier as playing a critical role in certain aspects of executive function. Indeed, both lack of spontaneity and echolalia can be seen as reflecting excessive dependence on external prompts in the absence of internal (executive) control.

Another feature of autistic communication is a high frequency of pronominal reversals and anaphoric errors (Frith, 1989). Indeed, individuals with autism not only mix up personal pronouns in their speech, but also show difficulty in integrating more than one viewpoint, such that all pronouns may become reduced to the third person (Baltaxe & Simmons, 1977). It is difficult to tell whether this difficulty results from a failure to integrate a large amount of information, as suggested by Frith's (1989) account of autistic impairments in "central coherence," or from a more direct problem in shifting mental set. Among more able, verbal individuals with autism, almost universal communicative deficits include verbal rituals and highly restricted topics of conversation (Wing & Gould, 1979). These forms of speech share not only a lack of regard for the listener's viewpoint (consistent, of course, with an impaired awareness of other people's mental states), but also extreme repetition, rigidity, and restrictedness—features that fit well with the predicted consequences of executive dysfunction.

Similar suggestions apply to both parents of children with autism (Hughes et al., 1997a; Landa et al., 1992) and children with semantic-pragmatic disorder (SPD), a disorder that is considered by many to be closely related to autism. Specifically, Bishop (1989) proposed that the unexpected and overliteral interpretations that characterize the conversations of children with SPD may arise from a failure to engage inhibitory processes that usually serve to suppress unwanted and irrelevant associations. Bishop's proposal is based on experimental evidence (see Gernsbacher, 1996) that on hearing a word, related concepts are activated, even if they do not apply to the current context (e.g., in a story about a cocktail party, the word "punch" primes both "drink" and "hit"). According to Gernsbacher (1996), the damping down of irrelevant meanings cannot be explained by passive decay, or by mutual inhibition between competing meanings. Instead, a "Structure Building Model" is postulated, in which irrelevant meanings are actively inhibited as part of the normal process of comprehension. The consequences of failure to inhibit irrelevant meanings predicted by this model are in many ways reminiscent of the communication problems found in autism. For example, failure to inhibit irrelevant meanings is posited to result in (a) mental structures that are less cohesive and less accessible than those of others; (b) tangential or irrelevant inferences, leading to odd changes of topic; and (c) similar impairments for nonverbal comprehension (e.g., picture sequencing). These predictions, based on experimental work with normal adults, are supported by clinical neuropsychological studies of children with closed head injuries (Dennis & Barnes, 1990).

The aforementioned ensemble of findings suggests strong evidence for a relation between executive function and a range of sociocommunicative skills. Of course, correlations say nothing about causal directions, so it is worth considering whether social impairment might lead to poor executive function (rather than vice versa). Indeed, Luria's (1966) own model of executive functions was strongly influenced by the Vygotskian view that social interactions play a vital part in fostering the development of flexible thinking and planning capacity (e.g., in the coordination of goals, or negotiation of conflict). This possibility is supported by animal social deprivation studies that suggest that social isolation can result in perseveration, self-stimulation, and difficulties with complex tasks (e.g., Blanc et al., 1980).

However, evidence for the opposite causal direction in autism also exists. In particular, increased structure in children's environments was shown in numerous autism intervention studies to result in less stereotypic and more social behaviors (e.g., Clark & Rutter, 1981; Dadds, Schwartz, Adams, & Rose, 1988; Schopler & Olley, 1982). That is, reducing the demands for executive control placed by everyday situations appears to facilitate social development in children with autism. Similarly, the results of two longitudinal studies of high-functioning adolescents with autism demonstrate that performance on a standard executive test (WCST, Grant & Berg, 1948) is a highly effective predictor of both progress in social understanding (Berger, van Spaendonck, & Horstinck, 1993) and social functioning in adulthood (Szatmari, Bartolucci, & Bremner, 1989). Thus executive functions may contribute to social ability across the entire span of development in individuals with autism. However, the influence of executive function on social skills may be indirect as well as direct. For example, functions such as cognitive flexibility may enable individuals to engage in social interactions, which in turn foster the development of more advanced social skills.

Alternatively, the relation between executive function and real-life sociocommunicative skills may be mediated by underlying associations with theory-of-mind development. Work with young typically developing children provides considerable evidence that theory-of-mind and executive-function performance are indeed closely associated (e.g., Hughes, 1998a, 1998b; Moore, 1996; Russell, Mauthner, Sharpe, & Tidswell, 1991). This association is also significant for high-functioning individuals with autism (Ozonoff et al., 1991). However its nature is interpreted in at least four different ways. Two of these views assume a functional link between theory of mind and EF. According to Pacherie (1997) and Russell (1996), some form of EF is necessary for the development of mental-state concepts. Alternatively, mental-state awareness may be a prerequisite for the development of executive control (Carruthers, 1996; Perner, 1991, 1999; Wimmer, 1989). In the two remaining accounts, the association between theory of mind and EF is caused by a third factor, be this the neuroanatomical proximity of distinct functional systems (Ozonoff et al., 1991; Pennington & Ozonoff, 1996) or the peripheral EF demands of theory-of-mind tasks (Davis & Pratt,

1995; Frye, Zelazo, & Palfai, 1995; Leslie & Polizzi, 1998). Exploring associations between EF performance and real-life sociocommunicative behavior provides a means of testing this last proposal. Specifically, regardless of its causal direction, if the association between theory of mind and EF is genuine, it should remain significant when real-life indices (rather than task measures) of theory-of-mind ability are used.

Links Between Executive Function and Repetitive Behaviors

The predicted consequences of executive dysfunction match closely with many of the everyday problems experienced by people with autism (difficulties in the face of changes to routines, repetitive behaviors, lack of flexibility of thought, and so forth). However, there are very few direct investigations of associations between EF and real-life problems in control of thought and behavior. One of these is Turner's (1997) set of detailed studies, on which the evidence reviewed in this section leans heavily.

Repetitive ritualistic behaviors are a striking feature of autism, as they present a challenging problem for caregivers and constitute one of the three behavioral criteria for diagnosis. Despite this, repetitive behaviors are rarely systematically investigated (see Charman & Swettenham, chap. 16, this volume). One reason for this neglect may be that such behaviors are not specific to autism, and so have often been considered as secondary to other impairments, such as mental retardation (Berkson & Davenport, 1962). Indeed, early accounts were based on studies of children with severe developmental delays and portrayed repetitive behaviors either as a coping mechanism for modulating maladaptive arousal levels (Hutt & Hutt, 1965) or as a conditioned response, reinforced by perceptual stimuli resulting from action (e.g., Lovaas, Newsom, & Hickman, 1987).

However, at least two points argue against the view that repetitive behaviors in autism are a nonspecific consequence of general developmental delay. First, even high-functioning children with autism show some degree of repetitive behavior (Bartak & Rutter, 1976). Second, the repetitive behaviors that characterize autism are qualitatively distinct from those seen in developmentally delayed children (Turner, 1999a). For example, a rigid insistence on sameness is common among individuals with autism but is rare among individuals with general developmental delay. Recognizing that repetitive behaviors in autism are unlikely to be simply secondary to general delay, more recent accounts focused on the cognitive abnormalities that characterize autism as possible causes of stereotypes and ritualized behavior. For example, repetitive acts and rituals may be an indirect consequence of impaired mentalizing ability. According to Baron-Cohen (1989) and Carruthers (1996), individuals with autism find social situations unpredictable because of their limited awareness of other people's mental states and therefore engage in repetitive behaviors as a means of imposing order and controlling their social anxiety. The clear prediction here is that repetitive behaviors should increase in situations with greater social demands. However, repetitive behaviors actually appear less frequent during periods of social interaction than in periods when the individual is alone (e.g., Clark & Rutter, 1981; Dadds et al., 1988; Donnellan, Anderson, & Mesaros, 1984), a finding that runs against this social-anxiety model.

In an alternative theory-of-mind account, Frith (1989) argued that it is not the simple presence of stereotypic behavior that sets people with autism apart, but rather a difference in frequency and kind. (Hair flicking and nail biting are normal, whereas hand flapping and rocking are not.) Frith (1989) suggests that this difference can be explained by a "liberating" consequence of a lack of theory of mind: Individuals with autism are less likely to care about what others think of them and so are less inhibited in their displays of stereotypes. In support of this proposal, in several first-hand accounts by high-functioning adults with autism (e.g., Cesaroni & Garber, 1991) stereotypic behaviors are reported to be more common in family situations, in which the individual presumably feels more relaxed. However, the fact that the same posited underlying deficit (poor mental-state awareness) can lead to opposite predictions raises questions as to the explanatory value of this type of account. More critically, Turner (1997) recently reported no difference in the frequency and severity of repetitive behaviors between individuals with autism who pass and who fail standard tests of theory-of-mind ability.

Another cognitive abnormality reported to be particularly characteristic of individuals with autism is a tendency to process information in terms of fragmentary parts rather than in terms of the coherent whole (Frith, 1989). The predicted consequence of this "weak central coherence" is a focus on minor details in the environment and a failure to process information in terms of underlying meaning. A fragmentary processing style could explain not only the surprisingly good performance shown by many individuals with autism on visuospatial tasks such as the block design and the Embedded Figures tests (Shah & Frith, 1993), but also the circumscribed interests and restricted repertoire of activities that are characteristic symptoms of autism. However, this account offers no clear predictions about which factors are likely to increase or decrease repetitive behaviors in autism, and so is rather difficult to test directly. In addition, Turner (1997) found that the frequency and severity of repetitive behaviors showed no association with performance on the Embedded Figures Test.

From the preceding, it appears that there is no good evidence that repetitive behaviors in autism are a consequence of deficits in either mental-state awareness or central coherence. One possible (if rather pessimistic) conclusion is that it is simply extremely difficult to obtain significant associations between ratings of everyday behavior and performance on cognitive tasks, since the contexts of each are so very different. Establishing that performance on executive function tasks is in fact related to everyday repetitive and inflexible behaviors is therefore a key challenge for research in this field. This predicted association is supported by at least three features of repetitive behaviors in autism. First, repetitive behavior is seen at many levels and in many forms; this pervasiveness suggests a general breakdown in the systems that control behavior (Ridley, 1994). Second, a primary impairment in executive control could explain why such behaviors are so prevalent, pervasive, and persistent in autism. Third, an executive account would predict that reducing the demands for internal control of behavior by increasing structure of the environment would lead to reduced stereotypy. This prediction is supported by the results of several independent studies (cited earlier).

How then does the executive account fare as an explanation of repetitive behaviors when put directly to the test? In the only study to address this question, Turner (1997) examined two areas of executive function that may be relevant for repetitive behaviors: inhibitory control and generativity. With regard to inhibitory control, Turner hypothesized that (a) perseverative task responses would be associated with everyday displays of repetitive behavior, and (b) different kinds of perseveration would be associated with distinct types of repetitive acts. The first predicted association was between recurrent perseveration (inappropriate repetition of a previous response) on a sequence-generation task and low-level stereotypes (e.g., hand flapping). The second predicted association was between "stuck in set" perseveration (failure to switch attention away from a previously salient dimension) on a set-shifting task and higher-level repetitive behaviors (e.g., circumscribed interests or elaborate verbal rituals). These predictions were fully supported for both high-functioning and learning disabled individuals with autism. In contrast, no association between task performance and everyday repetitive behavior was found for either comparison group. With regard to generativity, Turner (1997) employed three experimental tasks (see Turner, 1999b) and showed that for the autistic group only, the number of novel responses produced was significantly and inversely related to observational ratings of circumscribed interests.

In sum, Turner's studies (1997, 1999a) confirm that executive dysfunction is associated with real-life problems of repetitive behavior and also suggest that there are specific links between distinct aspects of executive function and different types of repetitive or inflexible behavior. For example impaired inhibitory control is likely to result in actions getting "stuck in a groove," whereas impaired generativity leads to a lack of variety in responses, particularly in open-ended unstructured situations. Thus, as noted earlier, within-group heterogeneity in executive dysfunction can be seen less as a problem in generalizability and more as an opportunity for elucidating specific mechanisms involved in particular behavioral symptoms of autism.

Of course the perennial caveat about inferring causality from correlational data applies here. However a reduction in repetitive behaviors with increased structure in the environment is directly predicted by the preceding executive account (external structure reduces the demand for internal control). In contrast, this reduction cannot readily be explained by accounts that either assume the reverse causal direction (repetitive behaviors lead to executive dysfunction) or invoke a "third factor" (e.g., neurobiological proximity) to explain the association between executive function and repetitive behavior. Overall then, there are good conceptual and empirical grounds for the view that executive dysfunction plays a direct and important role in the third area of the autistic triad of impairments—that of restricted, repetitive, and stereotyped patterns of behavior, interests, and activities.

Conclusions

Three questions were addressed in this chapter. The first concerned the issue of whether executive impairments in autism have a primary etiological significance or whether such deficits are more properly regarded as a general secondary consequence of neurological damage. This skeptical position is prompted by reports of executive dysfunction across a wide variety of developmental disorders, as well as by inconsistent evidence regarding executive impairments in very young children with autism.

In this chapter I argue that these problems of poor discriminant validity and contradictory findings may be largely attributed to the global and adult-oriented nature of traditional tests of executive function. Clearer discrimination between groups is reported in recent studies that use either (a) information-processing techniques to obtain a finer grain of analysis, (b) tasks tapping a broad array of neuropsychological functions to obtain an overall profile of intact and impaired abilities, or (c) simpler tasks that are developmentally more appropriate for assessing younger or less able children. In addition, independent support for the etiological significance of executive dysfunction in autism comes from four recent studies that demonstrate clear problems of executive control among parents and siblings of individuals with autism. Family and twin studies demonstrate that genetic influences on autism are extremely strong, accounting for approximately 90% of the variance in the population (Bailey et al., 1998) with strong support for a "broader autism phenotype" model of complex inheritance. Impaired executive control among close relatives of individuals with autism supports both this broader phenotype view and the primacy of executive functions in the etiology of autism.

The second topic was the question of how executive impairments in autism should be characterized. Three different problems create an obstacle for elucidating the exact nature of executive dysfunction in autism. The first is that current theoretical models are still very provisional and often too global to capture distinctions between different forms of a particular type of function (e.g., inhibitory control, see earlier). The second is that developmental studies of executive function are still in their infancy, such that there are a number of methodological issues that need to be resolved before sensitive and reliable measures of executive function in young children are readily available. The third obstacle is that within-group heterogeneities (e.g., related to age, ability, and symptomatology) may exist, so that attempts at identifying universal characteristics of executive dysfunction in autism may actually be misplaced. Despite these difficulties, convergent findings are beginning to emerge across studies. In particular, executive impairments in autism appear characteristically high-level and non-spatial, and this uneven profile of intact and impaired abilities may provide a first step toward elucidating the causes of executive dysfunction in autism.

The third question concerned the real-life implications of executive dysfunction in autism; this topic was divided in two parts. The first of these involved two assumptions: namely, that several aspects of sociability and communication place significant demands on diverse executive functions (e.g., online processing, rapid shifting of attention, anticipation of obstacles), and that multiple deficits contribute to the etiology of autism. These assumptions provided a platform for arguing that executive impairments in autism may contribute directly to the profound social and communicative abnormalities that characterize this disorder. The evidence reviewed suggests that associations with executive functions can be found for a variety of sociocommunicative skills, ranging from joint attention in infancy to high-level verbal rituals in adulthood. In addition, a role for executive functions is supported by reports in several studies of increased sociability and communication with increased structure of environment (Clark & Rutter, 1981; Schopler & Mesibov, 1985; Volkmar, Hoder, & Cohen, 1985). In the second part, repetitive behaviors are argued to result directly from functional impairments in executive control. This perspective contrasts both with early accounts of repetitive behaviors as nonspecific consequences of general developmental delay and with more recent cognitive accounts that focus on either the disabling or liberating consequences of reduced mental-state awareness in autism. Turner's (1997) detailed experimental and observational work provides the primary source of evidence for associations between executive function and real-life problems of repetitive behaviors and suggests a number of interesting leads for future studies. Overall, the executive account of autism, while still in need of further refinement, has proved fruitful. Future research should focus on developing appropriate means of assessing executive functions in very young children and on conducting longitudinal studies to examine potential developmental changes in the nature of executive impairments in autism.

ACKNOWLEDGMENTS

Please address correspondence to the Centre for Family Research, Social & Political Sciences Faculty, University of Cambridge, Free School Lane, Cambridge CB2 3RF, UK: e-mail: ch288@cam.ac.uk; tel: +44 (0)1223 334512.

REFERENCES

Alexander, G. E., Delong, M. R., & Strick, P. L. (1986). Parallel organisation of functionally segregated circuits linking basal ganglia & cortex. *Neuroscience, 9* (Annual Review), 357–381.

Alexander, M. P., Benson, D. F., & Stuss, D. T. (1989). Frontal lobes & language. *Brain & Language, 37,* 659–691.

American Psychiatric Association. (1994). *Diagnostic and statistical manual of mental disorders* (4th ed.). Washington, DC: Author.

Bailey, A., Palferman, S., Heavey, L., & Le Couteur, A. (1998). Autism: the phenotype in relatives. *Journal of Autism and Developmental Disorders, 28*(5), 381–404.

Baltaxe, C. A., & Simmons, J. Q. (1977). Bedtime soliloquies and linguistic competence in autism. *Journal of Speech & Hearing Disorders, 42,* 376–393.

Barkley, R. A. (1997). Behavioral inhibition, sustained attention and executive functions: Constructing a unified theory of ADHD. *Psychological Bulletin, 121,* 65–94.

Baron-Cohen, S. (1988). Social and pragmatic deficits in autism: Cognitive or affective? *Journal of Autism and Developmental Disorders, 18,* 379–401.

Baron-Cohen, S. (1989). Do autistic children have obsessions and compulsions? *British Journal of Clinical Psychology, 28*(3), 193–200.

Baron-Cohen, S. (1994). From attention-goal psychology to belief-desire psychology: The development of a theory of mind, and its dysfunction. In S. Baron-Cohen, H. Tager-Flusberg, & D. Cohen (Eds.), *Understanding other minds: Perspectives from autism* (pp. 59–82). Oxford, UK: Oxford University Press.

Baron-Cohen, S. (1995). *Mindblindness: An essay on autism and theory of mind.* Cambridge: MA: MIT Press.

Baron-Cohen, S., Cross, P., Crowson, M., & Robertson, M. (1994). Can children with Gilles de la Tourette syndrome edit their intentions? *Psychological Medicine, 24*(1), 29–40.

Bartak, L., & Rutter, M. (1976). Differences between mentally retarded and normally intelligent autistic children. *Journal of Autism and Childhood Schizophrenia, 6,* 109–120.

Bennetto, L., Pennington, B. F., & Rogers, S. J. (1996). Intact and impaired memory functions in autism. *Child Development, 67*(4), 1816–1835.

Berger, H. J. C., van Spaendonck, K. P. M., & Horstinck, M. W. I. M. (1993). Cognitive shifting as a predictor of progress in social understanding in high functioning adolescents with autism: A prospective study. *Journal of Autism & Developmental Disorders, 23,* 341–359.

Berkson, G., & Davenport, R. K. (1962). Stereotyped movements of mental defectives. *American Journal of Mental Deficiency, 66,* 849–852.

Bishop, D. (1993). Annotation: Autism, executive function and theory of mind: A neuropsychological perspective. *Journal of Child Psychology & Psychiatry, 34,* 279–293.

Bishop, D., & Adams, C. (1989). Conversational characteristics of children with semantic-pragmatic disorder: II. What features lead to a judgement of inappropriacy? *British Journal of Disorders of Communication, 24,* 211–239.

Blanc, G., Herve, D., Simon, H., Lisoprawski, A., Glowinski, J., & Tassin, J. (1980). Response to stress of mesocortical frontal depletion in rats after long term isolation. *Nature, 284,* 265–267.

Bolton, P., Macdonald, H., Pickles, A., Rios, P., Goode, S., Crowson, M., Bailey, A., & Rutter, M. (1994). A case-control family history study of autism. *Journal of Child Psychology & Psychiatry, 35,* 877–900.

Bouma, R., & Schweitzer, R. (1990). The impact of chronic childhood illness on family stress: A comparison between autism and cystic fibrosis. *Journal of Clinical Psychology, 46,* 722–730.

Bryson, S., Landry, R., & Wainwright, J. (1997). A componential view of executive dysfunction in autism: Review of recent evidence. In J. Burack & J. Enns (Eds.), *Attention, development, and psychopathology.* New York: Guilford.

Burack, J. A. (1994). Selective attention deficits in persons with autism: Preliminary evidence of an inefficient attentional lens. *Journal of Abnormal Psychology, 103,* 535–543.

Butterworth, G., & Grover, L. (1988). The origins of referential communication in human infancy. In L. Weiskrantz (Ed.), *Thought without language. A Fyssen Foundation symposium* (pp. 5–24). Oxford, UK: Clarendon Press/Oxford University Press.

Caplan, R., Chugani, H. T., Messa, C., Guthrie, D., Sigman, M., de Traversy, J., & Mundy, P. (1993). Hemispherectomy for intractable seizures, presurgical cerebral glucose metabolism and postsurgical nonverbal communication. *Developmental Medicine Child Neurology, 35,* 582–592.

Carruthers, P. (1996). Autism as mindblindness: An elaboration and partial defence. In P. Carruthers & P. K. Smith (Eds.), *Theories of theories of mind* (pp. 257–273). Cambridge, UK: Cambridge University Press.

Cesaroni, L., & Garber, M. (1991). Exploring the experience of autism through firsthand accounts. *Journal of Autism & Developmental Disorders, 21,* 303–313.

Chelune, G. J., Ferguson, W., Koon, R., & Dickey, T. O. (1986). Frontal lobe disinhibition in attention deficit disorder. *Child Psychiatry & Human Development, 16,* 221–234.

Clark, P., & Rutter, M. (1981). Autistic children's responses to structure and to interpersonal demands. *Journal of Autism & Developmental Disorders, 11,* 201–217.

Corkum, V., & Moore, C. (1998). The origins of joint visual attention in infants. *Developmental Psychology,* 28–38.

Courchesne, E., Townsend, J., Akshoomoff, N. A., & Saitoh, O. (1994). Impairment in shifting attention in autistic and cerebellar patients. *Behavioral Neuroscience, 108,* 848–865.

Cox, A., Klein, K., Charman, T., Baird, G., Baron-Cohen, S., Swettenham, J., Drew, A., & Wheelwright, S. (1999). Autism spectrum disorders at 20 and 42 months of age: Stability of clinical and ADI-R diagnosis. *Journal of Child Psychology & Psychiatry & Allied Disciplines, 40*(5), 719–732.

Dadds, M. R., Schwartz, S., Adams, T., & Rose, S. (1988). The effects of social context and verbal skill on the stereotypic and task-involved behavior of autistic children. *Journal of Child Psychology & Psychiatry, 29,* 669–676.

Davis, H. L., & Pratt, C. (1995). The development of children's theory of mind: The working memory explanation. *Australian Journal of Psychology, 47,* 25–31.

Dawson, G., Meltzoff, A., Osterling, J., & Rinaldi, J. (1998). Neuropsychological correlates of early symptoms of autism. *Child Development, 69*(5), 1276–1285.

Dennis, M., & Barnes, M. A. (1990). Knowing the meaning, getting the point, bridging the gap and carrying the message: Aspects of discourse following closed head injury in childhood and adolescence. *Brain & Language, 39,* 428–446.

Diamond, A., & Taylor, C. (1996). Development of an aspect of executive control: Development of the abilities to remember what I said and to "Do as I say, not as I do." *Developmental Psychobiology, 24,* 315–334.

Donnellan, A. M., Anderson, J. L., & Mesaros, R. A. (1984). An observational study of stereotypic behavior and proximity related to the occurrence of autistic child-family member interactions. *Journal of Autism & Developmental Disorders, 14,* 205–210.

Duncan, J. (1986). Disorganisation of behavior after frontal lobe damage. *Cognitive Neuropsychology, 3,* 271–290.

Fombonne, E., Siddons, F., Archard, S., Frith, U., & Happé, F. (1994). Adaptive behavior and theory of mind in autism. *European Child and Adolescent Psychiatry, 3,* 176–186.

Frith, U. (1989). *Autism: Explaining the enigma.* Oxford, UK: Blackwell Scientific.

Frith, U., Happé, F., & Siddons, F. (1994). Autism and theory of mind in everyday life. *Social Development, 3,* 108–124.

Frye, D., Zelazo, P. D., & Palfai, T. (1995). Theory of mind and rule-based reasoning. *Cognitive Development, 10,* 483–527.

Gernsbacher, M. A. (1996). The structure-building framework: What it is, what it might also be, and why. In B. K. Britton & A. C. Graesser (Eds.), *Models of understanding text* (pp. 289–311). Mahwah, NJ: Lawrence Erlbaum Associates.

Golden, C. J. (1981). The Luria-Nebraska Children's Battery: Theory and formulation. In G. W. Hynd & G. E. Obrzut (Eds.), *Neuropsychological assessment and the school-aged child* (pp. 277–302). New York: Grune & Stratton.

Goodman, R. (1994). A modified version of the Rutter parent questionnaire including items on children's strengths: A research note. *Journal of Child Psychology and Psychiatry, 35,* 1483–1494.

Grant, D. A., & Berg, E. A. (1948). A behavioral analysis of degree of reinforcement and ease of shifting to new responses in a Weigl-type card sorting problem. *Journal of Experimental Psychology, 38,* 404–411.

Grodzinsky, G., & Diamond, R. (1992). Frontal lobe functioning in boys with attention-deficit hyperactivity disorder. *Developmental Neuropsychology, 8,* 427–445.

Happé, F., & Frith, U. (1996). The neuropsychology of autism. *Brain, 119,* 1377–1400.

Harris, P. L., & Kavanaugh, R. D. (1993). Young children's understanding of pretense. *Monographs of the Society for Research in Child Development, 58(*1, Serial No. 231).

Hobson, P. (1993). *Autism and the development of mind.* Hove, UK: Lawrence Erlbaum Associates Ltd.

Hughes, C. (1998a). Executive function in preschoolers: Links with theory of mind and verbal ability. *British Journal of Developmental Psychology, 16,* 233–253.

Hughes, C. (1998b). Finding your marbles: Does preschoolers' strategic behavior predict later understanding of mind? *Developmental Psychology, 34*(6), 1326–1339.

Hughes, C., & Dunn, J. (1997). "Pretend you didn't know": Preschoolers' talk about mental states in pretend play. *Cognitive Development, 12,* 477–499.

Hughes, C., Leboyer, M., & Bouvard, M. (1997a). Executive function in parents of children with autism. *Psychological Medicine, 27*(1), 209–220.

Hughes, C., Plumet, M. -H., & Leboyer, M. (1999). Towards a cognitive phenotype for autism: Increased prevalence of executive dysfunction and superior spatial span amongst siblings of children with autism. *Journal of Child Psychology and Psychiatry, 40*(5), 705–718.

Hughes, C., Russell, J., & Robbins, T. W. (1994). Evidence for central executive dysfunction in autism. *Neuropsychologia, 32,* 477–492.

Hughes, C., Soares-Boucaud, I., Hochmann, J., & Frith, U. (1997b). Social behavior in pervasive developmental disorders: Effects of informant, group and "theory-of-mind." *European Child & Adolescent Psychiatry, 6,* 191–198.

Hutt, C., & Hutt, S. J. (1965). Effects of environmental complexity on stereotyped behaviors of children. *Animal Behavior, 13,* 1–4.

Jarrold, C., Boucher, J., & Smith, P. K. (1994). Executive function deficits and the pretend play of children with autism: A research note. *Journal of Child Psychology & Psychiatry, 35,* 1473–1482.

Jones, V., & Prior, M. (1985). Motor imitation abilities and neurological signs in autistic children. *Journal of Autism & Developmental Disorders, 15,* 37–46.

Kanner, L. (1961). *Early infantile autism. Feelings and their medical significance* (Vol. 3). Columbus, OH: Ross Laboratories.

Kasari, C., Sigman, M., Mundy, P., & Yirmiya, N. (1990). Affective sharing in the context of joint attention interactions of normal, autisitc and mentally retarded children. *Journal of Autism and Developmental Disorders (20),* 87–100.

Kochanska, G., Murray, K., Jacques, T. Y., Koenig, A. L., & Vandegeest, K. A. (1996). Inhibitory control in young children and its role in emerging internalization. *Child Development, 67,* 490–507.

Landa, R., Piven, J., Wzorek, M., Gayle, J., Chase, G., & Folstein, S. (1992). Social language use in parents of autistic individuals. *Psychological Medicine, 22,* 245–254.

Leslie, A. (1987). Pretense and representation: The origins of "theory of mind." *Psychological Review, 94,* 412–426.

Leslie, A. M., & Polizzi, P. (1998). Inhibitory processing in the false-belief task: Two conjectures. *Developmental Science, 1,* 247–254.

Lewis, V., & Boucher, J. (1988). Spontaneous, instructed and elicited play in relatively able autistic children. *British Journal of Developmental Psychology, 6,* 325–339.

Lovaas, O. I., Newsom, C., & Hickman, C. (1987). Self-stimulatory behavior and perceptual development. *Journal of Applied Behavior Analysis, 20,* 45–68.

Luciana, M., & Nelson, C. A. (1998). The functional emergence of prefrontally-guided working memory systems in four- to eight-year-old children. *Neuropsychologia, 36,* 273–293.

Luria, A. R. (1966). *Higher cortical functions in man* (1st ed.). New York: Basic Books.

McEvoy, R., Rogers, S. J., & Pennington, B. F. (1993). Executive function and social communication deficits in young autistic children. *Journal of Child Psychology & Psychiatry, 34,* 563–578.

Meltzoff, A. N. (1995). Understanding the intentions of others: Re-enactment of intended acts by 18-month-old children. *Developmental Psychology, 31,* 838–850.

Minshew, N. J., Goldstein, G., & Siegal, D. J. (1997). Neuropsychologic functioning in autism: Profile of a complex information processing disorder. *Journal of the International Neuropsychological Society, 3,* 303–316.

Moore, C. (1996). Evolution and the modularity of mindreading. *Cognitive Development, 11,* 605–621.

Mundy, P., & Sigman, M. (1989). Specifying the nature of the social impairment in autism. In G. Dawson (Ed.), *Autism: Nature, diagnosis, and treatment* (pp. 3–21). New York: Guilford.

Mundy, P., Sigman, M., & Kasari, C. (1994). Joint attention, developmental level, and symptom presentation in autism. *Development & Psychopathology, 6,* 389–401.

Ozonoff, S. (1995). Executive functions in autism. In E. Schopler & G. B. Mesibov (Eds.), *Learning and cognition in autism. Current issues in autism* (pp. 199–219). New York: Plenum.

Ozonoff, S. (1997). Components of executive function in autism and other disorders. In J. Russell (Ed.), *Autism as an executive disorder* (pp. 179–211). New York: Oxford University Press.

Ozonoff, S., & Jensen, J. (1999). Specific executive function profiles in three neurodevelopmental disorders. *Journal of Autism and Developmental Disorders, 29*(2), 171–177.

Ozonoff, S., Pennington, B. F., & Rogers, S. J. (1991). Executive function deficits in high functioning autistic children: Relationship to theory of mind. *Journal of Child Psychology & Psychiatry, 32,* 1081–1105.

Ozonoff, S., Rogers, S. J., Farnham, J. M., & Pennington, B. F. (1993). Can standard measures identify subclinical markers of autism? *Journal of Autism & Developmental Disorders, 23,* 429–441.

Pacherie, E. (1997). Motor-images, self-consciousness, and autism. In J. Russell (Ed.), *Autism as an executive disorder* (pp. 215–355). New York: Oxford University Press.

Pennington, B. F., & Ozonoff, S. (1996). Executive function and developmental psychopathology. *Journal of Child Psychology & Psychiatry, 37*(1), 51–87.

Perner, J. (1991). *Understanding the representational mind.* Cambridge, MA: MIT Press.

Perner, J., & Lang, B. (1999). Theory of mind and executive function: Is there a developmental relationship? In S. Baron-Cohen, H. Tager-Flusberg, & D. J. Cohen (Eds.), *Understanding other minds: Perspectives from autism and developmental cognitive neuroscience* (2nd ed.). Oxford, UK: Oxford University Press.

Pickles, A., Bolton, P., Macdonald, H., Bailey, A., Le Couteur, A., Sim, C. H., & Rutter, M. (1995). Latent-class analysis of recurrence risks for complex phenotypes with selection and measurement error: A twin and family history study of autism. *American Journal of Human Genetics, 57,* 717–726.

Piven, J., & Palmer, P. (1997). Cognitive deficits in parents from multiple incidence autism families. *Journal of Child Psychology and Psychiatry, 38,* 1011–1022.

Rakic, P., Bourgeois, J. P., Zecevic, N., Eckenhoff, M. F., & Goldman-Rakic, P. S. (1986). Concurrent overproduction of synapses in diverse regions of the primate cerebral cortex. *Science, 232,* 232–235.

Ridley, R. M. (1994). The psychology of perseverative and stereotyped behavior. *Progress in Neurobiology, 44,* 221–231.

Robbins, T. W. (1996). Dissociating executive functions of the prefrontal cortex. *Philosophical Transactions of the Royal Society: London, 351,* 1463–1471.

Rogers, S., & Pennington, B. (1991). A theoretical approach to the deficits in infantile autism. *Development & Psychopathology, 3,* 137–162.

Russell, J. (1996). *Agency: Its role in mental development.* Hove, UK: Lawrence Erlbaum Associate Ltd./Taylor and Francis.

Russell, J. (1997). How executive disorders can bring about an inadequate 'theory of mind'. In J. Russell (Ed.), *Autism as an executive disorder* (pp. 256–304). New York: Oxford University Press.

Russell, J., Jarrold, C., & Henry, L. (1996). Working memory in children with autism and with moderate learning difficulties. *Journal of Child Psychology & Psychiatry, 37,* 673–686.

Russell, J., Mauthner, N., Sharpe, S., & Tidswell, T. (1991). The "windows task" as a measure of strategic deception in preschoolers and autistic subjects. *British Journal of Developmental Psychology, 9,* 331–349.

Rutter, M. (1991). Autism as a genetic disorder. In P. McGuffin & R. Murray (Eds.), *The new genetics of mental illness* (pp. 225–244): Butterworth-Heinemann: The Mental Health Foundation.

Rutter, M., Dunn, J., Plomin, R., Simonoff, E., Pickles, A., Maughan, B., Ormel, J., Meyer, J., & Eaves, L. (1997). Integrating nature and nurture: Implications of person-environment correlations and interactions for developmental psychopathology. *Development and Psychopathology, 9*(2), 335–364.

Schopler, E., & Mesibov, G. (1985). *Communication problems in autism.* New York: Plenum.

Schopler, E., & Olley, J. (1982). Comprehensive educational services for autistic children: The TEACCH model. In C. R. Reynolds & T. B. Gutkin (Eds.), *Handbook of school psychology.* New York: Wiley.

Shah, A., & Frith, U. (1993). Why do autistic individuals show superior performance on the block design task? *Journal of Child Psychology & Psychiatry, 34,* 1351–1364.

Shallice, T. (1982). Specific impairments in planning. *Philosophical Transactions of the Royal Society of London, B298,* 199–209.

Smith, I., & Bryson, S. (1994). Imitation and action in autism: A critical review. *Psychological Bulletin, 2,* 259–273.

Swettenham, J., Baron-Cohen, S., Charman, T., Cox, A., Baird, G., Drew, A., Rees, L., & Wheelwright, S. (1998). The frequency and distribution of spontaneous attention shifts between social and nonsocial stimuli in autistic, typically developing, and nonautistic developmentally delayed infants. *Journal of Child Psychology & Psychiatry, 39,* 747–753.

Szatmari, P., Bartolucci, G., & Bremner, R. (1989). Asperger's syndrome and autism: Comparison of early history and outcome. *Developmental Medicine & Child Neurology, 31,* 709–720.

Taylor, M., & Carlson, S. (1997). The relation between individual differences in fantasy and theory of mind. *Child Development, 68,* 436–455.

Townsend, J., Harris, N. S., & Courchesne, E. (1996). Visual attention abnormalities in autism: Delayed orienting to location. *Journal of the International Neuropsychological Society, 2,* 541–550.

Turner, M. (1997). Towards an executive dysfunction account of repetitive behavior in autism. In J. Russell (Ed.), *Autism as an executive disorder* (pp. 57–100). New York: Oxford University Press.

Turner, M. A. (1999a). Annotation: Repetitive behavior in autism. *Journal of Child Psychology & Psychiatry,* 837–850.

Turner, M. A. (1999b). Generating novel ideas: Fluency performance in high-functioning and learning disabled individuals with autism. *Journal of Child Psychology & Psychiatry, 40,* 189–202.

Volkmar, F. R., Hoder, E. L., & Cohen, D. J. (1985). Compliance, 'negativism', and the effect of treatment structure in autism: a naturalistic behavioral study. *Journal of Child Psychology and Psychiatry, 26,* 865–877.

Wehner, E., & Rogers, S. J. (1994). *Attachment relationships of autistic and developmentally delayed children.* Paper presented at the bimonthly meeting of the Developmental Psychobiology Research Group, Denver, CO.

Welsh, M. C., Pennington, B. F., & Groisser, D. B. (1991). A normative-developmental study of executive function: A window on prefrontal function in children. *Developmental Neuropsychology, 7,* 131–149.

Wimmer, H. (1989). Common-Sense Mentalismus and Emotion: Einige entwicklungpsychologie Implikationen. In E. Roth (Ed.), *Denken und Fühlen.* Berlin: Springer Verlag.

Wing, L., & Gould, J. (1979). Severe impairments of social interactions and associated abnormalities in children: Epidemiology & classification. *Journal of Autism & Developmental Disorders, 9,* 11–30.

Youngblade, L. M., & Dunn, J. (1995). Social pretend with mother and sibling: Individual differences and social understanding. In A. Pellegrini (Ed.), *The future of play theory: Essays in honor of Brian Sutton-Smith* (pp. 221–240). New York: SUNY Press.

Zelazo, P. D., Frye, D., & Rapus, T. (1996). An age-related dissociation between knowing rules and using them. *Cognitive Development, 11,* 37–63.

IV

Social and Adaptive Behaviors

14

Communicative Intentions and Symbols in Autism: Examining a Case of Altered Development

Lisa L. Travis
Marian Sigman
University of California, Los Angeles

In her classic work on early language development, Bates (1979) poetically identifies "two moments at the dawn of language." According to Bates and others (e.g., Bruner, 1983; Harding & Golinkoff, 1979; Werner & Kaplan, 1963) two significant developmental reorganizations that set the stage for subsequent language acquisition occur around the end of the first year. The first "moment" involves the development of communicative intentions. Starting at around 9 months, infants begin to show awareness of the effects their signals have on others. This awareness brings about qualitative change, as signals become intentional messages directed to others. The second "moment" is the emergence of symbols. Starting at around 11 to 13 months, infants begin to comprehend signs as being both substitutable for, and yet separate from, their referents. This enables them to acquire communicative symbolic gestures and words. Of course, neither moment is actually a moment, but rather involves an extended course of development, beginning around the ages just mentioned. Autism provides an especially interesting perspective on these developmental reorganizations, as it involves specific impairment in both communicative and symbolic functioning. In fact, these impairments are even considered by several theoretical accounts to be central to the disorder (e.g., Baron-Cohen, 1995; Hobson, 1993; Leslie & Happé, 1989; Mundy, Sigman, & Kasari, 1993). Nevertheless, children with autism do show developmental change in communicative intent and symbolic functioning as mental age and linguistic skills increase. The purpose of this chapter is to integrate existing literature in order to provide a description of developmental change in autism. Contrasts between the course of development in autism and typical development are used to address issues regarding the nature of the impairments in autism as well as the nature of typical developmental processes.

In contrasting typical and atypical development, we follow the tradition of developmental psychopathology, which views typical and atypical development as reciprocally informative (Cicchetti, 1995). In this chapter, we hope to realize the goal of reciprocal informativeness in two ways. First, with respect to autism, we aim to provide a description of developmental change in key abilities that highlights similarities and differences with typical development. This description may be useful in helping to uncover how some individuals with autism are able to compensate for, or even overcome, certain deficits. It may also be informative with respect to theoretical issues regarding which deficits are primary and which are secondary in autism. Greater perturbation in developmental course may be one indication that deficiency in a particular ability is primary, rather than a secondary consequence of another deficit. Second, the opportunity to examine an atypical case can provide unique insights into typical development (Hodapp & Burack, 1990). Alterations in the typical organization and developmental paths of abilities can inform us about necessary prerequisites and facilitating factors for the development of a particular ability and help to separate them from incidentally co-occurring aspects of development. In particular, we discuss how autism is informative regarding two theoretical issues in typical development. The first issue concerns the degree of psychological understanding that should be attributed to infants based on their early communicative behaviors. The second concerns the contributions of cognitive and social factors to early symbolic development.

Drawing Inferences About Development in Autism by Integrating Across Studies: Some Limitations

Ideally, we would use information from longitudinal and cross-sectional studies to describe developmental change in specific abilities. In the case of autism, where chronological age and developmental level are often dissociated, cross-sectional designs would involve comparing groups at different developmental levels, as assessed by general measures of cognitive and language ability, rather than relying on chronological age as a metric of development. Unfortunately, even though a fairly large body of literature has focused on symbolic and communicative abilities in autism, very few studies have followed children longitudinally or employed cross-sectional designs. This does not reflect mere oversight on the part of autism researchers, but rather is due to limitations associated with studying a rare disorder. Although researchers are beginning to respond to the great need for developmental designs, at this point we are forced to get most of our information about developmental change by integrating studies that have employed the same or similar procedures to samples differing in average developmental level, as indexed by group means on standardized cognitive or language assessments. However, there are a number of difficulties associated with describing developmental change using this approach.

Perhaps the most serious limitation is that this method can only provide indirect evidence about individual trajectories of development. Comparing groups at different developmental levels does not necessarily reveal the developmental path of any individual. While this limitation applies to cross-sectional studies generally, the difficulties are exacerbated in the case of studies of autism because the samples are often very heterogeneous. Individuals within the same sample may vary greatly in cognitive and language abilities and in chronological age, as well as in the relations among these measures (i.e., they may be more or less delayed). A related problem is that the variability in developmental level may itself vary across studies. Two samples with the same mean mental age (MA), for example, may actually represent very different populations. Thus, characterizing the abilities of a sample with a particular mean mental age, for example, does not necessarily reveal the abilities of a typical individual at that mental age. Nevertheless, we can make some tentative inferences about the course of development by comparing across samples differing in developmental level. In order to remind the reader that we have only indirect evidence about the course of individual development, we will refer to abilities manifested by samples with a particular mean mental age, rather than stating that children with that mental age typically have that ability. In order to say that a certain MA, for example, is associated with a certain ability in individual children, longitudinal data, or at least cross-sectional data on fairly homogeneous groups, are necessary. We also acknowledge that because individuals with autism constitute a heterogeneous population, there may be no single common developmental path that characterizes all individuals with the disorder. However, we will try to identify patterns that are likely to characterize most individuals.

A practical issue associated with integrating studies by developmental level is that it is necessary to find a common metric of developmental level. Metrics of developmental level vary across studies. Some report language-age equivalents, and some mental-age equivalents. Even when two studies both report language-age equivalents, for example, different instruments may be used to derive these scores, with the result that they are not directly comparable. In order to address the problem of comparing studies that report only MA equivalents with those that report only LA equivalents, we examined discrepancies in MA and LA for all the studies we reviewed that report both. It is well established that language ability in children with autism lags behind their overall cognitive ability, but there is no ready formula for converting one into the other. Our analysis revealed evidence for more pronounced language impairment at higher levels of functioning.

Among the studies we examined, there was a natural division between those based on samples with average MAs below 32 months (Mundy, Sigman, Ungerer, & Sherman, 1987; McDonough, Stahmer, Schreibman, & Thompson, 1997; Sigman & Ruskin, 1999—sample at intake; Charman et al., 1997) (range 17 to 32 months, mean = 24 months) and those with average MAs in the 60-month range (Baron-Cohen, 1987; Riguet, Taylor, Benaroya, & Klein, 1981; Landry & Loveland, 1988; Loveland et al., 1988; Sigman & Ruskin, 1999—sample at follow-up) (range = 57 to 66 months, mean = 62.5 months). Two studies based on very high-functioning samples with average MAs of 85 and 90 months, respectively, were excluded from the higher functioning group (Charman & Baron-Cohen, 1994, 1997). For the lower ability samples, LAs lagged behind MAs an average of 7.2 months, range 6 to 10 months. For the higher ability samples, LAs lagged behind MAs an average of 27.8 months, range 15 to 33 months. We use these averages to provide a rough estimate of the missing score for studies supplying only one of the two, thereby allowing us to get a rough idea of the order of emergence of skills.

Our analysis only provides a rough guideline that allows us to order abilities, but not to identify the exact mental or language level at which particular skills emerge. At this level of resolution, we felt warranted in adopting the simplifying assumption that different measures of the same ability (e.g., different measures of language age) were comparable. In addition, we did not attempt to analyze differences in the variance in mental or language ages across studies.

In this chapter, primary emphasis is placed on developmental level as a factor influencing communicative and symbolic behavior. Emphasis on developmental level as measured by mental or language age disregards potentially important differences in chronological age and IQ. With respect to IQ, we run the risk of ignoring important distinctions between, for example, a slightly delayed 3-year-old and a severely delayed 12-year-old. With respect to chronological age, we run the risk of failing to consider the appropriateness and meaningfulness of particular behaviors for individuals of different ages. Chronological age undoubtedly influences others' responses to one's behaviors, and it may well influence one's predisposition to engage in behaviors independently from cognitive abilities. For example, symbolic play is probably not encouraged in adolescents, nor may it be attractive to them, even though they may have mental and language abilities that are in the range where symbolic play is typically shown. Undoubtedly, developmental level, IQ, and chronological age interact in complex ways as influences on the abilities we are examining. However, there is simply not enough information available at this time to gain a complete picture of these complex interactions. We have chosen to focus on developmental level because we believe it is likely to exert a particularly strong influence on early communicative and symbolic abilities.

Communicative Intentions

Typical Development

At about 9 months of age, a qualitative change in infants' signaling behavior occurs. Signals abound prior to this age, but the infant does not seem to be aware of the effects of these signals on a listener. The first signs of such awareness are apparent in two new behaviors, requesting (protoimperatives) and indicating (protodeclaratives). For example, in the case of requesting, when infants younger than about 9 months are interested in out-of-reach objects, they simply attempt to reach them. At around 9 months, infants begin to attempt to achieve their goals by communicating their desires to adults in order to enlist assistance. Bates (1979) outlines three signs that infant behaviors are based on intent to communicate. First, gaze alternation between the adult and the target object suggests that the infant is directing a message at the adult and monitoring its effectiveness. Second, infants' behaviors become contingent on adults' responses. For example, infants cease to signal when adults begin to assist them, rather than continuing to signal until the goal is achieved. Third, signals become ritualized and abbreviated. A full-blown reach is replaced by a schematic reaching gesture, which is eventually replaced by pointing.

Although naturalistic observations typically reveal the first signs of communicative intent at 8 to 9 months (e.g., Bates, Beningi, Bretherton, Camaioni, & Volterra, 1979), protoimperatives and protodeclaratives become more frequent, more flexible, and better organized over the period from 9 to 15 months (see Carpenter, Nagell, & Tomasello, 1998, for a review). For example, earliest pointing is restricted to nearby objects, but pointing is extended to distal objects by 15 months (Zinober & Martlew, 1985). Conventional forms such as pointing also come to play a more important role in children's repertoires. Noncommunicative pointing is often present from very early in infancy, but pointing is not typically the earliest form of communicative gesture. Communicative reaching, giving, and showing tend to emerge earlier than pointing (Carpenter, Nagell, et al., 1998; Lock, Young, Service, & Chandler, 1990). Recently, in an intensive study of the order of emergence of various prelinguistic communicative skills, Carpenter, Nagell, et al. (1998) found that when all the forms were considered together (i.e., showing, giving, and pointing), protodeclaratives emerged considerably earlier than protoimperatives (average age of emergence: 10.3 vs. 12.7 months).

As infants attain the ability to direct the attention and behavior of others, they also learn to respond to others' communicative efforts. Under maximally supportive conditions, infants as young as 6 months sometimes turn to look in the same direction as an adult (Butterworth & Jarrett, 1991; D'Entremont, Hains, & Muir, 1997; Scaife & Bruner, 1975). However, when stringent criteria are used to define gaze following, such as requiring that infants more frequently match rather than mismatch the direction of gaze of an adult partener, gaze following is not reliably present until 12 to 15 months (Corkum & Moore, 1995; Morissette, Ricard, & Gouin-Décarie, 1995). The ability to localize distant targets, to ignore distractor targets along the infant's scan path, and to follow gaze directed at a location behind the infant emerge between the ages of 12 and 18 months (Butterworth & Jarrett, 1991; Morissette et al., 1995). Point following is affected by similar factors and develops along a similar timetable (Desrochers, Morissette, & Ricard, 1995; Lempers, 1979; Murphy & Messer, 1977).

A few studies have addressed the issue of whether attention-directing or attention-following behaviors develop earlier. Comprehension of pointing emerges slightly before production of pointing (Desrochers et al., 1995; Lempers, 1979; Leung & Rheingold, 1981; Lock et al., 1990), but the differences in age of emergence are small, on the order of 1 month. Considering a wider range of behaviors, Carpenter, Nagell, et al. (1998) found that the age of emergence of particular communicative behaviors was dependent on the specific behavior more than it was on whether the behavior was attention-directing or attention-following. Most infants demonstrated attention directing in the form of sharing first (giving or showing a proximal object), then began to follow gaze and pointing, and finally began to use pointing to direct adults' attention to more distal objects.

Development in Autism

Perhaps the most obvious feature of the development of communicative behaviors in autism is extreme delay in relation to typical development. Whereas typically developing infants master basic prelinguistic skills between 9 and 15 months, children with autism acquire these skills in the mental-age range of 17 to 30 months. The following discussion focuses on the sequences in which various skills develop and the overall level of cognitive development that is associated with the appearance of particular skills.

One of the earliest communicative behaviors to emerge in children with autism appears to be point following. Some early signs of this ability are present even in the youngest, least able samples that have been studied (mean MAs in the 17- to 18-month range). For example, one group of children with autism with a mean MA of 17 months succeeded in following a point on 19% of trials (Mundy, Sigman, & Kasari, 1994), and in another group with a mean MA of 18 months and a CA of 2 years, 13% were able to follow a point (DiLavore & Lord, 1995). Point following improves with increasing mental age. DiLavore and Lord followed their sample longitudinally until they were 5 years old (MA not reported, though we can assume that it increased), by which time 79% were capable of point following. Samples with mean MAs over 30 months are nearly perfect in following the direction of a point (Atwood, Frith, & Hermelin, 1988; Baron-Cohen, 1989; Mundy et al., 1994; Sigman & Ruskin, 1999).

In typically developing children, spontaneous gaze following emerges at about the same time as point following, and may emerge earlier. For children with autism, gaze following presents more much difficulty than point following. Reliable gaze following is not present in children with autism with MAs less than 48 months (Leekam, Hunnisett, & Moore, 1998), and deficits may be apparent in some circumstances even at higher mental ages (Leekam, Baron-Cohen, Perrett, Milders, & Brown, 1997) (sample mean MA = 64 months).

Requesting skills appear to emerge early in development. In one study, a sample with a mean MA of 17 months made requests as frequently as an MA-matched mentally retarded control sample (Mundy et al., 1994). The autistic and control samples also did not differ in the distribution of higher level requests (giving or pointing) versus lower level requests (reaching to out-of-reach toys with or without eye contact). However, one difference between the early requesting skills of autistic and other children is that the early requests of children with autism are less likely to incorporate eye contact or gaze alternation between person and desired object. In a low-ability sample with mean MA of 17 months, Charman et al. (1997) found that children with autism presented with an interesting out-of-reach toy showed gaze alternation on only 8% of trials. Comparison with an MA-matched developmentally delayed control group highlighted the severity of the deficit. The control group showed gaze alternation on 83% of trials.

Although requesting is a relative strength in autism, because it begins to develop early and occurs with similar frequency as in comparison groups (e.g., Sigman & Ruskin, 1999), there are some unusual features of early requesting in autism that suggest possible deficiencies in communicative intent. One example is the lack of eye contact in conjunction with signaling. This is clearly true of less able samples. However, it is unclear whether lack of eye contact characterizes the requests of samples in the 25- to 40-month MA range. Whereas Mundy, Sigman, Ungerer, and Sherman (1986) and Mundy et al. (1994) found that samples of 27 and 30 months mean MA were not impaired in use of eye contact in conjunction with requesting, Phillips, Gomez, Baron-Cohen, Laa, and Riviere (1995) found that children with autism (mean MA = 39 months) used less eye contact while requesting than an MA-matched mentally retarded sample. It appears likely that children with autism do increase their use of eye contact in conjunction with requesting as they mature cognitively, but they may never use eye contact as frequently as other children. Children with autism may also be less flexible in their use of eye contact in a variety of requesting situations. One type of requesting situation that presents difficulty for more able children with autism is when information, rather than a concrete object or event, is the object of the request. Phillips, Baron-Cohen, and Rutter (1992) showed that when presented with an ambiguous social event (an adult blocking the child's actions, or offering and then withdrawing a toy) children with autism (mean MA = 38 months) are strikingly less likely to make eye contact. This failure to use eye contact in order to resolve social ambiguity suggests that even fairly able children with autism are impaired in their understanding of the adult as a potential communicative partner.

A second unusual feature of early requesting in autism is that it is more likely to involve physical manipulation of the partner's body. Children with autism have a tendency to lead, push, or pull an adult toward a desired item rather than to use a conventional gesture such as pointing. In addition, children with autism sometimes indicate requests for actions by placing the adult's hand on a desired item (e.g., a jar to be opened) (Lord, Rutter, & Le Couteur, 1994). Both forms of requesting are rare in typically developing children. As in the case of lack of eye contact, atypical forms of requesting may decrease with increasing mental age. Phillips et al. (1995) failed to find evidence for greater use of physical manipulation in an autistic sample with a mean MA of 39 months, possibly reflecting the fact that by this mental age, most children with autism have outgrown these strategies. Again, similar to the case of eye contact, in spite of improvement, subtle impairments probably remain. Phillips et al. did find differences between their autistic and control samples. Children with autism engaged in less schematic reaching, less pointing, and less gesturing toward distal objects than MA-matched mentally retarded children.

The most seriously impaired communicative behaviors in autism are those relating to sharing of attention. Whereas in typical development, protodeclaratives emerge somewhat earlier than protoimperatives, the opposite pattern occurs in autism. Indeed, across a wide range of developmental levels, children with autism are impaired in the frequency with which they initiate bids for joint attention (e.g., Sigman & Ruskin, 1999). At the time that protoimperatives are just beginning to emerge (17 to 18 months MA), protodeclaratives are almost completely absent (e.g., Mundy et al., 1994). This may partially reflect the fact that criteria for protoimperatives typically require that both gestures and eye contact be present. For children with autism, the earliest forms of protoimperatives may involve making eye contact while manipulating an object, without providing a clear accompanying gesture (Mundy et al., 1994). Samples with average MAs of 26 to 30 months produce some protodeclarative pointing and showing, but these behaviors are much less frequent than they are in MA-matched mentally retarded control groups (Mundy et al, 1994; Mundy et al., 1986). Protodeclarative, or joint attention behaviors, also appear to be more disorganized in form than are requesting behaviors. For example, use of eye contact in conjunction with requesting behavior appears prior to use of eye contact in conjunction with indicating or sharing behaviors (Mundy, Sigman, Ungerer, & Sherman, 1986). In addition, whereas it is common for typically developing children to express positive affect while engaged in attention sharing, children with autism rarely do so (Dawson, Hill, Spencer, Galpert, & Watson, 1990; Kasari, Sigman, Mundy, & Yirmiya, 1990).

Children with autism manifest impairments in attention sharing regardless of the setting, but some settings are more supportive of these behaviors than others. The studies just described have assessed abilities in structured laboratory situations designed to elicit demonstrations of competence. However, in unstructured situations, the joint-attention deficits of children with autism are even more apparent (e.g., Kasari, Sigman, & Yirmiya, 1993; Stone & Caro-Martinez, 1990).

In summary, both severe delay and atypical organization of development characterize the acquisition of communicative competence in autism. Behaviors that typically emerge at about 9 months of age are only beginning to appear by 17 months of MA in autism. One indication of altered organization is a dissociation between joint-attention and requesting behaviors. In typical development, these behaviors develop in tandem, with the earliest joint-attention behaviors appearing only slightly before the earliest requesting behaviors (Carpenter, Nagell, et al., 1998), whereas in autism, requesting precedes joint attention. A second difference is that responding to pointing appears to be a relative strength in autism, as it precedes initiating pointing and gaze following. In typical development, gaze following and point following emerge at approximately the same time, whereas gaze following presents exceptional difficulty for children with autism. Point following before use of pointing is characteristic of both typical and autistic development. Pointing lags further behind point following in autism, but it is not clear whether this represents an atypical developmental path, or simply reflects the slower pace of communicative development in autism. Children with autism also exhibit unusual forms of both joint-attention and requesting behaviors. Early on, children with autism often fail to make eye contact in conjunction with signaling, and they are also prone to using requesting strategies that involve physically manipulating the adult's body.

Accounting for the Developmental Course of Communicative Behaviors in Autism

Perturbations in the development of communicative behaviors in autism can be viewed from two perspectives. On the one hand, the pattern of impairments is quite consistent with views that typical development of specific communicative behaviors is part of the unfolding of a biologically based, social, or social-cognitive system, which is missing or impaired in autism. For example, lack of gaze following and eye contact are quite consistent with a deficient "shared attention mechanism" (Baron-Cohen, 1995) or with deficient metarepresentational abilities and consequent impairment in mental-state understanding (Leslie, 1991). Disproportionate impairment in initiating joint attention and lack of positive affect in conjunction with communication are consistent with impairments in Mundy's (1995) proposed "social-emotional approach system."

On the other hand, if the specific social impairment view is correct, it is also informative that even without the typical innate endowments, children with autism are able to make some progress in communicative behaviors as they advance cognitively. This progress suggests that behaviors that may typically be mediated by some specialized social mechanisms can be acquired by other means. What might be the alternative mechanisms of development in autism?

One possibility is that the child with autism's first inroads into the domain of communication are made using general-purpose learning tools, such as means–end analysis and operant conditioning. Delay may reflect the fact that these tools are not ideally suited to the task at hand, and the child with autism is faced with solving some difficult problems.

Consider how requesting behavior might be acquired if it were initially entirely dependent on means–end understanding. The human assistant is a means with a complex set of properties. In contrast with the use of a simple tool, no physical mechanism directly links one's own behavior and the attainment of a goal. Instead, the outcome is indirectly achieved by another person. The propensity to physically manipulate an adult's body in the early stages of requesting may reflect attempts by children with autism to bridge the physical gap between the means and the end. In other words, they may be inappropriately applying strategies that are successful in the physical world to social problems. Compounding the difficulty of the requesting problem is the fact that the effects of one's own behavior on a human "means" are probabilistic, in contrast to the simpler case in the physical world where effects of one's own behavior on outcomes are fairly regular. Successful requesting behavior without the benefit of underlying mentalistic understanding probably requires some rather sophisticated means–end analysis. This may explain why such an advanced level of means–end understanding (i.e., one associated with 20 to 30 months MA) is associated with the onset of requesting behavior in autism.

Responding to pointing may also be acquired through general-purpose learning tools. Operant conditioning seems a likely mechanism of development, and indeed, this mechanism is proposed to play a role in the typical development of this skill (e.g., Corkum & Moore, 1995). However, the difficulties experienced by children with autism suggest that this mechanism in isolation may be particularly ill suited to the task. One problem with this learning route is that, as anyone who has tried to use pointing to communicate with an animal or a young infant knows, the first serendipitous success is likely to be a long time in coming. Among persons with autism, additional factors—such as the demand for attention switching, which in itself presents difficulties for individuals with autism (Courchesne et al., 1994)—may hamper the learning process. Another problem is that the "reward" of following pointing (i.e., an interesting sight) may not be as intrinsically rewarding for those with autism as it might be for other individuals. Events that interest developmentally typical children and adults might not interest children with autism because the latter have more difficulty understanding the social context and because they may be absorbed by their own unusual and restricted interests.

If children with autism learn to make requests and follow pointing in the manner we have suggested, their skills at 20 to 25 months MA, though less advanced than in comparison groups, are actually impressive. Nonetheless, such skills may not be informative about these children's understanding of communicative intent. Rather, they may be instrumental behaviors that mimic behaviors that are associated with communicative intent in developmentally typical children. However, clearer signs for such understanding can be found in subsequent developments. Around 25 to 30 months MA, children with autism show at least some self-initiated attention sharing such as pointing and showing, increase their use of eye contact in conjunction with indicating and requesting, and decrease their use of requesting strategies involving direct manipulation of others' bodies. These behaviors are more difficult to connect with their apparent utility for nonsocial rewards, and hence are less easily explained by mechanisms such as operant conditioning. Thus, children with autism who show these communicative behaviors may have begun to develop some rudimentary understanding of communication as a process that is mediated by mental states. Although this understanding will be impaired throughout development, there is apparently an important qualitative shift at about 30 months MA that may signal the first emergence of true communicative intent.

Symbols

Theorists interested in early representational ability often distinguish between two senses of representation, conceptual and symbolic (Mandler, 1983). Conceptual representation involves building and using a knowledge system that is divorced from perception and action. Such representations have several advantages over earlier "enactive" or "sensorimotor" representations, including the capacity to be maintained and manipulated in the absence of perceptual support and the potential to incorporate abstract, non-perceptually-based content. Closely tied to the development of conceptual representations, yet separable from them, are symbols. Bates (1979) offers the following definition of symbol use: "The comprehension or use, inside or outside communicative situations, of a relationship between a sign and its referent, such that the sign is treated as belonging to and/or substitutable for its referent in a variety of contexts; at the same time the user is aware that the sign is separable from its referent, that is, not the same thing" (p. 43). Symbolizing involves selecting a part to stand for a whole, which is cognitively economical. One important property of symbols such as words and gestures is that they are "lightweight mental tokens" (Bates, 1979, p. 65) that can serve as proxy for more cumbersome full-blown conceptual representations. Symbols facilitate access to and manipulation of conceptual representations, thereby serving as powerful tools of thought. We review this distinction here because in what follows, we are going to focus narrowly on evidence relevant to the ability of children with autism to use symbols, rather than more broadly on their ability to use both conceptual and symbolic representation.

Four behaviors that emerge in the second year are considered important indicators of early conceptual and symbolic abilities: delayed imitation, pretend play, referential gestures, and referential words. In our review, we focus only on referential words and pretend play. Early referential gesturing has simply not been studied in autism, and although imitation has been studied extensively, we chose not to include it for two reasons. First, recent findings in cognitive development have challenged the Piagetian assumption that imitation is closely tied to symbolic development (Mandler, 1988). More important, imitation is a highly social ability that is compromised in autism (see Smith & Bryson, 1994, for a review). Because imitation deficits may derive either from social or symbolic impairments, imitation is a poor measure of symbolic ability in this particular population.

Typical Development

In typically developing children, protosymbolic behaviors begin to emerge around the end of the first year. These behaviors include first words, first conventional gestures, and first instances of functional play. Functional play involves using an object in play in a conventional way (e.g., comb hair with comb, drink from cup). Initially, however, such conventional uses of objects are not necessarily symbolic, because they do not satisfy Bates' two criteria of substitutability and separability. It is not clear that early words and play actions refer to and yet remain distinct from a class of objects or events. They may be simply parts of well-learned routines. For example, Bates describes a little girl who said "kitty" only after she threw her toy cat out of her crib, as a request for her father to return it to her. She did not say "kitty" to refer to any other cat, or in any other situation. Similarly, a child may perform a drinking gesture in response to seeing and holding a cup, without using this gesture to stand for a broader class of actions or objects. Gradually, by a process of *decontextualization*, these behaviors become more independent of perceptual support and less tied to their antecedents and consequents. As a result, protosymbols become more accessible in a variety of situations, and finally (somewhat magically) come to stand for classes of objects and events. Another aspect of the process of early symbolic development is that symbols become increasingly independent of overt behaviors. Eventually, symbols can be mentally evoked and manipulated without any accompanying overt behavior.

The first instances of gestures and words that are used with enough generality and flexibility to be credited with referring to classes of objects or events appear at about the same time, typically sometime early in the second year (Bates et al., 1979; Acredolo & Goodwyn, 1988). Functional play acts appear at about the same time, however, their status as symbolic behavior is unclear. Some theorists suggest that these actions function as "recognitory" acts, or "gestural names," serving to evoke a child's knowledge regarding an object or situation (Bates, 1979; Werner & Kaplan, 1963). While there are several reasons for crediting them with symbolic status (Shore, Bates, Bretherton, Beeghly, & O'Connell, 1990), they are not as unambiguously symbolic as words and gestures, because they require interaction with a concrete object. Only later-developing forms of pretend play, such as use of object substitution (e.g., use of a banana for a telephone) or use of absent objects (e.g., pantomime use of phone with no prop) provide unassailable evidence for symbolic functioning. These forms typically do not occur until toward the end of the second year (McCune-Nicolich, 1981).

Development in Autism

Symbolic abilities in autism have been fairly well investigated, and several reviews of research on this topic are available (Jarrold, Boucher, & Smith, 1993; Cicchetti, Beeghly, & Weiss-Perry, 1994; Wulfe, 1985). There has long been speculation that symbolic deficits may be central to the disorder (Hammes & Langdell, 1981; Ricks & Wing, 1975), and more recent conceptualizations hold that a highly specialized form of symbolic ability underlying both mental-state understanding and pretense is lacking in autism (Baron-Cohen, 1995; Leslie, 1991).

Words And Language. Lexical development, though delayed, is not highly deviant in its early stages. Autistic and Down syndrome children are similar in patterns of lexical acquisition during the MLU 1.0 to 2.0 range. Lexical diversity (the number of different root words used in 100 utterances) increases at comparable rates and the distribution of form classes (nouns, verbs, closed class words) are similar (Tager-Flusberg et al., 1990). Though linguistic measures, such as these, provide only indirect evidence regarding symbolic ability, gross atypicalities in symbol use are likely to affect these general measures of lexical development. Later stages of lexical development also do not appear to be deviant in individuals with autism. Older children with autism appear to have the same extensions for basic and superordinate level category terms (e.g., *dog* and *animal*; *hammer* and *tool*) as do typically developing children (Tager-Flusberg, 1985). This suggests that they do not have particular difficulty decontextualizing lexical symbols and acquiring concepts as abstract as *animal* or *tool*.

In spite of typical patterns of lexical acquisition, peculiarities in the use of language among individuals with autism may indicate impairments in more advanced levels of symbolic functioning. The language of people with autism is often described as rigid and concrete, partially due to their failure to comprehend nonliteral uses of language such as metaphor and idiom (Happé, 1995). Their interpretations of idiom tend to be completely literal. For example, Ricks & Wing (1975) described a girl who became quite distressed when she heard the phrase "crying your eyes out," and another who started anxiously searching when asked if he had "lost his tongue."

Children with autism are also prone to idiosyncratic uses of language. Use of neologisms (e.g., *diddle-up* for *shoe*) is more prevalent in autism than in other developmentally delayed groups (Volden & Lord, 1991), as is use of "metaphorical language," which is actually the use of idiosyncratic expressions for particular meanings. These idiosyncratic expressions appear to be traceable to original learning episodes. For example, Kanner (1973) cites the example of a boy who used the expression "Peter-eater" for saucepan, because his mother had been reciting the rhyme "Peter, Peter, pumpkin-eater" one day when she accidentally dropped a pan. Metaphorical language appears to reflect preservation of original private meanings either because of imperviousness to communication pressure or because of difficulty in reattaching a new symbol to an old meaning.

Analysis of language for underlying meaning also presents difficulty for individuals with autism. One sign of this difficulty is failure to exhibit clustering of semantically related items in recall (Hermelin & O'Connor, 1970; Tager-Flusberg, 1991). While reading text, individuals with autism have difficulty using sentence context to resolve the meanings of *homographs*, which are pairs of words that are orthographically identical, but with different pronunciations and meanings (e.g., *lead* the metal vs. *lead* the dog) (Frith & Snowling, 1983; Happé, 1997). Finally, relational terms such as verbs, prepositions, and comparative adjectives may present greater learning difficulty for children with autism than they do for typically developing children (Menyuk & Quill, 1985), possibly because these require deeper level analysis for meaning than do concrete nouns.

Functional Play. Even the youngest, lowest functioning samples of children with autism that have been studied produce some spontaneous functional play. Charman et al. (1997) found that 60% of a group of children with autism with a mean MA of 17 months produced at least some spontaneous functional play, and this rate was not different from a MA-matched control sample of developmentally delayed children. Similarly, Baron-Cohen (1987) found that 80% of a group of children with autism with a mean MA of 57 months produced some functional play, which again was not different from an LA-matched Down syndrome sample. However, a minority of children with autism fails to produce any functional play. Children with autism are overrepresented among mentally retarded children with MAs above 20 months who fail to produce any functional play (Wing, Gould, Yeates, & Brierley, 1977).

The clearest evidence for deficits in functional play comes from measures reflecting the quality of play produced. In a sample with mean MA of 25 months, Sigman & Ungerer (1984) found that there was less diversity in the functional-play actions produced and less combination of acts into meaningful 2- and 3-step sequences in autistic as compared to typical and MA-matched developmentally delayed control samples.

Within the autistic group, the amount of functional play produced is correlated with MA and LA (Ungerer & Sigman, 1981; Mundy, Sigman, Ungerer, & Sherman, 1987). However, it is not yet clear whether, or at what mental age, children with autism produce as much functional play as other children. Sigman & Ungerer (1984) found that a sample with mean MA of 25 months spent only about half as much time in functional play as a mentally retarded comparison group. Findings for children with higher MAs are not consistent, with one study reporting no differences in amount of time spent in functional play between a high-functioning autistic and LA-matched control group (Libby, Powell, Messer, & Jordan, 1998) (mean LA of autistic group 29 months, estimated MA of 57 months) and another study reporting less play in autistic than in LA-matched comparison groups (Lewis & Boucher, 1988) (mean MA of sample 65 months).

The findings just described might appear to indicate that deficits in quantity of functional play decline with increasing cognitive ability. However, several methodological issues complicate the deceptively simple issue of whether or not there are deficits in the quantity of functional play produced. For example, the criteria for matching comparison samples can make a critical difference in findings, and in the research just described it is confounded with developmental level. Whereas Sigman & Ungerer's (1984) study with less able children used mental-age matching, the two studies of more able children compared them to language-matched groups. Language matching imposes a stricter criterion for the demonstration of autism-specific deficits than does mental-age matching. Thus deficits that may be apparent when individuals with autism are matched based on mental age may disappear when language-age matching is employed. Which matching criterion is more appropriate is a particularly difficult issue in the case of an ability such as functional play, which is highly related to language ability. On the one hand, MA matching will put children with autism at a disadvantage in terms of linguistic ability. On the other hand, LA-matching may impose an unduly strict criterion. That is, it may preclude the possibility of finding group differences, because groups are matched on essentially the same ability on which they are compared.

Other factors also influence whether deficits in functional play are apparent. For example, deficits are particularly apparent in unstructured settings. Spontaneous play is typically assessed in settings where a large number of toys and other objects are spread about. Demonstration of functional play in this context requires the ability to ignore distraction and the ability to organize one's behavior based on an internal plan rather than on the perceptually available information. Not surprisingly, decreasing these demands by presenting objects singly or in thematically related groups substantially increases amount of play exhibited by all children. However, the benefits of such structured presentation are particularly great for children with autism (Sigman & Ungerer, 1984).

The composition of the comparison group can also affect whether or not deficits in play are identified. In a recent study combining Sigman and Ungerer's (1984) data with that from several other studies to yield a large sample with a mean MA of 25 months, Sigman and Ruskin (1999) found that children with autism produced as many different functional-play acts as typically developing and developmentally delayed children, though fewer than Down syndrome children. This finding points out that inclusion of Down syndrome children in control groups in many studies, including that of Sigman and Ungerer (1984), may lead to spurious findings of deficits in autistic samples because of the disproportionately good play abilities of DS children.

In summary, questions regarding deficits in the quantity of spontaneous functional play are difficult to resolve because of a variety of methodological issues. At this point, the best evidence for functional-play deficits comes from measures of the quality of play (Sigman & Ungerer, 1984) and from the fact that children with autism are overrepresented among those children with MAs greater than 20 months who fail to produce any functional play (Wing et al., 1977). Regarding quantity of play produced, it appears likely that if deficits do exist they are not large. Large, robust deficits would undoubtedly be apparent across studies despite methodological differences.

A number of studies include measures of elicited functional play, in which children's ability to reproduce actions modeled by an experimenter is assessed. Below about 20 months MA, children with autism appear to have difficulty reproducing modeled actions. For example, Charman et al. (1997) found that children with autism (mean MA = 17 months) were only successful in copying modeled actions on 20% of trials, whereas MA-matched developmentally delayed controls were successful on 60% of trials. However in a slightly more advanced sample (mean MA = 25 months), Sigman and Ungerer (1984) found that children with autism were as able to reproduce at least some types of functional play as controls. More able samples with MAs of 48 months and above appear to be virtually perfect in imitating simple actions on objects, such as pounding a nail with a hammer and combing a doll's hair (e.g., Charman & Baron-Cohen, 1994; Hammes & Langdell, 1981; Lewis & Boucher, 1988; Rogers, Bennetto, McEvoy, & Pennington, 1996).

Symbolic Play. Spontaneous symbolic play in children with autism is so rare that impairments in imaginative play are included among the diagnostic criteria for the disorder (DSM–IV, American Psychiatric Association, 1994). Although symbolic-play abilities improve along with language ability within the autistic group, (Mundy et al., 1987; Sigman & Ungerer, 1984), children with autism remain impaired in symbolic play relative to matched control groups even at advanced levels of linguistic and cognitive development. Impairments in symbolic play have been documented in samples ranging in mean MA from 17 to 57 months (Charman et al., 1997; Sigman & Ungerer, 1984; Libby et al., 1998; Baron-Cohen, 1987; Riguet, Taylor, Benaroya, & Klein, 1981). The symbolic play produced by children with autism is often stereotyped. In contrast to the flexible, creative use of pretense displayed by typically developing children, children with autism tend to display a limited repertoire of symbolic actions that they produce repeatedly (Wing et al., 1977). Two major theoretical views compete as accounts for symbolic play deficits in autism. According to the metarepresentational deficit account, symbolic play is absent in autism because children with autism lack the necessary representational abilities. These representational abilities are essential not only to the adoption of an "as if" attitude in pretense, but also to grasping mental states in others and developing a theory of mind (Leslie; 1991; Leslie & Roth, 1993) Within this account, absence of symbolic play in autism is somewhat analogous to absence of vision in a blind child. Highly specialized equipment that is essential for the function is damaged, with the result that competence is impaired in a fundamental and irremediable manner. The second major view is that children with autism have underlying competence in symbolic play that is masked by performance limitations. Executive-function impairments such as inability to generate ideas (Lewis & Boucher, 1995) or inability to override immediate perceptual input with mentally generated ideas (Harris, 1993) may be responsible for lack of symbolic play. In order to distinguish between these two accounts, researchers have examined symbolic play in circumstances where executive-function demands are decreased, specifically, when symbolic play is elicited by providing supportive contexts. Reduction of impairments in these supportive conditions would be most consistent with the production deficit view, whereas persistence of deficits in spite of support would be most consistent with the metarepresentation view.

Various methods have been used to elicit symbolic play, ranging from simply structuring the materials by presenting them in small, thematically related sets to modeling target play actions. For children with MAs below 30 months, symbolic play improves under elicited conditions, but not to the same level as observed in comparison groups (Sigman & Ungerer, 1984). More able children produce as much symbolic play as comparison groups under some circumstances (Charman & Baron-Cohen, 1997; Lewis & Boucher, 1995). However, even fairly able children have difficulty with some forms of symbolic play. Object substitution appears to be the easiest type of symbolic play for children with autism, both in spontaneous and elicited conditions. Play involving use of imaginary objects (pantomime) and attribution of false properties poses more difficulty (Hammes & Langdell, 1981; Rogers et al., 1996).

The fact that symbolic play can be elicited at all at first appears to support the production-deficit view. However, metarepresentation theorists counter that this does not provide strong evidence against a metarepresentational deficit. One objection to these highly structured situations is that children may succeed in producing target actions by adopting an "intelligent guessing" strategy (Baron-Cohen, 1990). They may simply relate two objects in the most obvious way, without actually adopting a pretend attitude. In cases where symbolic actions are modeled for the child, a more serious objection applies. As Baron-Cohen (1987) points out, it is difficult to discern whether resulting successful imitations are truly symbolic. When the experimenter models holding a banana to her ear and talking, the child may have represented "use the banana as a telephone," or "hold the banana to my ear." The second alternative would not involve symbolic pretense, though it would involve sophisticated imitative abilities. Thus successful imitation of "symbolic" actions does not unambiguously establish that children with autism have underlying symbolic competence. In order to resolve this ambiguity, researchers have employed alternative procedures that allow them to isolate specific aspects of symbolic-play competence, such as the ability to generate ideas for play (Lewis & Boucher, 1995), the ability to comprehend pretend scenarios (Jarrold, Smith, Boucher, & Harris, 1994), and willingness to use "counterfunctional" props (e.g., a pencil as a toothbrush) (Jarrold, Boucher, & Smith, 1994). Somewhat surprisingly, all of these studies failed to provide support for either metarepresentational or production-deficit accounts because they failed to find the anticipated symbolic-play deficits in any of their conditions. Even though lack of group differences does not reflect ceiling effects, failure to find deficits may result from these studies' focus on high-functioning individuals (mean LAs 57 to 65 months, estimated MAs at least 85 to 93 months). Symbolic-play deficits are likely to be more apparent in younger, less able samples. Studies aimed at differentiating between various accounts of symbolic-play deficits are most likely to succeed if they target children at lower developmental levels, where deficits are most apparent.

Unfortunately, little information is available regarding the underlying source of symbolic-play deficits in developmentally younger children with autism. However, one study of elicited symbolic play in samples of children with mean MAs of 26 and 30 months presents a challenge to the metarepresentation account (McDonough et al., 1997). The logic behind this study was that delayed imitation provides better evidence for symbolic encoding than does immediate imitation, because comprehension of meaning may be required for, or at least highly facilitative of, delayed recall. McDonough et al. found that delayed recall of familiar actions with novel "placeholder" objects (e.g., hold block to one's ear and talk) was the same for autistic and MA- and LA-matched typically developing comparison groups. All groups recalled more familiar actions on placeholder objects than comparable novel actions on objects, providing some evidence that children were sensitive to the symbolic substitution realized by the placeholders. Furthermore, all groups showed some flexibility in choice of placeholder objects to imitate a particular action (they did not necessarily choose the object that they had seen the action modeled with). This flexibility is good evidence that children had encoded the actions as involving a symbolic substitution. Children with autism were also as good as typically developing matched controls at delayed imitation of multiple-step play sequences involving object substitution. Although more work is needed to replicate and extend these findings, this study suggests that even younger, less able children with autism have the ability to grasp that one object can be used to represent another in play, which appears inconsistent with the metarepresentation account. However, arguments that object substitution may sometimes be accomplished by means other than metarepresentational abilities (Currie, 1996; Harris, 1994) point out a need for studies of the ability of developmentally younger children with autism to understand play involving attribution of false properties and use of imaginary objects.

Accounting for the Development of Symbolic Abilities in Autism

Considering the evidence from lexical and play development, disruption of symbolic functioning seems less a case of disorganized development, as some have suggested (Cicchetti, Beeghly, & Weiss-Perry, 1994), and more a case of delayed and arrested development. Earlier-developing forms of symbol use such as words and functional play appear fairly intact in autism, though they are considerably delayed. More advanced forms, such as understanding subtleties of language use and engaging in symbolic forms of pretense, do appear to be considerably impaired. In comparing the extent of developmental atypicality for communicative and symbolic abilities, it is clear that deviation from typical development is greater in the case of communicative functioning. Earlier, we suggested that the extent of developmental atypicality may be an indication of status of a deficit as "primary" or "secondary." Thus our developmental analysis returns us to the issue of whether symbolic deficits in autism are primary manifestations of the disorder or whether they may be secondary consequences of other deficits.

A number of existing accounts of autism do consider symbolic deficits to be secondary consequences of other deficits. For example, as previously mentioned, one hypothesis regarding symbolic play impairments is that they are production deficits reflecting underlying executive-function problems (Harris, 1993; Hughes & Russell, 1993; Lewis & Boucher, 1995; Ozonoff, 1995). Support for this view is found in the fact that limitations in symbolic functioning bear similarities to limitations in other domains of functioning. For example, restricted interests, resistance to change in routine, and stereotyped behaviors may have more than superficial similarity to rigidity in language use and to limited, stereotyped play. All of these features of autism may stem from the same underlying source.

Another hypothesis is that primary deficits in communicative intentions lead to secondary deficits in symbolic functioning, as Hobson (1993) has suggested. This may be particularly apparent in the case of language, although it may also extend more broadly to other forms of symbol use. According to Hobson, rigidity of language in autism may be an outgrowth of failing to appreciate the full range and subtlety of speakers' communicative intentions. In typical development, children's sensitivity to speakers' intentions and viewpoints may allow them to move beyond rigid word-meaning mappings. Pressure for successful communication may push them to accept multiple words for the same meaning, as well as to allow multiple meanings for the same symbol. Typically developing children are remarkably adept at both types of flexibility in linguistic symbol use. Brown (1977) provides an example of a child's flexibility in interpreting the same linguistic construction differently depending on the social context in his description of his subject Adam's grasp of the interrogative. Adam's mother used the construction in two ways (e.g., "why don't you play with your ball?" vs. "why are you playing with your ball?"). In spite of the similarity between the two constructions, from an early age Adam was able to identify one as a request for action and the other as a request for information. The second type of flexibility, use of different linguistic symbols to refer to the same, or very similar, meanings is also a remarkable strength in typically developing children. By preschool age, typically developing children readily accept two labels for the same object (e.g., Savage & Au, 1996). In contrast, children with autism are reputed to have difficulty when a new word is used to refer to an object for which they already have a name. For example, Ricks & Wing (1975) describe the case of a child who became confused when the word "bowl" was substituted for "dish" in reference to the item containing his dog's food.

Willingness to be flexible in word-meaning mappings in the service of successful communication may also help typically developing children to build more elaborate, richer semantic systems. Such flexibility is likely to help build multiple lexical entries for multiple closely related meanings, which in turn is likely to have desirable consequences. It may assist in reorganization and systematization of meanings, allowing underlying dimensions to be identified. For example, accepting "bowl" and "dish" for the same item may help the child to identify the relation between two meanings. Repeated exposure to similar examples may help the child to identify the dimensions on which critical differences exist. In the case of bowls, dishes, and other related terms, the child may eventually come to identify underlying dimensions such as shape, function, and material. An overly rigid approach toward language may preclude children with autism from important learning opportunities inherent in such situations. One outcome may be impairments in analyzing language for meaning—as is evident in the difficulty that individuals with autism have in resolving homographs—and failure to use semantic clustering in recall. Similarly, flexible use of a single word in many different contexts may help the child abstract across these contexts to identify the core, invariant meaning. Failure to engage in this kind of abstraction would result in idiosyncratic extensions for words, as in the case of neologisms and "metaphorical language" that are characteristic of autism.

Alternatively, it remains possible that symbolic impairments in autism are a primary manifestation of the disorder, essentially unrelated to underlying communicative or executive-function impairment. However, the fact that the developmental perturbation is greater in the case of communicative behaviors than it is in the case of symbolic function, in combination with the plausible links between communicative impairment and the particular forms of impairments in symbolic functioning, lend support to the view that symbolic impairments are secondary.

Application to Issues in Typical Development

"Rich" Versus "Lean" Interpretations of Early Communicative Behaviors

An active area of debate concerns the level of psychological understanding underlying the communicative behaviors of infants in the 12- to 18-month age range (see Baldwin & Moses, 1994, for a discussion). Some theorists are liberal in their willingness to attribute fledgling understanding of psychological states, albeit a limited set of them—such as attention and intention—understood in a nonreflective manner (Baldwin & Moses, 1994; Baron-Cohen, 1995; Tomasello, 1995; Wellman, 1993). These theorists point to a convergence of a number of changes in communicative and other behaviors suggesting qualitative change in social understanding. In addition to the emergence of gaze following and well-organized protoimperatives and protodeclaratives incorporating eye contact, infants begin to show sensitivity to adults' attention and intentions in a number of ways. For example, they appear to take account of the attentional focus of an adult, both in word-learning and social-referencing contexts (see Baldwin & Moses, 1994), and they begin to distinguish between intended and accidental actions (Carpenter, Akhtar, & Tomasello, 1998; Meltzoff, 1995). Although "rich" interpreters admit that no single behavior is sufficient to warrant crediting the infant with mentalistic understanding, they argue that the convergence of a number of developmental occurrences strongly supports the view that some form of mentalistic understanding emerges in the first half of the second year.

In contrast, other theorists shy away from attributing mentalistic understanding at such an early age. Taking a more reductive approach, they argue that behaviors such as gaze alternation in conjunction with pointing may reflect no more than checking to see whether the parent is likely to respond appropriately, and that even protodeclaratives may simply reflect pleasure in mastery over the mother's eye direction. These theorists argue that early communicative behaviors do not provide a window onto understanding of mental states (Moore & Corkum, 1994; Perner, 1991). There are also intermediate positions such as that of Butterworth (1994). He argues that infants directly perceive (in a Gibsonian sense) mental states, but that these are not conceived of as mental entities separate from behavior.

Atypicalities in the early communicative development of children with autism provide intriguing, albeit indirect, evidence that bears on this issue. Patterns of communication in autism may provide additional evidence for the rich interpretation of early behaviors in typically developing children, because they provide an informative contrasting case. Autism may provide us with an example illustrating how early social behaviors would appear in the absence of underlying mentalistic understanding. Thus the salient differences between the communicative behaviors of autistic and typically developing children early in development may highlight those aspects of typically developing children's repertoires that are particularly indicative of mentalistic understanding. Earlier, we identified four salient differences between the development of early joint-attention and requesting behaviors in typically developing children and children with autism. First, relative to other cognitive abilities, communicative behaviors are extremely delayed in autism. Second, the signaling of children with autism differs in form from that of typically developing children. The former are less likely to use eye contact while signaling (e.g., Charman et al., 1997; Mundy et al., 1986; Phillips et al., 1995) and more likely to use a form of requesting involving leading an adult or manipulating the adult's body than are typically developing children (Lord et al., 1994). Third, protoimperatives emerge earlier than protodeclaratives in autism (Mundy et al., 1994), whereas they appear in the opposite order in typical development. Finally, gaze following presents exceptional difficulty for children with autism, and it may remain a deficit throughout development (Leekam et al., 1997). The ability to follow a point is acquired much earlier than gaze following (Mundy et al., 1994), whereas in typical development these abilities appear at about the same time. Thus the fact that typical 12- to 14-month olds (a) use protodeclaratives and protoimperatives at all, rather than first showing these behaviors at 20 to 30 months; (b) fail to use leading strategies for requesting and make good use of eye contact; (c) do not show earlier development of protoimperatives than protodeclaratives; and (d) engage in gaze following, may be additional evidence in favor of early emergence of mentalistic understanding in typical development. Proponents of rich interpretations have already pointed to some of these features, such as early emergence of protodeclaratives, use of eye contact while signaling, and gaze following, as evidence for mentalistic understanding (Baldwin & Moses, 1994; Baron-Cohen, 1995; Tomasello, 1995; Wellman, 1993). Evidence from autism may add strength to their arguments with respect to these behaviors, as well as suggest other features of typical development that are potential indicators of mentalistic understanding, such as lack of physical manipulation as a protoimperative strategy and precocious emergence of skills in relation to other cognitive abilities.

Social and Cognitive Contributors to Symbolic Abilities

The early development of symbolic abilities in autism may also provide an informative contrast with typical development. A great deal of research is focused on the typically developing child's earliest use of linguistic symbols. This research is generally conducted within one of two approaches. One approach, inspired by Piaget, attempts to identify cognitive prerequisites of linguistic symbol use, with focus on abilities such as object permanence and means-end understanding. Another approach, inspired by Vygotsky (1962) and Bruner (1975; 1983), emphasizes that the discovery of linguistic symbols occurs within social, communicative interactions. This tradition focuses on identifying specific ways in which adults support children's language development, such as by engaging them in games and routines and in responding to their focus of attention. Although each approach acknowledges the importance of the other, intersection between them is minimal. The existence of two such differing research traditions reveals some divergence of opinion on the relative importance of cognitive and social factors.

Symbolic development in autism may prove to be an experiment in nature that is informative for both traditions. Autism presents a case where basic prelinguistic communicative intentions are substantially delayed, not only in relation to cognitive abilities, but also in relation to language. Based on patterns of performance across domains, it appears likely that some children with autism produce their earliest symbolic words prior to having well-developed communicative intentions, as indexed by regular, well-organized protoimperatives and protodeclaratives. This conjecture is based on our estimates for an average language delay of about 7 months in young children with autism. Thus at about 30 months MA, when children begin to exhibit regular, well-organized protoimperatives and protodeclaratives, at least some may have LAs in the 20-month range, indicating that they have already mastered a fairly substantial number of lexical symbols. We emphasize that this is a speculative conjecture based on the results of studies examining group means. However, if this anomalous path of development were confirmed, it could provide unique evidence regarding the contributions of cognitive and social factors to early symbolic functioning.

First, the appearance of lexical symbols prior to well-developed protoimperatives and protodeclaratives is surprising from both cognitive and social perspectives, because both postulate some continuity between early communicative signaling and later use of linguistic symbols. From the social perspective, there is important continuity in terms of the function behaviors serve for the child as well as in terms of the support provided by the communicative partner. Thus, in making the transition to naming, a child adopts new forms (i.e., words) to serve previously well-established functions (i.e., requesting and referring). In addition, the supportive communicative partner plays a key role in this process by providing consistent "formats" that serve to promote consistency in function despite changes in form. An illustration of a more cognitive perspective on the role of early communicative behaviors in the development of symbols is provided by Bates (1979), who contends that conventionalization and abbreviation of signals in protoimperatives and protodeclaratives may be an important first step in the process of decontextualization of symbols. This small step is important for symbolic development because it involves the first detachment of signal from its functional context. Increasing the separation between the signal and its functional context eventually culminates in mastery of highly abstract, context-free symbols such as words. The mastery of lexical symbols before communicative behaviors in some children with autism would suggest that refinement and extension of communicative behaviors is not the only possible route to symbol mastery. Furthermore, it would support a view of symbolic ability as separable from its communicative functions. Such a finding would be quite consistent with the view proposed by Bates (1979), who argues that although prelinguistic signaling precedes and may contribute to the emergence of true symbols, the symbolic function is a separate capacity.

Secondly, contrasts between typical development and development in autism may provide information regarding the contributions of social and cognitive factors to early symbolic development. Before about 30 months MA, the lack of communicative competence in children with autism is likely to limit their opportunity to benefit from the highly structured social exchanges that are believed to serve a critical role in supporting language development. Although parents may provide the appropriate support, children with autism are unlikely to be capable of perceiving and benefiting from it. The fact that symbolic development proceeds at all in this circumstance suggests that finely tuned social support is facilitative, but not necessary for acquisition of lexical symbols. Viewed from the other perspective, the substantial delay in acquisition of lexical symbols in autism highlights the facilitative power of supportive social contexts in typical symbolic development. The earliest symbolic words and gestures are acquired at about 12 to 15 months in typically developing children, while they do not begin to appear until 20 to 30 months MA in children with autism. This suggests that in order for symbolic behaviors to emerge at around 12 to 15 months of age, as they do in typical development, supportive social contexts are necessary. Thus, the view that both cognitive and social factors play an essential role in the typically developing child's symbolic development is supported.

We offer one further speculative suggestion about the course of development in autism: that basic communicative intentions eventually emerge in more able children with autism, though they are significantly delayed. Eventually, children with autism gain enough competence in pointing, showing, and coordinating eye contact with communicative gesturing that it is difficult to attribute these behaviors solely to their instrumental functions. How do some children with autism manage to achieve even basic competence in this domain if they lack underlying specialized cognitive mechanisms? One possibility is that for children with autism, symbolic abilities may facilitate communicative understanding, whereas typical development builds in the opposite direction. For children with autism, the cognitive economy of symbol use, rather than its communicative power, may be the driving force behind early symbolic development. Children with autism may initially use words to represent their concepts, to make them more accessible, and to facilitate more complex and abstract forms of thought. Of course, words are conventional symbols that must be socially transmitted. However, the use of neologisms and metaphorical language by children with autism suggest that they are less sensitive to pressure to use conventional forms than are other children. The predominance of conventional forms in their vocabularies may reflect the ready availability of these forms in their environments and the explicit teaching of these forms. Once lexical symbols are mastered, however, they lend themselves to social use. Social use of words, even for instrumental functions, may eventually propel the child with autism toward a basic understanding of communication.

Conclusions

Autism presents a unique window onto two developmental reorganizations that are thought to pave the way for language development: the emergence of communicative intentions and the emergence of symbolic ability. Despite specific impairments in both abilities, children with autism nevertheless show developmental progress in these areas as they mature cognitively. Contrasting the timing and course of this developmental progress with typical development is informative with respect to basic issues involving the nature of the impairments in autism and the nature of typical development. From a rough description gleaned by integrating studies of children with autism based on average developmental levels, we gather support for several conclusions. First, communicative development appears to be more disorganized than does symbolic development. The order of emergence of communicative skills is substantially altered. Protoimperatives emerge prior to protodeclaratives, and point following emerges prior to gaze following. Communicative behaviors are also disrupted in form; for example, communicative gesturing fails to incorporate eye contact, and early requesting strategies involve physical manipulation of the adult. Important changes in communicative behaviors occurring at about 25 to 30 months MA in children with autism suggest that true communicative intent may emerge at this time. Disruption in symbolic development is less dramatic, suggesting a course of delayed and arrested, rather than disorganized, development. In terms of the developmental relation between the course of communicative and symbolic functioning in autism, we suggest that symbolic impairments may derive from primary deficits in communicative functioning, and that, in contrast to typical development, in autism symbolic abilities may serve as the foundation for communicative intent. With respect to typical development, we argue that the patterns of impairment in autism offer support for the view that 12- to18-month-old typically developing infants may already have some rudimentary mentalistic understanding. In addition, we argue that the course of symbolic development in autism supports the view that although symbolic abilities can be acquired without finely tuned social support, they cannot be acquired as early as they are in typical development.

ACKNOWLEDGMENTS

Please address correspondence to the Department of Psychology, U.C.L.A., 1285 Franz Hall, Los Angeles, CA 90095-1563; Phone: (310) 794-5439; Fax: (310) 206-5895; e-mail: travis@psych.ucla.edu.

REFERENCES

Acredolo, L., & Goodwyn, S. (1988). Symbolic gesturing in normal infants. *Child Development, 59,* 450–466.

American Psychiatric Association. (1994). *Diagnostic and statistical manual of mental disorders* (4th ed.). Washington DC: Author.

Atwood, A., Frith, U., & Hermelin, B. (1988). The understanding and use of interpersonal gestures by autistic and Down's Syndrome Children. *Journal of Autism and Developmental Disorders, 18,* 241–257.

Baldwin, D. A., & Moses, L. J. (1994). Early understanding of referential intent and attentional focus: Evidence from language and emotion. In C. Lewis & P. Mitchell (Eds.), *Children's early understanding of mind* (pp. 133–156). Hove, UK: Lawrence Erlbaum Associates, Ltd.

Baron-Cohen, S. (1987). Autism and symbolic play. *British Journal of Developmental Psychology, 5,* 139–148.

Baron-Cohen,. S. (1989). Perceptual role-taking and protodeclarative pointing in autism. *British Journal of Developmental Psychology, 5,* 139–148.

Baron-Cohen, S. (1990). Instructed and elicited play in autism: A reply to Lewis & Boucher. *British Journal of Developmental Psychology, 8,* 207.

Baron-Cohen, S. (1995). *Mindblindness: An essay on autism and theory of mind.* Cambridge, MA: MIT Press.

Bates, E. (1979). Intentions, conventions and symbols. In E. Bates (Ed.), *The emergence of symbols: Cognition and communication in infancy* (pp. 33–68). New York: Academic Press.

Bates, E., Beningi, L., Bretherton, I., Camaioni, L., & Volterra, V. (1979). Cognition and communication from nine to thirteen months: Correlational findings. In E. Bates (Ed.), *The emergence of symbols: Cognition and communication in infancy* (pp. 69–140). New York: Academic Press.

Brown, R. (1977). Introduction. In C. E. Snow & C. A. Ferguson (Eds.), *Talking to children: Language input and acquisition.* Cambridge, UK: Cambridge University Press.

Bruner, J. (1975). The ontogenesis of speech acts. *Journal of Child Language, 2,* 1–19.

Bruner, J. (1983). *Child's talk: Learning to use language.* New York: Norton.

Butterworth, G. (1994). Theory of mind and the facts of embodiment. In C. Lewis & P. Mitchell (Eds.), *Children's early understanding of mind* (pp. 115–132). Hove, UK: Lawrence Erlbaum Associates, Ltd.

Butterworth, G., & Jarrett N. (1991). What minds have in common is space: Spatial mechanisms serving joint visual attention in infancy. *British Journal of Developmental Psychology, 9,* 55–72.

Carpenter, M., Akhtar, N., & Tomasello, M. (1998). Fourteen- through 18-month-olds' differentially imitate intentional and accidental actions. *Infant Behavior and Development, 21,* 315–330.

Carpenter, M., Nagell, K., & Tomasello, M. (1998). Social cognition, joint attention, and communicative competence from 9 to 15 months of age. *Monographs of the Society for Research in Child Development, 63* (4, Serial No. 255).

Charman, T., & Baron-Cohen, S. (1994). Another look at imitation in autism. *Development and Psychopathology, 6,* 403–413.

Charman, T., & Baron-Cohen, S. (1997). Brief report: Prompted pretend play in autism. *Journal of Autism and Developmental Disorders, 27*, 325–333.

Charman, T., Swettenham, J. S., Baron-Cohen, S., Cox, A., Baird, G., & Drew, A. (1997). Infants with autism: An investigation of empathy, pretend play, joint attention and imitation. *Developmental Psychology, 33*, 781–789.

Cicchetti, D. (1995). Perspectives on developmental psychopathology. In D. Cicchetti & D. J. Cohen (Eds.), *Developmental Psychopathology: Vol. 1 Theory and Methods* (pp. 3–20). New York: Wiley.

Cicchetti, D., Beeghly, M., & Weiss-Perry, B. (1994). Symbolic development in children with Down Syndrome and in children with autism: An organizational, developmental psychopathology perspective. In A. Slade & D. Palmer Wolf (Eds.), *Children at play: Clinical and developmental approaches to meaning and representation* (pp. 206–237). New York: Oxford University Press.

Corkum, V., & Moore, C. (1995). Development of joint visual attention in infants. In C. Moore & P. J. Dunham (Eds.), *Joint attention: Its origins and role in development* (pp. 61–83). Hillsdale, NJ: Lawrence Erlbaum Associates.

Courchesne, E., Townsend, J. P., Akshoomoff, N. A., Yeung-Courchesne, R. Y., Press, G. A., Murakama, J. W., Lincoln, A., James, H., Saitoh, O., Egaas, B., Haas, R. H., & Schreibman, L. (1994). A new finding: Impairment in shifting attention in autistic and cerebellar patients. In S. H. Broman & J. Grafman (Eds.), *Atypical cognitive deficits in developmental disorders: Implications for brain function* (pp. 101–137). Hillsdale, NJ: Lawrence Erlbaum Associates.

Currie, G. (1996). Simulation theory, theory-theory, and the evidence from autism. In P. Carruthers and P. K. Smith, (Eds.), *Theories of theories of mind.* Cambridge, UK: Cambridge University Press.

Dawson, G., Hill, D., Spencer, A., Galpert, L., & Watson, L. (1990). Affective exchanges between young autistic children and their mothers. *Journal of Abnormal Child Psychology, 18*, 335–345.

D'Entremont, B., Hains, S., & Muir, D. (1997). A demonstration of gaze following in 3- to 6-month-olds. *Infant Behavior and Development, 20*, 569–572.

Desrochers, S., Morissette, P., & Ricard, M. (1995). Two perspectives on pointing in infancy. In C. Moore & P. J. Dunham (Eds.), *Joint attention: Its origins and role in development* (pp. 85–101) Hillsdale, NJ: Lawrence Erlbaum Associates.

DiLavore, P., & Lord, C. (1995). Do you see what I see? Requesting and joint attention in young autistic children. Poster presented at the Biennial Conference of the Society for Research in Child Development. Indianapolis, IL.

Frith, U., & Snowling, M. (1983). Reading for meaning and reading for sound in autistic and dyslexic children. *Journal of Developmental Psychology, 1*, 329–342.

Hammes, J. G. W., & Langdell, T. (1981). Precursors of symbol formation and childhood autism. *Journal of Autism and Developmental Disorders, 11*, 331–346.

Happé, F. G. E. (1995). Understanding mind and metaphors: Insights from the study of figurative language in autism. *Metaphor and Symbol, 10*, 275–295.

Happé, F. G. E. (1997). Central coherence and theory of mind in autism: Reading homographs in context. *British Journal of Developmental Psychology, 15*, 1–12.

Harding, C. G., & Golinkoff, R. M. (1979). The origins of intentional vocalization in prelinguistic infants. *Child Development, 50*, 33–40.

Harris, P. (1993). Pretending and planning. In S. Baron-Cohen, H. Tager-Flusberg, & D. J. Cohen (Eds.), *Understanding other minds: Perspectives from autism* (pp. 228–246). Oxford, UK: Oxford University Press.

Harris, P. (1994). Understanding pretense. In C. Lewis & P. Mitchel (Eds.), *Children's early understanding of mind* (pp. 235–258). Hove, UK: Lawrence Erlbaum Associates, Ltd.

Hermelin, B., & O'Connor, N. (1970). *Psychological experiments with autistic children.* Oxford, UK: Pergamon.

Hobson, R. P. (1993). *Autism and the development of mind.* Hove, UK: Lawrence Erlbaum Associates. Ltd.

Hodapp, R. M., & Burack, J. A. (1990). What mental retardation teaches us about typical development: The examples of sequences, rates and cross-domain relations. *Development and Psychopathology, 2,* 213–225.

Hughes, C., & Russell, J. (1993). Autistic children's difficulty with mental disengagement from an object: Its implications for theories of autism. *Developmental Psychology, 29,* 489–510.

Jarrold, C., Boucher, J., & Smith, P. K. (1993). Symbolic play in autism: A review. *Journal of Autism and Developmental Disorders, 23,* 281–307.

Jarrold, C., Boucher, J., & Smith, P. K. (1994). Executive function deficits and the pretend play of children with autism: A research note. *Journal of Child Psychology and Psychiatry, 35,* 1473–1482.

Jarrold, C., Smith, P., Boucher, J., & Harris, P. (1994). Comprehension of pretense in children with autism. *Journal of Autism and Developmental Disorders, 24,* 433–455.

Kanner, L. (1973). *Childhood psychosis: Initial studies and new insights.* New York: Wiley.

Kasari, C., Sigman M., & Yirmiya, N. (1993). Focused and social attention of autistic children in interaction with familiar and unfamiliar adults: A comparison of autistic, mentally retarded and normal children. *Developmental Psychopathology, 5,* 403–414.

Kasari, C., Sigman, M., Mundy, P., & Yirmiya, N. (1990). Affective sharing in the context of joint attention interactions of normal, autistic and mentally retarded children. *Journal of Autism and Developmental Disorders, 20,* 87–100.

Landry, S. H., & Loveland, K. A. (1988). Communicative behaviors in autism and developmental language delay. *Journal of Child Psychology and Psychiatry, 29,* 621–634.

Leekam, S., Baron-Cohen, S., Perrett, D., Milders, M., & Brown, S. (1997). Eye-direction detection: A dissociation between geometric and joint attention skills in autism. *British Journal of Developmental Psychology, 15,* 77–95.

Leekam, S. R., Hunnisett, E., & Moore, C. (1998). Targets and cues: Gaze-following in children with autism. *Journal of Child Psychology and Psychiatry and Allied Disciplines, 39,* 951–962.

Lempers, J. D. (1979). Young children's production and comprehension of nonverbal deictic behaviors. *Journal of Genetic Psychology, 135,* 93–102.

Leslie, A. M. (1991). The theory of mind impairment in autism: Evidence for a modular mechanism of development? In A. Whiten (Ed.), *Natural theories of mind.* Cambridge, MA: Basil Blackwell.

Leslie, A. M., & Happé, F. (1989). Autism and ostensive communication: The relevance of metarepresentation. *Development and Psycopathology, 1,* 205–212.

Leslie, A. M., & Roth, D. (1993). What autism teaches us about metarepresentation. In S. Baron-Cohen, H., Tager-Flusberg, & D. J. Cohen (Eds.), *Understanding other minds: Perspectives from autism* (pp. 83–110). Oxford, UK: Oxford University Press.

Leung, E. H. L., & Rheingold, H. L. (1981). Development of pointing as a social gesture. *Developmental Psychology, 17,* 215–220.

Lewis, V., & Boucher, J. (1988). Spontaneous, instructed and elicited play in relatively able autistic children. *British Journal of Developmental Psychology, 6,* 325–339.

Lewis, V., & Boucher, J. (1995). Generativity in the play of young people with autism. *Journal of Autism and Developmental Disorders, 25,* 105–121.

Libby, S., Powell, S., Messer, D., & Jordan, R. (1998). Spontaneous play in children with autism: A reappraisal. *Journal of Autism and Developmental Disorders, 28,* 487–497.

Lock, A., Young, A., Service, V., & Chandler, P. (1990). Some observations on the origins of the pointing gesture. In V. Volterra & C. J. Erting (Eds.), *From gesture to language in hearing and deaf children* (pp. 42–55). New York: Springer-Verlag.

Loveland, K. A., Landry, S. H., Hughes, S. O., Hall, S. K., & McEvoy, R. M. (1988). Speech acts and the pragmatic deficits of autism. *Journal of Speech and Hearing Research, 31,* 593–604.

Lord, C., Rutter, M., & Le Couteur, A. (1994). Autism Diagnostic Interview-Revised: A revised version of a diagnostic interview for caregivers of individuals with possible pervasive developmental disorders. *Journal of Autism and Developmental Disorders, 24,* 659–685.

Mandler, J. (1983). Representation. In J. H. Flavell & E. M. Markman (Eds.), *Handbook of Child Psychology, (Vol. 3)* (pp. 420–483). New York: Wiley.

Mandler, J. M. (1988). How to build a baby: On the development of an accessible representational system. *Cognitive Development, 3,* 113–136.

McCune-Nicholich, L. (1981). Toward symbolic functioning: Structure of early pretend games and potential parallels with language. *Child Development, 52,* 785–797.

McDonough, L., Stahmer, A., Schreibman, L., & Thompson, S. J. (1997). Deficits, delays and distractions: An evaluation of symbolic play and memory in children with autism. *Development and Psychopathology, 9,* 17–41.

Meltzoff, A. N. (1995). Understanding the intentions of others: Re-enactment of intended acts by 18-month-old children. *Developmental Psychology, 31,* 838–850.

Menyuk, P., & Quill, K. (1985). Semantic problems in autistic children. In E. Shopler & G. Mesibov (Eds.), *Communication problems in autism* (pp. 127–145). New York: Plenum.

Moore, C., & Corkum, V. (1994). Social understanding at the end of the first year of life. *Developmental Review, 14,* 349–372.

Morissette, P., Ricard, M., & Gouin-Décarie, T. (1995). Joint visual attention and pointing in infancy: A longitudinal study of comprehension. *British Journal of Developmental Psychology, 15,* 163–177.

Mundy, P. (1995). Joint attention and social-emotional approach in children with autism. *Developmental Psychopathology, 7,* 63–82.

Mundy, P., Sigman, M., & Kasari, C. (1993). The theory of mind and joint attention in autism. In S. Baron-Cohen, H. Tager-Flusberg, & D. Cohen (Eds.), *Understanding other minds: Perspectives from autism* (pp. 181–203). Oxford, UK: Oxford University Press.

Mundy, P., Sigman, M., & Kasari, C. (1994). Joint attention, developmental level, and symptom presentation in autism. *Development and Psychopathology, 6,* 389–401.

Mundy, P., Sigman, M., Ungerer, J., & Sherman, T. (1986). Defining the social deficits of autism: The contribution of non-verbal communication measures. *Journal of Child Psychology and Psychiatry, 27,* 657–669.

Mundy, P., Sigman, M., Ungerer, J., & Sherman, T. (1987). Nonverbal communication and play correlates of language development in autistic children. *Journal of Autism and Developmental Disorders, 17,* 349–364.

Murphy, C. M., & Messer, D. J. (1977). Mothers, infants and pointing: A study of gesture. In H. R. Schaffer (Ed.), *Studies in mother–infant interaction* (pp. 325–354). New York: Academic Press.

Ozonoff, S. (1995). Executive functions in autism. In E. Schopler & G. Mesibov (Eds.), *Learning and cognition in autism* (pp. 199–219). New York: Plenum.

Perner, J. (1991). *Understanding the representational mind.* Cambridge, MA: MIT Press.

Phillips, W., Baron-Cohen, S., & Rutter, M. (1992). The role of eye contact in goal-detection: Evidence from normal infants and children with autism or mental handicap. *Development and Psychopathology, 4,* 375–383.

Phillips, W., Gomez, J. C., Baron-Cohen, S., Laa, V., & Riviere, A. (1995). Treating people as objects, agents, or "subjects": How young children with and without autism make requests. *Journal of Child Psychology and Psychiatry, 36,* 1383–1398.

Ricks, D. M., & Wing, L. (1975). Language, communication and use of symbols in normal and autistic children. *Journal of Autism and Childhood Schizophrenia, 5,* 191–222.

Riguet, C. B., Taylor, N. D., Benaroya, S., & Klein, L. S. (1981). Symbolic play in autistic, Down's, and normal children of equivalent mental age. *Journal of Autism and Developmental Disorders, 11,* 439–448.

Rogers, S. J., Bennetto, L., McEvoy, R., & Pennington, B. F. (1996). Imitation and pantomime in high-functioning adolescents with autism spectrum disorders. *Child Development, 67,* 2060–2073.

Savage, S. L., & Au, T. K. (1996). What word learners do when input contradicts the Mutual Exclusivity Assumption. *Child Development, 67,* 3120–3134.

Scaife, M., & Bruner, J. (1975). The capacity for joint visual attention in the infant. *Nature, 253,* 265–266.

Shore, C., Bates, E., Bretherton, I., Beeghly, M., & O'Connell, B. (1990). Vocal and gestural symbols: Similarities and differences from 13 to 28 months. In V. Volterra and C. Erting (Eds.), *From gesture to language in hearing and deaf children.* New York: Springer-Verlag.

Sigman, M., & Ruskin, E. (1999). Continuity and change in the social competence of children with autism, Down Syndrome and Developmental Delays. *Monographs of the Society for Research in Child Development, 64* (1, Serial No. 256).

Sigman, M., & Ungerer, J. (1984). Cognitive and language skills in autistic, mentally retarded, and normal children. *Developmental Psychology, 20,* 293–302.

Smith, I. M., & Bryson, S. E. (1994). Imitation and action in autism: A critical review. *Psychological Bulletin, 11,* 259–273.

Stone, W. L., & Caro-Martinez, L. M. (1990). Naturalistic observations of spontaneous communication in autistic children. *Journal of Autism and Developmental Disorders, 20,* 437–453.

Tager-Flusberg, H. (1985). The conceptual basis for referential word meaning in children with autism. *Child Development, 56,* 1167–1178.

Tager-Flusberg, H. (1991). Semantic processing in the free recall of autistic children: Further evidence for a cognitive deficit. *British Journal of Developmental Psychology, 9,* 417–430.

Tager-Flusberg, H., Calkins, S., Nolin, T., Baumberger, T., Anderson, M., & Chadwick-Dias, A. (1990). A longitudinal study of language acquisition in autistic and Down Syndrome children. *Journal of Autism and Developmental Disorders, 20,* 1–21.

Tomasello, M. (1995). Joint attention as social cognition. In C. Moore & P. J. Dunham (Eds.), *Joint attention: Its origins and role in development* (pp. 103–130). Hillsdale, NJ: Lawrence Erlbaum Associates.

Ungerer, J., & Sigman, M. (1981). Symbolic play and language comprehension in autistic children. *Journal of the American Academy of Child Psychiatry, 20,* 318–337.

Volden, J., & Lord, C. (1991). Neologisms and idiosyncratic language in autistic speakers. *Journal of Autism and Developmental Disorders, 21,* 109–130.

Vygotsky, L. S. (1962). *Thought and Language.* New York: Wiley.

Wellman, H. (1993). Early understanding of mind: The normal case. In S. Baron-Cohen, H. Tager-Flusberg, & D. J. Cohen (Eds.), *Understanding other minds: Perspectives from autism* (pp. 10–39). Oxford, UK: Oxford University Press.

Werner, H., & Kaplan, B. (1963). *Symbol formation.* New York: Wiley.

Wing, L., Gould, J., Yeates, S. R., & Brierley, L. M. (1977). Symbolic play in severely mentally retarded and in autistic children. *Journal of Child Psychology and Psychiatry, 18,* 167–178.

Wulfe, B. (1985). The symbolic and object play of children with autism: A review. *Journal of Autism and Developmental Disorders, 15,* 139–148.

Zinober, B., & Martlew, M. (1985). Developmental changes in four types of gesture in relation to acts and vocalization from 10 to 21 months. *British Journal of Developmental Psychology, 3,* 293–306.

15

Social Emotions and Social Relationships: Can Children With Autism Compensate?

Connie Kasari
Brandt Chamberlain
University of California, Los Angeles
Nirit Bauminger
Bar-Ilan University, Ramat Gan, Israel

Autism is associated with significant social impairments. Diagnostic criteria include an inability to develop adequate social relationships, including peer interactions and friendships, and difficulty with recognizing and understanding emotions in self and other (APA, 1994; Hobson, 1993). Most studies focus on children who are young or children who also are mentally retarded. Thus, the types of skills examined are confined to developmentally young ones—e.g., peer interactions or basic emotions (e.g., happy, sad, angry, scared). Few studies focus exclusively on high-functioning children with autism—children who conceivably could engage in higher level social relationships (e.g., friendships) and complex emotions. We currently know less, then, about the emotional understandings and social relationships of children with autism who have normal cognitive abilities.

The study of social emotions and social relationships in high-functioning children with autism could provide important information for both typical and atypical development. For example, social emotions, such as guilt and embarrassment, require appraisal of others' views of oneself. As a result, they pose a special challenge for children with autism, who often have difficulty with reasoning about other people's thoughts and feelings (Baron-Cohen, Leslie, & Frith, 1985). Children also learn about social emotions through interactions with others, and interactions with others are improved through experiencing social emotions. Due to limited experiences with others, children with autism may be at a disadvantage in furthering their knowledge of social emotions and social relationships. However, the degree to which children depend on experiences with others and require certain types of knowledge to have friendships or to experience certain emotions remains unclear. Studying children with autism may help us to better understand these developmental links.

In this chapter, we first consider the emergence of the social emotions pride, empathy, embarrassment, and guilt in children with autism as well as factors associated with their emergence. We also consider possible limitations to the understanding of social emotions for children with autism and the effect of these limitations on their social relationships. Finally, we consider whether and how children with autism might engage in compensatory strategies. The issue of compensatory strategies, or the issue of "making up" for a mismatch between the skills a person possesses and the demands of the environment (Dixon & Backman, 1995), is an underexamined issue within autism and developmental psychopathology in general. Here, however, it may be the case that children with autism are using their intellectual abilities to get around their inability to "naturally" understand these social emotions and social situations. Although speculative at this time, a perspective that cuts across these children's skills to examine how the skills they do possess can compensate for skills that are more difficult to acquire seems an important addition to developmentally oriented work with children with autism.

SOCIAL EMOTIONS

Unlike primary or basic emotions like happy and sad, which are believed biologically based and present from birth, social emotions emerge later in development (Izard & Harris, 1995). Social emotions are also referred to as self-conscious, complex, or secondary emotions, reflecting the acknowledgment that these emotions require certain cognitive and social experiences. Although many studies have examined children's expression of, responsiveness to, and understanding of basic emotions, far fewer studies have examined children's use and understanding of social emotions.

Two explanations for the limited attention to children's social emotions include the complex nature of the emotions and the lack of consistent, reliable measurement. First, social emotions are considered complex because they require a blending of cognitive and social skills. These skills include the differentiation of self from other and, particularly, the ability to put oneself in the place of the other. Self–other differentiation begins in the second year of life when children react to their mirror image and later when children begin to use personal pronouns and to understand *theory of mind* (the idea that others have feelings, thoughts, and beliefs that are distinct from self) (Lewis, 1995).

These skills often become realized in the context of interactions and experiences with others. For example, children learn about culturally relevant standards and rules for behavior through their interactions with others, and they use this information to know what kinds of behavior are either pride-worthy or shameful (Stipek, Recchia, & McClintic, 1992). Social emotions are invariably connected with real or imagined social interactions, where experiences with others centrally influence their development (Barrett, 1995).

A second reason that the study of social emotions remains limited is that social emotions have no reliable facial indices that are associated with them. Researchers, however, have recently identified a number of associated bodily expressions and actions for emotions like guilt, pride, empathy, and embarrassment. For example, open-hand expressions and looking up to others in the context of finishing a task are associated with expressions of pride in young children (Heckhausen, 1984). Gaze aversion and silly smiles are associated with embarrassment in children (Lewis, 1995). However, because these same associated behaviors may also index guilt or shame, researchers recognize that the context in which the behaviors occur is important in determining the emotion. Thus, careful coding of behavior, facial expression, and context are necessary in determining social emotion, which complicates the study of social emotions in young or nonverbal children.

In the next section, we examine the social emotions of pride, empathy, embarrassment, and guilt. We consider factors associated with their emergence and issues in their measurement.

Pride

Pride is a positive, self-conscious emotion that depends on one's views of both self and other (Lewis & Brooks-Gunn, 1979; Lewis, Sullivan, Stanger, & Weiss, 1989). Children experience pride when they know they have exceeded the expected standard for performance and when they feel personally responsible for their success. Pride depends, then, on a number of cognitive skills, including an accurate sense of self and one's behaviors, the ability to compare one's performance against an established standard, and the ability to reflect upon one's own accomplishment.

Children's pride emerges due in part to the aforementioned cognitive skills and in part to the child's socialization experiences. Through multiple interactions with others, children learn what others consider to be pride-worthy, and this knowledge, in turn, affects how children view their own accomplishments (Stipek, Recchia, & McClintic, 1992). For example, caregiver praise provided when preschool-aged children complete an achievement-related task increases expressions of pride (Stipek et. al., 1992), whereas too much assistance by caregivers decreases feelings of pride (Lutkenhaus, 1984; Stipek, et al., 1992). The role of others, then, becomes a critical consideration both in the completion of a task and in the recognition of what is pride-worthy.

But pride also changes as the child develops (Mascolo & Fischer, 1995). Although very young children are more likely to show behavioral manifestations of pride in the presence of others, they are less likely to compare their own performance to that of others when asked to give an example of a time when they felt pride. By 7 or 8 years of age, however, children readily recognize the role that others play in the evaluation of their own accomplishments. Reference to an audience is noted in the majority of school-aged children's descriptions of pride-evoking events. The comparison of self to others changes again by adulthood when references to an audience decrease as feelings of pride become more internalized (Seidner, Stipek, & Feshbach, 1988).

In a study of young children with autism, Kasari, Sigman, Baumgartner, & Stipek (1993) examined the behavioral manifestations of pride as children completed puzzles with and without praise from an adult. Behavioral manifestations of pride include looking up to another person with a closed smile, an open posture—body stretched and hands open or held high—and verbal or behavioral means of drawing another's attention to the completed task (Heckhausen, 1984; Stipek, et al., 1992). The young children with autism in this study smiled when they completed the puzzles, but they did not look up to others to share their satisfaction or to draw attention to their accomplishment. Praise from an adult did not encourage children with autism to respond more positively, and in fact, many children turned away from the praising adult. The pattern of responses suggests that children with autism do not yet display self-reflective, socially mediated pride. From these findings, however, one could not rule out the possibility that the nature of pride (e.g., the degree to which it is socially mediated) and the situations in which it is experienced (e.g., social versus independent) may be different for children with and without autism.

To examine the nature of pride in older, high-functioning children with autism, we assessed pride understanding in children aged 8 to 14 years (Kasari, Paparella, & Bauminger, 1999). In this study, children were asked to provide an example of a time they had felt pride and to estimate how frequently they had felt pride during the last two weeks. They were also asked to identify the emotion in situations designed to elicit pride and to tell how much pride they would feel in situations that varied as to how much assistance others provided in accomplishing a task.

Children with autism reported feeling pride and revealed understandings of conditions that elicit pride as often as did typically developing children. However, they were more likely to provide examples that were general and less personal. For example, children with autism often gave general examples as "I felt proud when I got an A" compared to developmentally typical children who might suggest feeling proud "when I got an A on a really difficult algebra test in Mr. Graham's class." Children with autism also included references to an audience less often in their personal examples of pride and were more likely to give examples that were external and uncontrollable, e.g., "I was proud because my dad was tall."

Children with autism include references to pride less often in illustrated pictures of situations designed to elicit pride, but their answers often are in the correct hedonic tone. For example, they most often said "happy" rather than "proud" to describe how a boy felt when he won a race and received a trophy. In responding to vignettes that described the success of children in situations in which they sometimes received help and sometimes did not, the children with autism more often attributed similar levels of pride regardless of how much help they received. In contrast, developmentally typical children felt more pride when they did not receive help, but accomplished a task on their own. Since pride is an achievement-related emotion, success due to high effort should produce emotions distinct from those elicited by success due to help from others. When success is due to high effort attributed to self and not to others, greater pride is experienced (Graham, 1988; Graham & Barker, 1990). Considering the role of self and other in the understanding of pride, these findings suggest that high-functioning children with autism have limited or underdeveloped understandings of pride.

Qualitative differences in pride understanding are also found in a study by Capps, Yirmiya, and Sigman (1992). These authors found that children with autism took longer in recalling an example of pride and that their examples were general and nonspecific. The authors suggest that the additional "think" time needed to describe a pride-eliciting experience compared to a happy or sad experience may be due to the increased cognitive workload for children with autism. The longer response latency may be explained as reflecting a learned association rather than a subjective experience of pride, and may reflect a means of compensating for a lack of subjective experience.

Empathy

At an early age, children show concern for distress in others, whether they have caused the distress themselves or merely witnessed it. Indeed, Hoffman (1975; Sagi & Hoffman, 1976) suggests that empathic concern for others is biologically based and evidenced in the contagious crying of infants. Responding with personal distress over the distress of others, then, may be considered as the beginning of empathy.

Empathy differs from guilt in that the sympathetic response can occur without having caused the distress (Zahn-Waxler & Robinson, 1995). Thus, empathy refers to the vicarious experience of another person's emotional, physical, or psychological states. It has both cognitive and affective components, reflecting the capacity to understand, imagine, and affectively share the others' emotional states. In children as young as 1 year of age, empathy becomes manifested in prosocial behaviors (help, sharing, comforting) indicative of concern for others (Zahn-Waxler & Robinson, 1995). Empathy is also often linked with moral behavior. From very early ages, children understand the differences between right and wrong, evidencing a " moral sense" (Kagan & Lamb, 1987).

As with the other social emotions, certain social and cognitive foundations are considered prerequisites. In order for children to respond to others with other-oriented behaviors of sympathetic concern (as opposed to self-oriented personal distress) they must differentiate self from other (Asendorpf & Baudonniere, 1993; Bischof-Kohler, 1991; Zahn-Waxler, Radke-Yarrow, Wagner, & Chapman, 1992). Self–other differentiation is also important for understanding standards for behavior and for judging the behavior of self and other.

In young children, measurement of empathic concern has centered on affective and behavioral responses. Although infants may respond to distress in others with their own personal distress, toddlers begin to provide comfort to others in distress. Comfort to others increases over age and includes behaviors of hugging, patting, touching, sympathetic facial expressions, and soothing vocalizations or statements. Empathy in older children has most often been examined by asking children how they feel in response to vignettes designed to elicit sympathetic or empathic concern (Feshbach, 1982).

Studies of children with autism have employed a normative model of empathy development. In young children with autism, studies have focused on responses to distress and discomfort in others (Bacon, Fein, Morris, Waterhouse, & Allen, 1998; Charman, 1997; Sigman, Kasari, Kwon, & Yirmiya, 1992). For example, children from developmentally matched 3- to 6-year-old autistic, mentally retarded, and typically developing samples watched as each of their mothers pretended to cry after she hit her finger with a pounding toy and as the mother feigned illness (Sigman et al., 1992). In the latter case, the mother lay moaning on a sofa during a free-play episode with the child.

Most of the children remained neutral, and few responded with personal distress themselves. But the children with mental retardation and the children who were typically developing were very attentive to the adult's expressions in the experimental situations. In contrast, many of the children with autism appeared to ignore or to not notice the adults showing these negative affects. Thus, little empathy in the form of personal distress, prosocial behaviors, or even attention to the other was found in these young children with autism.

As with typical children (Feshbach, 1982), high-functioning school-aged children with autism were asked how the protaganist felt and how they felt after viewing videotaped segments designed to elicit empathic responses (Yirmiya, Sigman, Kasari, & Mundy, 1992). Compared with typically developing children, the children with autism performed less well on labeling the emotion of the protaganists and on empathy—the degree to which their own reported feeling matched the protaganist's feeling. Moreover, children with autism took longer to respond and used more "I think" terms in reporting an emotion (Capps et al., 1992). Thus, the authors suggest that the empathetic responses of children with autism, similar to their pride understandings, reflect an increased cognitive workload when completing emotion-related tasks.

Embarrassment

Embarrassment generally occurs when a person fails some standard and there is public observation of the failure. According to Lewis (1995), embarrassment occurs when a person is aware that he or she is the center of attention and that he or she is being judged. The presence of another person is thus implicit.

Negative evaluation, however, is not always necessary to elicit embarrassment. For example, a person may become embarrassed when introduced with praise, or when he or she walks into a room and everyone stops talking. In these examples, embarrassment occurs merely through exposure or self-awareness (Griffin, 1995).

Embarrassment develops early in life. Lewis (1995) suggests that a rudimentary embarrassment exists in young children prior to their acquisition of the ability to self-evaluate. Thus, embarrassment emerges some time during the middle of the second year of life. Not until somewhere between the second and third year of life does embarrassment also reflect self-evaluation. Others, however, suggest that embarrassment emerges only after children can self-evaluate (Miller, 1995). In order to be embarrassed, then, one must both understand and care about others' evaluations of self.

Two studies of embarrassment have been reported, both concerning older, high-functioning children with autism (Capps et al., 1992; Kasari et al., 1999). Both studies found that children with autism were more likely to give a general example of embarrassment that was external and uncontrollable compared with typical children, who gave more specific, personally related examples that were internal and controllable. Thus, a child with autism might report embarrassment when "I fell down" compared to a typical child who reports, "I was embarrassed when I tripped over my own foot, and fell in front of the class." Miller (1995) found that 65% of embarrassment examples given by typically developing children involve individual behaviors, e.g., actions that violate a person's idealized self-image, cause accidental harm, or are concerned with violations of norms. For example, a child might report feeling embarrassed when "At a special dinner party, I knocked over my glass of milk and it spilled all over me." Similarly, in the Kasari et al. (1999) study, 68% of typically developing children gave individual behavior examples. In contrast, only 18% of the children with autism did so.

Children with autism were more likely to describe situations in which embarrassment was provoked by others (e.g., being teased when they had done nothing wrong): 42% of the examples of children with autism versus only 6% of the examples of typically developing children mentioned direct provocation. These data suggest that the conditions that elicit embarrassment among children with autism are often different from those reported by typically developing children. Children with autism may be less aware of their own behavior in the presence of others and more likely to respond with embarrassment when they are the direct target of others' provocations. Only then might children with autism recognize that they are the salient focus of others' attention.

Guilt

In general, guilt is distinguished from shame in that guilt is associated with outward movement aimed at reparation of a wrongdoing, and shame is associated with withdrawal from social contact. Both shame and guilt experiences contribute in important ways to the child' s development of a sense of self. These experiences highlight the consequences of the child's behavior and how others view the child and help the child to learn how to evaluate him or herself. Certain broad cognitive understandings are important for guilt. One concerns self-knowledge. Another is the development of standards and rules for behavior and personal responsibility for behavior. But socialization is crucial to the development of guilt. Socialization causes the child to care about the opinions of others, making the child want to follow social standards. It teaches the child about rules and standards for behavior and endows particular standards with significance. For example, the child who frequently breaks another's toys may amend more often (Barrett, 1995), so that experience with violating a standard ultimately helps the child to develop the self, and in turn to develop the social emotion of guilt.

We have recently examined children's understanding of guilt in MA- and IQ-matched samples of high-functioning children with autism and typically developing children (Kasari, Chamberlain, & Bauminger, 2000). In this study, we asked children to provide a personal example of guilt. As for other social emotions, the examples of guilt were then coded for a number of elements, including specificity and locus of control. Additionally, the examples were coded for social-script elements and in terms of the type of harm caused. For example, in terms of social scripts, the child could provide a self-evaluative statement—"I'm the only one who forgot" (Shaver, Schwartz, Kirson, & O' Connor, 1987). The type of harm caused might include reference to rule-breaking or damage to things versus physical or emotional harm to another person or relationship.

Results indicated that children with autism had more difficulty providing an example of guilt than did typically developing children, but reported similar frequency of experiencing guilt. Compared with typically developing children, children with autism also made proportionally fewer self-evaluative comments and were more likely to describe situations of rule-breaking, disruptiveness, and property damage and less likely to report feeling guilt over causing physical or emotional harm to others (Kasari et al., 2000).

For children with autism, then, guilt appears to be defined not in interpersonal empathetic terms, but in terms of memorizable rules and actions toward things (e.g., taking toys from school, stealing cookies, running away, defacing property). Typically developing children, in contrast, were more concerned about hurting other people or their feelings, or about trying to shift their own guilt onto others (e.g., leaving a friend out of a game, lying, breaking a window and blaming a brother). This "compound guilt"—blaming others for one's own transgressions—was nonexistent in the responses of children with autism, but appeared several times among their typically developing age-mates. Perhaps the children with autism could not manipulate such counterfactual material due to difficulties in representing false beliefs (Baron-Cohen, 1991; Harris, 1989). In general, the children with autism seem to lack a sense of the effects of their actions on others; as a result, their guilt scenarios tend to lack an interpersonal component.

Summary

Generally, studies of social emotions in autism have been limited to high-functioning, older children with autism. Few studies have examined social emotions in developmentally young children, and this should be an area of focus in future investigations. The findings from studies of older children, however, share several themes. First, compared with typically developing children, children with autism report similar frequency in feeling an emotion, but understand the emotion less well. When providing an example of feeling a particular emotion, children with autism more often report scripted, less personally-related examples. And when asked to give an example of their own experience of pride, guilt, and embarrassment, children with autism often identified unusual self–other dimensions. Thus, guilt was often reported in response to breaking things, not in hurting others, and embarrassment was provoked by others and less focused on the self. Indeed, individual characteristics of children may shed light on these understandings. Future studies need to examine further the role of mental age, theory of mind, and other social, emotional, and cognitive skills in children' s understanding of social emotions.

How Do Cognitive or Experiential Deficits Affect the Development of Social Emotions?

Do deficits in cognitive abilities affect the development of social emotions in autism? This seems a critical question given the theoretical importance of certain cognitive skills for the development of social emotions in typical development. For example, autism is associated with deficits in self-development. Spiker and Ricks (1984) noted that children with autism do not demonstrate coy or self-conscious affect in response to their mirror image, and thus may not possess a distinct self-concept. Children with autism also demonstrate problems with personal pronouns, often confusing and misusing them in reference to self and other. Additionally, they have difficulty with theory-of-mind tasks, often failing to understand that others have different perspectives or beliefs from their own (Baron-Cohen, Leslie, & Frith, 1985; Hobson, 1990).

Capps et al. (1992), Kasari et al. (1999), and Yirmiya et al. (1992) all found that higher cognitive abilities were associated with better performance on social-emotion measures in autistic but not in developmentally typical children.

Interestingly, Kasari et al. (2000) found that general cognitive abilities were associated with better performance on measures of guilt understanding in children with autism, but that performance on theory-of-mind tasks was a better predictor of performance on an embarrassment measure. Thus, embarrassment and guilt may require specific sets of cognitive abilities in children with autism.

Fewer social experiences with others (e.g., reciprocal peer interactions) may also affect the development of social emotions in autism. Developmentally normal children are attuned to interact with their surrounding environment from the moment they are born. Through these interactions they learn about the self and about how others have thoughts and feelings that are different from their own. They discover which types of behaviors are right and which ones are wrong. They also discover what happens when they fail or succeed, hurt others, or see others get hurt. In the course of typical interactions, children are socialized to experience social emotions, and through them, to learn about relationships and about the self. These are likely critical experiences.

Children with autism may experience fewer reciprocal interactions with others. In spite of being in "contact" with other children (through school, community, and family contacts), children with autism tend not to seek out other children, express interest in them, or engage them (APA, 1994). Thus, their own behaviors may counteract their involvement with peers and others, thereby limiting their ability to learn from these relationships. In these situations, children with autism, then, have reduced opportunities to learn about themselves and others and to understand standards and rules for behavior and for their personal responsibility.

To what extent are these reciprocal interactions necessary to children's learning about social emotions? How can one compensate for experiences that one has not had, or for development that one is unaware of? These types of questions have rarely been addressed in autism research, but represent critical gaps in our knowledge of children's emotional development.

Can Children With Autism Compensate?

What is compensation and when does it occur? Compensation originates in a mismatch between the skills a person possesses and the demands of the environment (Dixon & Backman, 1995). The mismatch can be the result of a person's deficit with relatively constant environmental demands or of an increase in environmental demands that are not matched by an increase in the person's skills. Both Backman and Dixon (1992) and Salthouse (1995) concur that compensation occurs when a person develops or activates substitutable skills or invests more time or effort to achieve the same degree of competence that a person without the deficit possesses.

A classic example of compensation is seen in older typists. Despite the slower perceptual-motor speed of older typists, Salthouse (1984) found that both older and younger typists performed at the same level in transcription typing. Similar performance was found because older typists had larger eye-hand spans than did younger typists. That is, older typists processed the to-be-typed text farther ahead than did younger typists, thus compensating for their slower perceptual-motor speed.

How might compensation apply to the emotional deficits we see in children with autism? A possible explanation for the similar responses of children with autism and typically developing children is that children with autism can compensate for their lack of emotional understanding by using their high-level cognitive abilities. Thus, in Capps et al. (1992), children with autism use longer latencies to come up with personal examples of embarrassment and pride. They use more "I think" terms as evidence of this greater cognitive effort.

This interpretation is consistent with Hermelin and O'Connor' s (1985) logico-affective hypothesis that children with autism learn strategies to recognize and express emotions that "come naturally" to nonautistic individuals. For example, children with autism may have to learn rules for recognizing emotions. However, it is unclear if children with autism make deliberate, conscious efforts to compensate for deficits in emotional development, or if their compensatory efforts are successful (Grandin, 1995).

Children with autism may be unable to fully compensate for their emotional deficits. The idea of partial compensation—that is, when efforts to compensate are only partially successful—may be more accurate. Thus, children with autism may take longer to describe an experience of embarrassment or pride and may fall short in their description, as when they less often give a personally-related, detailed example or less often identify an audience in their example. Their incomplete or scripted answers seem to suggest less experience with the sought-for emotion. Children with autism may compensate by giving a learned or memorized answer that does not reflect an actual feeling or experience.

In certain studies, attempts at compensation are not evident or compensatory efforts, if present, fall short. Thus, in a recent study of children's friendship-development, high-functioning children with autism, although reporting fewer friends than more typically developing controls, each identified at least one friend (Bauminger & Kasari, 2000). Typically developing children comprehend what a friend is and what it means when a friend is not around. Children with autism likewise demonstrated understandings of friendship, but these understandings were not utilized to reduce feelings of loneliness. Indeed, children with autism reported significantly higher levels of loneliness than did typical children.

As suggested by Hobson (1993), individuals with autism might lack the necessary intersubjective sharing with others needed to really understand the concept of friendship and associated social emotions like loneliness. Thus, individuals with autism "stand outside social relationships and merely watch behaviors" (Hobson, 1993, p. 5). Children with autism may form friendships that are superficial, rarely achieving the depth, reciprocity, and closeness that are necessary to develop higher level emotional understandings. Compensation, therefore, may only be partially successful in that friendships can be counted, but the qualitative benefits of friendships are absent or limited. A goal of future studies should be to examine evidence of compensatory strategies by children with autism in situations eliciting social emotions and social relationships.

CONCLUSIONS AND FUTURE DIRECTIONS

Children with autism differ from developmentally typical children in their conceptions of pride, empathy, embarrassment, and guilt. For example, children with autism tend to provide scripted, general examples of their own experiences of these emotions and less often recognize the role that others may play in their feelings. Indeed, they tend not to identify an audience in an emotional situation in which an audience is a critical element, e.g., in embarrassing situations. However, they also seem to have less of a sense of their own agency in emotion-eliciting situations. These differences seem to stem largely from difficulties in conceiving how the self relates to others, and specifically how the views of others may influence one's self-evaluations.

In the context of an emotional experience, the ability to perceive "what I think you think of me" and to incorporate that social cognition into a self-concept requires an ability to manipulate multiple social variables simultaneously (Griffin, 1995; Mascolo & Fischer, 1995) and to maintain a concept of "self" over time (Harter, 1986). Particularly in their descriptions of guilt and embarrassment, children with autism have difficulty understanding their own roles as social agents who may cause harm to others and as social objects who come under others' observation and evaluation. Thus, deficits in self -knowledge may seriously hinder the development of social emotions.

Because children with autism may have superficial relationships with peers, or fewer such relationships, they may also fail to experience the functional benefits of social emotions. For example, feeling guilty often includes the impetus to make reparations and to restore harmonious interactions with others. As noted by Baumeister, Stillwell, and Heatherton (1995), "Guilt causes people to act in ways that will be beneficial to relationships, such as expressing affection, paying attention, and refraining from transgressions" (p. 256). Having consistent and sustained experiences with others likely assists in the emergence of social emotions that in turn facilitate the development of interpersonal understanding. Current studies are limited in defining links between emotional knowledge, social relationships, and other cognitive skills. For example, verbal IQ was associated with better performance on social-emotion measures in some studies (Capps et al., 1992; Kasari et al., 2000; Yirmiya et al., 1992).

But other important capabilities are often not examined, including theory of mind and engagement in social relationships. Theory of mind may be essential to children's understanding of social emotions that rely on an audience (e.g., embarrassment) as suggested by Kasari et al. (2000) in their study of guilt and embarrassment. Also important in future investigations would be following-up over time to determine what types of skills are necessary for emotional understanding in children with autism and the point at which children gain (or fail to gain) emotional understandings. Such information should assist in designing better and more timely interventions with children with autism.

Finally, evidence exists that children with autism engage in some compensatory strategies to cope with deficits in emotional knowledge. Thus, they take longer to respond in situations requiring emotional knowledge and appear to invest more effort in such situations (Capps et al., 1992). The concept of compensation in high-functioning children with autism may prove especially critical to these children's social outcomes. If children with autism can learn compensatory strategies, interventions can be designed to help them in the critical areas of social emotions and social relationships. Future studies need to first examine the ways in which children are trying to compensate if they are indeed making such attempts. Studies should also examine socialization practices as a means of teaching children critical concepts and strategies for compensation.

ACKNOWLEDGMENTS

This work was supported by NIH/NICHD grant HD35470. We gratefully acknowledge the comments of Robert Hodapp on earlier versions of the chapter. Correspondence may be sent to Connie Kasari, Graduate School of Education & Information Studies, UCLA, Los Angeles, CA. 90095. E-mail: Kasari@gseis.UCLA.edu.

REFERENCES

American Psychiatric Association. (1994). *Diagnostic and statistical manual of mental disorders* (4th ed.). Washington, DC: Author.

Asendorpf, J. B., & Baudonniere, P. M. (1993). Self-awareness and other-awareness: Mirror self-recognition and synchronic imitation among unfamiliar peers. *Developmental Psychology, 29,* 88–95.

Backman, L., & Dixon, R. A. (1992). Psychological compensation: A theoretical framework. *Psychological Bulletin, 112,* 259–283.

Bacon, A. L., Fein, D., Morris, R., Waterhouse, L., & Allen, D. (1998). The responses of children with autism to the distress of others. *Journal of Autism and Developmental Disorders, 28,* 129–142.

Baron-Cohen, S. (1991). The development of a theory of mind in autism: Deviance and delay? In M. Konstantareas & J. Beitchman (Eds.), *Psychiatric Clinics of North America, 14,* 33–51.

Baron-Cohen, S., Leslie, A. M., & Frith, U. (1985). Does the autistic child have a "theory of mind"? *Cognition, 21,* 37–46.

Barrett, K. C. (1995). A functionalist approach to shame and guilt. In J. P. Tangney & K. W. Fischer (Eds.), *Self-conscious emotions: The psychology of shame, guilt, embarrassment, and pride* (pp. 25–63). New York: Guilford.

Baumeister, R. F., Stillwell, A. M., & Heatherton, T. F. (1995). Interpersonal aspects of guilt: Evidence from narrative studies. In J. P. Tangney & K. W. Fischer (Eds.), *Self-conscious emotions: The psychology of shame, guilt, embarrassment, and pride* (pp. 255–273). New York: Guilford.

Bauminger, N. & Kasari, C. (2000). Loneliness and friendship in high-functioning children with autism. *Child Development, 71,* 447–456.

Bischof-Kohler, D. (1991). The development of empathy in infants. In M. E. Lamb & H. Keller (Eds.), *Infant development: Perspectives from German-speaking countries* (pp. 1–33). Hillsdale, NJ: Lawrence Erlbaum Associates.

Capps, L., Yirmiya, N., & Sigman, M. (1992). Understanding of simple and complex emotion in high-functioning children with autism. *Journal of Child Psychology and Psychiatry, 33,* 1169–1182.

Charman, T. (1997). The relationship between joint attention and pretend play in autism. *Development & Psychopathology, 9,* 1–16.

Dixon, R. A., & Backman, L. (1995). Concepts of compensation: Integrated, differentiated, and Janus-faced. In R. A. Dixon & L. Backman (Eds.), *Compensating for psychological deficits and declines: Managing losses and promoting gains* (pp. 3–19). Mahwah, NJ: Lawrence Erlbaum Associates.

Feshbach, N. (1982). Sex differences in empathy and social behavior in children. In N. Eisenberg (Ed.), *The development of prosocial behavior* (pp. 315–338). New York: Academic Press.

Graham, S. (1988). Children's developing understanding of the motivational role of affect: An attributional analysis. *Cognitive Development, 3,* 71–88.

Graham, S., & Barker, G. P. (1990). The down side of help: An attributional-developmental analysis of helping behavior as a low-ability cue. *Journal of Educational Psychology, 82,* 7–14.

Grandin, T. (1995). How people with autism think. In E. Schopler & G. Mesibov (Eds.), *Learning and cognition in autism* (pp. 137–156). New York: Plenum.

Griffin, S. (1995). A cognitive-developmental analysis of pride, shame, and embarrassment in middle childhood. In J. P. Tangney & K. W. Fischer (Eds.), *Self-conscious emotions: The psychology of shame, guilt, embarrassment, and pride* (pp. 219–236). New York: Guilford.

Harris, P. L. (1989). *Children and emotion: The development of psychological understanding*. Oxford, UK: Blackwell.

Harter, S. (1986). Cognitive-developmental processes in the integration of concepts about emotions and the self. *Social Cognition, 4,* 119–151.

Heckhausen, H. (1984). Emergent achievement behavior: Some early developments. In J. Nicholls (Ed.), *Advances in motivation and achievement (Vol 3): The development of achievment motivation* (pp. 1–32). Greenwich, CT: JAI Press.

Hermelin, B., & O'Connor, N. (1985). The logico-affective disorder in autism. In E. Schopler & G. B. Mesibov (Eds.), *Communication problems in autism* pp. 283–310. New York: Plenum Press.

Hobson, R. P. (1990). On the origins of self and the case of autism. *Development and Psychopathology, 2,* 163–181.

Hobson, R. P. (1993). *Autism and the development of mind.* Hillsdale, NJ: Lawrence Erlbaum Associates.

Hoffman, M. L. (1975). Developmental synthesis of affect and cognition and its implications for altruistic motivation. *Developmental Psychology, 11,* 605–622.

Izard, C. E., & Harris, P. (1995). Emotional development and developmental psychopathology. In D. Cicchetti & D. J. Cohen (Eds.), *Developmental psychopathology, Vol. 1: Theory and methods* pp. 467–503. New York: Wiley.

Kagan, J., & Lamb, S. (Eds.). (1987). *The emergence of morality in young children.* Chicago: University of Chicago Press.

Kasari, C., Chamberlain, B., & Bauminger, N. (2000). Theory of mind in the understanding of guilt and embarrassment by children with autism. Manuscript under review.

Kasari, C., Paparella, T., & Bauminger, N. (1999). Pride in high-functioning children with autism. Manuscript under review.

Kasari, C., Sigman, M. D., Baumgartner, P., & Stipek, D. J. (1993). Pride and mastery in children with autism. *Journal of Child Psychology and Psychiatry, 34,* 353–362.

Lewis, M. (1995). Embarrassment: The emotion of self-exposure and evaluation. In J. P. Tangney & K. W. Fischer (Eds.), *Self-conscious emotions: The psychology of shame, guilt, embarrassment, and pride* (pp. 198–218). New York: Guilford.

Lewis, M., & Brooks-Gunn, J. (1979). *Social cognition and the acquisition of self.* New York: Plenum.

Lewis, M., Sullivan, M. W., Stanger, C., & Weiss, M. (1989). Self-development and self-conscious emotions. *Child Development, 60,* 146–156.

Lutkenhaus, P. (1984). Pleasure derived from mastery in three-year-olds: Its function for persistence and the influence of maternal behavior. *International Journal of Behavioral Development, 7,* 343–358.

Mascolo, M., & Fischer, K. W. (1995). Developmental transformations in appraisals for pride, shame, and guilt. In J. P. Tangney & K. W. Fischer (Eds.), *Self-conscious emotions: The psychology of shame, guilt, embarrassment, and pride* (pp. 64–113). New York: Guilford.

Miller, R. (1995). Embarrassment and social behavior. In J. P. Tangney & K. W. Fischer (Eds.), *Self-conscious emotions: The psychology of shame, guilt, embarrassment, and pride* (pp. 322–339). New York: Guilford.

Sagi, A., & Hoffman, M. L. (1976). Empathic distress in the newborn. *Developmental Psychology, 12,* 175–176.

Salthouse, T. A. (1995). Refining the concept of psychological compensation. In R. A. Dixon & L. Backman (Eds.), *Compensating for psychological deficits and declines: Managing losses and promoting gains* (pp. 21–34). Mahwah, NJ: Lawrence Erlbaum Associates.

Salthouse, T. A. (1984). Effects of age and skill in typing. *Journal of Experimental Psychology-General, 113,* 345–371.

Seidner, L. B., Stipek, D. J., & Feshbach, N. D. (1988). A developmental analysis of elementary school-aged children's concepts of pride and embarrassment. *Child Development, 59,* 367–377.

Shaver, P., Schwartz, J., Kirson, D., & O'Connor, C. (1987). Emotion knowledge: Further exploration of a prototype approach. *Journal of Personality and Social Psychology, 52,* 1061–1086.

Sigman, M., Kasari, C., Kwon, J. H., & Yirmiya, N. (1992). Responses to the negative emotions of others by autistic, mentally retarded, and normal children. *Child Development, 63,* 796–807.

Spiker, D., & Ricks, M. (1984). Visual self-recognition in autistic children: Developmental relationships. *Child Development, 55,* 214–225.

Stipek, D. J., Recchia, S., & McClintic, S. (1992). Achievement-related self-evaluation in young children. *SRCD Monographs, 57.*

Yirmiya, N., Sigman, M., Kasari, C., & Mundy, P. (1992). Empathy and cognition in high-functioning children with autism. *Child Development, 63,* 150–160.

Zahn-Waxler, C., Radke-Yarrow, M., Wagner, E., & Chapman, M. (1992). Development of concern for others. *Developmental Psychology, 28,* 126–136.

Zahn-Waxler, C., & Robinson, J. (1995). Empathy and guilt: Early origins of feelings of responsibility. In J. P. Tangney & K. W. Fischer (Eds.), *Self-conscious emotions: The psychology of shame, guilt, embarrassment, and pride* (pp. 143–173). New York: Guilford.

16

Repetitive Behaviors and Social-Communicative Impairments in Autism: Implications for Developmental Theory and Diagnosis

Tony Charman
Institute of Child Health
University College London, England
John Swettenham
University College London, England

When first described by Leo Kanner (1943), two types of psychological dysfunction were said to underlie characteristic autistic behavior: "autistic aloneness" and "an obsessive insistence on sameness." Current diagnostic criteria have not substantially altered the defining characteristics of the disorder. They require that an individual demonstrate impairments in three behavioral domains: (i) reciprocal social interaction; (ii) verbal and nonverbal communication, and in imaginative activity; and (iii) a markedly restricted repertoire of activities and interests (DSM–IV: APA, 1994; ICD–10: WHO, 1993). Despite the initial interest shown by the early pioneers of experimental psychological research into autism in the third axis of impairments, which includes sensory, perceptual, attentional, and repetitive behaviors (Frith, 1970, 1972; Hermelin & O'Connor, 1964; Lovaas, Schreibman, Koegel, & Rehm, 1971; Ornitz, 1969; Ritvo, Ornitz, & La Fanchi, 1968), more recent concentration of research efforts on the social and communicative impairments has resulted in the relative disregard of these third-axis behaviors (Rutter, 1996).

This relative neglect of repetitive behaviors, restricted interests, and preference for sameness is a disservice to both the clinical and research enterprises in autism. Understanding the nature and the developmental course of these behaviors has important implications for critical aspects of our attempts to solve the puzzle of autism. For example, consideration of whether these behaviors are unique and universal in individuals with autism impacts on the syndromal approach taken to diagnosing autism, and on our understanding of the relation between autism and other neurodevelopmental conditions. Similarly, identifying the extent to which repetitive and restricted behaviors are associated with the social and communicative impairments over the life course has implications for our understanding of the pathogenesis of autism, and therefore for developmental models that attempt to explain autism at the neurobiological, genetic, and psychological levels. Clinically, repetitive and stereotyped behaviors impact considerably on families; a better understanding of their nature and cause would be of benefit to both parents and professionals. In this chapter we examine the available empirical evidence that bears on these questions and identify directions for the research that will be required in order to answer them.

The Specificity and Universality of Third-Axis Behaviors to Autism

Under the present categorical diagnostic systems, autism is understood to be a syndrome, in that a particular number of symptoms in a particular combination of these domains are required for the diagnosis to be applied (Boucher, 1996; Pennington, 1991). In general terms, *syndromes* are understood to be conditions in which a set of behaviors are present that co-occur more commonly than by chance. However, whereas the primary rationale for the current classification systems is intended to ensure reliability of diagnosis between clinicians (Clark, Watson, & Reynolds, 1995), their empirical status is less sure. For example, the cutoffs for reaching threshold and the particular combination of behaviors in the particular number of domains required to fulfil the diagnostic criteria are arbitrary, and the "à la carte" approach to the diagnostic menu system leads to considerable within-category heterogeneity. Although autism is not unique among neurodevelopmental disorders in this regard, empirical research cannot disregard considerations of the validity of the current classification systems.

One question that follows from this is whether repetitive and stereotyped behaviors, along with social and communicative impairments, cluster together only in individuals with autism. Are these domains of behavior related more generally in typically developing individuals and in individuals with other developmental disabilities? In their landmark epidemiological study of a population of developmentally delayed children in London, UK, Wing and Gould (1979) found that repetitive and stereotyped behaviors were present in almost all severely developmentally delayed children who were socially impaired, but were present to a markedly lesser extent in the group of sociable severely delayed children. This association held both for those children who met formal diagnostic criteria for autism and for those who presented with the broader "triad of impairments." A similar finding was demonstrated in a survey of the adult population of a mental handicap hospital in the UK (Shah, Holmes, & Wing, 1982). Thus, it appears that social and communicative impairments and repetitive behaviors tend to co-occur in individuals with the broader "triad of impairments" that characterize the pervasive developmental disorders (PDDs), whether or not they show a sufficient number or severity of impairments in all three domains to meet formal diagnostic criteria for autism.

The repetitive and restricted activities and interests that characterize autism include stereotyped and repetitive motor mannerisms, persistent preoccupation with parts of objects or nonfunctional elements of play materials (including their odor, taste, or feel), attachment to unusual objects, a marked distress over changes made in trivial aspects of environment, an insistence on following routines in precise detail, and stereotyped and restricted patterns of interest (DSM–IV; ICD–10). A helpful, detailed descriptive taxonomy (Turner, 1999) and a review of the instruments employed to measure such behaviors (Lewis & Bodfish, 1998) have recently been published, to which readers are referred. Clinically, some behaviors seem so peculiar and so specific to autism that they are almost syndrome defining. Indeed, using a signal-detection analysis, Siegel, Vukicevic, Elliott, and Kraemer (1989) found that "persistent preoccupation with parts of an object" was the second most characteristic DSM–III–R symptom of autism, following "marked lack of awareness of the existence or feelings of others." What is the empirical evidence that these behaviors are unique to autism?

Repetitive and ritualistic behaviors are a feature of typical development, at least as a transient phenomenon and particularly in the preschool years (Evans et al., 1997). However, repetitive, ritualistic, and stereotyped behaviors are more common and more enduring in individuals with developmental delay (mental handicap) than among typically developing individuals, and their prevalence and severity increase as the severity of delay increases (Bodfish et al., 1995; Campbell et al., 1990). Repetitive and stereotyped behaviors are also found in individuals with other clinical disorders including schizophrenia, obsessive-compulsive disorder and Tourette syndrome, as well as in individuals with sensory disabilities including blindness and deafness (for reviews, see C. D. Frith & Done, 1990; Ridley, 1994). Preference for routines and insistence on sameness, accompanied by distress if routines or the environment is changed, are described in obsessive-compulsive disorder (Leonard et al., 1992), Tourette syndrome (Pauls, Towbin, Leckman, Zahner, & Cohen, 1986), and in individuals with general developmental delay (Bodfish et al., 1995). Thus, there is no clear evidence that any particular type of third-axis behavior is unique to autism.

However, what may be unique are the combination, the severity, or both of these features in individuals with autism. Hermelin and O'Connor (1963) reported that individuals with autism engaged in significantly more and longer bouts of stereotyped movements than did individuals with general developmental delay matched for age and ability. Matson et al. (1996) found stereotypes in over 75% of individuals with autism with severe or profound mental retardation versus only 7% in the comparison group without autism. In addition, repetitive and stereotyped behaviors, including circumscribed interests and highly developed routines, are also found in individuals with autism and Asperger's syndrome who have intellectual abilities in the average and even above-average range (Bartak & Rutter, 1976; Frith, 1991; Szatmari, Bartolucci, & Bremner, 1989), rates that are higher than for nonautistic psychiatric controls (Szatmari et al., 1989). Prior and Macmillan (1973) found that insistence on sameness was associated with higher cognitive level in a sample of children with autism. Turner (1997) also found that both high- and low-IQ individuals with autism showed repetitive and stereotyped behaviors, significantly more frequently than in comparison to both average-IQ psychiatric outpatients and low-IQ developmentally delayed controls. Baron-Cohen and Wheelwright (1999) found that the content of obsessions in individuals with autism and Asperger's syndrome differed from that found in individuals with Tourette syndrome. Individuals with autism and Asperger's syndrome showed an obsessional interest in "how things worked," whereas individuals with Tourette syndrome showed an obsessional interest in action and sensory phenomena. Thus, although no individual third-axis behavior is unique to autism, there appears to be some degree of specificity in the combination and in the severity of repetitive, stereotyped, and restricted behaviors found in autism.

Third-Axis Behaviors in PDDs and the Broader Phenotype

Individuals with PDD are characterized either by an atypicality in age of onset, range, or severity of symptoms of autism. Are the repetitive and stereotyped behaviors that characterize autism also found in the related PDDs? Tanguay, Robertson, and Derrick (1998) factor-analyzed scores on social and communication items from the ADI-R for a sample of individuals who met DSM–IV criteria for autism, Asperger's syndrome, and PDD. They derived three main factors that they labeled "affective reciprocity," "joint attention," and "theory of mind." They found that all three factors correlated highly with ADI-R domains scores for the social and communicative domain, but that none correlated with the restricted, repetitive, and stereotyped interests domain score. Tanguay et al. also found that a subset of individuals who met diagnostic criteria for PDD but not autism per se did not show third-axis behaviors. They argued that the necessity for symptoms in this domain to be present for a PDD diagnosis might need to be rethought. There is some circularity to their argument as they state that "Subjects with PDD-NOS [N = 17] were almost all ones who had marked abnormalities in the first two DSM–IV domains, but not in the third" (Tanguay et al., 1998, p. 273). That these participants did not show repetitive behaviors but clearly showed social and communicative impairments would, at least in part, explain the lack of association between the factors derived from the first two axes and the ADI-R domain scores measuring stereotyped, restricted, and repetitive behaviors.

Employing factor analysis of items from the Childhood Autism Rating Scale (CARS; Schopler, Reichler, De Vellis, & Daly, 1980), Stella, Mundy, and Tuchman (1999) found that whereas some third-axis behaviors (odd sensory exploration) did not discriminate between children with autism and those with PDD, other third-axis behaviors (stereotypies) were rated less severe in the individuals with PDD. Stella et al. conclude that scores on the social and communicative factor-based scales derived from the CARS may be more important than third-axis behaviors when considering diagnosis, especially of more intellectually able children with PDD. Thus, there is some evidence that individuals can meet diagnostic criteria for related PDDs (though not for childhood autism) without showing significant repetitive, stereotyped, and restricted behaviors. Does this suggest that these behaviors are more uniquely defining of the core nature of autism compared to related PDDs than are those in the social and communicative domains?

Designing a clear research strategy to answer such a question is fraught with methodological pitfalls, not least in the application of the diagnostic criteria in sample selection. We know that PDD is a less reliable diagnosis than Asperger's syndrome and childhood autism (Mahoney et al., 1998), perhaps especially so in younger children (Cox et al., 1999; Stone et al., 1999). However, in our anecdotal clinical experience, when one sees a child who clearly meets criteria for childhood autism or Asperger's syndrome, one always sees (by definition) notable repetitive, stereotyped, and restricted behaviors—although these can vary from severe and persistent body rocking to a fascination with subway routes and highway maps. However, in a child who receives a PDD diagnosis such features are often less clear. In fact, this is often precisely the reason why a diagnosis of PDD rather than autism is given. We do not know of any systematic data that bear on this issue. However, we suspect that clinically (at least outside of individuals with severe and profound mental retardation) a significant proportion of children who receive a PDD diagnosis display sufficient symptoms in the first two domains to meet full criteria for autism in these domains, but not in the third domain.

Outside the clinical field, there is increasing research interest in the extent to which a milder, "broader phenotype" of autism may characterize family members of individuals with autism (Bailey, Palferman, Heavey, & Le Couteur, 1998; see Bauminger and Yirmiya, chap. 4, this volume). What is the evidence for the universality of third-axis behaviors in individuals with the broader phenotype? In contrast to the consistent findings of increased levels of milder autistic-like social and communicative impairments in monozygotic and dizygotic twins of autistic probands, in siblings and parents, and in extended family members (e.g., Bolton et al., 1994; Le Couteur et al., 1996), evidence for the presence of repetitive and stereotyped behaviors in less clear. For example, Wolff, Narayan, and Moyes (1988) found no increased rate of single-mindedness in parents of children with autism. Bailey et al. (1995) found a higher rate of circumscribed interests, rigidity, and repetitive behaviors in first-degree relatives of probands, compared with controls. However, these behaviors were present at a lower rate than that of the social and communicative impairments and never appeared in isolation. Piven et al. (1994) did not find increased rates of rigidity and conscientiousness in parents of children with autism. Murphy et al. (1998) reported higher rates of these traits among parents of individuals with autism, but they were associated with a general-anxiety personality factor and were not associated with the social and communicative atypicalities that make up the broader autism phenotype. Bailey et al. (1998) noted that the lower ascertainment of these third-axis behaviors in a milder form may be due to inadequate measurement sensitivity. However, it may be (in common with the findings previously discussed for PDD) that repetitive and stereotyped behaviors are less apparent as part of the broader autism phenotype than in the core disorder.

Strength of Association Between Repetitive and Social-Communicative Symptoms

Only a few studies have directly measured the association between repetitive and social-communicative symptoms within a group of individuals with autism. In some studies the severity of social and communicative symptoms were positively correlated with severity of stereotypies (Campbell et al., 1990) and with degree of insistence on sameness behavior (Prior & Macmillan, 1973). These associations held independently of IQ, to which the overall level of repetitive and stereotyped behaviors were correlated in both autistic and nonautistic individuals. In contrast, Lord and Pickles (1996) found that whereas several social and communicative abnormalities were associated with level of language ability in a group of individuals with autism, there was no association between level of language ability and repetitive, stereotyped, and restricted behaviors.

One difficulty in examining the association between the severity of symptoms on the three axes of behavior that define autism is the heterogeneity of presentation across individuals. The menu or algorithm approach to the syndromal categorization of autism used in the DSM and ICD classification systems means that not every individual will show the same set of symptoms. Perhaps as a result, more effort is expended on identifying subtypes who show different patterns of symptoms than on examining the degree of association between behaviors from the three axes. Sevin et al. (1995) cluster-analyzed scores derived from standardized behavior rating and adaptive behavior scales on a small (N = 34) heterogeneous sample of individuals with autism and identified four subtypes. The first subtype had mild social and language impairments, accompanied by mild sensory, repetitive, and stereotyped behaviors. The second and third subtypes both had moderate social and language impairments, one accompanied by few sensory, repetitive, and stereotyped behaviors but the other by severe third-axis symptoms. The last subtype had severe symptoms in all three domains. Similarly, Roux, Adrien, Bruneau, Malvy, and Barthélémy (1998) employed correspondence analysis of item scores on the Behavior Summarized Evaluation Scale–Revised (BSE–R; Barthélémy et al., 1997) on a large (N = 145), more homogeneous group of children referred for diagnostic assessment. They also found subgroups of children characterized by different patterns of symptoms. One subgroup was characterized by an absence of bizarre responses to auditory stimuli, and another by an absence of bizarre responses to auditory stimuli *and* an absence of stereotyped sensorimotor activity. The latter group existed only in children with a development age below 2 years (Roux et al., 1998).

These studies suggest that among individuals who meet diagnostic criteria for autism and related PDDs, there may be a subgroup of individuals who show few repetitive, stereotyped, and restricted behaviors (and perhaps the associated sensory abnormalities that are commonly noted). Roux et al.'s (1998) finding also suggests that individuals may be more likely to have this profile of symptoms if they are young or developmentally immature. Examining the presence of third-axis behaviors and their association with social and communicative symptoms over the life course may give us clues as to their centrality in the diagnosis of autism and PDDs.

Repetitive Behaviors Across the Life Span

As part of a prospective screening study to identify autism in infancy (Baird et al., 2000; Baron-Cohen et al., 1996), Cox et al. (1999) assessed parental report of past and present symptoms using the ADI-R (Lord et al., 1994) at ages 20 months and 42 months. An unexpected finding was that impairments on the third dimension of repetitive and stereotyped behaviors were not reported at the definite level of abnormality at age 20 months in many children who went on to receive a diagnosis of autism at 42 months (and even fewer in children with PDD). For example, the most commonly reported third-axis behaviors definitely present at 20 months were hand and finger and other complex mannerisms, but these were present in only 25% of the children with autism and in none of the children with PDD. Third-axis behaviors were present in most individuals with autism by age 42 months, though again sometimes only at the possible rather than definite level of certainty. Once again, third-axis behaviors were even less common in children with a diagnosis of PDD at 42 months. This contrasted to abnormalities in social and communication domains that were present in the majority of children with autism and PDD at the possible, and often the definite, level of certainty at the younger as well as the older age point. These findings differ from those of Lord's (1995) study of a clinic sample seen at age 2 years 6 months and followed up 1 year later. Lord (1995) found that abnormalities on the third axis of the ADI-R—including hand and finger mannerisms, unusual sensory behaviors, unusual preoccupations, and whole-body mannerisms—were present at both the younger and older time points. These differences may reflect the older age of Lord's (1995) sample and their lower IQs. Another possibility is that the nature and extent of difficulties in this domain differs in young preschool children with autism from that seen in older 4- and 5-year-old children with autism (the age at which the authors of the ADI-R indicate that autistic symptomatology is most prototypical). However, the Cox et al. (1999) group of children with autism and related PDDs were the youngest studied to date. We cannot rule out that in at least some children with autism abnormalities on the third dimension of behaviors only begin to emerge after infancy, at a time later than the social and communication impairments are apparent.

Other more indirect sources of information regarding early development in autism are retrospective parental reports and home videos taken before the child is diagnosed (for reviews, see Charman, 2000; Stone, 1997). Both of these methodologies have limitations in that they rely, on the one hand, on retrospective parental report that may introduce bias, and on the other hand, on selective and often unsystematic samples of children's behavior. However, to date we have no prospective method by which the behavior of children with autism can be studied in the first year of life. With appropriate caution is it worth considering what can be learned about the early development of individuals with autism from these sources. From parents' retrospective accounts, there is evidence that social and communicative abnormalities *and* repetitive and stereotyped behaviors and sensory abnormalities are found in the first two years of life (e.g., DeMeyer, 1979; Dahlgren & Gillberg, 1989; Gillberg et al., 1990; Hoshino et al., 1982; Ornitz, Guthrie, & Farley, 1977; Stone, Hoffman, Lewis, & Ousley, 1994). However, third-axis behaviors were present in fewer of the children than social and communicative impairments. Further, in the majority of studies, when parents reported concerns about third-axis behaviors, these were noticed during the second year of life and less frequently in the first year.

From retrospective reviews of home videos taken by parents of children with autism, several researchers have identified impairments in social and communicative behaviors in the first and second year of life. Discriminating items included lack of social smile, lack of appropriate facial expression, ignoring people, preference for aloneness, lack of eye contact, and lack of appropriate gestures (Adrien et al., 1993; Osterling & Dawson, 1994). Notably, few third-axis behaviors appeared to be present in these samples of early behavior. For example, Osterling and Dawson (1994) found that, compared to typically developing children, those with autism were not more likely to show self-stimulatory behavior. Baranek (1999) found that from videos taken between 9 and 12 months of age, children with autism were distinguished from developmentally delayed children by an increase in mouthing objects. However, several other third-axis behaviors were more commonly found in the comparison group, including unusual posturing, stereotyped play with objects, and visual staring or fixation on objects. Again, despite the limitations of these selective, retrospective video analyses, these enterprising studies consolidate the information elicited from retrospective parental accounts of early symptoms. The abnormalities that most clearly differentiate children with autism from other children are abnormalities or delays in emotional or empathic response, joint-attention behaviors such as pointing and use of eye contact to monitor attention, imitation, and imaginative and pretend play. Although there is also evidence in some studies for the presence of early abnormalities in sensory, repetitive, and stereotyped behaviors, the best discriminators in the first two years of life appear to be the social and communicative impairments.

One recent experimental study involving a cohort a young preschoolers with autism produced an unexpected finding that may be consistent with the view that third-axis abnormalities are less common or severe in very young children with autism. Griffith, Pennington, Wehner, and Rogers (1999) investigated executive abilities in preschool children with autism and IQ-matched controls, as dysfunction in executive systems may underlie many of the behavioral abnormalities shown by individuals with autism (for reviews, see Hughes, chap. 13, this volume; Ozonoff, 1997; Pennington & Ozonoff, 1996). The notion that problems in planning, flexibility, and attention shifting are in some way related to the repetitive, routine-bound, and restricted interests that are included in the third-axis criteria for autism certainly has strong face validity as a hypothesis. Griffith et al. (1999) tested 3-year-old children with autism on a series of nonverbal experimental tasks measuring aspects of executive ability (Diamond, Prevor, Callender, & Druin, 1997; see Griffith et al., 1999, for details). Contrary to their predictions and to findings with older samples of individuals with autism, Griffith et al. found that these young children with autism performed no worse, and on some tasks performed better than, children in the comparison group. In contrast, autism-specific impairments in joint-attention behavior were found. Griffith et al. (1999) followed up some of this sample one year later. No autism-specific deficit in executive ability was apparent, although there was a slight trend to the developmentally delayed control group showing improved executive ability (in contrast to the children with autism). Thus, in the youngest sample in which executive deficits were investigated, no autism-specific executive impairments were identified. One possible explanation is that the measures used were not sensitive to the nature or the degree of the executive impairments found in these preschool children. Alternatively, these findings are consistent with the notion that repetitive and stereotyped behaviors may have a relatively later onset in autism, compared with that of social and communicative symptoms.

Adopting an alternative developmental approach—looking at later as opposed to earlier symptoms—shows a different pattern of findings. Piven, Harper, Palmer, and Arndt (1996) used the ADI (Le Couteur et al., 1989) to examine parental report of current versus retrospective report of symptoms at 5 years of age among a cohort of high-functioning (high IQ) adolescents and young adults with autism. They found that for most individuals symptoms in the social reciprocity and communication domains improved over development. In contrast, there was less improvement in the repetitive and restricted interests domains, with almost half of the group showing no improvement in their score on this domain over time. Piven et al. (1996) cautioned that this might be an instrument effect, in that many of the social and communicative abnormalities included on the schedule are more readily applicable to children than to the high-functioning adolescents and adults in their study. However, they suggested that the developmental course of the third-axis behaviors might differ from that of the social and communicative domains. In a prospective longitudinal study, Eaves and Ho (1996) also found that third-axis behaviors such as rigidity, sensory disturbance, and a narrow range of interest were among the symptoms that improved the least at follow-up in a group of individuals with autism and PDD, in contrast to greater improvements in social and communicative behaviors. One possible explanation is that social and communicative impairments are more frequently the target of intervention and educational approaches than are repetitive and stereotyped behaviors, and improvement in these symptoms over time reflects the effect of these programs as well as that of development. It may also be the case that the former behaviors are more amenable to learning and modification than are the latter behaviors. Longitudinal and intervention studies are necessary to map the changing pattern of symptoms across the three defining domains of behavior in autism throughout the life span and to assess the role of development and intervention in their course.

How Might Psychological Theory Help Us Understand the Pattern of Symptoms in Autism?

The empirical evidence we reviewed on the presence, course, and associations of repetitive, stereotyped, and restricted behaviors presents challenges to both the research and the clinical enterprise in autism. In terms of research, an integrated, developmental theory of pathogenesis in autism is needed to account for the apparent changes in symptoms of autism over development, as well as for differences between individuals with autism and related PDDs, especially if the latter are less characterized by repetitive and stereotyped behaviors. In terms of the clinical enterprise, the applicability of the current diagnostic criteria to all individuals regardless of age and IQ may need to be questioned. Of course, the clinical and research enterprises are not separate. There is an implicit assumption that co-occurrence of a set of symptoms that characterize a syndrome may signify the developmental manifestation of some primary etiological mechanism or substrate that is responsible for the pathogenesis of the condition (Sonuga-Barke, 1998). While the primary rationale for the current classification systems is to ensure reliability of diagnosis between clinicians, their empirical status should continue to be tested against models of the pathogenesis.

In terms of psychological theory, the dominant theoretical accounts of autism are the theory of mind (Baron-Cohen, 1993, 1995, 2000; see Tager-Flusberg, chap. 9, this volume), the executive dysfunction (Ozonoff, 1997; Pennington et al., 1997, see Hughes, chap. 13, this volume), and the weak central coherence accounts (Frith & Happé, 1994, see Happé, chap. 12, this volume). How do these accounts explain the co-occurrence of third-axis and social-communicative abnormalities in autism, at either the cognitive or the behavioral levels? Baron-Cohen (1989) suggested that repetitive behavior may be a coping strategy to reduce anxiety in the face of a world that is rendered unpredictable due to an inability to understand others' mental states and thus predict their behavior. Similarly, Carruthers (1996) argued that repetitive and stereotyped behaviors represented a withdrawal from a social world that individuals with autism are unable to understand. Conversely, the increasing empirical evidence for an association between executive deficits and theory-of-mind ability among autistic (see Pennington et al., 1997, for a review), developmentally delayed (e.g. Zelazo, P. D. Burack, Benedetto, & Frye, 1996), and typically developing children (Hughes, 1998), led to the suggestion that executive deficits may underlie theory-of-mind deficits (see Russell, 1997, for various versions of this thesis). In its initial inception, it was also suggested that weak central coherence may in some way explain both mentalizing impairments and third-axis behaviors in autism (Frith, 1989). Although Frith later revised her position and suggested that weak central coherence and theory-of-mind impairment might exist as independent deficits in autism (Frith & Happé, 1994), some recent evidence emerged that these processes may be related in autism and in typical development (Jarrold, Butler, Cottingham, & Jimenez, 2000).

More recently, many proponents of these theories moved toward multiple deficit theories that do not assume a direct superordinate association between these cognitive characteristics. Thus, impairments in executive or frontal abilities, impairments in theory-of-mind understanding, and a weak drive for coherence in processing stimuli may exist as independent deficits (e.g., Baron-Cohen & Swettenham, 1997; Happé & Frith, 1996; Pennington et al., 1997). "Multiple deficit" accounts of autism are probably necessary given the heterogeneity of brain damage with which the disorder is associated (Bishop, 1993; Goodman, 1989; Waterhouse, Fein, & Modahl, 1996), and it may be that no unitary explanation at the psychological level is possible.

A number of researchers have examined more primary processing deficits in attention (Burack, Enns, Stauder, Mottron, & Randolph, 1997; Courchesne et al., 1994; Swettenham, Milne, Plaisted, Campbell, & Coleman, 2000) or perception (Mottron & Burack, chap. 7, this volume; Plaisted et al., 1998, 1999; Plaisted, chap. 8, this volume). Impairments in these processes may underlie the social and communicative impairments in autism and also the third-axis behaviors, including sensory abnormalities and fixation on parts of objects, that are not easily explained by higher-level cognitive accounts, such as theory-of-mind deficit or executive-dysfunction accounts.

Dynamic Versus Static Accounts of Pathogenesis in Autism and Implications for Diagnosis

However, any cogent psychological theory of autism—in terms of either unitary or multiple deficits—needs to take a clear developmental perspective. Autism is not unique among neurodevelopmental disorders in this respect. Recent reviews by Bishop (1997) and Karmiloff-Smith (1997, 1998) tackle similar issues with reference to other disorders. Bishop (1997), using the example of specific language impairment, demonstrated that at a cognitive level there is considerable interaction over development between levels of representation that some have argued are dissociable or even modular cognitive systems. According to Bishop, when applied to developing cognitive systems, the dominant methodologies and theoretical models of adult neuropsychology—demonstration of double dissociation in single-case studies and localization of brain systems involved in particular cognitive processing—may not be appropriate. Thus, at the level of neurobiological organization and cognitive representation, specification of function (or "modularity" of function) may only appear over time. Impairment in one developing system may therefore have secondary consequences on other systems. Karmiloff-Smith (1997, 1998) also argued for a more dynamic approach to modeling cognitive systems in both typical and in atypical cases (using the example of Williams syndrome). One strength of these approaches to understanding psychopathology is that they emphasize the role of development in the crucial associations between the genetic and neurobiological substrate that underlies neurodevelopmental disorders and the cognitive and behavioral levels of explanation.

A similar account was elucidated with reference to autism by Mundy and colleagues (Mundy & Markus, 1997; Mundy & Neal, 2000). The frontal cortical and medial temporal neurological systems are the likely foci for the social-communicative impairments that characterize autism (e.g., Damasio & Maurer, 1978; Dawson, 1996; Minshew, 1996). Mundy and colleagues examined the possibility that impairments to such systems are the "downstream" consequences of earlier impairments in the caudal brain systems (Courchesne et al., 1994;

Damasio & Maurer, 1978). Mundy and Markus (1997) proposed a "social orienting" model of autistic pathology, whereby disturbances to frontally mediated neuroaffective motivation systems that serve to prioritize social information processing (Dawson & Lewy, 1989; Hobson, 1993; Mundy, 1995) are apparent in development in advance of cognition as the primary regulator of behavior. There is experimental evidence of a deficit in social orienting in preschool children (Dawson, Meltzoff, Osterling, Rinaldi, & Brown, 1998) and in infants with autism (Swettenham et al., 1998). Mundy and Neal (in press) suggested that the primary neurobiological deficits of social orienting that impact on optimal behavioral responses in the first few months of life lead to secondary neurological and later representational disturbance via the interaction of the developing brain system with the organization of input available to the children from their processing of and interaction with the environment ("experience expectant neural development," Greenough, Black, & Wallace, 1987).

Other models that attempt to integrate neurobiolgical and behavioral developmental evidence have been proposed, notably Courchesne's account of disturbed cerebellum development (Courchesne et al., 1994) and the ambitious attempt by Waterhouse, Fein, and Modahl (1996) to link specific autistic symptoms to disruption of four neurofunctional mechanisms: canalesthesia, impaired assignment of affective significance of stimuli, asociality, and extended selective attention. Although these accounts present elegant hypotheses and add considerable impetus to further empirical study, confirming evidence to support one account over the other is not yet available.

These accounts are consistent with the notion that the neurological substrate that guides later aspects of behavior as the brain develops may in turn have its development affected by damage to, or reorganization of, other brain systems. The time course during which this brain development and organization occurs extends from birth throughout infancy and beyond. Therefore, there may be a neurobiological basis to a pattern of different symptoms of autism emerging at different times over this time period. We accept that the available empirical evidence is insufficient to develop anything but a tentative account as yet. However, some third-axis behaviors may emerge after the social and communicative impairments in autism have manifested themselves. This may be due to pathogenic developmental processes at the neurobiological, rather than the psychological or the behavioral, level.

A further tentative suggestion is that different types of third-axis behaviors may be due to different neuropathological processes and have different developmental courses. For example, impairments in basic low-level brain processes such as those suggested by Mottron and Burack (chap. 7, this volume), Plaisted (chap. 8, this volume), and Courchesne et al. (1994) might underlie sensory and attentional abnormalities. Secondary effects of these impairments on the development of brain systems that regulate higher level social and cognitive development might underlie the impairments in social and communicative development, as well as the stereotyped and restricted patterns of interest that characterize autism. The developmental course, amenability to intervention, and relation to social and communicative impairments of these subtypes of third-axis behaviors may differ (see Turner, 1997). What is required to test such hypotheses are longitudinal studies of very early-identified infants with autism that track symptoms as they emerge and change over the course of development, as well as intervention studies that attempt to change this developmental course. This enterprise is clearly not one that psychologists can pursue in isolation, and the call to arms for properly integrated cross-specialism research has already been sounded (Yeung-Courchesne & Courchesne, 1997).

Clinical Implications

Whether or not this or another theoretical account of pathogenesis in autism is supported by future empirical evidence, several aspects of this review warrant our clinical attention, in particular in relation to the diagnosis of autism. Although defined as a developmental disorder within the current classification systems (DSM–IV; ICD–10), the diagnostic criteria allow only consideration of particular symptoms in relation to developmental level. For example, consideration of abnormality or delay in language ability or peer relationships is conducted with regard to developmental level. Our reading of the available empirical literature suggests that a more radical developmental stance may be required. If, for example, certain third-axis behaviors are less severe or less common (and certainly not universal) in very young individuals with autism, then the diagnostic criteria need to be modified to take this into account.

Alternatively, the specification of the type of third-axis abnormalities that are currently within the diagnostic criteria may need to be extended to include rigid and repetitive behaviors that characterize younger children with autism. That is, the type of ritualized or "stuck in set" behaviors that characterize very young children with autism might not be those suggested by the current versions of DSM or ICD. Little evidence is available about the continuities between early and late third-axis behaviors, and it is too early to suggest what these "early third-axis" behaviors might be. One fruitful line of investigation might be to consider what types of early behavior would be affected by the accounts of psychological and neurological pathogenesis just outlined (Mottron & Burack, chap. 7, this volume; Mundy & Neal, 2000; Plaisted, chap. 8, this volume; Waterhouse et al., 1996). These diagnostic considerations deserve attention, as it is clear that better surveillance methods are increasing the number of children referred for diagnosis in the third and even the second year of life (e.g., Lord, 1995; Stone et al., 1999; for a review, see Filipek et al., 1999).

Another diagnostic consideration is whether atypical or less severe presentations of autism, currently subsumed under various subcategories of PDD, are particularly characterized by atypicality or milder symptoms in the third axis. There is presently no specification of the symptom domains in which the atypicalities are likely to be found. However, the primary diagnostic features of individuals with PDDs might be their social and communication impairments. These impairments may or may not be accompanied by repetitive and stereotyped behaviors. Such profiles of symptoms might vary according to IQ or to age. We know at present that the reliability of the diagnostic criteria for PDDs is moderate at best (and may be especially difficult in young preschool children). It may be that if greater specification could be given as to which sets of symptoms cluster together in different individuals at which developmental age, the reliability and the clinical utility of the PDD category may be enhanced. The degree to which the three characteristic domains of impairment that characterize autism co-occur and the degree to which they may be separable is a critical consideration for furthering our understanding of the core disorder and its boundaries. This will have implications for the research enterprise across a number of fields, including psychology and genetics (Szatmari, Jones, Zwaigenbaum, & MacLean, 1998), as well as clinical diagnostic practice.

Conclusions

At the heart of this chapter is a question that is central to understanding autism at both a behavioral and pathogenic level. Although the presence of abnormalities in repetitive, restricted, and stereotyped behaviors has been axiomatic to a diagnosis of the "classic" condition from Kanner's time to the present day, our understanding of how these features are associated with the social and communicative abnormalities remains limited. These domains may be united (far back in development) at a neurobiological level, or they may be connected further "downstream" of the pathogenic pathway at a cognitive or a behavioral level. Alternatively, there may be no pathogenic association whatsoever, with different genetic liability acting on separately developing brain systems, and it is only at the classificatory level that they are united. If a true association is determined, investigation of whether these associations are unique to autism or universal in development (for instance, in individuals with other neurodevelopmental disorders or sensory impairments) will further illuminate this challenging and disrupting disorder. It is already apparent that developmental theories of autism are likely to be multifaceted and multifactorial. This presents considerable challenges for us to take forward into the next stage of empirical research into autism.

ACKNOWLEDGMENTS

The authors are grateful to the colleagues, parents and individuals with autism with whom discussions have informed their thinking on this topic.

Please address all correspondence to: Tony Charman, Behavioural Sciences Unit, Institute of Child Health, 30 Guilford Street, London WC1N 1EH UK; e-mail: t.charman@ich.ucl.ac.uk.

REFERENCES

Adrien, J. L., Lenoir, P., Martineau, J., Perrot, A., Hameury, L., Larmande, C., & Sauvage, D. (1993). Blind ratings of early symptoms of autism based on family home movies. *Journal of the American Academy of Child and Adolescent Psychiatry, 33,* 617–626.

American Psychiatric Association. (1994). *Diagnostic and Statistical Manual of Mental Disorders* (4th ed.) (DSM–IV). Washington, DC: Author.

Bailey, A., Le Couteur, A., Gottesman, I., Bolton, P., Simonoff, E., Yuzda, E., & Rutter, M. (1995). Autism as a strongly genetic disorder: Evidence from a British twin study. *Psychological Medicine, 25,* 63–77.

Bailey, A., Palferman, S., Heavey, L., & Le Couteur, A. (1998). Autism: The broader phenotype in relatives. *Journal of Autism and Developmental Disorders, 28,* 369–392.

Baird, G., Charman, T., Baron-Cohen, S., Cox, A., Swettenham, J., Wheelwright, S., Drew, A., & Kemal L. (2000). A screening instrument for autism at 18 month of age: A six-year follow-up study. *Journal of the American Academy of Child and Adolescent Psychiatry, 39,* 694–702.

Baranek, G. (1999). Autism during infancy: A retrospective analysis of sensory-motor and social behaviors at 9–12 months of age. *Journal of Autism and Developmental Disorders, 29,* 213–224.

Baron-Cohen, S. (1989). Do autistic children have obsessions and compulsions? *British Journal of Clinical Psychology, 28,* 193–200.

Baron-Cohen, S. (1993). From attention-goal psychology to belief-desire psychology: The development of a theory of mind and its dysfunction. In S. Baron-Cohen, H. Tager-Flusberg, & D. Cohen (Eds.), *Understanding other minds: perspectives from autism* (pp. 59–82). Oxford, UK: Oxford University Press.

Baron-Cohen, S. (1995). *Mindblindness: An essay on autism and theory of mind.* Cambridge, MA: MIT Press.

Baron-Cohen, S. (2000). Theory of mind and autism: A fifteen-year review. In S. Baron-Cohen, H. Tager-Flusberg, & D. Cohen (Eds.), *Understanding other minds: Perspectives from autism and developmental cognitive neuroscience* (2nd ed.) (pp. 3–20). Oxford, UK: Oxford University Press.

Baron-Cohen, S., Cox, A., Baird, G., Swettenham, J., Nightingale, N., Morgan, K., Drew, A., & Charman, T. (1996). Psychological markers of autism at 18 months of age in a large population. *British Journal of Psychiatry, 168,* 158–163.

Baron-Cohen, S., & Swettenham, J. (1997). Theory of mind in autism: Its relationship to executive function and central coherence. In D. J. Cohen & F. R.

Volkmar (Eds.), *Handbook of autism and pervasive developmental disorders* (2nd ed.) (pp. 880–893). New York: Wiley.

Baron-Cohen, S., & Wheelwright, S. (1999). "Obsessions" in children with autism and Asperger syndrome. *British Journal of Psychiatry, 175,* 484–490.

Bartak, L., & Rutter, M. (1976). Differences between mentally retarded and normally intelligent autistic children. *Journal of Autism and Childhood Schizophrenia, 6,* 109–120.

Barthélémy, C., Roux, S., Adrien J. L., Hameury, L., Guérin, P., Garreau, B., & Lelord, G. (1997). Validation of the Revised Behavior Summarized Evaluation Scale (BSE–R). *Journal of Autism and Developmental Disorders, 27,* 137–151.

Bishop, D. V. M. (1993). Annotation: Autism, executive functions and theory of mind: A neuropsychological perspective. *Journal of Child Psychiatry and Psychology, 34,* 279–293.

Bishop, D. V. M. (1997). Cognitive neuropsychology and developmental disorders: Uncomfortable bedfellows. *The Quarterly Journal of Experimental Psychology, 50A,* 899–923.

Bodfish, J. W., Crawford, T. W., Powell, S. B., Parker, D. E., Golden, R. N., & Lewis, M. H. (1995). Compulsions in adults with mental retardation: Prevalence, phenomenology, and comorbidity with stereotypy and self-injury. *American Journal of Mental Retardation, 100,* 183–192.

Bolton, P., MacDonald, H., Pickles, A., Rios, P., Goode, S., Crowson, M., Bailey, A., & Rutter, M. (1994). A case-controlled family history study of autism. *Journal of Child Psychology and Psychiatry, 35,* 877–900.

Boucher, J. (1996) What could possibly explain autism? In P. Carruthers & P. K. Smith (Eds.), *Theories of theories of mind* (pp. 223–241). Cambridge: Cambridge University Press.

Burack, J. A., Enns, J. T., Stauder, J. E. A., Mottron, L., & Randolph, B. (1997). Attention and autism: Behavioral and electrophysiological evidence. In D. J. Cohen & F. R. Volkmar (Eds.), *Handbook of autism and pervasive developmental disorders* (pp. 266–282). New York: Wiley.

Campbell, M., Locascio, J. J., Choroco, M. C., Spencer, E. K., Malone, R. P., Kafantaris, V., & Overall, J. E. (1990). Stereotypies and tardive dyskinesia: Abnormal movements in autistic children. *Psychopharmalogical Bulletin, 26,* 260–266.

Carruthers, P. (1996). Autism as mindblindness: An elaboration and partial defence. In P. Carruthers & P. K. Smith (Eds.), *Theories of theories of mind* (pp. 257–273). Cambridge, UK: Cambridge University Press.

Charman, T. (2000). Theory of mind and the early diagnosis of autism. In S. Baron-Cohen, H. Tager-Flusberg, & D. Cohen (Eds.), *Understanding other minds: Perspectives from autism and developmental cognitive neuroscience* (2nd ed.) (pp. 422–441). Oxford, UK: Oxford University Press.

Clark, L. A., Watson, D., & Reynolds, S. (1995). Diagnosis and classification of psychopathology: Challenges to the current system and future directions. *Annual Review of Psychology, 46,* 121–153.

Courchesne, E., Townsend, J. P., Akshoomoff, N. A., Yeung-Courchesne, R., Press, G. A., Murakami, J. W., Lincoln, A. J., James, H. E., Saitoh, O., Egass, B., Haas, R. H., & Schreibman, L. (1994). A new finding: Impairment in shifting attention in autistic and cerebellar patients. In S. H. Broman & J. Grafman (Eds.), *Atypical cognitive deficits in developmental disorders: Implications for brain function* (pp. 101–137). Hillsdale, NJ: Lawrence Erlbaum Associates.

Cox, A., Klein, K., Charman, T., Baird, G., Baron-Cohen, S., Swettenham, J., Wheelwright, S., & Drew, A. (1999). Autism spectrum disorders at 20 and 42 months of age: Stability of clinical and ADI–R diagnosis. *Journal of Child Psychology and Psychiatry, 40,* 719–732.

Dahlgren, S. O., & Gillberg, C. (1989). Symptoms in the first two years of life: A preliminary population study of autism. *Archives of Psychiatry and Neurological Science, 238,* 169–174.

Damasio, A., & Maurer, R. (1978). A neurological model of childhood autism. *Archives of Neurology, 35,* 777–786.

Dawson, G. (1996). Brief report: Neuropsychology of autism: A report of the state of science. *Journal of Autism and Developmental Disabilities, 26,* 179–184.

Dawson, G., & Lewy, A. (1989). Arousal, attention and the socioemotional impairments of individuals with autism. In G. Dawson (Ed.), *Autism: Nature, diagnosis and treatment* (pp. 144–173). New York: Guilford.

Dawson, G., Meltzoff, A. N., Osterling, J., Rinaldi, J., & Brown, E. (1998). Children with autism fail to orient to naturally occurring social stimuli. *Journal of Autism and Developmental Disorders, 28,* 479–485.

DeMyer, M. K. (1979). *Parents and children in autism.* Washington, DC: Winston.

Diamond, A., Prevor, M. B., Callender, G., & Druin, D. P. (1997). Prefrontal cortex deficits in children treated early and continuously for PKU. *Monographs of the Society for Research in Child Development, 62,* 1–205.

Eaves, L. C., & Ho, H. H. (1996). Brief report: Stability and change in cognitive and behavioral characteristics of autism through childhood. *Journal of Autism and Developmental Disorders, 26,* 557–569.

Evans, D. W., Leckman, J. F., Carter, A., Reznick, S., Henshaw, D., King, R. A., & Pauls, D. (1997). Ritual, habit, and perfectionism: The prevalence and development of compulsive-like behavior in normal young children. *Child Development, 68,* 58–68.

Filipek, P. A., Accardo, P. J., Baranel, G. T., Cook, E. H., Dawson, G., Gordon, B., Gravel, J. S., Johnson, C. P., Kallen, R. J., Levy, S. E., Minshew, N. J., Prizant, B. M., Rapin, I., Rogers, S. J., Stone, W. L., Teplin, S., Tuchman, R. F., & Volkmar, F. R. (1999). The screening and diagnosis of autistic spectrum disorders. *Journal of Autism and Developmental Disorders, 29,* 439–484.

Frith, C. D., & Done, D. J. (1990). Stereotyped behavior in madness and in health. In S. J. Cooper & C. T. Dourish (Eds.), *Neurobiology of behavioral stereotypy* (pp. 232–259). Oxford, UK: Oxford University Press.

Frith, U. (1970). Studies in pattern detection in normal and autistic children: II Reproduction and production of color sequences. *Journal of Experimental Child Psychology, 10,* 120–135.

Firth, U. (1972). Cognitive mechanisms in autism: Experiments with color and tone sequence production. *Journal of Autism and Childhood Schizophrenia, 2,* 160–173.

Frith, U. (1989). *Autism: Explaining the enigma.* Oxford, UK: Blackwell.

Frith, U. (Ed.). (1991). *Autism and Asperger syndrome.* Cambridge, UK: Cambridge University Press.

Frith, U., & Happé, F. (1994). Autism: Beyond "theory of mind." *Cognition, 50,* 115–132.

Gillberg, C., Ehlers, S., Schaumann, H., Jakobsson, G., Dahlgren, S. O., Lindblom, R., Bagenholm, A., Tjuus, T., & Blinder, E. (1990). Autism under age 3 years: A clinical study of 28 cases referred for autistic symptoms in infancy. *Journal of Child Psychology and Psychiatry, 31,* 921–34.

Goodman, R. (1989). Infantile autism: A syndrome of multiple primary deficits? *Journal of Autism and Developmental Disorders, 19,* 409–424.

Greenough, W. T., Black, J. E., & Wallace, C. S. (1987) Experience and brain development. *Child Development, 58,* 539–559.

Griffith, E. M., Pennington, B. F., Wehner, E. A., & Rogers, S. J. (1999). Executive functions in young children with autism. *Child Development, 70,* 817–832.

Happé, F. G. E., & Frith, U. (1996) The neuropsychology of autism. *Brain, 119,* 1377–1400.

Hermelin, B., & O'Connor, N. (1963). The response and self-generated behavior of severely disturbed children and severely subnormal controls. *British Journal of Social and Clinical Psychology, 2,* 37–43.

Hermelin, B., & O'Connor, N. (1964). Effects of sensory input and sensory dominance on severely disturbed autistic children and subnormal controls. *British Journal of Psychiatry, 55,* 201–206.

Hobson, R. P. (1993). *Autism and the development of mind.* London: Lawrence Erlbaum Associates, Ltd.

Hoshino, Y., Kumashiro, H., Yashima, Y., Tachibana, R., Watanabe, M., & Furukawa, H. (1982). Early symptoms of autistic children and their diagnostic significance. *Folia Psychiatrica et Neurologica, 36,* 267–374.

Jarrold, C., Butler, D. W., Cottingham, E. M., & Jimenez, F. (2000). Linking theory of mind and central coherence bias in autism and in the general population. *Developmental Psychology, 36,* 126–138.

Kanner, L. (1943). Autistic disturbances of affective contact. *Nervous Child, 2,* 217–250.

Karmiloff-Smith, A. (1997). Crucial differences between developmental cognitive neuroscience and adult neuropsychology. *Developmental Neuropsychology, 13,* 513–524.

Karmiloff-Smith, A. (1998). Development itself is the key to understanding developmental disorders. *Trends in Cognitive Neuroscience, 2,* 389–398.

Le Couteur, A., Rutter, M., Lord, C., Rios, P., Robertson, S., Holdgrafer, M., & McLennan, J. (1989). Autism Diagnostic Interview: A standardized investigator-based instrument. *Journal of Autism and Developmental Disorders, 19,* 363–387.

Le Couteur, A., Bailey, A., Goode, S., Pickles, A., Robertson, S., Gottesman, I., & Rutter, M. (1996). A broader phenotype of autism: The clinical spectrum in twins. *Journal of Child Psychology and Psychiatry, 37,* 785–801.

Leonard, H., Lenane, M., Swedo, S., Rettew, D. C., Gershon, E. S., & Rapoport, J. L. (1992). Tics and Tourette's syndrome: A 2- to 7-year follow-up of 54 obsessive-compulsive children. *American Journal of Psychiatry, 149,* 1244–1251.

Lewis, M. H., & Bodfish, J. W. (1998). Repetitive behavior disorders in autism. *Mental Retardation and Developmental Disabilities Research Reviews, 4,* 80–89.

Lord, C. (1995). Follow-up of two-year-olds referred for possible autism. *Journal of Child Psychology and Psychiatry, 36,* 1365–1382.

Lord, C., Rutter, M., & Le Couteur, A. (1994). Autism Diagnostic Interview–Revised. *Journal of Autism and Developmental Disorders, 24,* 659–686.

Lord, C., & Pickles, A. (1996). Language level and nonverbal social-communicative behaviors in autistic and language-delayed children. *Journal of the American Academy of Child and Adolescent Psychiatry, 35,* 1542–1550.

Lovaas, I., Schreibman, L., Koegel, R., & Rehm, R. (1971). Selective responding by autistic children to multiple sensory input. *Journal of Abnormal Psychology, 77,* 211–222.

Mahoney, W. J., Szatmari, P., MacLean, J. E., Bryson, S. E., Bartolucci, G., Walter, S. D., Jones, M. B., & Zwaigenbaum, L. (1998). Reliability and accuracy of differentiating pervasive developmental disorder subtypes. *Journal of the American Academy of Child and Adolescent Psychiatry, 37,* 278–285.

Matson, J., Baglio, C., Smiroldo, B., Hamilton, M., Packlowskyi, T., Williams, D., & Kirkpatrick-Sanchez, S. (1996). Characteristics of autism as assessed by the Diagnostic Assessment for the Severely Handicapped–II (DASH–II). *Research into Developmental Disability, 17,* 135–143.

Minshew, N. (1996). Brief report: Brain mechanisms in autism: Functional and structural. *Journal of Autism and Developmental Disorders, 26,* 205–209.

Mundy, P. (1995). Joint attention and social-emotional approach behavior in children with autism. *Development and Psychopathology, 7,* 63–82.

Mundy, P., & Markus, J. (1997). On the nature of the communication and language impairment in autism. *Mental Retardation and Developmental Disabilities Research Reviews, 3,* 343–349.

Mundy, P., & Neal, R. (2000). Neural plasticity, joint attention and a transactional social-orienting model of autism. *Mental Retardation and Developmental Disabilities Research Reviews, 20,* 139–168.

Murphy, M., Bolton, P., Pickles, A., Fombonne, E., Piven, J., & Rutter, M. (1998). Personality traits of the relatives of autistic probands. Unpublished manuscript (cited in Bailey et al., 1998).

Ornitz, E. M. (1969). Disorders of perception common to early infantile autism and schizophrenia. *Comprehensive Psychiatry, 10,* 259–274.

Ornitz, E. M., Guthrie, D., & Farley, A. J. (1977). The early development of autistic symptoms. *Journal of Autism and Childhood Schizophrenia, 7,* 207–229.

Osterling, J., & Dawson, G. (1994). Early recognition of children with autism: A study of first birthday home videotapes. *Journal of Autism and Developmental Disorders, 24,* 247–257.

Ozonoff, S. (1997). Components of executive function in autism and other disorders. In J. Russell (Ed.), *Executive functioning and autism* (pp. 179–211). New York: Oxford University Press.

Pauls, D., Towbin, K., Leckman, J., Zahner, G. E., & Cohen, D. J. (1986). Gilles de la Tourette syndrome and obsessive-compulsive disorder: Evidence supporting a genetic relationship. *Archives of General Psychiatry, 43,* 1180–1182.

Pennington, B. F. (1991). *Diagnosing learning disorders.* New York: Guilford.

Pennington, B. F., & Ozonoff, S. (1996). Executive functions and developmental psychopathology. *Journal of Child Psychology and Psychiatry, 37,* 51–87.

Pennington, B. F., Rogers, S., Bennetto, L., Griffiths, E. M., Reed, D. T., & Shyu, V. (1997). Validity tests of the executive dysfunction hypothesis of autism. In J. Russell (Ed.), *Executive Functioning and Autism* (pp. 143–178). New York: Oxford University Press.

Piven, J., Harper, J., Palmer, P., & Arndt, S. (1996). Course of behavioral change in autism: A retrospective study of high-IQ adolescents and adults. *Journal of the American Academy of Child and Adolescent Psychiatry, 35,* 523–529.

Piven, J., Wzorek, M., Landa, R., Lainhart, J., Bolton, P., Chase, G. A., & Folstein, S. (1994). Personality characteristics of the parents of autistic individuals. *Psychological Medicine, 24,* 783–795.

Plaisted, K. C., O'Riordan, M., & Baron-Cohen, S. (1998). Enhanced discrimination of novel, highly similar stimuli by adults with autism during a perceptual learning task. *Journal of Child Psychology and Psychiatry, 39,* 765–775.

Plaisted, K. C., Swettenham, J., & Rees, L. (1999). Children with autism show local precedence in a divided attention task and global precedence in a selective attention task. *Journal of Child Psychology and Psychiatry, 40,* 733–742.

Prior, M., & Macmillan, M. B. (1973). Maintenance of sameness on children with Kanner's syndrome. *Journal of Autism and Childhood Schizophrenia, 3,* 154–167.

Ridley, R. M. (1994). The psychology of perseverative and stereotyped behavior. *Progress in Neurobiology, 44,* 221–231.

Ritvo, E. R., Ornitz, E. M., & La Fanchi, S. (1968). Frequency of repetitive behaviors in early infantile autism and its variants. *Archives of General Psychiatry, 19,* 341–347.

Roux, S., Adrien, J. L., Bruneau, N., Malvy, J., & Barthélémy, C. (1998). Behavior profiles within a population of 145 children with autism using the Behavior Summarised Evaluation Scale. *Autism: The International Journal of Research and Practice, 2,* 345–366.

Russell, J. (Ed.). (1997). *Executive functioning and autism.* New York: Oxford University Press.

Rutter, M. (1996). Autism research: Prospects and priorities. *Journal of Autism and Developmental Disorders, 26,* 257–275.

Schopler, E., Reichler, R. J., DeVellis, R. F., & Daly, K. (1980). Toward objective classification of childhood autism: Childhood Autism Rating Scale (CARS). *Journal of Autism and Developmental Disorders, 10,* 91–103.

Sevin, J. A., Matson, J. L., Coe, D., Love, S. R., Matese, M. J., & Benavidez, D. A. (1995). Empirically derived subtypes of pervasive developmental disorders: A cluster analytic study. *Journal of Autism and Developmental Disorders, 25,* 561–578.

Shah, A., Holmes, N., & Wing, L. (1982). Prevalence of autism and related conditions in adults in a mental handicap hospital. *Applied Research in Mental Retardation, 3,* 303–317.

Siegel, B., Vukicevic, J., Elliott, G. R., & Kraemer, H. C. (1989). The use of signal detection theory to assess DSM–III-R criteria for autistic disorder. *Journal of the American Academy of Child and Adolescent Psychiatry, 28,* 542–548.

Sonuga-Barke, E. (1998). Categorical models of childhood disorder: A conceptual and empirical analysis. *Journal of Child Psychology and Psychiatry, 39,* 115–133.

Stella, J., Mundy, P., & Tuchman, R. (1999). Social and nonsocial factors in the childhood autism rating scale. *Journal of Autism and Developmental Disorders, 29,* 307–317.

Stone, W. L. (1997). Autism in infancy and early childhood. In D. J. Cohen & F. R. Volkmar (Eds.), *Handbook of autism and pervasive developmental disorders* (2nd ed.) (pp. 266–282). New York: Wiley.

Stone, W. L., Hoffman, E. L., Lewis, S. E., & Ousley, O. Y. (1994). Early recognition of autism: Parental reports vs. clinical observation. *Archives of Pediatric and Adolescent Medicine, 148,* 174–179.

Stone, W. L., Lee, E. B., Ashford, L., Brissie, J., Hepburn, S. L., Coonrod, E. E., & Weiss, B. H. (1999). Can autism be diagnosed accurately in children under three years? *Journal of Child Psychology and Psychiatry, 40,* 219–226.

Swettenham, J., Charman, T., Baron-Cohen, S., Cox, A., Baird, G., Drew, A., Wheelwright, S., & Reece, L. (1998). The frequency and distribution of spontaneous attention shifts between social and non-social stimuli in autistic, typically-developing and non-autistic developmentally delayed infants. *Journal of Child Psychology and Psychiatry, 39,* 747–754.

Swettenham, J., Milne, E., Plaisted, K., Campbell, R., & Coleman, M. (2000). Visual orienting in response to social stimuli in typically developing children and children with autism. Poster presentation at the Cognitive Neuroscience Conference 2000. San Francisco, CA, April 2000.

Szatmari, P., Bartolucci, G., & Bremner, R. (1989). Asperger's syndrome and autism: Comparison of early history and outcome. *Developmental Medicine and Child Neurology, 31, 709–*720.

Szatmari, P., Jones, M. B., Zwaigenbaum, L., & MacLean, J. E. (1998). Genetics of autism: Overview and new directions. *Journal of Autism and Developmental Disorders, 28,* 351–368.

Tanguay, P. E., Robertson, J., & Derrick, A. (1998). A dimensional classification of autism spectrum disorder by social communication domains. *Journal of the American Academy of Child and Adolescent Psychiatry, 37,* 271–277.

Turner, M. (1997). Towards an executive dysfunction account of repetitive behavior in autism. In J. Russell (Ed.), *Executive functioning and autism* (pp. 57–100). New York: Oxford University Press.

Turner, M. (1999). Annotation: Repetitive behavior in autism: A review of psychological research. *Journal of Child Psychology and Psychiatry, 40,* 839–849.

Waterhouse, L., Fein, D., & Modahl, C. (1996). Neurofunctional mechanisms in autism. *Psychological Review, 103,* 457–489.

Wing, L., & Gould, J. (1979). Severe impairments of social interaction and associated abnormalities in children: Epidemiology and classification. *Journal of Autism and Developmental Disorders, 9,* 11–29.

Wolff, S., Narayan, S., & Moyes, B. (1988). Personality characteristics of parents of autistic children. *Journal of Child Psychology and Psychiatry, 29,* 143–154.

World Health Organization (1993). *Mental disorders: A glossary and guide to their classification in accordance with the 10th revision of the International Classification of Diseases (ICD–10).* Geneva, Switzerland: Author.

Yeung-Courchesne, R., & Courchesne, E. (1997). From impasse to insight in autism research: From behavioral symptoms to biological explanations. *Development and Psychopathology, 9,* 389–419.

Zelazo, P. D., Burack, J. A., Benedetto, E., & Frye, D. (1996). Theory of mind and rule use in individuals with Down's syndrome: A test of the uniqueness and specificity claims. *Journal of Child Psychology and Psychiatry, 37,* 479–484.

Author Index

A

B

C

D

I

J

K

L

N

S

T

U

V

W

Y

Z

Subject Index

D

R

S

T